MW01670877

SPEAKING PAKISTANI PUKHTO

A practical guide to learning the language of Khyber Pukhtunkhwa

Robert Sampson

InterLit Foundation
Peshawar, Pakistan

2012

Copyright © 2011 Sampson, Robert

All Rights Reserved. No part of this book may be used or reproduced in any manner whatsoever without written permission, except in the case of brief quotations.

Published by InterLit Foundation
U.P.O Box 879, Peshawar, Pakistan
www.interlitfoundation.org

First edition 2012

Illustrations by Robert Sampson

Cover Design by An-Phuong Ly

Printed by PanGraphics (PvT) Limited
G-7/1, Islamabad
pangraph@isb.comsats.net.pk

ISBN: 978-969-8343-45-3

Dedicated to the memory of Muhammad Ashraf of Oghi.

A generous friend

and patient mentor of a generation of Pukhto learners.

Table of Contents

Preface

When I first came to live in north west Pakistan, I began picking up the language by sitting with friends and students and listening to what they said. What was missing at the time were the tools to help in learning the language that surrounded me – the modern Pukhto of Khyber Pukhtunkhwa.

This book is an attempt to fill that gap. It is designed to be used with Pukhtun friends as helpers, rather than as a formal textbook. The original outline for the book was based on *Speaking Afghan Pashto* written by Randall Olson. Several Pukhtun friends have worked with me over the years to improve and develop the book. It has slowly evolved through a number of unpublished editions. My plan was to make it available to anyone as excited as me about speaking this lovely frontier language.

The staff at InterLit provided the impetus and expertise to add the standard IPA system of phonetics and finally get the book into print. My goal has been to keep the language learning process as simple as possible. There is grammar in *Speaking Pakistani Pukhto*, but I have tried not to overwhelm the student with complicated terminology. My overall aim remains the desire to motivate and empower those who wish to learn Pakistani Pukhto. I have included proverbs and poetry because these are highly valued in Pukhtun culture and act as bridges for growing relationships.

Robert Sampson
Peshawar, 2012

Acknowledgements

The production of this book has been a team effort. Above all it has relied on the kindness and generosity of Pukhtuns who have extended their warm hospitality to me and my family. My thanks also to the many helpers who have worked to produce this first published edition of *Speaking Pakistani Pukhto*. I especially want to especially thank Muhammad Shahid and Momin Khan, who began to work with me on the first hand-written versions of the book over 20 years ago. As the book evolved from Momin's lovely calligraphy into various computerized versions a succession of gifted students and linguists have improved the text. Particular thanks to Sherbaz Khan, Sabir Hussain, Jawad Babar, Kamran Akhtar, Muhammad Jehangir, Umar Ghani, Khanzeb Khan, Rose Chugg, Lori Fulghum, Susan Smith and the staff of the InterLit Foundation.

Introduction

This book is intended to be a guide for those wishing to begin learning the Yusufzai dialect of Pakistani Pukhto that is spoken in and around Peshawar, Mardan and the Swat valley.

Each lesson is divided into dialogue, grammar points and drills that help in forming new language habits. The parts of the dialogues marked 'L' (for 'learners') should be memorised. Repeat each phrase many times with your helper until you match their intonation, speed and rhythm.

A small digital recorder is invaluable: record key sections of each lesson to practise when the helper is not around. When making a recording, have your language helper repeat each sentence twice at normal speed with pauses between each sentence so you can repeat it yourself. Audio-lessons are being developed to accompany this book, and when they are ready they will save you from having to make your own recordings.

Every lesson contains a vocabulary list. The vocabulary lists are arranged alphabetically according to Pukhto script, and provide information about the part of speech, gender and, where important, the number of each word. For more help with vocabulary you may find *A Dictionary of Spoken Pukhto* to be useful.[1]

The most important part is practice in real settings. The method of learning outlined by Tom Brewster in *Language Acquisition Made Practical (LAMP)*[2] is of particular help, but the main resource will always be Pukhtuns. You will not progress in your language learning until you go out into the bazaars and homes and begin to use what you are learning. Most people will be delighted to help you practice your Pukhto, and from these conversations your ability to communicate will rapidly develop.

---

[1] Sampson, Robert. *A Dictionary of Spoken Pashto*, 2nd printing. Peshawar, Pakistan. InterLit Foundation. 2010.

[2] Brewster, Tom and Brewster, Elizabeth S. *Language Acquisition Made Practical (LAMP): Field methods for language learners*, 5th printing. Pasadena, CA 91182. Lingua House. 1984.

Pukhtun tribes

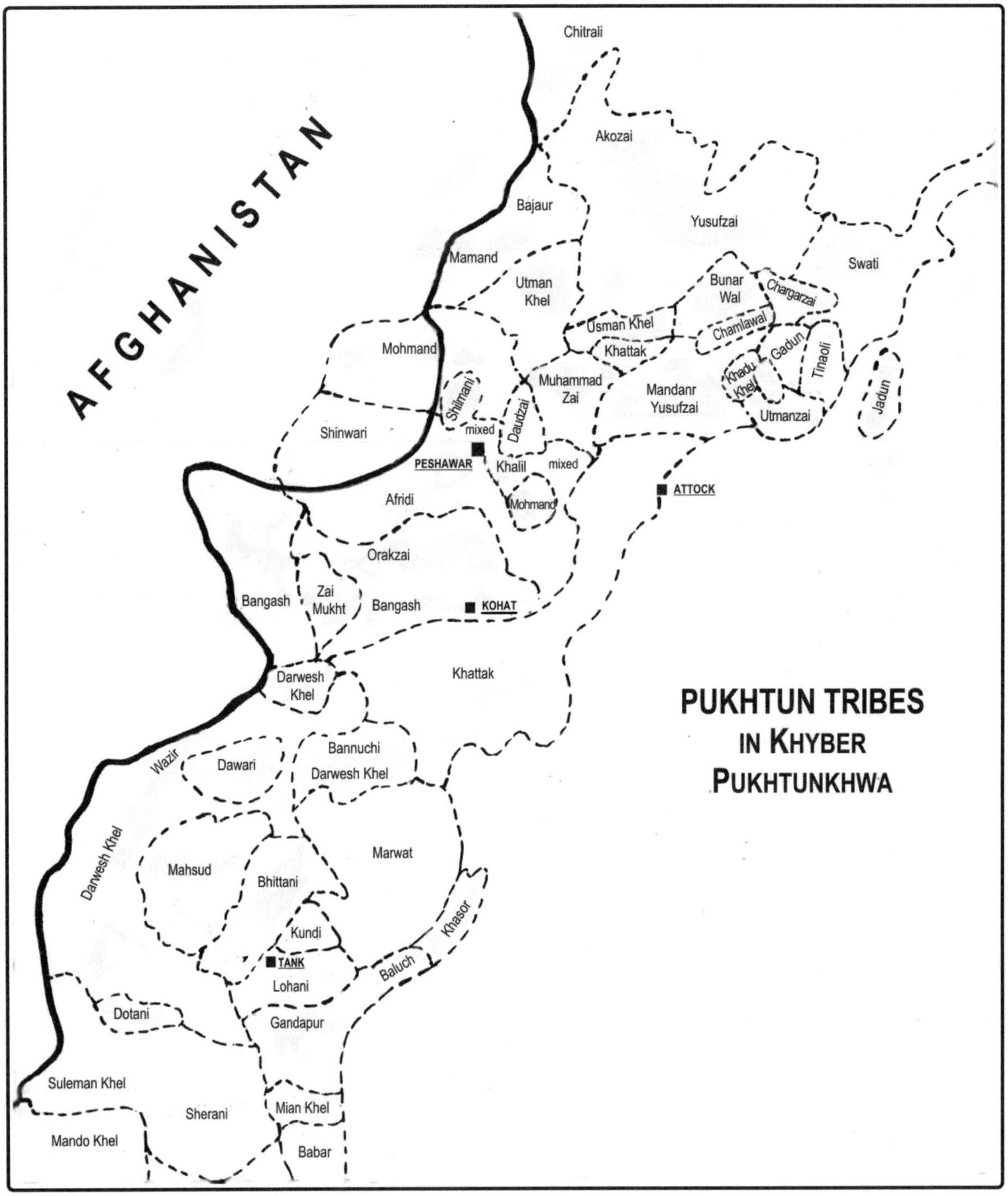

The sounds of Pukhto

The first challenge in learning Pukhto is to hear and then produce the different sounds that have to be mastered. These early exercises will have to be revisited frequently to teach the tongue new habits.

A number of sounds found in Pukhto are not found in English. It is helpful to be able to write these new sounds in phonetic form. This book uses a modified version of the International Phonetic Alphabet to help you. Phonetics simply provide a guide to the sounds, which can only be learned from a Pukhtun patient enough to correct you. You can best master the new sounds by repeating what you hear from a Pukhtun helper.

In addition, the sounds of Pukhto vary according to region. There are some major differences in the sounds of the various Pukhto dialects, even within Khyber Pukhtunkhwa. The phonetic chart below represents the sounds of the language as spoken in and around Peshawar and the Swat valley, although some indication of dialect differences has been given.

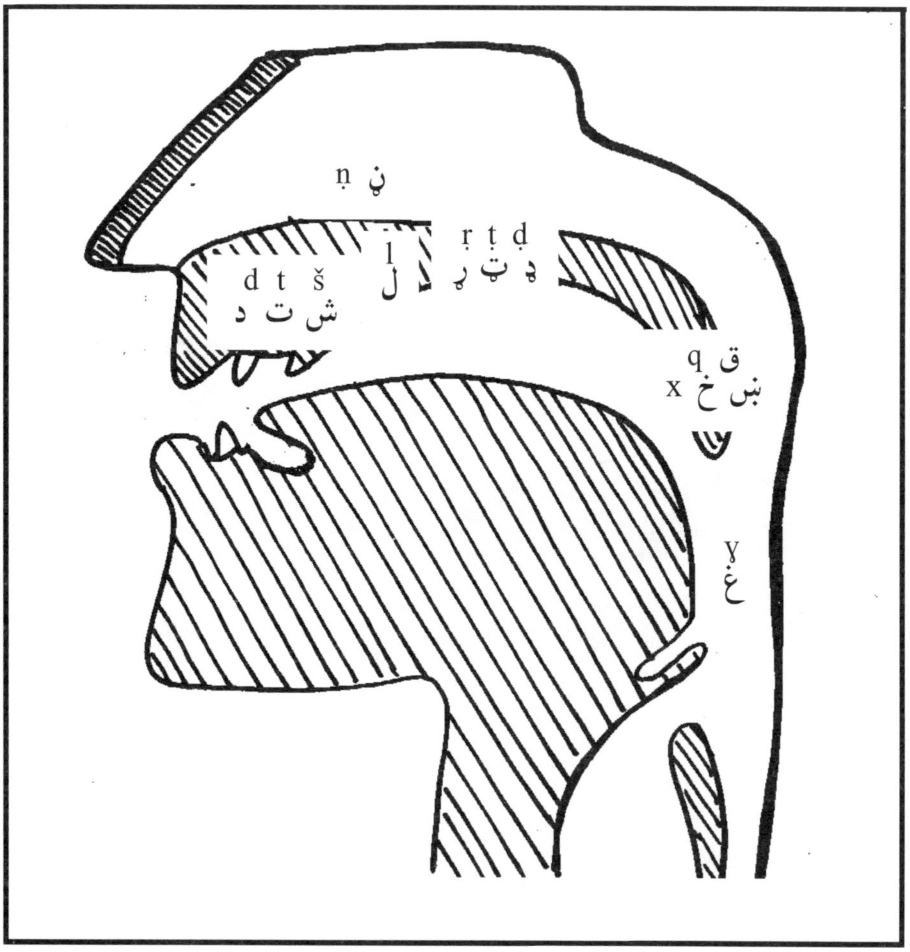

A summary of the sounds of Yusufzai Pukhto

Pukhto has a reputation for being a harsh-sounding language. The harshness is generated by guttural sounds that are made at the back of the throat. These 'hard' or 'retroflex' sounds are made when the tongue is held deep in the mouth and flicked forward. In this book the hard sounds appear with a dot underneath: / ṛ / ړ , / ḍ / ډ , / ṭ / ټ and / ṇ / ڼ. With a little practice most learners can soon master these hard consonants, as well as the sounds / x / (kh) خ and / ɣ / (gh) غ.

But Pukhto is not all guttural. There are also 'soft' or 'dental' sounds that are made with the tongue on the back of the teeth. Again, there are no exact equivalents of these sounds, which include / d / د , / t / ت and / r / ر . In fact to begin with many learners find they are unable to hear the difference between the hard and soft sounds, let alone make them.

Again, lots of practice and attentive listening will be the key to correct usage. (Please note that the charts below are arranged in an order similar to that of the English alphabet.)

Practice these sounds with your language helper using the following chart and tables.[3] Repeat each of the words after your language helper. The meanings of the words are not important.

Consonants

Few of the consonants are exactly the same as those used in English, and many are not found in English at all. It will take constant repetition to form new habits of pronunciation for these sounds, but working hard at it now will reap big dividends for years to come. These are the distinctive sounds that give Pukhto its special identity.

Phonetic symbol	Pukhto letter	Explanation of sounds	Sample words	
b	ب	Similar to English / b / but less aspirated	ba'dām	بادام
č	چ	Like the consonant cluster / ch / as in 'chair'	čay	چائي
d	د	The soft, dental / d /; a Spanish dental / d /; there is no English equivalent	dwa wā'də ā'zād	دوه وادهٔ آزاد
ḍ	ډ	The retroflex or hard / d /; tongue is flexed at the back of the palate	ḍo'ḍəy gəḍ	ډوډۍ ګډ
f	ف	Similar to the English / f /	far'mān	فرمان
g	ګ، ږ	Like the English / g / as in the word 'glove'	grān	ګران

[3] A indicates that action needs to be taken by the teacher or language helper, or by the student and teacher or helper working together.

Phonetic symbol	Pukhto letter	Explanation of sounds	Sample words	
ɣ	غ	The voiced counterpart of / x / formed in the lower throat; no English equivalent; in other phonetic alphabets is sometimes written as / gh /	ɣar'ma 'daɣa bāɣ	غرمه دغه باغ
h	ح، ه	Like English / h /	hā'lat	حالت
ǰ	ج	Like English / j /	ǰa'du	جادُو
ǰ (ž)	ژ	Often pronounced like an English / j /, but in some dialects similar to the middle consonant sound in the English words 'measure' and 'seizure'	žwənd	ژوند
k	ک	Like English / k /	kɪ'tāb	کِتاب
l	ل	Similar to an English / l / when at the beginning of a word, as in the word 'leave', but the tongue is higher in the mouth; also like a Spanish / l /	lās li'kəl	لاس ليکل
m	م	Like English / m /	mār	مار
n	ن	Like English / n /	nim	نيم
ṇ	ڼ	The retroflex or hard / n /; tongue is flexed at the back of the palate; a slight / r / sound at the end	pa'ṇa tar'kāṇ	پاڼه ترکاڼ
p	پ	Similar to English / p / but less aspirated	plār	پلار
q	ق	This sound is like the English / k / but much farther back in the throat. This sound is usually indistinguishable from / k /, though some literate people will make an effort at differentation	qi'sa haqi'qət ra'fiq	قيصه حقيقت رفيق
r	ر	A trilled / r /; not a flat English / r /; similar to the rolling / r / used in Spanish	rang pa'run kor	رنگ پرُون کور
ṛ	ړ	The retroflex, or hard / r /; tongue is flexed at the back of the palate	ṛund sa'ṛey ǰoṛ	ړُوند سړے جوړ

Phonetic symbol	Pukhto letter	Explanation of sounds	Sample words	
s	س، ص، ث	Like English / s /	spək	سپک
š	ش	Like the English consonant cluster / sh / in the word 'shoe' or 'sheep' but with more emphasis	špa pi'šo	شپه پیشو
t	ت، ط	A dental or soft / t / with the tongue on the back of the upper teeth, not aspirated; like the Spanish dental / t /; no English equivalent	tor ki'tāb zyāt	تور کتاب زَیات
ṭ	ټ	The retroflex or hard / t /. The tongue is flexed at the back of the palate; no English equivalent	ṭo'pək māl'ṭa pəṭ	ټوپک مالټه پټ
ts	څ	Like the sound found in English words 'hats' and 'cats', but occurs in all three positions (beginning, middle and end of words); in some dialects it is reduced to a simple / s /	'tsumra ku'tsa hits	څومره کوڅه هیڅ
β	و	Somewhat like a / v / sound but with both lips together instead of the upper teeth touching the lower lip	'šɪβe	شوي
w	و	Between an English / v / and / w / (sounding more like 'victor'); in the initial position, similar to an English / w / though mouth is not rounded	'wəge u'wə	وږي اووۀ
x	خ، ښ	Somewhat similar to the German or Scottish / ch / in words like 'bach' and 'loch'; or like the Spanish / j / in words like 'jefe' and 'ojo'; in other phonetic alphabets is sometimes written as / kh /	xpəl pəx'to ux	خپل پښتو اوخ
y	ی	Like English / y / when in the initial position	yār	یار
z	ځ، ذ، ز، ظ، ض	Like English / z /	zo'kām	زُکام

Vowels

Phonetic symbol	Pukhto letter	Explanation of sounds	Sample words	
ā	ا، ع	A long / a / sound, similar to the vowel sound in English words 'father' and 'ahhhh' (open mouth)[4]	ās'mān pākɪ'stān kā'kā ām	آسمان پاکستان کاکا عام
a	ا، ه، ع	A short / a /sound as in 'banana' (American pronunciation); not as long or open as / ā /; between the / a / of 'hat' and the / u / of 'but'; when stressed is closer to / a /, when unstressed is closer to / u /	gawən'ḍey ha'ɣa poza adət	گاونډے هغه پوزه عادت
e	ې، ا، ع	Similar to the vowel sounds in the words 'eight' and 'bait', but covers a range of sounds – therefore also like the vowel sound in 'bet' and 'let'; not as lengthy as / ey / (below); like the Spanish / e /	'dāse mez eǰā'zət kena e'lāǰ	داسې مېز اِجازت کښېنه علاج
ey	ے ائ	As in the English words 'they' and 'day'; no diphthong; stronger than / e / (above); ے indicates masculine gender when at the end of words	lar'gey sa'ṛey xo'dey	لرگے سړے خُدائ
i	ـيـ، ي، ی	As in the English words 'beet' and 'meat'; no diphthong	'mina sa'ṛi	مينه سړی
ɪ	ا، ع	An / i / sound, as in the English words 'bit' and 'lit'	ɪs'lām ɪlm	اِسلام عِلم
o	و	A pure / o / sound; no diphthong; similar to the vowel sound in the words 'boat', 'note' and 'bone'	dost pi'šo	دوست پيشو

[4] The three vowel sounds / ā /, / a / and / ə / are quite fluid in Pukhto, particularly between / ā / and / a / and between / a / and / ə /. Regional differences in pronunciation mean that some speakers will use a clear / ā / sound while a speaker from another area might pronounce the same letter with more of an / a /. Likewise, one speaker will use an / a / where another might use an / ə /. You will need to listen carefully to your tutor to catch these distinctions.

Phonetic symbol	Pukhto letter	Explanation of sounds	Sample words	
u	و ، ا	A pure / u / sound, no diphthong, as in 'food', 'boot' and 'rule'	u'bə du'kān ka'du	أُبَهٔ دُوکان کدُو
ə	usually no character; ۀ at end of words	The schwa sound, which is always unstressed in English, but commonly stressed in Pukhto; similar to the sound in English words 'another' and 'but'. When in final position it is similar to the sound in 'hook'	wā'də (stressed) pəx'to (unstressed)	وادهٔ پښتو

NOTE:

The vowel chart is simply a guide to pronunciation. The letters listed for each vowel are only some of the possibilities, as vowel sounds in Pukhto are very fluid. In addition, vowels are not always written, but can be indicated by a diacritical mark (as in Arabic, Farsi, etc). For example, the most common vowel sound in Pukhto / ə / is usually not written as a separate letter, even though it exists as a distinct sound.

Diphthongs

Diphthongs are made by gliding from one vowel sound to another vowel sound. Diphthongs are often found at the end of words in Pukhto as gender markers.

Phonetic symbol	Pukhto letter	Explanation of sounds	Sample words	
ay	ائي ای	This sound combines / ā / and / y / glide (dipthong); pronounced as the English word 'lie'. In some dialects this sound is pronounced / e / or / ey /	čay zay	چائي ځای
əy	ئ / ی	This sound combines the schwa with a / y / glide (diphthong); there is no English equivalent; indicates feminine gender	spəy 'kenəy	سپی کښېنئ
uy	وئ	A combination of / u / and / əy /; there is no English equivalent	luy	لوئ

Sound recognition

☝ The following exercises will help you differentiate between similar sounding letters. Have your helper read a word, and then you point to which of the two letters you think the word contains. The focus here is on the sounds, so ignore the meaning of the words altogether.

Focus on: ṛ ړ r ر

ورور، ورځ، کارُوبار، ړُوند، مانړۍ، راشه، لاړ شه، روغ، ناجوړه، بیمار،
تکړه، شرابی سترګې، مار، لړم، تیارهٔ، رنړا، موړ، نهار، تور، زېړ، فکر،
زاړه، ښار، خوړل، خړخړ

Focus on: ḍ ډ d د

درُوند، ډیوه، دوه، ډوډۍ، ډرامه، دوست، بنډل، بندول، ډېر،
دشمن، لنډ، اُوږد، ډنډه، دنګه، انګلینډ، ډز، ګنډل، ګډول،
ګودام، دولس، ډُوب

Focus on: ṭ ټ t ت

ټول، تول، ټېپر، توره، ټماټر، ترکاری، باتینګڼ، ټافی،
غوټۍ، ناشپاتئ، ټوپک، توره، ټېپ، فیته، ټاپ، ټاس،
ترماس، اتهٔ، آټ، تیکې، توپ، ټوټه، تُوت

Focus on: q ق k ک

قلم، قسم، قدم، قابِل، قاتِل، قاضی، قانُون، قُدرت، قبر،
قافله، کِتاب، کلام، کمال، کَرم، کار، کابل، کُرسۍ، لیکل،
مکَار، سَائیکل، ګلکار، ترکاڼ، مقبره، مکمل، مُقابله،
قِسمت، سکُول، دُوکَان، امریکه، تُرکی

Focus on: ā آ, ا a اَ

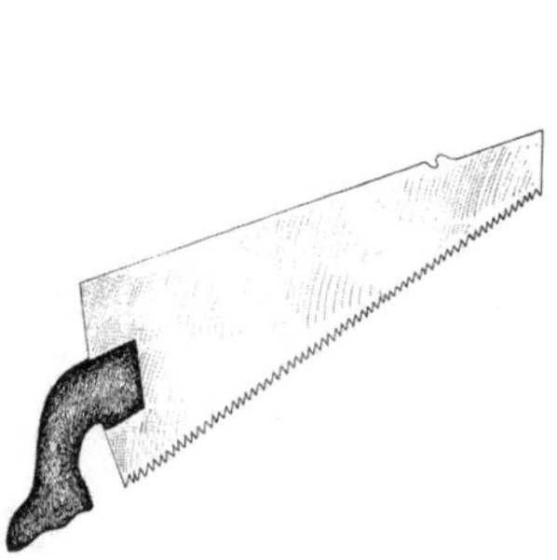

کاهِله، بلا، نوکره، کمره، بنګله، لالا، فاصِله، وفاداره،
خانَسامه، ښځه، قابِله، هوښیاره، نیکهٔ، تابِعدارَه، حُسنداره،
آسمانی، نارنجی، ماما، پاپا، بابا، ماریه، نائله، سونیا،
سومیا، صبا

Focus on: ɣ غ   x خ

غُصه، شُغل، مُغل، غُسل، باغ، داغ، غم، غاښ، غضب، مغز، ماښام، خِدمت، رُخصت، فارِغ، غیبت، تاریخ، اغوستل، غوښه، خندل، خوږ، خوګ، تریخ، غوښتل، خارِج، خواهش

Focus on: ey ے əy ۍ

شپیلے، شپیلۍ، ژوندے، ژوندۍ، خاپیرے، خاپیرۍ، کابلے، کابلۍ، سپے، سپۍ، جینۍ، سړے، المارۍ، کړکۍ، لیونے، لیونۍ

Key to abbreviations

A number of abbreviations are used in this book to indicate gender and to classify words grammatically. A key to these abbreviations is listed below:

1st pn.pl.	first person plural
1st pn.s.	first person singular
2nd pn.pl.	second person plural
2nd pn.s.	second person singular
3rd pn.pl.	third person plural
3rd pn.s.	third person singular
adj.	adjective
adv.	adverb
comp.	compound
conj.	conjunction
dem.	demonstrative
f.	feminine
fig.	figuratively
f.pl.	feminine plural
f.s.	feminine singular
ft.v.m.	future verb marker
inf.	infinitive
interject	interjection
lit.	literally
m.	masculine
m.pl.	masculine plural
m.s.	masculine singular
n.	noun
neg.	negative
obj.	object
ph.	phrase
pl.	plural
pa.p.	past participle
pn.	person
poss.	possessive
post.	postposition
prep.	preposition
pro.	pronoun
pr.t.	present tense
q.	question
s.	singular
v.	verb
v.i.	intransitive verb
v.t.	transitive verb

In addition, a forward slash (/) is used to divide the singular and plural forms while a comma or a semicolon is used to separate different meanings. Alternative pronunciations or spellings are indicated by [ ].

The Pukhto alphabet

چ č	ځ z	ج ǰ	ث s	ټ ṭ	ت t	پ p	ب b	آ ā	ا a, e, i, ɪ, u, o
ژ ǰ	ز z	ړ ṛ	ر r	ذ z	ډ ḍ	د d	خ x	ح h	څ ts, s
غ ɣ	ع a, e, ɪ	ظ z	ط t	ض z	ص s	ښ x	ش š	س s	ږ g
ه h	و w, o	ڼ ṇ	ن n	م m	ل l	ګ g	ک k	ق q	ف f
								ے y, e	ی y, e, i

āˈwal saˈbəq اول سبق

Lesson One

Dialogue one: Greetings

Where L is you, the Language Learner, and H is your Language Helper.

L: ˈāsalām aˈlekum! Peace be upon you!	السلام علیکم!
H: waˈālekum a-saˈlām! And peace be upon you!	وعلیکم السلام!
L: ˈtsənga ye? ǰoṛ ye? How are you? Are you well?	څنګه يې؟ جوړ يې؟
H: merabāˈni, ˈxə yɪm. Thanks, I'm fine.	مِهرباني، ښۀ يم.
L: zə pəxˈto ɪzˈda kaˈwəm. I`m learning Pukhto.	زۀ پښتو زده کوم.
H: ḍer xə! Very good!	ډېر ښۀ!
L: zəˈmā həm ˈdumra ɪzˈda da. This is all I know.	زما هم دومره زده ده.
H: čay ske? Would you like to drink tea?	چائې څښې؟
L: merabāˈni, byā ba ˈrāšəm. Thanks, I will come again.	مِهرباني، بيا به راشم.
L: təkˈlif ˈməkawa. eǰāˈzət dey? Don`t go to any trouble. Is there permission (to leave)?	تکليف مۀ کوه. اِجازت دے؟
H: pa ˈməxa de ˈxa! May you face only good!	په مخه دې ښه!
L: də xoˈdey pa āˈmān! May you go in God's peace!	د خُدائ په آمان!

NOTES:

1. The question *čay ske*? (چائې څښې؟) is an invitation to drink tea. It is polite to automatically refuse the first invitation by saying *merabāˈni* (مِهرباني). If the offer is repeated several times the invitation is sincere and can be accepted by saying *təkˈlif ˈməkawa* (تکليف مۀ کوه).
   In addition to *čay ske?* the expression *če ske?* is also commonly heard.

2. The phrase *pa 'məxa de 'xa* (په مخه دې ښه) is useful for saying goodbye to someone who is leaving.

Pronunciation drill

Repeat these sentences after your teacher. Then, contrast the words in focus. The meaning of the sentences is not important.

1. Contrasting / **t** / ت with / **d** / د

dā tura da.	دا تُوره ده	dā tars dey.	دا ترس دے.
dā duṛa da.	دا دُوړه ده.	dā dars dey.	دا درس دے.

Make a conscious effort to make these sounds 'dental', with the tongue well forward on the teeth. Old grammar books would often characterize the sounds / t / and / d / as / th / or / dh / to emphasise how far forward the tongue needs to be placed.

2. Contrasting / **e** / ې with / **i** / ی

mā'lum ba še.	معلُوم به شي.
mā'lum ba ši.	معلُوم به شی.
'mina la'rəm.	مینه لرم.
'wera 'məkawa.	وېره مهٔ کوه.
wir 'məkawa.	ویر مهٔ کوه.

Singular subject pronouns and the verb 'to be'

Person	Pronoun			Verb		
First person singular	zə	I	زهٔ	yım	am	یم
Second person singular	tə	you	تهٔ	ye	are	یې
Third person singular masculine	dey	he	دے	dey	is	دے
	ha'ɣa	he	هغه			
Third person singular feminine	dā	she	دا	da	is	ده
	ha'ɣa	she	هغه			

NOTE:

The pronouns for 'he' and 'she' are *dey* (دے) and *dā* (دا) when the person is in the presence of the speaker. In their absence both 'he' and 'she' become *ha'ɣa* (هغه).

Gender in Pukhto

Gender is an important issue in both Pukhtun culture and language. The clue to a word's gender is its ending. For example, nouns ending in / -ey / (ے -) and those ending with a consonant are usually masculine.

Pronouns used with masculine nouns

zə pəx'tun yım.	I am a Pukhtun.	زهٔ پښتُون يم.
tə tā'lıb ye?	Are you a (religious) student?	تهٔ طالِب يې؟
dey af'ɣān dey?	Is he an Afghan?	دے افغان دے؟
ha'ɣa špun'key dey.	He is a shepherd.	هغه شپُونکے دے.

NOTE:
There is no definite article in Pukhto, but the number 'one' (*yo* يو) is used to convey the idea of indefiniteness.

Recognising masculine singular noun endings

1. As seen in the example above, nouns ending in the suffix / -ey / (ے -) are masculine.

ha'ɣa sa'ṛey dey.	He is a man.	هغه سړے دے.

2. Most nouns ending in a consonant are also masculine.

zə plār yım.	I am a father.	زهٔ پلار يم.
tə ha'lək ye.	You are a boy.	تهٔ هلک يې.
ha'ɣa mā'šum dey.	He is a child.	هغه ماشُوم دے.

3. Nouns referring to a profession and ending in / -i / (ی -) are masculine.

zə qā'zi yım.	I am a judge.	زهٔ قاضی يم.
ha'ɣa mā'li dey.	He is a gardener.	هغه مالی دے.

Questions with positive and negative replies

Q:	tə tālı'bıləm ye?	Are you a student?	تهٔ طالبعلم يې؟
A:	āw, tālı'bıləm yım.	Yes, I'm a student.	آو، طالبعلم يم.
Q:	tə mis'tri ye?	Are you a mechanic?	تهٔ مستری يې؟
A:	na, mis'tri nə yım.	No, I'm not a mechanic.	نه، مستری نهٔ يم.

NOTE:
Unlike English, the Pukhto negative verb marker *nə* نۀ (not) comes in front of the verb.

☝ Practice simple questions and answers using the words that have been introduced in this lesson.

Memorising moment

ma'təl (proverb)

Nothing expresses deeply held cultural values more aptly than a proverb (متل). Using them appropriately will always elicit a warm smile.

☝ Memorise these proverbs after you have discussed the meaning and usage with your helper.

تادی کار دَ شېطان دے.

tā'di kār də še'tān dey.

A speedy job is of Satan.

کارغۀ هوښیار دے.

kār'ɣə ux'yār dey.

The crow is wise.

Exercises for Lesson One

1. Use the correct pronoun to complete the following sentences:

   a. ________________ ha'lək dey. — ________________ هلک دے.

   b. ________________ qā'zi ye? — ________________ قاضی یې؟

   c. ________________ mā'šum dey. — ________________ ماشُوم دے.

   d. ________________ mā'li yım. — ________________ مالی یم.

2. Use the correct form of the 'to be' verb in the following sentences:

   a. dey tālı'bıləm ________________. — دے طالبعلم ________________.

   b. tə sa'ṛey ________________. — تۀ سړے ________________.

   c. zə mā'li ________________. — زۀ مالی ________________.

   d. ha'ɣa špun'key ________________. — هغه شپُونکے ________________.

Vocabulary for Lesson One

ā'mān	آمان	*m.*	*n.*	peace, security
eǰā'zət [eǰā'za]	اِجازت [اِجازه]	*m.*	*n.*	permission
af'ɣān	افغان	*m.s.*	*n., adj.*	(an) Afghan
af'ɣānān, af'ɣānāno	افغانان، افغانانو	*m.pl.*		
af'ɣāna, af'ɣāne	افغانه، افغانې	*f.s.*		
af'ɣāniāne, af'ɣānāne	افغانیانې، افغانانې	*m.pl.*		
byā	بیا		*adv.*	again; then, later
pəx'to	پښتو	*f.s.*	*n.*	Pukhto
pəx'tun / pəxtā'nə	پښتُون / پښتانهٔ	*m.*	*n.*	Pukhtun
plār / plā'rān	پلار / پلاران	*m.*	*n.*	father
tək'lif	تکلیف	*m.s.*	*n.*	trouble, difficulty
tə	تهٔ	*m., f.*	*pro.*	you
ǰoṛ	جوړ	*m.*	*adj.*	healthy, well, sound
'ǰoṛa / 'ǰoṛe	جوړه / جوړې	*f.*		
čay [če]	چائې	*f.pl.*	*n.*	tea
skəl	څښل		*v.t.*	to drink; to smoke
'tsənga	څنګه		*q., adv.*	how, in what manner
xānsā'ma	خانسامه	*m.*	*n.*	cook
xo'dey	خُدائ	*m.s.*	*n.*	God
dā	دا	*f.s.*	*pro.*	she (near)
dey	دے	*m.s.*	*pro.*	he (near)
ḍer	ډېر	*m.*	*adj., adv.*	much, more, very
rāt'ləl	راتلل		*v.i*	to come
ız'da ka'wəl	زده کول		*v.t.*	to learn
zə'mā	زما	*m., f.*	*pos. pro.*	my, mine
zə	زهٔ	*m., f.*	*pro.*	I
sa'ṛey / sa'ṛi	سړے / سړی	*m.*	*n.*	man
špun'key	شپُونکے	*m.s.*	*n.*	shepherd

xa	ښه		*interject.*	OK, well, fine, good, ah (indicating agreement)
xə	ښهٔ		*adj.*	fine, good, well, OK
tāˈlıb	طالِب	*m.s.*	*n.*	(religious) student
tāˈlıbıləm / tālıbılˈmān	طالبعلم / طالبعلمان	*m.*	*n.*	student
qāˈzi	قاضی	*m.s.*	*n.*	judge
māˈšum / māšuˈmān	ماشُوم / ماشُومان	*m.*	*n.*	child
māˈli	مالی	*m.s.*	*n.*	gardener
maˈtəl / mataˈluna	متل / متلُونه	*m.*	*n.*	proverb
ˈməxa / ˈməxe	مخه / مخې	*f.*	*n., adv.*	front, before
misˈtri	مستری	*m.*	*n.*	mechanic, craftsman
merabāˈni	مِهربانی	*f.s.*	*n.*	thanks, kindness
na	نه		*adv.*	no
nə	نهٔ		*adv.*	not, no
haˈɣa	هغه	*m., f.*	*pro.*	he, she (far)
haˈlək / haləˈkān	هلک، هلکان	*m.*	*n.*	boy
həm ˈdumra	هم دومره		*adv.*	only this much

dwem sa'bəq دويم سبق

Lesson Two

Dialogue two: Introductions

L: pa xer 'rāɣle! Welcome! (*Lit.* You came in peace!)	په خير راغلې!
H: xo'dey de 'ubaxa! May you live in peace!	خُدائ دې اوبخښه!
L: 'tsənga ye? si'hət de xə dey? How are you? Is your health good?	څنګه يې؟ صحت دې ښۀ دے؟
H: xə yɪm. tə 'tsənge ye? I'm fine. How are you?	ښۀ يم. ته څنګه يې؟
L: də xo'dey 'fəzəl dey, xə yɪm. By the grace of God, I'm well. zə'mā num ǰān dey. My name is John. stā num tsə dey? What is your name?	د خُدائ فضل دے، ښۀ يم. زما نُوم جان دے. ستا نُوم څۀ دے؟
H: zə'mā num ɪm'dād dey. My name is Imdad.	زما نُوم امداد دے.
L: tə də kəm zay ye? *or* tə də kəm zay na rāɣəley ye? Where are you from?	تۀ د کُوم ځائ يې؟ (يا) تۀ د کُوم ځائ نه راغلے يې؟
H: zə də mar'dān yɪm. *or* zə də mar'dān na rāɣəley yɪm. I'm from Mardan.	زۀ د مردان يم. (يا) زۀ د مردان نه راغلے يم.
L: zə də lan'dən yɪm. I'm from London.	زۀ د لندن يم.

NOTE:

Names are not usually exchanged until the initial conversation is almost finished.

Pronunciation drill

1. Contrasting / ṭ / ټ with / ḍ / ډ

zə ṭāl la'rəm. زۀ ټال لرم.

zə ḍāl la'rəm. زۀ ډال لرم.

ṭol šta. ټول شته.

ḍol šta. ډول شته.

ˈhalta ṭak šo. هلته ټک شو.

dā ḍak šo. دا ډک شو.

dā tāl dey. دا تال دے.

dā ṭāl dey. دا ټال دے.

2. Contrasting / **ā** / ا with / **a** / (may not have a character in script form)

dā xār dey. دا ښار دے.

dā xar dey. دا خر دے.

ˈhaɣa ɣār dey. هغه غار دے.

ˈhaɣa ɣar dey. هغه غر دے.

Demonstrative pronouns: 'this' *dā* and 'that' *ˈdaɣa, ˈhaɣa* دا، دغه، هغه

dā	دا	this
ˈdaɣa	دغه	that (nearby objects)
ˈhaɣa	هغه	that (distant objects)

'this' *dā* and 'that' *ˈdaɣa, ˈhaɣa* with masculine nouns and adjectives

Pronoun	Adjective	Noun	Verb	
dā	lənḍ	pɪnˈsəl	dey.	دا لنډ پنسل دے. This is a short pencil.
dā	ˈugəd	qaˈləm	dey.	دا اُوږد قلم دے. This is a long pen.
ˈdaɣa	drund	mez	dey.	دغه دروُند میز دے. That is a heavy table.
ˈdaɣa	spək	kiˈtāb	dey.	دغه سپک کتاب دے. That is a light book.

'haɣa	tor	war	dey.	هغه تور ور دے. That is a black door.
'haɣa	spin	kā'ɣəz	dey.	هغه سپین کاغذ دے. That is a white paper.
dā	ha'lək	xə	dey.	دا هلک ښهٔ دے. This boy is good.
dā	ki'tāb	xa'rāb	dey.	دا کتاب خراب دے. This book is bad.
'daɣa	ba'laxt	šin	dey.	دغه بالخت شین دے. This pillow is green.
'haɣa	spey	ɣaṭ	dey.	هغه سپے غټ دے. That male dog is big.
'haɣa	sa'ṛey	wa'ṛukey	dey.	هغه سړے وړُوکے دے. That man is small.

☝ Have the teacher point to objects that are close and far away, substituting nouns already introduced. Don't introduce new vocabulary. Use the question *dā tsə šey dey?* (دا څهٔ شے دے؟) 'What is this?' to elicit new vocabulary.

NOTES:

1. Demonstrative pronouns do not change in form for plural nouns.
2. *dā* (دا) is used for an object in the hand, or within easy reach.
3. *šin* (شین) can mean either 'green' or 'blue'.

Subject pronouns with masculine adjectives

Pronoun	Adjective	Verb	
zə	'stəṛey	yım.	زهٔ ستړے یم. I am tired.
ha'ɣa	'xkwəley	dey.	هغه ښکُلے دے. He is handsome.
tə	ǰoṛ	ye?	تهٔ جوړ یې؟ Are you well?

ˈhaɣa	ɣaṭ	dey.	هغه غټ دے. That/he is big.
dey	naˈrey	dey.	دے نرے دے. He is thin.
dā	drund	dey.	دا دروند دے. This is heavy.

NOTE:

When two consecutive adjectives are used, *āw* (او) 'and' is inserted between the two adjectives. For example:

dā ɣaṭ āw drund mez dey.	This is a large and heavy table.	دا غټ او دروند مېز دے.
ˈhaɣa moˈṭər tor āw spin dey.	That car is black and white.	هغه موټر تور او سپین دے.

Questions and answers

tə ˈstəṛey ye?	Are you tired?	تۀ ستړے يې؟
na, ḍer ˈstəṛey nə yım.	No, I'm not very tired.	نه، ډېر ستړے نۀ يم.
dā ɣaṭ kiˈtāb dey?	Is this a big book?	دا غټ کتاب دے؟
āw, dā ɣaṭ kiˈtāb dey.	Yes, this is a big book.	آو، دا غټ کتاب دے.
tə ˈtəgey ye?	Are you (*m.*) thirsty?	تۀ تږے يې؟
āw, zə ḍer ˈtəgey yım.	Yes, I (*m.*) am very thirsty.	آو، زۀ ډېر تږے يم.
ˈhaɣa moˈṭər kəm rang dey?	What colour is that car?	هغه موټر کُوم رنګ دے؟
ˈhaɣa spin āw sur dey.	It's white and red.	هغه سپین او سُور دے.
ˈdaɣa mez drund dey?	Is this table heavy?	دغه مېز دروند دے؟
na, ˈdaɣa mez drund nə dey, spək dey.	No, this table is not heavy, it's light.	نه، دغه مېز دروند نۀ دے، سپک دے.

Questions and answers with: 'what?' *tsə* and 'how?' *ˈtsənga* څۀ، څنګه

ˈdaɣa tsə šey dey?	What is that?	دغه څۀ شے دے؟
ˈdaɣa qaˈləm dey.	It's a pen.	دغه قلم دے.

dā qa'ləm 'tsənga dey?	How is this pen?	دا قلم څنګه دے؟
dā xə qa'ləm dey.	It is a good pen.	دا ښۀ قلم دے.
'haɣa tsə šey dey?	What thing is that?	هغه څۀ شے دے؟
'haɣa mo'ṭər dey.	That is a car.	هغه موټر دے.
'haɣa mo'ṭər 'tsənga dey?	How is that car?	هغه موټر څنګه دے؟
'haɣa mo'ṭər ḍer xa'rāb dey.	That car is very bad.	هغه موټر ډېر خراب دے.

Memorising moment

mata'luna

په هر چا خپل وطن کشمير دے.

pa har čā xpəl wa'tən kaš'mir dey.

For everyone his own country is Kashmir.

خپل عمل دَ لارې مل دے.

xpəl a'məl də 'lāre məl dey.

Your own deeds are with you on your path.

NOTE:

Be careful to listen to the pronunciation of place names like Kashmir. Many are quite different from the English way of saying them.

Find out and use the Pukhto pronunciations of Peshawar, Nowshera, Swat and Pakistan, etc.

Exercises for Lesson Two

1. Use the correct form of the verb 'to be' in the following sentences.

a. 'daɣa mez drund ________________. — دغه مېز درُوند ________________.

b. 'haɣa mo'ṭər ɣaṭ ________________. — هغه موټر غټ ________________.

c. tə ḍer 'stəṛey ________________. — تۀ ډېر سترے ________________.

d. dā qaˈləm tor nə ________________.   ________________ دا قلم تور نهٔ.

e. zə ḍer ˈtəgey nə ________________.   ________________ زهٔ ډېر تږے نهٔ.

f. stā num tsə ________________?   ________________ ستا نُوم څهٔ؟

2. Use the correct pronoun to complete the following sentences:

a. ________________ ˈwəgey nə yım.   وږے نهٔ یم ________________.

b. ________________ xə saˈṛey ye.   ښهٔ سړے یې ________________.

c. ________________ tor kiˈtāb nə dey.   تور کتاب نهٔ دے ________________.

d. ________________ ḍer ˈstəṛey yım.   ډېر ستړے یم ________________.

e. ________________ mez ˈugəd dey.   مېز اُوږد دے ________________.

f. ________________ tsənga ye?   څنګه یې؟ ________________

Vocabulary for Lesson Two

āw	او		*conj.*	and
ˈugəd / ugˈdə	اُوږد / اُوږدهٔ	*m.*	*adj.*	long
ugˈda / ugˈde	اُوږده / اُوږدې	*f.*		
baˈlaxt / balaxˈtuna	بالخت / بالختُونه	*m.*	*n.*	pillow
pınˈsəl	پِنسل	*m.s.*	*n.*	pencil
ˈtəgey	تږے	*m.s.*	*adj.*	thirsty
tor	تور	*m.*	*adj.*	black
ˈtora / ˈtore	توره / تورې	*f.*		
zay	ځائ	*m.s.*	*n.*	place, space
tsə	څهٔ		*q., pro.*	what
xaˈrāb	خراب	*m.*	*adj.*	bad, spoiled, ruined, decayed, faulty, poor quality
xaˈrāba / xaˈrābe	خرابه / خرابې	*f.*		
xer	خېر		*adj.*	OK, fine, good; 'peace' (in greetings)
dā	دا	*m., f.*	*dem. pro.*	this, it
drund / drāˈnə	درُوند / درانهٔ	*m.*	*adj.*	heavy; important, esteemed
draˈna / draˈne	درنه / درنې	*f.*		
ˈdaɣa	دغه	*m., f.*	*dem. pro.*	that, it
rang	رنګ	*m.s.*	*n.*	colour, dye, paint; kind, manner
spək	سپک	*m.*	*adj.*	light; worthless, dishonourable
ˈspəka / ˈspəke	سپکه / سپکې	*f.*		
spəy	سپۍ	*f.*	*n.*	bitch (female dog)
spey / spi	سپے / سپی	*m.*	*n.*	dog
spin	سپین	*m.*	*adj.*	white
ˈspina / ˈspine	سپینه / سپینې	*f.*		
ˈstəṛey / ˈstəṛi	ستړے / ستړی	*m.*	*adj.*	tired, exhausted, weary, fatigued

sur / srə	سُور / سرهٔ	*m.*	*adj.*	red; hot, scorching
sra / sre	سره / سرې	*f.*		
šin / šnə	شین / شنهٔ	*m.*	*adj.*	green; blue; clear (cloudless blue sky); fine
šna / šne	شنه / شنې	*f.*		
ˈxkwəley / ˈxkwəli	ښکُلے / ښکُلی	*m.*	*adj.*	handsome, beautiful, pretty, lovely, nice, good-looking
ˈxkwəle	ښکُلې	*f.*		
siˈhət	صحت	*m.*	*n.*	health
ɣaṭ	غټ	*m.*	*adj.*	big, large, fat
ˈɣaṭa / ˈɣaṭe	غټه / غټې	*f.*		
ˈfəzəl	فضل	*m.*	*n.*	grace, blessing
qaˈləm	قلم	*m.s.*	*n.*	pen
kāˈɣəz / kāɣəzˈuna	کاغذ / کاغذونه	*m.*	*n.*	paper
kiˈtāb / kitābˈuna	کتاب / کتابونه	*m.*	*n.*	book
kəm [kum]	کُوم	*m.*	*q., pro.*	which
kəma [kuma]	کُومه	*f.*		
lənḍ	لنډ	*m.*	*adj.*	short
ˈlənḍa / ˈlənḍe	لنډه / لنډې	*f.*		
moˈṭər	موټر	*m.s.*	*n.*	car, motor, truck, automobile
mez / mezˈuna	مېز / مېزونه	*m.*	*n.*	table, desk
naˈrey	نرے	*m.s.*	*adj.*	thin
naˈrəy	نرۍ	*f.s.*		
num / nuˈmuna	نُوم / نومُونه	*m*	*n.*	name
war	ور	*m.s.*	*n.*	door
waˈṛukey	وړُوکے	*m.s.*	*n., adj.*	small, little; child; boy
ˈhaɣa	هغه	*m., f.*	*dem. pro.*	that, it

drem saˈbəq دریم سبق

Lesson Three

Dialogue three: Shopping

H: ˈtsənga hāl dey? How are you?	څنګه حال دے؟
L: merabāˈni, xə yım. ˈtāso ˈtsənga yəy? Thanks, I'm fine. How are you?	مِهربانی، ښهٔ یم. تاسو څنګه یئ؟
L: de tə pəxˈto ke tsə ˈwaye? What do you call this in Pukhto?	دې ته پښتو کښې څهٔ وائی؟
H: dā pyāz di. These are onions.	دا پیاز دی.
L: pyāz kiˈlo pa tso di? How much is a kilo of onions?	پیاز کلو په څو دی؟
H: āβˈyā ruˈpəy kilo. Seventy rupees a kilo.	اویا روپۍ کلو.
L: yo pāw ˈrāka. Give me one *pao* (quarter of a kilo).	یو پاؤ راکه.
L: darˈzən keˈle pa tso di? How much are a dozen bananas?	درزن کیلې په څو دی؟
H: pa tsalˈwext ruˈpəy di. They are forty rupees.	په څلوېښت روپۍ دی.
L: ˈḍere ˈgrāne di, ləge arˈzāne ˈrāka! They are very expensive. Give me a little cheaper!	ډېرې ګرانې دی، لږې ارزانې راکه!
H: xer dey, pa pinˈzə derš ruˈpəy ˈrāka! It's OK, give me thirty-five rupees.	خیر دے، په پینځهٔ دېرش روپۍ راکه.
L: ṭik da. That's fine.	ټیک ده.
H: nor tsə šey paˈkār dey? Do you want anything else?	نور څهٔ شے پکار دے؟
L: na bas dey, yār. No that is enough, friend.	نه بس دے، یار.
L: ṭole ˈtsumra peˈse šwe? How much does it all come to?	ټولې څومره پیسې شوې؟

NOTE:

yār (یار) means 'friend'. It is not appropriate for women to use *yār* when speaking to men. Ladies can use the phrase *na bas dey, merabāˈni.* (نه بس دے، مِهربانی.) instead.

Ladies' dialogue: Making friends

L: ˈāsalām aˈlekum! Peace be upon you!	السلام عليکم!
H: waˈālekum a-saˈlām! And upon you be peace!	وعليکم السلام!
L: zə ˈhalta oˈsegəm āw zə pəxˈto ɪzˈda kaˈwəm. I live over there and I am learning Pukhto.	زۀ هلته اوسيږم او زۀ پښتو زده کوم.
H: xa! dəˈnəna ˈrāša! Good! Come in!	ښه! دننه راشه!
L: pəxˈto ˈgrāna da āw zəˈmā ləg maˈdəd paˈkār dey. Pukhto is difficult and I need a little help.	پښتو گرانه ده او زما لږ مدد پکار دے.
H: xo zə pa liˈkəlo ˈbānde nə poˈhigəm. But I don't know writing.	خو زۀ په ليکلو باندې نۀ پوهيږم.
L: xer dey. āse zəˈmā swāl dey če tə ləg zəˈmā təlaˈfuz ṭik kaˈwəley še? That's OK. My request is, can you simply correct my pronunciation?	خير دے. هسې زما سوال دے چې ته لږ زما تلفُظ ټيک کولے شې؟
H: ˈbɪlkəl! be ˈɣama ša! Sure! Don't be worried!	بِلکل! بې غمه شه!
L: dā tsə dey? What is this?	دا څۀ دے؟

NOTE:

While Pukhtun women are very hospitable, they are also very busy. It is hard for language learners to find ladies to visit simply for brief conversations. It takes time to have tea, and be polite. So, relax and enjoy new friendships.

Numbers one to ten

1	yo	يو	۱	6	špəg	شپږ	۶
2	dwa	دوه	۲	7	uˈwə	اووۀ	۷
3	dre	درې	۳	8	āˈtə	اتۀ	۸
4	tsaˈlor	څلور	۴	9	ˈnəhə	نهۀ	۹
5	pinˈzə	پينځۀ	۵	10	ləs	لس	۱۰

NOTE:

Urdu numbers are also commonly used, especially in the bigger cities.

A shopping list

☝ This list is a starting point only. In the space provided, add other things you often need to buy. You will find that the words you use are the words you will remember. Role play shopping with your language helper.

Dried Food

ˈwriǰe rice	وریژې
oˈṛə flour	اوړهٔ
čiˈni sugar	چینی
ˈgarma masāˈla curry powder	گرمه مساله

Vegetables

gul goˈpi cauliflower	گُل گوپی
ṭeˈpər turnip	ټیپر
muˈləy radish	مُولی
maˈṭər peas	مټر

Fruit

ānˈgur grape	انگور
ām mango	آم
keˈla banana	کیله
seβ, maˈṇa apple	سېو، منړه
āmˈrud guava	امرُود
mālˈṭa orange	مالټه
našpāˈtəy pear	ناشپاتئ

Other Useful Items

šāt honey	شات
maˈhe fish	مهی
ˈɣaṭa ˈɣwaxa beef	غټه غوښه
naˈrəy ˈɣwaxa mutton	نری غوښه
māsˈtə yogurt	ماستهٔ
ˈmālga salt	مالگه

NOTE:

How is your pronunciation going? Pukhtuns are so pleased you are learning their language that they will seldom correct you. You will have to find other ways to check yourself. One good test is to go to a shop and ask for an item without pointing to it. You know you are doing well when you get what you asked for. If you are having particular trouble with one sound, ask for something with that sound in it.

When you can get peas (/ ṭ / ټ), beef (/ ɣ / غ) and flour (/ ṛ / ړ) without any trouble, you are doing well. The ultimate test is to go into a shop that does not stock the item you find hard to pronounce. Because the word is out of context you will only be understood if your pronunciation is accurate.

Pronunciation drill

Contrasting / **r** / ر and / **ṛ** / ړ

dā sur dey.	This is red.	دا سُور دے.
dā soṛ dey.	This is cold.	دا سوړ دے.
ˈhaɣa ɣwaṛ dey.	That is oily.	هغه غوړ دے.
ˈhaɣa war dey.	That is a door.	هغه ور دے.
zə ˈlāṛəm.	I went.	زهٔ لاړم.
zə laˈrəm.	I have.	زهٔ لرم.
dā zoṛ saˈṛey ṛund dey.	This old man is blind.	دا زوړ سړے ړُوند دے.

Plural subject pronouns

Person	Pronoun		Verb	
we	mung	مُونږ	yu	يو
you	ˈtāso	تاسو	yəy	يئ
they	hayˈwi	هغوی	di	دی

Masculine plural nouns

Nouns in Pukhto agree by changing their endings. The two most common masculine plural endings are / -i / ی - and / -ān / ان - .

saˈṛey (a man)	سړے	changes to	saˈṛi (men)	سړی
ḍākˈṭər (a doctor)	ډاکټر	changes to	ḍākṭəˈrān (doctors)	ډاکټران

Here are some examples:

zə tālıˈbıləm yim.	I am a student.	زۀ طالبعلم يم.
ˈtāso tālıbılˈmān yəy?	Are you students?	تاسو طالبعلمان يئ؟
haˈɣa špunˈkey dey.	He is a shepherd.	هغه شپُونکے دے.
haɣˈwi špunˈki di.	They are shepherds.	هغوی شپُونکی دی.

NOTE:
Nouns can be either singular or plural (number), masculine or feminine (gender), and be one of two basic cases; direct or oblique. Depending on whether they are in the direct or oblique case, nouns undergo a number of inflections which will be introduced later.

Changing masculine nouns to their plural forms

Have your helper say the sentence in the singular form. You make it plural.

Endings in / -ey / ے- change to / -i / ی-

haˈɣa kamˈyāb saˈṛey dey.	He is a successful man.	هغه کامیاب سړے دے.
haɣˈwi kamˈyāb saˈṛi di.	They are successful men.	هغوی کامیاب سړی دی.

Consonant endings become / -ān / ان-

haˈɣa məšaˈhur ḍākˈṭər dey.	He is a famous doctor.	هغه مشهُور ډاکټر دے.
haɣˈwi məšaˈhur ḍākṭəˈrān di.	They are famous doctors.	هغوی مشهُور ډاکټران دی.
tə yo klək musalˈmān ye?	Are you a strong Muslim?	تهٔ یو کلک مُسلمان يې؟
ˈtāso klək musalmāˈnān yəy?	Are you strong Muslims?	تاسو کلک مسلمانان يئ.
dey yo mālˈdār māˈlək dey.	He is a rich tribal leader.	دے یو مالدار ملک دے.
haɣˈwi mālˈdāra maləˈkān di.	They are rich tribal leaders.	هغوی مالداره ملکان دی.

Endings in / -ā / ا- and / -i / ی- change to / -ān / ان-

ˈhaɣa muˈlā ɣaṭ dey.	That mullah is fat.	هغه مُلا غټ دے.
ˈhaɣa mulaˈyān ɣaṭ di.	Those mullahs are fat.	هغه مُليان غټ دی.
haˈɣa səst isāˈi dey.	He is a lazy Christian.	هغه سست عیسائی دے.

hayˈwi səst isāˈyān di.	They are lazy Christians.	هغوی سست عیسایان دی.

Certain nouns change to / -ānə / انهٔ-

dey kuṇ pəxˈtun dey.	He is a deaf Pukhtun.	دے کُوڼ پښتُون دے.
hayˈwi kāˈṇə pəxtāˈnə di.	They are deaf Pukhtuns.	هغوی کانړهٔ پښتانهٔ دی.
dā drund melˈma dey.	He is an important guest.	دا درُوند مېلمه دے.
hayˈwi drāˈnə melmāˈnə di.	They are important guests.	هغوی درانهٔ مېلمانهٔ دی.

NOTE:
drund (درُوند) literally means 'heavy', but also refers to an important or honourable person. In contrast, a worthless person is considered *spək* (سپک).

Personal pronouns

Person	Singular			Plural		
1st	my, mine	zəˈmā	زما	our, ours	zmung	زمُونږ
2nd	your, yours	stā	ستا	your, yours	ˈstāso	ستاسو
3rd m.	his	də də	د دهٔ	their, theirs (near)	də di, də dwi	د دی، د دوئ
3rd f.	hers	də de	د دې	their, theirs (near)	də di, də dwi	د دی، د دوئ
3rd m.	his (far)	də haˈɣə	د هغهٔ	their, theirs (far)	də haɣˈi, də haɣˈwi	د هغئ، د هغوی
3rd f.	hers (far)	də haˈɣe	د هغې	their, theirs (far)	də haɣˈi, də haɣˈwi	د هغئ، د هغوی

NOTE:
Refer also to the introduction of possessive pronouns in Lesson Seven.

Irregular family names

Here are four irregular plural forms of kinship terms:

zəˈmā trə ḍer xəˈfa dey.	My uncle is very upset.	زما ترهٔ ډېر خفه دے.
zəˈmā ˈtruna ḍer xəˈfa di.	My uncles are very upset.	زما ترُونه ډېر خفه دی.
haˈɣa xə plār dey.	He is a good father.	هغه ښهٔ پلار دے.
hayˈwi xə plāˈrān di.	They are good fathers.	هغوی ښهٔ پلاران دی.

stā wror ḍer takˈṛa dey. — Your brother is very strong. — ستا ورور ډېر تکړه دے.

stā ˈwruṇa ḍer takˈṛa di. — Your brothers are very strong. — ستا وروڼه ډېر تکړه دي.

zəˈmā mor ˈstəṛe da. — My mother is tired. — زما مور ستړې ده.

zmung ˈmyende ˈstəṛi di. — Our mothers are tired. — زمونږ میاندې ستړې دي.

Comprehension drill: Counting

This is the first drill where you will act like a soldier on parade. Simply obey the instructions without comment. The more vigorously you do so the more easily new words will stick. Teach your helper to slowly add new words according to your success, and keep going back and mixing them up.

ˈyəwa ˈguta xkāˈra ka! — یوه ګوته ښکاره که!

dwa ˈgute xkāˈra ka! — دوه ګوتې ښکاره که!

dre ˈgute xkāˈra ka! — درې ګوتې ښکاره که!

ləs ˈgute xkāˈra ka! — لس ګوتې ښکاره که!

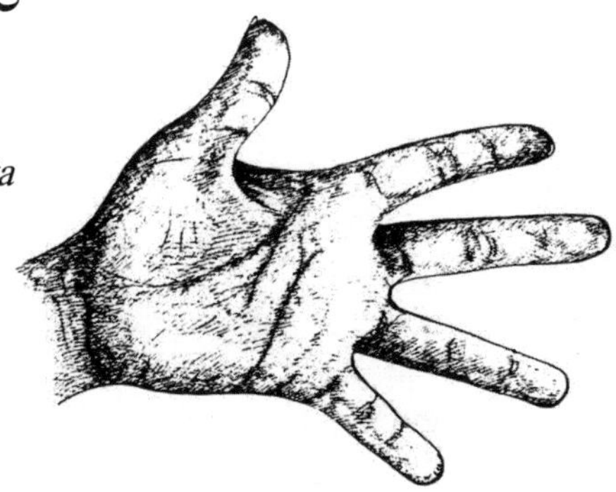

NOTE:

Pukhto is a rhyming language. Here the / -a / ـه - ending on *ˈguta* ګوته (a finger) modifies the *yo* یو (one) to *ˈyəwa* یوه.
More on this later.

Memorising moment

mataˈluna

په پردی لاس مار وژل هم ښۀ نۀ دی.

pa praˈdi lās mār waˈǰəl həm xə ˈnə di.

Even a snake shouldn't be killed by another's hand.

دَ اُوښ غلا په ټيټه ملا نۀ کيږی.

də ux ɣlā pa ˈṭiṭa mlā ˈnə kigi.

A camel can't be stolen with a bent back.

خپل څادر سره خپې غزوه.

xpəl tsā'dər sa'ra xpe ɣəzawa.

Stretch your feet according to your cover.

Reminder: First learn the proverbs and then explore their meanings with your new friends.

Exercises for Lesson Three

1. Substitute the words below for the underlined word in the sentence:

   ☝ Have your helper say the first sentence and then call out the words to be substituted in. This pattern of practice is best limited to known vocabulary words.

   pyāz pa tso di? پیاز په څو دی؟

māl'ṭa مالټا	ā'lu آلو	mrəč / marčakey مرچ / مرچکے	ṭamā'ṭər ټماټر

2. Make the following sentences plural:

   a. ha'ɣa wa'ṛukey mā'šum dey. هغه وړوکے ماشُوم دے.

   ____

   b. zə klək isā'i yım. زۀ کلک عیسائی یم.

   ____

   c. dey xə mel'ma dey. دے ښۀ مېلمه دے.

   ____

   d. tə ḍer 'stəṛey ye. تۀ ډېر ستړے يې.

   ____

   e. zə pəx'tun yım. زۀ پښتُون یم.

   ____

   f. zə 'wəgey yım. زۀ وږے یم.

   ____

   g. ha'ɣa 'xkwəley dey. هغه ښکُلے دے.

   ____

3. Use the correct form of the present tense of the verb 'to be' to complete each sentence:

a. zə pəxtun ________________. — زهٔ پښتُون ________________.

b. mung melmāˈnə ________________. — مُونږ مېلمانهٔ ________________.

c. ˈtāso ˈstəṛi ________________. — تاسو سترې ________________.

d. haˈɣa haˈlək ________________. — هغه هلک ________________.

e. mung ˈtəgi ________________. — مُونږ تږې ________________.

f. hayˈwi qāziˈān ________________? — هغوی قاضيان ________________؟

g. mung ˈstəṛi ________________. — مُونږ سترې ________________.

h. hayˈwi haləˈkān ________________. — هغوی هلکان ________________.

4. Substitution: Use the words below to change the basic sentence:

zə ḍākˈṭər yım. — زهٔ ډاکټر يم.

a.	dey	دے	f.	hayˈwi	هغوی
b.	tāˈlıbıləm	طالبعلم	g.	pəxtāˈnə	پښتانهٔ
c.	məšaˈhur	مشهُور	h.	musalmāˈnān	مسلمانان
d.	ˈstəṛi	سترې	i.	ḍākṭərˈān	ډاکټران
e.	mung	مُونږ	j.	ˈtāso	تاسو

Vocabulary for Lesson Three

ām	آم	m.	n.	mango
ā'tə	اتۀ		n., adj.	eight
ar'zān	ارزان	m.	adj.	cheap, inexpensive
ar'zāna / ar'zāne	ارزانه / ارزانې	f.		
ām'rud	امرُود	m.	n.	guava
ān'gur	انګُور	m.pl.	n.	grapes
o'ṛə	اوړۀ	m.pl.	n.	flour
ose'dəl	اوسېدل		v.t.	to live, to stay, to reside
u'wə	اووۀ		n., adj.	seven
āβ'yā	اويا		n., adj.	seventy
'bānde	باندې		prep., post.	on, above, up; about
bas	بس		adv.	enough; just; OK; stop
'bılkəl	بِلکل		adv.	entirely, wholly, absolutely, exactly
pāw	پاؤ	m.	n.	*pao* (= quarter kilo)
pa'kār	پکار		prep. ph.	need
pohe'dəl	پوهېدل		v.t.	to know, to understand
pa tso	په څو		q. adv.	how much
pe'se	پېسې	f.pl.	n.	money
pyāz	پياز	m.	n.	onion
pin'zə	پينځۀ		n., adj.	five
pin'zə derš	پينځۀ دېرش		n., adj.	thirty-five
'tāso	تاسو	m., f.	pro.	you (plural or formal)
tak'ṛa	تکړه	m., f.	adj.	strong, energetic, healthy; skilful
trə	ترۀ	m.	n.	uncle (paternal)
təla'fuz	تلفُظ	m.	n.	pronunciation
ṭol	ټول		adj.	all, whole

ṭe'pər	ټېپر	*m.*	*n.*	turnip
ṭik	ټیک	*m.*	*adj.*	OK
či'ni	چینی	*f.*	*n.*	sugar
tsa'lor	څلور		*n., adj.*	four
tsal'wext	څلوېښت		*n., adj.*	forty
'tsumra	څومره		*q., adj.*	how much, how many
hāl	حال	*m.s.*	*n.*	condition of health, state, mood
xə'fa [xə'pa]	خفه [خپه]	*m., f.*	*adj.*	upset, angry, mad, sad, unhappy, gloomy, discouraged
xo	خو		*q., adv., conj*	but
dar'zən	درزن	*m.*	*n.*	dozen
dre	درې		*n., adj.*	three
də'nəna	دننه		*adv.*	inside, interior
dwa	دوه		*n., adj.*	two
ḍāk'ṭər	ډاکټر	*m.s.*	*n.*	doctor
rāka'wəl	راکول		*v.t.*	to give me
ru'pəy	روپۍ	*f.*	*n.*	rupee
ṛund / ṛān'də	ړُوند / ړاندهٔ	*m.*	*adj. n.*	blind; blind person
ṛan'da / ṛan'de	ړنده / ړندې	*f.*		
zmung	زمُونږ	*m., f.*	*pos. pro.*	our
stā	ستا	*m., f.*	*pos. pro.*	your
səst	سست	*m.*	*adj.*	lazy; loose; weak
'səsta / 'səste	سسته / سستې	*f.*		
swāl / swāl'una	سوال / سوالونه	*m.*	*n.*	request, question, query; begging
soṛ	سوړ	*m.*	*adj.*	cold
seβ	سېو	*m.*	*n.*	apple

šāt	شات	*m.pl.*	*n.*	honey
špəg	شپږ		*n., adj.*	six
šey	شے	*m.*	*n.*	thing, object, matter, substance
isāˈi / isāˈyān	عیسائی / عیسایان	*m.*	*n.*	Christian; A.D.
ˈɣaṭa ˈɣwaxa	غټه غوښه	*f.s.*	*n.*	beef
ɣəm	غم	*m.*	*n.*	sorrow, worry, anxiety
ɣwaṛ	غوړ	*m.*	*adj.*	oily
kamˈyāb	کامیاب	*m.*	*adj.*	successful
ke	کښې		*post.*	in, inside
klək	کلک	*m.*	*adj.*	hard, firm, solid; staunch
ˈkləka / ˈkləke	کلکه / کلکې	*f.*		
kiˈlo	کلو	*m.*	*n.*	1000 grams, 1 kilogram
kuṇ / kāˈṇə	کُوڼ / کاڼهٔ	*m.*	*adj.*	deaf
kaˈṇa / kaˈṇe	کڼه / کڼې	*f.*		
keˈla	کیله	*f.s.*	*n.*	banana
grān	ګران	*m.*	*adj.*	expensive, costly; dear (i.e. special); difficult
ˈgrāna / ˈgrāne	ګرانه / ګرانې	*f.*		
ˈgarma masāˈla	ګرمه مساله [مصالحه]	*f.s.*	*n.*	curry powder
gul goˈpi	ګُل ګوپی	*f.*	*n.*	cauliflower
ˈguta / ˈgute	ګوته / ګوتې	*f.*	*n.*	finger; toe; ring
ləg	لږ	*m.*	*adj.*	little, less, few, a few
ˈləga / ˈləge	لږه / لږې	*f.*		
ləs	لس		*n., adj.*	ten
liˈkəl	لیکل		*v.t.*	to write
māsˈtə	ماستهٔ	*m.pl.*	*n.*	yoghurt [yogurt]
mālˈṭa	مالټه	*f.s.*	*n.*	orange

māl'dār	مالدار	*m.*	*adj.*	rich, wealthy
māl'dāra / māl'dāre	مالداره / مالداري	*f.*		
mā'lək / mālə'kān	ملک / ملکان	*m.*	*n.*	chieftain, tribal leader, village head
'mālga	مالگه	*f.*	*n.*	salt
ma'ṭər	مټر	*m.*	*n.*	peas
ma'dəd	مدد	*m.*	*n.*	aid, help, assistance
musal'mān / musalmā'nān	مُسلمان / مسلمانان	*m.*	*n.*	Muslim
məša'hur	مشهُور	*m.*	*adj.*	famous, renowned, well-known
mu'lā / mulā'yān	مُلا / مُلیان	*m.*	*n.*	mullah
ma'ṇa	منڼه	*f.s.*	*n.*	apple
mor / 'myende	مور / میاندې	*f.*	*n.*	mother
mu'ləy	مُولۍ	*f.s.*	*n.*	radish
mung	مُونږ	*m., f.*	*pro.*	we
ma'he	مهی	*m.s.*	*n.*	fish
mel'ma / melma'nə	مېلمه / مېلمانهٔ	*m.*	*n.*	guest
našpā'təy	ناشپاتئ	*f.s.*	*n.*	pear
na'rəy 'ɣwaxa	نرۍ غوښه	*f.s.*	*n.*	sheep or goat's meat
nor	نور	*m.*	*adj., adv.*	more; other
'nəhə	نههٔ		*n., adj.*	nine
wror / 'wruṇa	ورور / ورونړه	*m.*	*n.*	brother
'wriǰe	وريژې	*f.pl.*	*n.*	rice
haɣ'wi	هغوی	*m., f.*	*pro.*	they (far)
'halta	هلته		*adv.*	there
yār	یار	*m.*	*n.*	friend
yo	یو		*n., adj.*	one

tsaloˈrəm saˈbəq څلورم سبق

Lesson Four

Dialogue four: A learner's role

L: zə pəxˈto ɪzˈda kaˈwəl ˈɣwāṛəm. I want to learn Pukhto.	زهٔ پښتو زده کول غواړم.
H: ḍer xə, yār. Very good, friend.	ډېر ښهٔ، يار.
L: ˈasəl ke zəˈmā pəxtāˈnə ḍer xwax di. Actually I like Pukhtuns a lot.	اصل کښې زما پښتانهٔ ډېر خوښ دي.
H: xo pəxˈto ḍera ˈgrāna da. But Pukhto is very difficult.	خو پښتو ډېره ګرانه ده.
L: zə rozāˈna yo dwa ˈnewi ˈṭɪki ɪzˈda kaˈwəm. I learn a few new words every day.	زهٔ روزانه يو دوه نوي ټکي زده کوم.
H: xa! dāˈna dāˈna če yo zay ši ɣər ši. Good! A speck on a speck makes a mountain.	ښه! دانه دانه چې يو ځای شي غر شي.
L: bɪlˈkəl! zə ˈdəlta byā rātˈləl ˈɣwāṛəm. Exactly! I want to come back here again.	بِلکل! زهٔ دلته بيا راتلل غواړم.
H: har ˈkəla ˈrāša. pa ˈməxa de xə! Come anytime. May you face good!	هر کله راشه. په مخه دې ښه!
L: də xoˈdey pa aˈmān! May you be found in God's peace!	د خُدای په آمان!

Pronunciation drill

1. Contrasting / ṭ / ټ and / t / ت

dā ṭāl dey.	This is a swing.	دا ټال دے.
dā tār dey.	This is a thread.	دا تار دے.

ˈdaɣa ṭol šo.	That has rolled-up.	دغه ټول شو.
ˈdaɣa tor dey.	That is black.	دغه تور دے.
ṭop	jump	ټوپ
top	cannon	توپ

2. Contrasting / **u** / وُ and / **o** / و

dā ˈtura da.	This is a sword.	دا تُوره ده.
dā ˈtora da.	This is black.	دا توره ده.
haˈɣa zəˈmā lur da.	That is my daughter.	هغه زما لُور ده.
ˈhaɣa zəˈmā lor dey.	That is my sickle.	هغه زما لور دے.
dā tut dey.	This is a mulberry.	دا تُوت دے.
dā tod dey.	This is warm.	دا تود دے.

Plural sentences

Demonstrative adjective	Noun	Adjective	Verb	
dā	kitāˈbuna	xə	di.	دا کتابونه ښۀ دی. These books are good.
dā	āluˈgān	xaˈrāb	di.	دا آلُوګان خراب دی. These potatoes are bad.
ˈdaɣa	qaləˈmuna	naˈri	di.	دغه قلمُونه نری دی. These pens are thin.
ˈdaɣa	məngəˈkān	šetāˈnān	di.	دغه منږکان شيطانان دی. These mice are bothersome.
ˈhaɣa	wārˈuna	spin	di.	هغه ورونه سپين دی. Those doors are white.
ˈhaɣa	uˈxān	ɣaṭ	di.	هغه اُوښان غټ دی. Those camels are big.

NOTE:

šeˈtān (شيطان) 'the devil' is also an adjective meaning 'naughty' or 'troublesome'.

Making masculine nouns plural

Inanimate nouns ending in a consonant are inflected to / -una / -ونه

dā luy kor dey.	This is a big house.	دا لوئ کور دے.
dā luy ko'runa di.	These are big houses.	دا لوئ کورونه دی.

/ -ey / ے endings become / -i / ی -

stā spey wa'ṛukey dey.	Your dog is small.	ستا سپے وړُوکے دے.
stā spi wā'ṛə di.	Your dogs are small.	ستا سپی واړهٔ دی.

Animate nouns ending in a consonant are changed to / -ān / -ان

'haɣa mār lənḍ dey.	That snake is short.	هغه مار لنډ دے.
'haɣa mār'ān 'lənḍi di.	Those snakes are short.	هغه ماران لنډی دی.
'daɣa xatar'nāk la'ṛəm dey.	That is a dangerous scorpion.	دغه خطرناک لړم دے.
'daɣa xatar'nāk laṛəmā'nān di.	Those are dangerous scorpions.	دغه خطرناک لړمانان دی.

NOTE:
Notice how the adjective *lənḍ* (لنډ) rhymes with the verb by adding / ī / ی to become *lənḍī* (لنډی). This type of agreement is like Cockney rhyming slang and is best learned by mimicry rather than by following rules.

Inanimate nouns ending in / -u / are changed to / -gān / or / -wān / -وان، -ګان

dā ālu məzi'dār dey.	This potato is delicious.	دا آلُو مزیدار دے.
dā ālu'gān məzi'dār di.	These potatoes are tasty.	دا آلُوګان مزیدار دی.
'haɣa ka'du xa'rāb dey.	That squash is rotten.	هغه کدُو خراب دے.
'haɣa kad'wān xa'rāb di.	Those squash [squashes] are rotten.	هغه کدوان خراب دی.

An exercise in making masculine nouns plural

☝ Have your helper make simple singular sentences with the following nouns. Then try to make them plural.

mā'šum	child	ماشُوم	sa'ṛey	man	سړے	'ləxta	stick	لښته

gul	flower	گُل	bɪs'təra	mattress	بِستره	'gāḍey	vehicle	ګاډے
məč	fly	مچ	'māše	mosquito	ماشي	'kəley	village	کلے
bāɣ	garden	باغ	qa'ləm	pen	قلم			
mā'li	gardener	مالی	'gaḍa	sheep	ګډه			

Subject markers for verbs

It is common to drop the subject out of the sentence in colloquial speech. For example you will often hear sentences like: *pəx'tun yɪm* (پښتُون يم) "I am a Pukhtun", rather than the more formal *zə pəx'tun yɪm* (زهٔ پښتُون يم). Therefore, it becomes important to recognise and use the subject markers – the only clue as to who the speaker is talking about:

Person	Singular		Person	Plural	
I	-ɪm	يم	we	-u	و
you	-e	ې	you (plural & for elders)	-əy	ئ
he, she, it	-i	ی	they	-i	ی

NOTES:

1. The second person singular pronoun *tə* (تهٔ) and the second person singular subject marker / -e / ې are used in informal conversation. *tə* (تهٔ) is the normal pronoun used to speak to family, friends and children. It is also used in everyday conversation outside the house.
2. The second person plural form *'tāso* (تاسو) and the second person plural subject marker / -əy / ئ are used to address people with extra politeness. For example, *'tāso* (تاسو) might be used when talking to a respected leader or elder. Note, although *'tāso* (تاسو) is plural in form, it can be used to address one person. The nearest English equivalent is the royal 'we'.

Asking questions

'who?' *tsok?* څوك؟

zə'mā num __________ dey.	My name is __________.	زما نُوم __________ دے.
ha'ɣa tsok dey?	Who is he?	هغه څوک دے؟
yo məša'hur us'tāz dey.	A famous teacher.	یو مشهُور اُستاذ دے.

'how many?', 'how much?' *tso?, tsumra?*		څو؟، څومره؟
tso kaˈsān di?	How many people are there?	څو کسان دي؟
ˈtsumra ābāˈdi da?	What is the population?	څومره آبادي ده؟
ˈtāso ˈtsumra ˈwruṇa yəy?	How many brothers are you?	تاسو څومره ورُوڼه يئ؟

'with whom?' *čā saˈra?*		چا سره؟
xə qaˈləm ˈčā saˈra dey?	Who has a good pen?	ښۀ قلم چا سره دے؟
xə qaˈləm ˈmā saˈra dey.	I have a good pen.	ښۀ قلم ما سره دے.
ˈḍere peˈse čā saˈra di?	Who has a lot of money?	ډېرې پېسې چا سره دي؟
ˈhɪ-čā saˈra ˈništa.	No one has any.	هيچا سره نشته.

'where?' *čerta?*		چرته؟
šāˈhɪd ˈčerta dey?	Where is Shahid?	شاهد چرته دے؟

Postpositions

The preposition *pa* (په) 'in' is often followed by a noun and another preposition to form a 'split' prepositional phrase, which is translated as a single preposition in English. The sentences below illustrate how a noun can be sandwiched between two prepositions. The preposition which follows the noun is called a postposition. The words *bānde* (باندې) 'above' and *ˈlande* (لاندې) 'below' are examples of postpositions in Pukhto.

'in' *pa ____ ke*		په ____ کښې
stā wror ˈčerta dey?	Where is your brother?	ستا ورور چرته دے؟
haˈɣa pa xār ke dey.	He is in the city.	هغه په ښار کښې دے.
haˈɣa pa kor ke dey.	He is in the house.	هغه په کور کښې دے.
tsok pa klās ke dey? *or* pa klās ke tsok di?	Who is in the classroom?	څوک په کلاس کښې دے؟ (يا) په کلاس کښې څوک دي؟
usˈtāz pa klās ke dey.	The teacher is in the classroom.	اُستاذ په کلاس کښې دے.

'on' *pa ____ 'bānde* په ____ باندې

qa'ləm pa ba'kəs ke dey?	Is the pen in the suitcase?	قلم په بکس کښې دے؟
na, pa ba'kəs 'bānde dey.	No, it is on the suitcase.	نه، په بکس باندې دے.
ni'sār pa čət 'bānde dey?	Is Nisar on the roof?	نثار په چت باندې دے؟
na, pa kam'ra ke dey.	No, he is in the room.	نه، په کمره کښې دے.

NOTE:
Again, colloquial speech is often shortened. The common expression *čay 'bānde di* (چائې باندې دی), meaning 'The tea is on', may be a contraction of *čay pa čo'la 'bānde di* (چائې په چوله باندې دی) 'The tea is on the stove'.

'under' *də ____ 'lande* د ____ لاندې

pın'səl 'čerta dey?	Where is the pencil?	پنسل چرته دے؟
pın'səl də mez 'lande dey.	The pencil is under the table.	پنسل د میز لاندې دے.

☝ With the help of your teacher, use the above drill to ask the location of different objects that are at hand. Remember to make use of objects you already know the name of so that you are not learning names and postpositions at the same time.

Some parts of the body

☝ Ask your helper to drill you in the names for these parts of the body. Respond to the words by touching the appropriate parts.

Working with money

☝ Collect a variety of notes and coins, and practice using them with your helper by taking turns asking and giving various amounts.

špəg ruˈpəy ˈrāka! Give me six rupees! شپږ روپۍ راکه!

Memorising moment

mataˈluna

دانه دانه چې یوځای شی غر ترې جوړ شي.

dāˈna dāˈna če yo zay ši ɣər tre ǰoṛ ši.

A grain on a grain makes a mountain.

چې اُوښان ساتې نو دروازې به دنګې ساتې.

če uˈxān sāˈte, no darwāˈze ba ˈdənge sāˈte.

If you keep camels, then you should have tall doors.

Exercises for Lesson Four

1. Using the question *dā ˈtsə šey dey?* (دا څهٔ شے دے؟) 'What is this?', point and reply to the following parts of the body:

a.	sər	سر	d.	ɣwəg	غوږ
b.	maṛˈwand	مړوند	e.	lās	لاس
c.	məx	مخ	f.	maˈrəy	مرۍ

2. Make the following sentences plural:

a. haˈɣa xatarˈnāk mār dey. هغه خطرناک مار دے.

____

b. dā sur kiˈtāb dey. دا سُور کتاب دے.

____

c. tə usˈtāz ye? تهٔ اُستاذ یې؟

____

3. Fill in the correct plural suffix in each sentence.

a.	dā qaˈləm ________________ di.	دا قلم ________________ دی.
b.	mung melm ________________ yu.	مُونږ میلم ________________ یو.
c.	haˈɣa war ________________ di.	هغه ور ________________ دی.
d.	ˈtāso səst ________________ yəy?	تاسو سست ________________ یئ؟
e.	dā kitāb ________________ xə di.	دا کتاب ________________ ښۀ دی.
f.	ˈhaɣa ux ________________ ɣaṭ di.	هغه اُوښ ________________ غټ دی.
g.	dā āˈlu ________________ məziˈdār di.	دا آلُو ________________ مزېدار دی.
h.	haɣˈwi məšaˈhur saṛ ________________ di.	هغوی مشهُور سړ ________________ دی.

4. Substitute the following pairs of words for the underlined words in the sentence:

<u>ustaˈzān</u> pa <u>skul</u> ke di. — <u>اُستاذان</u> په <u>سکُول</u> کښې دی.

a.	haɣˈwi	moṭər	موټر	هغوی
b.	haləˈkān	klās	کلاس	هلکان
c.	muˈlā	ǰuˈmāt	جُماعت	مُلا
d.	māˈli	bāɣ	باغ	مالی
e.	məngəˈkān	kor	کور	منږکان

5. Use the words listed below to transform the following sentence:

haˈɣa ḍākˈṭər dey. — هغه ډاکټر دے.

a.	tə	تۀ		f.	pəxtāˈnə	پښتانۀ
b.	haɣˈwi	هغوی		g.	melmāˈnə	مېلمانۀ
c.	ˈstəṛi	ستړی		h.	musalmāˈnān	مسلمانان
d.	mung	مُونږ		i.	zə	زۀ
e.	ˈtāso	تاسو		j.	isāˈi	عیسائی

Vocabulary for Lesson Four

ābā'di	آبادی	*f.s.*	*n.*	population
ālu / ālu'gān	آلو / آلوګان	*m.*	*n.*	potato
us'tāz / ustā'zān	اُستاذ / اُستاذان	*m.*	*n.*	teacher
us'tāza / us'tāzāne	اُستاذه / استاذانې	*f.*		
ux / u'xān	اُوښ / اُوښان	*m.*	*n.*	camel
'uxa / 'uxe	اُوښه / اُوښې	*f.*		
bāɣ / bāɣ'una	باغ / باغونه	*m.*	*n.*	garden, park, orchard
bɪs'təra	بِستره	*f.s.*	*n.*	mattress
ba'kəs	بکس	*m.s.*	*n.*	case, suitcase
pa ____ 'bānde	په ____ باندې		*prep., post.*	on, above, up, over
pa ____ ke	په ____ کښې		*prep., post.*	in
tār	تار	*m.s.*	*n.*	thread; cable
top	توپ	*m.s.*	*n.*	cannon
tut	تُوت	*m.pl.*	*n.*	mulberry
tod	تود	*m.*	*adj.*	warm
'tura	تُوره	*f.s.*	*n.*	sword
ṭāl	ټال	*m.s.*	*n.*	swing
'ṭɪkey	ټکے	*m.s.*	*n.*	word
ǰu'māt / ǰumā'tuna	جُماعت / جُماعتُونه	*m.*	*n.*	mosque
'čā sa'ra	چا سره		*q.*	with whom
čət	چت	*m.s.*	*n.*	roof
'čerta	چرته		*q.*	where
čo'la	چوله	*f.s.*	*n.*	stove
tsok	څوک		*q.*	who
xatar'nāk	خطرناک	*m.*	*adj.*	dangerous, risky
xatar'nāka / xatar'nāke	خطرناکه / خطرناکې	*f.*		

xwax ˈxwaxa / ˈxwaxe	خوښ خوښه / خوښې	m. f.	adj.	happy, glad, pleased
də ____ ˈlande	د____ لاندې		prep., post.	under
dāˈna	دانه	f.s.	n.	bit; item; speck, a single grain
ˈdəlta	دلته		adv.	here
rozāˈna	روزانه		adj.	daily, every day
sər	سر	m.s.	n.	head; top
skul	سکُول	m.s.	n.	school
šeˈtān / šetāˈnān	شیطان / شیطانان	m.	n., adj.	the devil, Satan; naughty, bothersome, troublesome
xār	ښار	m.s.	n.	city
ɣər / ɣruna	غر / غرُونه	m.	n.	mountain, hill
ɣwəg / ɣwəˈguna	غوږ / غوږُونه	m.	n.	ear
ɣoxˈtəl	غوښتل		v.t.	to want, to ask (for), to request; to demand
kaˈdu	کدُو / کدوان	m.	n.	squash
kas / kaˈsān	کس / کسان	m.	n.	person, someone, somebody
klās	کلاس	m.s.	n.	classroom, class
ˈkəley / ˈkəli	کلے / کلی	m.	n.	village
kamˈra / kamˈre	کمره / کمرې	f.	n.	room
kor / korˈuna	کور / کورونه	m.	n.	house
ˈgāḍey	ګاډے	m.s.	n.	vehicle
ˈgaḍa	ګډه	f.s.	n.	female sheep, ewe
gul / guˈluna	ګُل / ګُلُونه	m.	n.	flower
lās / lāˈsuna	لاس / لاسُونه	m.	n.	hand
laˈṛəm	لړم	m.s.	n.	scorpion
ˈləxta	لښته	f.s.	n.	stick
lur / ˈluṇa	لُور / لُونړه	f.	n.	daughter

lor	لور	*m.s.*	*n.*	sickle
luy	لوئ	*m.*	*adj.*	big, great
luya / luyəy	لویه / لوی	*f.*		
mār / mār'ān	مار / ماران	*m.*	*n.*	snake
'māše	ماشي	*f.pl.*	*n.*	mosquito
məč	مچ	*f.s.*	*n.*	fly
məx	مخ	*m.s.*	*n.*	face
ma'rəy	مری	*f.s.*	*n.*	throat
maṛ'wand	مړوند	*m.s.*	*n.*	wrist
məzi'dār	مزېدار	*m.*	*adj.*	tasty, delicious; enjoyable
məzi'dāra / məzi'dāre	مزېداره / مزېداري	*f.*		
mən'gək / məngə'kān	منږک / منږکان	*m.*	*n.*	mouse / mice
'ništa	نشته		*neg* 'be' *v.*	he is not, she is not, there is not, there are not
'newe	نوي	*f.*	*adj.*	new
'newey / 'newi	نوے / نوی	*m.*		
har 'kəla	هر کله		*adv.*	anytime, always
'hı-čā	هیچا		*adv.*	no one, nobody

pinˈzəm saˈbəq پينځم سبق

Lesson Five

Dialogue five: Ladies talk

L:	ˈwādə ˈšɪβe ye? Are you married?	وادهٔ شوي يې؟
H:	āw, špəg ˈkāla ˈkigi če ˈwādə ˈšɪβe yɪm. Yes, it is six years since I have been married.	آو ، شپږ کاله کېږی چې وادهٔ شوي يم.
L:	baˈči de xə di? Are your children well?	بچی دې ښهٔ دی؟
H:	āw, xə di? Yes, they are well.	آو ، ښهٔ دی.
L:	stā tso māšuˈmān di? How many children do you have?	ستا څو ماشُومان دی؟
H:	ˈmāšalla, zəˈmā tsaˈlor māšuˈmān di. I have four children, thank God. ˈyəwa lur āw dre zāˈmən di. One daughter and three sons.	ماشاءالله، زما څلور ماشُومان دی. يوه لُور او درې زامن دی.
L:	ˈšukər dey! Be grateful!	شُکر دے!
L:	stā xāˈwənd tsə kār kaˈwi? What job does your husband do?	ستا خاوند څهٔ کار کوی؟
H:	haˈɣa dukanˈdār dey. He is a shopkeeper.	هغه دُوکاندار دے.

NOTE:

The greetings used in previous lessons are left out in this and future dialogues – be sure to use them though.

Men's talk

L:	tā ˈwādə ˈkəṛey dey? Are you married?	تا وادهٔ کړے دے؟
H:	āw, wāˈdə me ˈkəṛey dey. Yes, I'm married.	آو ، وادهٔ مې کړے دے.
L:	stā tso māšuˈmān di? How many children do you have?	ستا څو ماشُومان دی؟
H:	zəˈmā yo zwe āw dwa ǰinaˈkəy di. I have one son and two daughters.	زما يو زوئ او دوه جينکۍ دی.

H: āw stā? And you?	او ستا؟
L: na, wā'də me nə-dey 'kəṛey. No, I haven't married.	نه، وادۀ مې نۀ دے کړے.
L: 'tāso tsə kār ka'wəy? What work do you do?	تاسو څۀ کار کوئ؟
H: zə dukan'dār yım. I'm a shopkeeper.	زۀ دُوکاندار يم.
L: kār 'tsənga ra'wān dey? How is business going?	کار څنګه روان دے؟
H: xə dey. It's good.	ښۀ دے.

NOTE:
When discussing marriage status (i.e., whether someone is married or not), men refer to it using the active voice, while females use the passive voice.

Some professions

nān-bā'i	bread maker	نانبائی	fo'ǰi	soldier	فوجي
nā'i	barber	نائی	sıpa'i	policeman	سپائی
maz'dur	labourer	مزدُور	molā'nā	religious scholar	مولانا
zami'dār	farmer	زميدار	tabli'ɣi	preacher	تبليغی
tsoki'dār	watchman	څوکيدار	lo'hār	blacksmith	لوهار
'benk walā	banker	بېنک والا	zar'gər	goldsmith	زرګر
qa'sāb	butcher	قصاب	čam'yār	cobbler	چميار
xānsā'ma	cook	خانسامه	gıl'kār	mason	ګلکار
dar'zi	tailor	درزی	tar'kāṇ	carpenter	ترکاڼ
ḍā'ki	postman	ډاکی	špun	shepherd	شپُون

In some cases, the addition of the word *tob* (توب) to the profession describes the activity undertaken. See the examples below:

dar'zi	tailor	درزی	darzi'tob	tailoring	درزی توب
mā'li	gardener	مالی	māli'tob	gardening	مالی توب
mu'lā	mullah	مُلا	mulā'tob	work of a mullah	مُلا توب

fo'ǰi	soldier	فوجی	foǰi'tob	soldiering	فوجی توب
špun	shepherd	شپُون	špun'tob	shepherding	شپُون توب

Pronunciation drill

1. Contrasting / ḍ / ډ and / d / د

ḍo'ḍəy šta?	Is food available?	ډوډی شته؟
də 'də tsə num dey?	What is his name?	د دهٔ څهٔ نُوم دے؟
ḍək 'rāwṛa.	Bring it full.	ډک راوړه.
dā xə dey.	This is good.	دا ښهٔ دے.
zṛə me ḍā'ḍa šo.	My heart became bold.	زړهٔ مې ډاډه شو.
zṛə me bəd šo.	I became upset.	زړهٔ مې بد شو.

2. Contrasting / u / وُ and / ə /

tə maz'dur ye?	Are you a labourer?	تهٔ مزدُور يې؟
'tāso zar'gər yəy?	Are you [polite] a goldsmith?	تاسو زرګر يئ؟
pa pul pu'ra dwa mo'ṭərey zay'igi.	There is room for two cars on the bridge.	په پُل پُوره دوه موټرې ځائيږی.
pa haf'ta ke pu'ra u'wə 'wrəze di.	There are seven days in a week.	په هفته کښې پُوره اووهٔ ورځې دی.

Feminine pronouns

There are two feminine singular pronouns. For people in sight, *dā* (دا) is used. For people who are 'over there' (i.e. far away or out of sight) *'haya* (هغه) is used.

The verb 'to be' becomes *da* (ده). For example, 'she is' becomes *dā da* (دا ده) or *ha'ya da* (هغه ده) depending on where the person is, in relation to you.

Feminine singular nouns

Pronoun	Feminine noun	Verb	
zə	ḍāk'ṭəra	yım.	زهٔ ډاکټره يم. I am a doctor.

tə	uˈstāza	ye?	تهٔ اُستاذه يې؟ Are you a teacher?
dā	āfɣāˈna	da?	دا افغانه ده؟ Is she an Afghan?
haˈɣa	pəxtaˈna	da.	هغه پښتنه ده. She is a Pukhtun.

NOTE:

The addition of / -a / ه - or ـه - to a noun indicates that it is feminine. You may also hear an extra / -a / ه - or ـه - added at the end of verbs to make a rhyme:

zə ḍākˈṭəra̱ ˈyım-a̱. I (*f.*) am a doctor. زهٔ ډاکټره يمه.

Feminine singular adjectives

Pronoun	Feminine noun	Verb	
zə	ˈstəṛe	yım.	زهٔ ستړې يم. I am tired.
tə	ˈǰoṛa	ye?	تهٔ جوړه يې؟ Are you well?
dā	naˈrəy	da.	دا نرۍ ده. She is thin.
dā	draˈna	da.	دا درنه ده. This is heavy.
haˈɣa	ˈxkwəle	da.	هغه ښکُلې ده. She is beautiful.
haˈɣa	ˈɣaṭa	da.	هغه غټه ده. She is big.

NOTE:

Adjectives are declined in one of the following ways:

	Big		Tired		Thin	
m.s.	ɣaṭ	غټ	ˈstəṛey	ستړے	naˈrey	نرے
f.s.	ˈɣaṭa	غټه	ˈstəṛe	ستړې	naˈrəy	نرۍ

Recognising feminine nouns and adjectives

The all-purpose / -a / ، -ه

tā sa'ra spin čərg šta?	Do you have a white cock?	تا سره سپین چرګ شته؟
tā sa'ra 'spina 'čərga šta?	Do you have a white hen?	تا سره سپینه چرګه شته؟
zə'mā nars pəx'tun dey.	My nurse (male) is a Pukhtun.	زما نرس پښتُون دے.
zə'mā 'narsa pəxta'na da.	My nurse (female) is a Pukhtun.	زما نرسه پښتنه ده.
dey xatar'nāk ɣəl dey.	He is a dangerous thief.	دے خطرناک غل دے.
dā xatar'nāka ɣla da.	She is a dangerous thief.	دا خطرناکه غله ده.

Some nouns are always feminine

dā 'ḍera maz'buta 'wəna da.	This is a very strong tree.	دا ډېره مضبُوطه ونه ده.
dā 'ḍera xa'rāba ma'ṇa da.	This is a very rotten apple.	دا ډېره خرابه منړه ده.

Nouns ending with / -əy / ۍ -

'haɣa ǰɪ'nəy 'xkwəle da.	That girl is beautiful.	هغه جینۍ ښکُلې ده.
dā ālma'rəy 'ɣaṭa da.	This wardrobe is big.	دا المارۍ غټه ده.
dā kur'səy u'čəta da.	This is a tall chair.	دا کُرسۍ اُوچته ده.
'haɣa war'koṭe spəy da.	That is a small bitch.	هغه ورکوټې سپۍ ده.
dā ḍo'ḍəy mazi'dāra da.	This food is delicious.	دا ډوډۍ مزېداره ده.
'daɣa kɪṛ'kəy 'pləna da.	This window is wide.	دغه کړکۍ پلنه ده.

Nouns and adjectives ending in / -e / ې-

zə 'newey us'tāz yɪm.	I am a new (male) teacher.	زهٔ نوے اُستاذ یم.
zə 'newe us'tāza yɪm.	I am a new (female) teacher.	زهٔ نوې اُستاذه یم.
stā mal'gərey ux'yār dey.	Your (male) friend is wise.	ستا ملګرے هوښیار دے.
stā mal'gəre ux'yāra da.	Your (female) friend is wise.	ستا ملګرې هوښیاره ده.

NOTE:

A masculine noun ending in / -ey / ے- is made feminine by changing the ending to / -e / ې-. The sounds / ey / ے and / e / ې differ only in length, and not in quality.

Endings in / -o / and / -ā / are feminine -و، -ا

zə'mā 'yəwa 'xkwəle pi'šo šta.	I have one beautiful cat.	زما يوه ښکُلې پيشو شته.
zə'mā nyā 'halta da.	My grandmother is there.	زما نيا هلته ده.
'haɣa ɣwā 'ɣaṭa da.	That cow is big.	هغه غوا غټه ده.
zə'mā ba'bo 'dəlta da.	My aunty is here.	زما ببو دلته ده.
'ḍera xan'dā xə nə da.	Much laughter is not good.	ډېره خندا ښهٔ نهٔ ده.
'ḍera ǰa'ṛā xə nə da.	Much crying is not good.	ډېره ژړا ښهٔ نهٔ ده.

Feminine because of gender

zə'mā mor mera'bāna da.	My mother is kind.	زما مور مهربانه ده.
stā tror bu'ḍəy da.	Your aunt is old.	ستا ترور بوُډۍ ده.
zə'mā xor 'məšra da.	My sister is older.	زما خور مشره ده.
stā lur 'ḍera xāy'sta da.	Your daughter is very pretty.	ستا لُور ډېره ښائسته ده.

NOTES:

1. All these nouns end in a consonant, and strictly speaking should be masculine – but natural gender overrules.
2. The adjective *xāy'sta* (ښائسته) 'pretty' can also be used with masculine nouns.

Feminine nouns ending in / -i / ی-

dos'ti xə da.	Friendship is good.	دوستی ښهٔ ده.
dušma'ni xə nə da.	Enmity is not good.	دُشمنی ښهٔ نهٔ ده.

Numbers eleven to twenty

☝ Write down the numbers as the teacher says them to you.

You may write them in English, or may wish to learn how to write the numbers in Pukhto. Don't repeat the sentence, just listen and obey the command. Start with 1-10, and then add numbers up to 20.

ˈyo-ləs ˈolika!	Write eleven!	۱۱	یوولس ولیکه!
do-ləs ˈolika!	Write twelve!	۱۲	دولس ولیکه!

13	ˈdyār-ləs	دیارلس	۱۳	17	uˈwə-ləs	اووۀ لس	۱۷
14	ˈtswār-ləs	څوارلس	۱۴	18	āˈtə-ləs	اتۀ لس	۱۸
15	pinˈzə-ləs	پینځلس	۱۵	19	ˈnuləs	نُولس	۱۹
16	ˈšpāṛəs	شپاړس	۱۶	20	šɪl	شل	۲۰

Memorising moment

šer (poem)[5]

هغه یار چې بې وفا دے څۀ یار نۀ دے،

او هغه کار چې بې بقا دے څۀ کار نۀ دے.

ˈhaɣa yār če be waˈfā dey tsə yār nə dey,

āw ˈhaɣa kār če be baˈqā dey tsə kār nə dey.

That friend who is unfaithful is no friend at all,

And that work which is temporal is no work at all.

mataˈluna

زۀ په طمع تۀ بې غمه.

zə pa ˈtəma tə be ˈɣəma.

I am expectant and you don't care.

---

[5] A *šer* (شعر) is rhyming poetry. The *šer* selected for memory work are so well known that they act like proverbs in Pukhtun society.

چې سر حيات وي ټوپۍ ډېرې.

če sər ha'yāt wi ṭo'pəy 'ḍeri.

If the head is living caps are many.

چې څهٔ کرے هغه به ريبې.

če tsə kə'rey ha'ɣa ba 'rebey.

As you sow so shall you reap.

Exercises for Lesson Five

1. Replace the underlined word in the question:

stā 'tso <u>ba'či</u> di? ستا څو بچی دی؟

a.	zā'mən	زامن	d.	melmā'nə	مېلمانهٔ
b.	kitā'buna	کتابونه	e.	'wruṇa	ورُونړه
c.	qalam'una	قلمُونه	f.	mal'gəri	ملګری

2. Change the following sentences into feminine ones:

a. tə 'newey tālı'bıləm ye? تهٔ نوے طالبعلم يې؟

____

b. 'haɣa lwəṛ ux dey. هغه لوړ اُوښ دے.

____

c. dey yo drund pəx'tun dey. دے يو درُوند پښتُون دے.

____

d. zə ḍer 'stəṛey yım. زهٔ ډېر ستړے يم.

____

e. dā čərg spin 'nə-dey? دا چرګ سپين نهٔ دے؟

____

f. 'daɣa še'tān mā'šum dey. دغه شېطان ماشُوم دے.

____

g. tə ḍer xə mal'gərey ye. تهٔ ډېر ښهٔ ملګرے يې.

____

h. tə ḍer xə o'stāz ye! تهٔ ډېر ښهٔ استاذ يې!

____

3. Substitute the underlined word in this sentence, using the words listed below:

'haɣa mez dey. هغه مېز دے.

'xəza	ښځه	pi'šo	پیشو
sa'ṛey	سړے	'wəna	ونه
špun'key	شپُونکے	nars	نرس
ās	اس	spey	سپے
ḍo'ḍəy	ډوډۍ	almā'rəy	الماری
kıṛ'kəy	کړکۍ	ɣəl	غل

4. Replace the underlined words to make sentences:

zə'mā pa kor ke 'yəwa 'xəza da. زما په کور کښې يوه ښځه ده

a.	sā'ṛey	سړے	d.	mā'šum	ماشُوم
b.	mel'ma	مېلمه	e.	čərg	چرګ
c.	gawən'ḍi	ګاونډی	f.	spey	سپے

Vocabulary for Lesson Five

ā'tə-ləs	اتۀ لس		n., adj.	eighteen
ās / ā'suna	اس / اسُونه	m.	n.	horse (stallion)
'āspa / 'āspe	اسپه / اسپې	f.	n.	horse (mare)
ālma'rəy	الماری	f.	n.	cupboard, cabinet, wardrobe
u'čət	اُوچت	m.	adj.	tall, high, lofty; loud
u'wə-ləs	اووۀ لس		n., adj.	seventeen
ba'bo	ببو	f.s.	n.	aunt
ba'či	بچی	m.pl.	n.	children
bəd	بد	m.	adj.	bad (situation); incorrect; upset
'bəda / 'bəde	بده / بدې	f.		
bu'ḍā / buḍa'gān	بُوډا / بُوډاګان	m.	adj. n.	old, elderly; old man
bu'ḍəy / buḍa'gāne	بُوډۍ / بوډېګانې [بوډۍ ګانې]	f.	adj. n.	old, elderly; old woman
'benk walā	بېنک والا	m.	n.	banker
pul	پُل	m.s.	n.	bridge
'plən	پلن	m.	adj.	wide
'pləna / 'pləne	پلنه / پلنې	f.		
pi'šo	پیشو	f.s.	n.	cat
pin'zə-ləs	پینځلس		n., adj.	fifteen
tabli'ɣi	تبلیغی	m.s.	n.	preacher, one proselytizing
tar'kāṇ	ترکاڼ	m.s.	n.	carpenter
tror / tror'yāne	ترور / تروریانې	f.	n.	aunt (paternal)
ǰɪ'nəy / ǰɪna'kəy	جینۍ / جینکۍ	f.	n.	girl, unwed woman
čərg / čər'gān	چرګ / چرګان	m.	n.	cockerel, cock
'čərga / 'čərge	چرګه / چرګې	f.	n.	hen, chicken
čam'yār	چمیار	m.s.	n.	cobbler

ˈtswār-ləs	څوارلس		n., adj.	fourteen
tsokiˈdār [čokiˈdār]	څوکيدار	m.s.	n.	watchman
xāˈwənd	خاوند	m.s.	n.	husband; owner
xanˈdā	خندا	f.	n.	laughter
xor / ˈxwende	خور / خوېندې	f.	n.	sister
darˈzi	درزی	m.s.	n.	tailor
dušmaˈni	دُشمنی	f.s.	n.	enmity, feud
dosˈti	دوستی	f.s.	n.	friendship
dukanˈdār	دُوکاندار	m.s.	n.	shopkeeper
do-ləs	دولس		n., adj.	twelve
ˈdyār-ləs	ديارلس		n., adj.	thirteen
ḍāˈki	ډاکی	m.s.	n.	postman
ḍoˈḍəy	ډوډۍ	f.s.	n.	food, meal; bread
rāwˈṛəl	راوړل		v.t.	to bring (inanimate objects)
raˈwān	روان	m.	adj.	going, flowing
raˈwāna / raˈwāne	روانه / رواني	f.		
zarˈgər	زرگر	m.s.	n.	goldsmith
zṛə	زړهٔ	m.s.	n.	heart
zamiˈdār	زميدار	m.s.	n.	farmer
zwe / zāˈmən	زوئ / زامن	m.	n.	son
ǰaˈṛā	ژړا	f.s.	n.	crying, weeping
sıpaˈi	سپائی	m.s.	n.	policeman
ˈšpāṛəs	شپاړس		n., adj.	sixteen
šta	شته		'to be' v.	he is, she is, it is, there is, there are
ˈšukər	شُکر	m	interject.	grateful
šıl	شل		n., adj.	twenty
xāyˈsta	ښائسته	m., f.	adj.	pretty

ˈxəza / ˈxəze	ښځه / ښځې	*f.*	*n.*	woman, wife, married female
ɣəl	غل	*m.*	*n.*	thief
ɣla / ɣle	غله / غلې	*f.*		
ɣwā	غوا	*f.s.*	*n.*	cow
foˈǰi	فوجی	*m.s.*	*n.*	soldier
qaˈsāb	قصاب	*m.s.*	*n.*	butcher
kār	کار	*m.*	*n.*	work, business, job
kār kaˈwəl	کار کول		*comp. v.t.*	to work
kāl / kāˈluna	کال / کالُونه	*m.*	*n.*	year
kurˈsəy	کُرسۍ	*f.s.*	*n.*	chair
kıṛˈkəy	کړکۍ	*f.s.*	*n.*	window
gawənˈḍi / gawənḍˈyān	ګاونډی / ګاونډیان	*m.*	*n.*	neighbour
gawənˈḍi / gawənḍˈyāne	ګاونډۍ / ګاونډیانې	*f.*		
gılˈkār	ګِلکار	*m.s.*	*n.*	mason
loˈhār	لوهار	*m.s.*	*n.*	blacksmith
ˈmāšalla	ماشاءالله		*ph.*	thanks be to God
mazˈdur	مزدُور	*m.s.*	*n.*	labourer
ˈməšar / məšaˈrān	مشر / مشران	*m.*	*adj.*	elder, senior, chief, leader
ˈməšra / ˈməšre	مشره / مشرې	*f.*		
mazˈbut	مضبُوط	*m.*	*adj.*	firm, strong, sturdy
malˈgəre	ملګرې	*f.*	*n.*	friend
malˈgərey / malˈgəri	ملګرے / ملګری	*m.*		
moläˈnā	مولانا	*m.s.*	*n.*	religious scholar
nān-bāˈi	نانبائی	*m.s.*	*n.*	bread maker
nāˈi	نائی	*m.s.*	*n.*	barber
ˈnarsa / ˈnarse	نرسه / نرسې	*f.*	*n.*	nurse
ˈnuləs	نُولس		*n., adj.*	nineteen

nyā / nyā'gāne	نیا / نیاګانې	*f.*	*n.*	grandmother
wā'də	وادۀ	*m*	*n.*	wedding, marriage
wā'də ke'dəl	وادۀ کېدل		*comp. v.i.*	to be married; to become married
wā'də ka'wəl	وادۀ کول		*comp.v.t.*	to marry
wrəz	ورځ	*f.s.*	*n.*	day
war'koṭe	ورکوټی	*m.*	*adj.*	small
'wəna	ونه	*f.s.*	*n.*	tree
haf'ta	هفته	*f.*	*n.*	week
ux'yār / uxyā'rān	هوښیار / هوښیاران	*m.*	*adj.*	wise, intelligent, prudent
ux'yāra / ux'yāre	هوښیاره / هوښیارې	*f.*		
'yo-ləs	یوولس		*n., adj.*	eleven

špəˈgəm saˈbəq شپږم سبق

Lesson Six

Dialogue six: A guest at your door

L: pa xer ˈrāɣle. Welcome.	په خېر راغلې.
L: har ˈkəla ˈrāša. Always welcome.	هر کله راشه.
L: ˈkena! ˈkena! Sit! Sit!	کښېنه! کښېنه!
L: čay xo ba sku, xo āˈwal ˈrāta ˈowaya če ḍoˈḍəy de xoˈṛəle da, kə na? We will drink tea, but first tell me if you have eaten food, or not?	چائې خو به څښُو، خو اول راته ووايه چې ډوډۍ دې خوړلې ده، کۀ نه؟
H: nə me da xoˈṛəle. I haven't eaten. kə tā ta təkˈlif nə wi, no ṭik da. If it's no trouble to you, then fine.	نۀ مې ده خوړلې. کۀ تا ته تکليف نۀ وی نو ټيک ده.
L: če tsə taˈyār wi, haˈɣa də ˈyār wi. Whatever is ready is for a friend.	چې څۀ تيار وی هغه د يار وی.
H: bas ṭik da. That's OK.	بس ټيک ده.
L: tə xə ye? Are you fine?	تۀ ښۀ يې؟
H: āw, xə yım. Yes, I'm fine.	آو، ښۀ يم.
L: kor ke xer dey, bāl bəč de xə dey? Is everything OK at your house? Are the children OK? xer xo dey kəna, tsənga ˈrāɣle? Is everything fine? Why did you come?	کور کښې خېر دے، بال بچ دې ښۀ دے؟ خېر خو دے کنه، څنګه راغلې؟
H: zəˈmā ləg kār dey no zəˈmā xyāl dey če ˈtā saˈra ba špa ˈokəm. I have a little work and I think I will spend the night with you.	زما لږ کار دے نو زما خيال دے چې تاسره به شپه وکم.
L: ḍer de xə ˈoka. You did very well.	ډېر دې ښۀ وکه.

NOTE:

Unstinting hospitality is a highly cherished virtue in Pukhtun society.

Pronunciation drill

1. Contrasting / ɣ / غ and / x / خ

ɣa'dār me 'olido.	I saw a deceitful man.	غدار مې وليدو.
xor me 'olida.	I saw a sister.	خور مې وليده.
dā ɣwā da.	This is a cow.	دا غوا ده.
dā xwā da.	This is the side.	دا خوا ده.
'daɣa ɣər dey.	This is a mountain.	دغه غر دے.
'daɣa xər dey.	This is a donkey.	دغه خر دے.
dā 'ɣaṭa da.	This is big.	دا غټه ده.
dā 'xaṭa da.	This is mud.	دا خټه ده.

Try this tongue twister:

زما غوا د کور په خوا کښې ده.

zə'mā ɣwā də kor pa xwā ke da.

My cow is close to the house.

2. Contrasting / o / و and / ə / ۀ or no character in script

tso la're?	How many do you have?	څو لرې؟
tsə la're?	What do you have?	څۀ لرې؟
dey moṛ šo.	He is full (from eating).	دے موړ شو.
dey məṛ šo.	He died.	دے مړ شو.

A complete listing of subject pronouns and the verb 'to be'

Person	Pronoun/Verb (Singular)			Pronoun/Verb (Plural)		
1st	zə yım	I am	زۀ يم	mung yu	we are	مونږ يو
2nd	tə ye	you are	ته يې	'tāso yəy	you are	تاسو يئ
3rd	ha'ɣa dey	he is	هغه دے	haɣ'wi di	they are	هغوی دی
	dey dey		دے دے			
	ha'ɣa da	she is	هغه ده	dwi di	they are	دوئ دی
	dā da		دا ده			

NOTES:

1. You will hear speakers using both *haɣi* (هغی) and *haɣ'wi* (هغوی) to mean 'they'; referring to people who are being talked about, but who are not present.
2. *dwi* (دوئ) is used to describe more than one person or animal; referring to people / animals which are close at hand and visible.
3. Commonly anything close at hand is often called *dā* (دا), but it is only by listening to the verb ending that you know whether this refers to 'he', 'she', 'they', etc.

Feminine plural nouns

tā sa'ra 'tsumra 'čərge šta?	How many hens do you have?	تا سره څومره چرګې شته؟
'tsumra kur'səy pa'kār di?	How many chairs are needed?	څومره کُرسۍ پکار دی؟
'tāso talıbıl'māne yəy?	Are you (female) students?	تاسو طالبعلمانې يئ؟
dwi ḍākṭər'āne di?	Are they (female) doctors?	دوئ ډاکټرانې دی؟
haɣ'wi nars'āne di.	They are nurses.	هغوی نرسانې دی.

NOTE:

The majority of feminine plural nouns are declined with the plural suffix / -e / ې- , but a few feminine plural nouns also end in / -əy / ۍ- ; some add / -ane / انې- .

Feminine plural adjectives

Pronoun	Adjective	Verb	
mung	'stəṛe	yu.	مونږ ستړې يو. We are tired.

hay'wi	'xkwəle	di.	هغوی ښکُلي دی. They are beautiful.
'tāso	'ǰoṛe	yəy?	تاسو جوړي يئ؟ Are you well?
ha'ɣa	'ɣaṭe	di.	هغه غټي دی. Those are big.
dā	dra'ne	di.	دا درني دی. They are heavy.

NOTE:
With *di* (دی), the 3rd person (plural) form of the verb 'to be', only the adjective ending indicates gender.

Some useful adjectives in their masculine and feminine forms

It would help to memorise the following chart:

Masculine singular	Masculine plural	Feminine singular	Feminine plural
ar'zān ارزان cheap, inexpensive	ar'zān ارزان	ar'zāna ارزانه	ar'zāne ارزاني
bad'rənga بدرنگه ugly	bad'rənga بدرنگه	bad'rənga بدرنگه	bad'rənge بدرنگي
bəd بد bad, incorrect	bəd بد	'bəda بده	'bəde بدي
bu'ḍā بُوډا elderly	buḍa'gān بُوډاگان	bu'ḍəy بُوډۍ	buḍa'gāne بُوډۍ گاني

Masculine singular	Masculine plural	Feminine singular	Feminine plural
paxwā'ney پخوانے old, ancient, former	paxwā'ni پخوانی	paxwā'nəy پخوانۍ	paxwā'nəy پخوانۍ
'təgey تږے thirsty	'təgi تږی	'təge تږې	'təge تږې
tak'ṛa تکړه strong	tak'ṛa تکړه	tak'ṛa تکړه	tak'ṛa تکړه
xa'rāb خراب bad, ruined, faulty	xa'rāb خراب	xa'rāba خرابه	xa'rābe خرابې
xə'fa [xə'pa] خفه sad, mad	xə'fa [xə'pa] خفه	xə'fa [xə'pa] خفه	xə'fa [xə'pa] خفه
drund درُوند heavy	drā'nə درانۀ	dra'na درنه	dra'ne درنې
zoṛ زوړ old	zā'ṛə زاړۀ	za'ṛa زړه	za'ṛe زړې
ǰwan'dey ژوندے alive	ǰwan'di ژوندی	ǰwan'dəy ژوندۍ	ǰwan'dəy ژوندۍ
spək سپک light	spək سپک	'spəka سپکه	'spəke سپکې
'stəṛey ستړے tired	'stəṛi ستړی	'stəṛe ستړې	'stəṛe ستړې
səst سست weak, lazy	səst سست	'səsta سسته	'səste سستې
xāy'sta ښائسته pretty	xāy'sta ښائسته	xāy'sta ښائسته	xāy'sta ښائسته
'xkwəley ښکُلے pretty	'xkwəli ښکُلی	'xkwəle ښکُلې	'xkwəle ښکُلې
xə ښۀ good	xə ښۀ	xə ښۀ	xe ښې
ɣaṭ غټ big, large, fat	ɣaṭ غټ	'ɣaṭa غټه	'ɣaṭe غټې
kuṇ کُوڼ fat	kā'ṇə کاڼۀ	ka'ṇa کڼه	ka'ṇe کڼې

Masculine singular	Masculine plural	Feminine singular	Feminine plural
grān گران expensive	grān گران	ˈgrāna گرانه	ˈgrāne گرانې
ləg لږ little, few	ləg لږ	ˈləga لږه	ˈləge لږې
lənḍ لنډ short	lənḍ لنډ	ˈlənda لنډه	ˈlənde لنډې
lwəṛ لوړ high, tall	lwəṛ لوړ	ˈlwəṛa لوړه	ˈlwəṛe لوړې
luy لوئ big, great	luy لوئ	ˈluya لويه	luyəy لوۍ
məṛ مړ dead	mṛə مړهٔ	mṛa مړه	mṛe مړې
moṛ موړ full	māˈṛə ماړهٔ	maˈṛa مړه	maˈṛe مړې
narˈey نرے thin, skinny	naˈri نري	naˈrəy نرۍ	naˈrəy نرۍ
waˈṛukey وړُوکے small	wāˈṛə واړهٔ	wāˈṛa وړه	wāˈṛe وړې
ˈwəgey وږے hungry	ˈwəgi وږي	ˈwəge وږې	ˈwəge وږې

☝ Practice the use of these adjectives until they become second nature. Using the illustrations in *Picture it in Dari and Pashto*[6] or generating some simple pictures to go with this chart will enable you to practice these adjectives with your language helper as well as illiterate friends. Find pictures of masculine singular and plural, and feminine singular and plural objects, then get your helper or friend to drill you. Here is an example using trees and books with the adjectives *ɣaṭ* (غټ) and *arˈzān* (ارزان):

dā ˈɣaṭa ˈwəna da. *(f.s.)*

دا غټه ونه ده.

dā ˈɣaṭe ˈwəne di. *(f.p.)*

دا غټې ونې دي.

[6] Language and Orientation Programme, International Assistance Mission. *Picture It in Dari and Pashto.* Peshawar, Pakistan. InterLit Foundation. 2004, reprinted 2011.

dā arˈzān kiˈtāb dey. *(m.s.)*

دا ارزان کِتاب دے.

dā arˈzān kiˈtābuna di. *(m.s.)*

دا ارزان کِتابونه دی.

Now you can substitute other adjectives from the list.

Recognising feminine plural nouns and adjectives

1. Feminine singular and adjectives ending in / -a / ـه- are declined with the suffix / -e / ې- for their plural forms.

haˈɣa qāˈbɪla ˈxəza da.	She is a capable woman.	هغه قابِله ښځه ده.
hayˈwi qāˈbɪle ˈxəze di.	They are capable women.	هغوی قابِلې ښځې دی.
ˈhaɣa ˈāspa mṛa da.	That mare is dead.	هغه اسپه مړه ده.
ˈhaɣa ˈāspe mṛe di.	Those mares are dead.	هغه اسپې مړې دی.
haˈɣe saˈra ˈyəwa mālˈṭa da.	She has one orange.	هغې سره يوه مالټه ده.
haˈɣe saˈra dwa mālˈṭe di.	She has two oranges.	هغې سره دوه مالټې دی.

2. Feminine nouns ending in / -əy / ۍ- do not change in their plural forms.

zəˈmā tsaˈpləy xaˈrāba da.	My sandal is bad.	زما څپلۍ خرابه ده.
zəˈmā tsaˈpləy xaˈrābe di.	My sandals are bad.	زما څپلۍ خرابې دی.

3. Feminine nouns ending in / -o / و- and / -a / ـه- add the suffix / -gāne / ګانې- for their plural forms.

zəˈmā piˈšo ṛanˈda da.	My cat is blind.	زما پيشو ړنده ده.
zəˈmā pišoˈgāne ṛanˈde di.	My cats are blind.	زما پيشوګانې ړندې دی.
stā ɣwā ˈɣaṭa da.	Your cow is big.	ستا غوا غټه ده.
stā ɣwaˈgāne ˈɣaṭe di.	Your cows are big.	ستا غواګانې غټې دی.

4. Words that end in a consonant are normally masculine, but there are a few feminine inanimate nouns that also end in a consonant. They become plural by adding / -e / ې- .

ˈhaɣa zaˈṛa bṛəsˈtən da.	That is an old quilt.	هغه زړه بړستن ده.
ˈhaɣa zaˈṛe bṛəsˈtəne di.	They are old quilts.	هغه زړې بړستنې دی.

5. Natural gender words for family members are declined as follows:

	singular		plural	
mother	mor	مور	ˈmyende	مياندې
sister	xor	خور	ˈxwende	خوېندې
daughter	lur	لُور	ˈluṇa / lurˈyāne	لُونړه / لُورياني

NOTE:

It is very easy to confuse the following:

full	moṛ	موړ
dead	məṛ	مړ
mother	mor	مور

Try these sentences:

zə moṛ yım.	I am full.	زهٔ موړ يم.
zə məṛ yım.	I am dead.	زهٔ مړ يم.
dā zəˈmā mor da.	She is my mother.	دا زما مور ده.
mung māˈṛə yu.	We are full.	مُونږ ماړه يو.
mung mṛə yu.	We are dead.	مُونږ مړهٔ يو.

The use of *šta* and *ˈništa* شته، نشته

šta (شته) and *ˈništa* (نشته) are commonly used forms of the 'to be' verb, expressing 'presence' and 'absence'.

ˈməšra ˈxəza pa kor ke šta?	Is the senior lady of the house in?	مشره ښځه په کور کښې شته؟
na, ˈdəlta ˈništa.	No, she is not here.	نه، دلته نشته.
usˈtāz sāˈhıb šta?	Is the teacher present?	أُستاذ صاحب شته؟
āw, ˈdəlta šta dey.	Yes, he is here.	آو، دلته شته دے.
pa pakıˈstān ke girˈja šta?	Is there a church in Pakistan?	په پاکِستان کښې گرجا شته؟
āw, ˈḍere šta dey.	Yes there are many.	آو، ډيرې شته دے.
tsok zanāˈna xo ˈništa.	Are there no ladies?	څوک زنانه خو نشته.
pa kor ke tsok həm ˈništa.	There is no one at home.	په کور کښې څوک هم نشته.

prɪnsɪˈpəl seb pa dəfˈtər ke šta?	Is the principal in his office?	پرنسپل صېب په دفتر کښې شته؟
āw, nāst dey.	Yes, he is sitting.	آو، ناست دے.
stā pa ǰeb ke tsə šta?	Is there is anything in your pocket?	ستا په جيب کښې څۀ شته؟
na, ˈhits ˈništa.	No, nothing.	نه، هيڅ نشته.

NOTES:

1. *seb* (صېب) is a term of respect, rather like the English word 'sir'. It is the contracted form of *sāˈhɪb* (صاحب).
2. The expression *tsok zanāˈna xo ˈništa?* (څوک زنانه خو نشته؟) is useful for men to ask before entering a place where women might be present.

The verb *keˈdəl* 'to become' in the present and future tenses کېدل

ˈtāso ˈstəṛi ˈkegəy?	Are you getting tired?	تاسو ستړی کېږئ؟
na, nə ˈstəṛi ˈkegu.	No, we are not getting tired.	نه، نۀ ستړی کېږُو.
tə ˈɣosa ˈkege?	Are you getting angry?	تۀ غُصه کېږې؟
na, nə ˈɣosa ˈkegəm.	No, I am not getting angry.	نه، نۀ غُصه کېږم.
dā kār ˈkigi kə ˈnə kigi?	Will this work happen or not happen?	دا کار کېږی کۀ نۀ کېږی؟
āw, ˈkigi.	Yes, [it will] happen.	آو، کېږی.
māšuˈmān ˈudə ˈkigi?	Are the children going to sleep?	ماشُومان اُودۀ کېږی؟
na, nə ˈudə ˈkigi.	No, they are not going to sleep.	نه، نۀ اُودۀ کېږی.
dā ˈwādə ˈkigi?	Is she getting married?	دا وادۀ کېږی؟
na, nə ˈwādə ˈkigi.	No, she is not getting married.	نه، نۀ وادۀ کېږی.
tə ba ˈtsumra muˈda ˈdəlta ˈpāte ˈkege?	How long will you be staying here?	تۀ به څومره موده دلته پاتې کېږې؟
zə ba ˈdwəo ˈkālo ˈpore ˈpāte ˈkegəm.	I will be staying here for two years.	زۀ به دوو کالُو پورې پاتې کېږم.
dā mṛa ˈkigi?	Is she dying?	دا مړه کېږی؟
āw, har yo kas ba məṛ ˈkigi.	Yes, everyone will die.	آو، هر يو کس به مړ کېږی.

NOTES:

1. The verb *ke'dəl* (کېدل) is an auxiliary verb, used with nouns and adjectives to form intransitive compound verbs. For example, *mṛə ke'dəl* (مړ کېدل) 'to become dead' (i.e. 'to die') and *wā'də ke'dəl* (وادۀ کېدل) 'to become married'. These types of combinations are common in Pukhto.
2. Transitive and intransitive verbs are introduced in more detail in Lessons Seven and Eight.

Recognising plural nouns

There are several nouns, especially liquids and grains, which are considered plural in Pukhto. It is worth memorizing the more common ones. Here are a few of them:

čay [če]	tea	چائې	*f.pl.*
čo'le	beans	چولې	*f.pl.*
ɣə'nəm	wheat	غنم	*m.pl.*
ǰā'me	clothes	جامې	*f.pl.*
ǰu'ār	maize	جوار	*m.pl.*
mās'tə	yogurt	ماستۀ	*m.pl.*
māz'ɣə	brain	مازغۀ	*m.pl.*
or'bəše	barley	وربشې	*f.pl.*
pəy	milk	پئ	*f.pl.*
šāt	honey	شات	*m.pl.*
šo'le	rice (plant)	شولې	*f.pl.*
šom'le	curd	شملې	*f.pl.*
tel	oil	تېل	*m.pl.*
u'bə	water	اوبۀ	*f. pl.*
'zəhar	poison	زهر	*m.pl.*

NOTE:

These plural words include uncountable nouns like čay (چائې) 'tea' and pəy (پئ) 'milk', and a few countable nouns such as māz'ɣə (مازغۀ) 'brain'.

Comprehension drill: Identifying numbers on a calendar

Use a calendar to learn the numbers 1-31.

First learn the numbers in order, and then try practising them out of order. Start by pointing to the numbers as your teacher calls them out, then try to name the correct number as your teacher points. The new numbers are:

21	'yo-iš	يوويشت	۲۱
22	'dwa-iš	دوه ويشت	۲۲
23	'dər-wišt	درويشت	۲۳
24	tsaler-išt	څليريشت	۲۴
25	pin'z-išt	پينځۀ ويشت	۲۵
26	'špəg-išt	شپږ ويشت	۲۶
27	u'wə-išt	اووۀ ويشت	۲۷
28	ā'tə-wišt	اتۀ ويشت	۲۸
29	yo kəm derš	يو کم دېرش	۲۹
30	derš	دېرش	۳۰
31	'yo-derš	يو دېرش	۳۱

More parts of the body

These examples are all feminine in gender:

Memorising moment

mataˈluna

خُدائ چې څهٔ کړی، هغه ښهٔ کړی.

xoˈdey če tsə kṛi, haˈɣa xə kṛi.

What God does, he does well.

څهٔ ژرنده ورانه اؤ څهٔ دانے لمدے.

tsə ǰranˈda wrāˈna āw tsə dāˈney ləmˈdey.

Partly the mill is broken, partly the grain is damp.

دَ غل په ږیره خس وی.

də ɣəl pa ˈgira xəs wi.

There's a straw in the thief's beard.

In collecting language information it is helpful to be able to write in phonetic script. Try writing the phonetics for this *ma'təl* after your language helper has said it a few times:

لږ خوره تل خوره ډېر خوره ګنده خوره.

____

Eat a little, eat forever; eat a lot, eat garbage.

Now memorise it and learn its usage.

Exercises for Lesson Six

1. Practice describing people, animals and objects with the following sentences:

ha'ɣa sa'ṛey dey.	He is a man.	هغه سړے دے.
ha'ɣa 'tsənga sa'ṛey dey?	What kind of man is he?	هغه څنګه سړے دے؟
ha'ɣa tak'ṛa sa'ṛey dey.	He is a strong man.	هغه تکړه سړے دے.

Now start with these sentences:

a. dā lur da. دا لُور ده. ______

b. pa kor ke spey šta? په کور کښې سپے شته؟ ______

c. stā ās šta? ستا اس شته؟ ______

d. dā 'xəza da. دا ښځه ده. ______

e. hay'wi pəxta'ne di. هغوی پوښتنې دی. ______

Find a children's picture book or use *Picture It in Dari and Pashto* and have friends give adjectives to describe the pictures. Make a list of the adjectives you have learned.

2. Replace the underlined word in the following sentence with the words listed below:

zə'mā dā <u>ki'tāb</u> xwax dey. زما دا <u>کتاب</u> خوښ دے.

a.	qa'ləm	قلم	b.	mo'ṭər	موټر	c.	mā'šum	ماشُوم
d.	rang	رنګ	e.	kor	کور	f.	mez	مېز

Then make the sentences negative.

3. Repeat exercise 2. with these feminine nouns:

a.	piˈšo	پیشو	c.	ˈwəna	ونه
b.	ḍoˈḍəy	ډوډۍ	d.	bṛəˈstən	بړستن

4. Make the following singular feminine nouns and adjectives plural.

a.	piˈšo	پیشو	______	k.	tsaˈpləy	څپلۍ	______
b.	mālˈṭa	مالټه	______	l.	ˈnarsa	نرسه	______
c.	draˈna	درنه	______	m.	bṛəˈstən	بړستن	______
d.	malˈgəre	ملګرې	______	n.	ḍoˈḍəy	ډوډۍ	______
e.	ˈspəka	سپکه	______	o.	ˈxkwəle	ښکلې	______
f.	lur	لُور	______	p.	mor	مور	______
g.	ɣwa	غوا	______	q.	maˈṇa	مڼه	______
h.	pəxtaˈna	پوښتنه	______	r.	xra	خره	______
i.	ˈxəza	ښځه	______	s.	kaˈṇa	کڼه	______
j.	arˈzāna	ارزانه	______	t.	xor	خور	______

5. Using the question *dā tsə šey dey?* (دا څهٔ شے دے؟) point to the following parts of the body:

a.	xpa	خپه
b.	ˈxeṭa	خېټه
c.	siˈna	سینه
d.	ˈpoza	پوزه
e.	ˈstərga	سترګه
f.	ˈwruza	ورُوځه

Vocabulary for Lesson Six

ā'tə-wišt	اتهٔ ویشت		n., adj.	twenty-eight
u'bə	اوبهٔ	f.pl.	n.	water
u'də	اُودهٔ	m., f.	adj., v.	asleep, sleeping
u'də ke'dəl	اُودهٔ کېدل		v.i.	to go to sleep, to sleep, to go to bed
ā'wal	اول	m	adj.	first
u'wə-išt	اووهٔ ویشت		n., adj.	twenty-seven
bad'rəng	بدرنګ	m.	adj.	ugly
bad'rənga / bad'rənge	بدرنګه / بدرنګې	f.		
bṛəs'tən	بړستن	f.	n.	quilt
'pāte ke'dəl	پاتې کېدل		v.i.	to stay, to remain
pakı'stān	پاکِستان	m.	n.	Pakistan
paxwā'ney / paxwā'ni	پخوانے / پخوانی	m.	adj.	ancient, former, old
paxwā'nəy	پخوانۍ	f.		
'pore [də _ 'pore]	پورې [د _ پورې]		prep.	up to, until
'poza	پوزه	f.s.	n.	nose
pəy	پئ	f.pl.	n.	milk
pin'z-išt	پینځهٔ ویشت		n., adj.	twenty-five
ta'yār	تیار	m.	adj.	ready, made, prepared
ta'yāra / ta'yāre	تیاره / تیارې	f.		
tel	تېل	m.pl.	n.	oil
ǰā'me	جامې	f.pl.	n.	clothes
ǰu'ār	جوار	m.pl.	n.	corn, maize
ǰeb	جیب	m.s.	n.	pocket
čo'le	چولې	f.pl.	n.	beans
tsa'pləy	څپلۍ	f.	n.	sandal, shoe
tsaler-išt	څلیریشت		n., adj.	twenty-four

xpa / xpe	خپه / خپې	*f.*	*n.*	foot
ˈxəṭa	خټه	*f.*	*n.*	mud
xər	خر	*m.*	*n.*	donkey
xəs	خس	*m.*	*n.*	small speck, small piece of straw, chip of wood
xwā	خوا	*m.*	*n.*	side, direction
xoˈṛəl	خوړل		*v.t.*	to eat, to consume, to bite
ˈxeṭa	خېټه	*f.s.*	*n.*	stomach
xyāl	خيال	*m.*	*n.*	idea, thought, notion
ˈdər-wišt	درويشت		*n., adj.*	twenty-three
dəfˈtər	دفتر	*m.s.*	*n.*	office
ˈdwa-iš	دوه ويشت		*n., adj.*	twenty-two
dwi	دوئ	*m., f.*	*pro.*	they (near)
derš	دېرش		*n., adj.*	thirty
zoṛ / zāˈṛə	زوړ / زاړۀ	*m.*	*adj.*	old
zaˈṛa / zaˈṛe	زړه / زړې	*f.*		
zanāˈna	زنانه	*f.pl.*	*n.*	ladies
ˈzəhar	زهر	*m.pl.*	*n.*	poison
ǰwanˈdey / ǰwanˈdi	ژوندے / ژوندی	*m.*	*adj.*	alive, living
ǰwanˈdəy	ژوندۍ	*f.*		
ˈstərga / ˈstərge	سترګه / سترګې	*f.*	*n.*	eye
siˈna	سينه	*f.*	*n.*	chest
ˈšpəg-išt	شپږ ويشت		*n., adj.*	twenty-six
špa	شپه	*f.s.*	*n.*	night
šomˈle	شملې	*f.pl.*	*n.*	curd
šoˈle	شولې	*f.pl.*	*n.*	rice (plant)
sāˈhıb [seb]	صاحب [صېب]	*m.*	*n.*	sir; boss
ɣaˈdār	غدار	*m.*	*n.*	villain, deceiver

ɣoˈsa	غُصه	f.	n. adj	anger, fury, rage; angry
ˈɣosa keˈdəl	غُصه کېدل		v.i.	to become angry
ɣəˈnəm	غنم	m.	n.	wheat
qāˈbɪl	قابِل	m.	adj.	able, capable, worthy, skilled
keˈdəl	کېدل		v.i.	to be, to become, to happen, to be possible
kenaˈstəl	کښېناستل [کېناستل]		v.i.	to sit (down)
girˈǰa	ګرجا	f.	n.	church
lwəṛ	لوړ	m.	adj.	high, tall
ˈlwəṛa / ˈlwəṛe	لوړه / لوړې	f.		
māzˈɣə	مازغهٔ	m.pl.	n.	brain
məṛ / mṛə	مړ / مړهٔ	m.	adj.	dead
mṛa / mṛe	مړه / مړې	f.		
məṛ keˈdəl	مړ کېدل		v.i.	to die
moṛ / māˈṛə	موړ / ماړهٔ	m.	adj.	full
maˈṛa / maˈṛe	مړه / مړې	f.		
nāst	ناست	m.	adj., v.	sitting, seated
ˈnāsta / ˈnāste	ناسته / ناستې	f.		
orˈbəše	وربشې	f.pl.	n.	barley
ˈwruza / ˈwruze	ورُوځه / ورُوځې	f.	n.	eyebrow
ˈwəgey	وږے	m.	adj.	hungry
ˈyo-derš	يو دېرش		n.adj.	thirty-one
yo kəm derš	يو کم دېرش		n., adj.	twenty-nine
ˈyo-iš	يوويشت		n., adj.	twenty-one
har yo kas, har ča	هر يو کس، هر څوک		pro.	everyone
ˈhits	هيڅ	m.	n.	nothing, none

u'wəm sa'bəq اووم سبق

Lesson Seven

Dialogue seven: *rıš'ka* 'rickshaw'

L: 'sədər ta ze? Are you going to Saddar?	صدر ته ځي؟
H: 'kena, zə če zu! Sit down, let's go!	کښېنه، ځه چي ځُو!
L: 'tsumra pe'se ba 'axle? How much money will you take?	څومره پیسي به اخلي؟
H: tsə če de 'xwaxa wi. (or) tsə če 'darta muna'sıb 'xkāri. Whatever you like. (or) Whatever seems proper to you.	څۀ چي دي خوښه وی. (یا) څۀ چي درته مُناسب ښکاری.
L: na, mā ta 'owaya. No, tell me.	نه، ما ته ووایه.
H: āβ'yā ru'pəy. Seventy rupees.	اویا روپۍ.
L: na, dā 'ḍere di. ləg kəm ša. No, that's too much. Make it less.	نه، دا ډېري دی. لږ کم شه.
H: pin'zə špe'ta ru'pəy 'rāka. Give me sixty-five rupees.	پینځۀ شپېته روپۍ راکه.
L: xa, špe'ta ru'pəy ba 'darkəm. OK, I'll give you sixty.	ښه، شپېته روپۍ به درکم.
L: 'dəlta xi ta'raf-ta 'tāw ša. Turn right here.	دلته ښی طرف ته تاؤ شه.
'dəlta gəs ta'raf-ta 'tāw ša. Turn left here.	دلته گَس طرف ته تاؤ شه.
'sida za. Go straight on.	سیده ځه.
'dəlta me kuz ka. Let me off here.	دلته مي کُوز که.
'dəlta 'odrega! brek ša! Stop here! Brake!	دلته ودرېگه! بریک شه!

NOTE:

zə če (ځه چي) literally means 'come that you may', and is an idiomatic way of saying 'let's'.

Pronunciation drill

1. Contrasting / ts / څ and / s / ص

dey xə tseˈra laˈri.	He has a good-looking face.	دے ښهٔ څېره لرى.
dā xə surat laˈri.	She has a good image.	دا ښهٔ صُورت لرى.
dā kuˈtsa da.	This is a street.	دا کوڅه ده.
dā ɣoˈsa da.	She is angry.	دا غُصه ده.

2. Contrasting / -ə / humza on final letter (e.g. ۀ) and / -a / ـه-

zə la de saˈra wāˈdə kaˈwəm.	I am getting married to her.	زۀ له دې سره وادۀ کوم.
zə la haˈɣa saˈra waˈda kaˈwəm.	I am making her a promise.	زۀ له هغه سره وعده کوم.
dā larˈgi kāˈgə di.	These bits of wood are bent.	دا لرګى کاږۀ دى.
dā ˈwəna kaˈga da.	This tree is bent.	دا ونه کږه ده.
dā xwāˈgə di.	These are sweet.	دا خواږۀ دى.
dā xwaˈga da.	This is sweet.	دا خوږه ده.

Possessive pronouns

The personal pronouns *zəˈmā* (زما) 'mine', *də də* (د دۀ) 'his', etc., introduced in Lesson 3, form the possessive case, answering the question *də čā?* (د چا؟) 'whose?'.

Person	Singular			Plural		
1st	my, mine	zəˈmā	زما	our, ours	zmung	زمُونږ
2nd	your, yours	stā	ستا	your, yours	ˈstāso	ستاسو
3rd m.	his	də də	د دۀ	their, theirs (near)	də di, də dwi	د دى، د دوئ
3rd f.	her, hers	də de	د دې	their, theirs (near)	də di, də dwi	د دى، د دوئ
3rd m.	his (far)	də haˈɣə	د هغۀ	their, theirs (far)	də haˈɣi, də haɣˈwi	د هغئ، د هغوى
3rd f.	her, hers (far)	də haˈɣe	د هغې	their, theirs (far)	də haˈɣi, də haɣˈwi	د هغئ، د هغوى

NOTE:

You will find that some speakers will habitually use either *dwi* (دوئ) or *di* (دى) for objects close at hand, and *haɣˈwi* (هغوى) or *haˈɣi* (هغئ) for objects out of sight. This seems to be an issue of habit or dialect.

Statements with possessive adjectives

Possessive pronoun	Noun	Adjective	Verb	
zəˈmā	mez	plən	dey.	زما مېز پلن دے. My table is wide.
zmung	kor	waˈṛukey	dey.	زمُونږ کور وړُوکے دے. Our house is small.
stā	wror	ɣaṭ	dey.	ستا ورور غټ دے. Your brother is fat.
ˈstāso	ˈməšar	malˈdār	dey?	ستاسو مشر مالدار دے؟ Is your elder rich?
də də	gaˈṛəy	ˈgrāna	da.	د دهٔ گړی گرانه ده. His watch is expensive.
də haˈɣə	xor	ˈxkwəle	da.	د هغهٔ خور ښکُلې ده. His sister is pretty.
də de	kaˈmis	lund	dey.	د دې قمیص لوند دے. Her shirt is wet.
də haˈɣe	mor	ˈstəṛe	da.	د هغې مور ستړې ده. Her mother is tired.
də dwi	moˈṭər	zoṛ	dey.	د دوئ موټر زوړ دے. Their (nearby) car is old.
də hayˈwi	saˈbəq	grān	dey.	د هغوی سبق گران دے. Their (distant) lesson is hard.
də ˈčā	ḍoˈḍəy	xə	da?	د چا ډوډی ښهٔ ده؟ Whose food is good?

NOTE:
plən (پلن) 'wide' finds a special use in the aggressive challenge: *plən ba de kaˈwəm* (پلن به دې کوم) 'I will make you wide'.

Statements and questions with possessive pronouns

dā stā kiˈtāb dey?	Is this your book?	دا ستا کتاب دے؟
āw, dā zəˈmā kiˈtāb dey.	Yes, this is my book.	آو، دا زما کتاب دے.

zəˈmā piˈšo ˈčerta da?	Where is my cat?	زما پیشو چرته ده؟
stā piˈšo pa bām ˈbānde da.	Your cat is on the roof.	ستا پیشو په بام باندې ده.
ˈstāso zwe nā-ˈǰoṛa dey?	Is your son sick?	ستاسو زوئ ناجوړه دے؟
āw, zmung zwe nā-ˈroɣa dey.	Yes, our son is sick.	آؤ، زمُونږ زوئ ناروغه دے.
ˈstāso noˈkər pa baˈzār ke dey?	Is your servant in the market?	ستاسو نوکر په بازار کښې دے؟
na, zmung noˈkər pa kor ke dey.	No, our servant is in the house.	نه، زمُونږ نوکر په کور کښې دے.
də haˈɣə tsaˈpləy ˈdəlta di?	Are his sandals here?	د هغهٔ څپلۍ دلته دی؟
na, də haˈɣə tsaˈpləy ˈdəlta ˈništa.	No, his sandals are not here.	نه، د هغهٔ څپلۍ دلته نشته.
də haˈɣə wāsˈkaṭ tor dey, kə spin?	Is his waistcoat black or white?	د هغهٔ واسکټ تور دے کهٔ سپین؟
də haˈɣə wāsˈkaṭ tor dey.	His waistcoat is black.	د هغهٔ واسکټ تور دے.
də de ˈstərga xug da?	Is her eye hurt?	د دې سترګه خوږ ده؟
āw, də de ˈstərga xug da.	Yes, her eye is hurt.	آو، د دې سترګه خوږ ده.
də haˈɣe xor ˈčerta da?	Where is her sister?	د هغې خور چرته ده؟
də haˈɣe xor pa yunɪwersɪˈṭəy ke da.	Her sister is at university.	د هغې خور په یونیورستۍ کښې ده.
ˈhaɣa ˈstāso ˈluxi di?	Are those your pots?	هغه ستاسو لوښی دی؟
na, ˈhaɣa də dwi ˈluxi di.	No, those are their pots.	نه، هغه د دوئ لوښی دی.
də haɣˈwi lur ˈčerta da?	Where is their daughter?	د هغوی لُور چرته ده؟
də haɣˈwi lur ˈhalta ˈnāsta da.	Their daughter is sitting there.	د هغوی لُور هلته ناسته ده.
ˈhalta də čā kiˈtāb prot dey?	Whose book is lying there?	هلته د چا کتاب پروت دے؟
ˈhaɣa zəˈmā kiˈtāb dey.	That is my book.	هغه زما کتاب دے.
də čā zwe uxˈyār dey?	Whose son is intelligent?	د چا زوئ هوښیار دے؟

də hay'wi zwe ux'yār dey.	Their son is intelligent.	د هغوی زوئ هوښیار دے.
də čā ṭo'pəy 'tora da?	Whose hat is black?	د چا ټوپۍ توره ده؟
stā ṭo'pəy 'tora da.	Your hat is black.	ستا ټوپۍ توره ده.

NOTE:

Words like *nāst* (ناست) 'sitting' and *prot* (پروت) 'lying' function as adjectives and are inflected for both gender and number.

Possessive pronouns in questions and answers

dā ki'tāb də čā dey?	Whose book is this?	دا کتاب د چا دے؟
dā ki'tāb zə'mā dey.	This book is mine.	دا کتاب زما دے.
'haya mo'ṭər də čā dey?	Whose car is that?	هغه موټر د چا دے؟
'haya mo'ṭər zmung dey.	That car is ours.	هغه موټر زمونږ دے.
dā pın'səl də čā dey?	Whose pencil is this?	دا پنسل د چا دے؟
dā pın'səl 'stāso dey.	This pencil is yours.	دا پنسل ستاسو دے.
'haya tore tsa'pləy 'stāso di?	Are those black sandals yours?	هغه تورې څپلۍ ستاسو دی؟
āw, 'haya zmung di.	Yes, they are ours.	آو، هغه زمونږ دی.
dā sur qa'ləm də də dey?	Is this red pen his?	دا سور قلم د دهٔ دے؟
na, dā də de dey.	No it is hers.	نه، دا د دې دے.
dā 'xkwəle pi'šo də ha'yə da?	Is this lovely cat his?	دا ښکلې پیشو د هغهٔ ده؟
na, dā də ha'ye da.	No, this is hers.	نه، دا د هغې ده.
'haya ux'yār ha'lək də čā dey?	Whose wise boy is that?	هغه هوښیار هلک د چا دے؟
'haya ha'lək də dwi dey.	That boy is theirs.	هغه هلک د دوئ دے.
'haya tas'wir də čā dey?	Whose picture is that?	هغه تصویر د چا دے؟
'haya də mu'sā dey.	That is Moses's.	هغه د موسیٰ دے.
dā xə šer də čā dey?	Whose good poem is this?	دا ښهٔ شعر د چا دے؟
dā də hā'fız dey.	This is Hafiz's.	دا د حافظ دے.

NOTE:

stāso (ستاسو) is used as a polite way to talk to a respected elder.

For example the sentence:

dā pɪnˈsəl ˈstāso dey? Is this pencil yours? دا پِنسل ستاسو دے؟

Object pronouns

When pronouns become receivers of action they take on this inflected form.

Person	Singular			Plural		
1st	mā	Me	ما	mung	us	مُونږ
2nd	tā	You	تا	ˈtāso	you	تاسو
3rd m.	də	him (near)	دهٔ	dwi	them (near)	دوئ
3rd f.	de	her (near)	دے	dwi	them (near)	دوئ
3rd m.	haˈɣə	him (far)	هغهٔ	haɣˈwi	them (far)	هغوی
3rd f.	haˈɣe	her (far)	هغې	haɣˈwi	them (far)	هغوی
Question	čā?	whom?	چا؟	čā?	whom?	چا؟

NOTES:

1. Object pronouns are receivers of action rather than doers of action, and precede prepositions such as 'with' *saˈra* (سره) and 'to' *ta* (ته).
2. Oblique case forms of singular pronouns are different from one another. For example the subject pronoun 'I' *zə* (زهٔ), becomes the object pronoun 'me' *mā* (ما).
   The oblique case is introduced in Lesson 8.
3. Object pronouns are also used in past tense transitive sentences as 'subject pronouns' (see Lesson 20).

Object pronouns used with *saˈra* 'with' سره

zəˈmā kiˈtāb <u>tā</u> saˈra dey?	Is my book with <u>you</u>?	زما کتاب <u>تا</u> سره دے؟
āw, stā kiˈtāb <u>mā</u> saˈra dey.	Yes, your book is with <u>me</u>.	آو، ستا کتاب <u>ما</u> سره دے.
zmung usˈtāz <u>de</u> saˈra dey?	Is our teacher with <u>her</u>?	زمُونږ اُستاذ <u>دې</u> سره دے؟
āw, haˈɣa <u>de</u> saˈra dey.	Yes, he is with <u>her</u>.	آو، هغه <u>دې</u> سره دے.

haɣ'wi čā sa'ra di?	Who are they with?	هغوی چا سره دی؟
haɣ'wi ha'san sa'ra di.	They are with Hassan.	هغوی حَسن سره دی.
dā 'tāso sa'ra šta?	Is it with you?	دا تاسو سره شته؟
āw, mung sa'ra šta.	Yes, it is with us.	آو، مُونږ سره شته.
də də da'ru tā sa'ra di?	Is his medicine with you?	د دهٔ دارُو تا سره دی؟
na, də də da'ru mā sa'ra 'ništa.	No, his medicine is not with me.	نه، د دهٔ دارُو ما سره نشته.
stā mo'ṭər čā sa'ra dey?	Who has your car?	ستا موټر چا سره دے؟
ha'ɣa ǰān sa'ra dey.	It is with John.	هغه جان سره دے.

NOTE:

The following expression is very useful when trying to match a piece of cloth at the tailors.

dā 'tāso sa'ra šta?	Do you have this?	دا تاسو سره شته؟

Transitive verbs

There are two kinds of verbs in Pukhto, and recognising them is as important as getting the masculine and feminine endings right. Verbs are either transitive or intransitive.

Transitive verbs are active or 'doing' verbs. They act on something, so they require a direct object. For example, to call, to send, to see, to write, to win, to take, to eat, to wash, to kill, to lick, to give, to spit, to beat, etc.

The transitive verb *ka'wəl* 'to do' used as an auxiliary verb — کول

'tāso 'čerta kār ka'wəy?	Where are you working?	تاسو چرته کار کوئ؟
mung pa dəf'tər ke kār ka'wu.	We work in an office.	مُونږ په دفتر کښې کار کوو.
dā tā sa'ra kār ka'wi?	Does she work with you?	دا تاسره کار کوی؟
na, mā sa'ra kār 'nə-kawi.	No she doesn't work with me.	نه، ما سره کار نهٔ کوی.
ka'rim 'sehen ǰā'ru kəy?	Is Karim sweeping the yard?	کریم صِحن جارُو کوی؟
na, ha'ɣa ko'ṭa ǰā'ru kəy.	No, he is sweeping the room.	نه، هغه کوټه جارُو کوی.
hafi'za tsə kəy?	What is Hafiza doing?	حافظه څهٔ کوی؟
ha'ɣa ka'pre is'tri kəy.	She is ironing the cloth.	هغه کپړې استری کوی.

zə'mā xor 'ḍere xa'bare kəy.	My sister talks a lot.	زما خور ډېرې خبرې کوي.
dā čā sa'ra xa'bare kəy?	Who does she talk with?	دا چا سره خبرې کوي؟
dā mal'gəre sa'ra xa'bare kəy.	She talks with her friend.	دا ملګرې سره خبرې کوي.
māšu'mān os 'čerta 'lobe kəy?	Where are the children playing now?	ماشُومان اوس چرته لوبې کوي؟
haɣ'wi pa bāɣ ke 'lobe kəy.	They are playing in the park.	هغوی په باغ کښې لوبې کوي.
tə pəx'to das'tur ız'da kawe?	Are you learning Pukhto culture?	تهٔ پښتو دستور زده کوې؟
āw, zə pəx'to das'tur ız'da ka'wəm.	Yes, I'm learning Pukhto culture.	آو، زهٔ پښتو دستور زده کوم.
ha'bib wā'də kəy?	Is Habib getting married?	حبيب وادهٔ کوي؟
na, ha'ɣa os wā'də nə-kəy.	No, he is not getting married now.	نه، هغه اوس وادهٔ نهٔ کوي.

NOTE:
The *ka'wəl* (کول) verb endings are often shortened in speech. For example, in the sentences above the ending *ka'wi* (کوي) is often shortened in speech to *kəy* even though the written form of the verb remains the same.

Comprehension drill: Learning numbers thirty to nine thousand

Ask your helper to give you numbers divisible by 10 (e.g. 20, 360, 7890). You then repeat that number plus the next nine in the series. For example, 360, 361, 362 through to 369. After this, let him randomly call out numbers from 1 to 1,000. Your response should only be to write them down as you hear them. Have your helper check your answers.

30	derš	دېرش	۳۰	100	sıl	سل	۱۰۰
40	tsal'wext	څلوېښت	۴۰	200	dwa sa'wa	دوه سوه	۲۰۰
50	pan'zos	پنځوس	۵۰	300	dre sa'wa	درې سوه	۳۰۰
60	špe'tə	شپېته	۶۰	1,000	zər	زر	۱۰۰۰
70	āβ'yā	اويا	۷۰	2,000	dwa za'ra	دوه زره	۲۰۰۰
80	āt'yā	اتيا	۸۰	9,000	'nəhə za'ra	نههٔ زره	۹۰۰۰
90	'nawi, ləs kəm sıl	نوي، لس کم سل	۹۰				

Memorising moment

mata'luna

په پوښتنه پوښتنه سړے کابل ته رسيد ے شي.

pa pox'təna pox'təna sa'ṛey kā'bəl ta rase'dey ši.

By asking and asking a man can reach Kabul.

خر چې دَ خر نه کم وی غوږ يې دَ پرې کولو وی.

xər če də xra na kəm wi ɣwəg ye də pre ka'wəlo wi.

If a donkey is less than a donkey it's ear should be cut.

الوتې مرغۍ په لاس نۀ راځی.

ālwə'te mar'ɣəy pa lās nə 'rāzi.

The bird that has flown can't come to the hand.

Exercises for Lesson Seven

1. Replace each of the words listed below for the underlined word in the sentence:

   zə 'ɣwāṛəm če pəx'to ız'da kṛəm. — زۀ غواړم چې پښتو زده کړم.

   a. fār'si فارسی   b. ur'du اُردو   c. angre'zi انګریزی

2. Substitute the appropriate words in the sentence.

   zə os kār ka'wəm. I am working now. — زۀ اوس کار کوم.

   a. ǰā'ru kəy جارُو کوی

   ____

   b. pa ko'ṭa ke په کوټه کښې

   ____

   c. kor کور

   ____

   d. sa'bəq سبق

   ____

   e. pəx'to پښتو

   ____

   f. xa'bare kəy خبرې کوی

   ____

   g. pa dəf'tər ke په دفتر کښې

   ____

   h. mung مُونږ

   ____

i. kār ka'we کار کوي

m. xob kəy خوب کوی

j. də de māšu'mān د دي ماشُومان

n. ha'bib حبیب

k. 'lobe kəy لوبې کوی

o. wā'də kəy وادهٔ کوی

l. pa bāɣ ke په باغ کښې

3. Substitute the pairs of words for the underlined words in this sentence:

dā zə'mā kor dey. This is my house. دا زما کور دے.

a. zmung زمونږ ki'tāb کتاب

e. də haɣ'wi د هغوی tsa'pləy څپلۍ

b. də ha'ɣə د هغه pɪn'səl پنسل

f. 'stāso ستاسو 'stərga سترګه

c. də dwi د دوئ dəf'tər دفتر

g. stā ستا bāɣ باغ

d. də ha'ɣe د هغې us'tāz اُستاذ

h. də haɣ'wi د هغوی u'xān اُوښان

4. In response to the question

tə 'čā sa'ra kār ka'we? Who works with you? تهٔ چا سره کار کوي؟

Reply using the following words in your answer:

a. mor مور

b. zwe زوئ

c. wror ورور

____

d. lur لُور

____

e. haɣ'wi هغوی

____

f. yo mā'šum یو ماشُوم

____

5. Replace the underlined parts in the sentence
<u>stā pi'šo</u> <u>mā</u> sa'ra da. Your cat is with me. <u>ستا پیشو</u> <u>ما</u> سره ده.

a. zmung pe'se, tāso زمُونږ پېسې، تاسو

____

b. də ha'ɣe ka'mis, də čā د هغې قمیص، د چا

____

c. də de lur, mung د دې لُور، مُونږ

____

d. stā wror, də ستا ورور، دهٔ

____

Vocabulary for Lesson Seven

āt'yā	اتیا		n., adj.	eighty
āxɪs'təl	اخستل		v.t.	to buy, to take, to get
ur'du	اُردو	f.s.	n.	Urdu language
us'tāz	اُستاذ	m.s.	n.	teacher
is'tri ka'wəl	اِستری کول		comp. v.t.	to iron
angre'zi	انګرېزی		n.	English language
os	اوس		adv.	now
āβ'yā	اویا	m.	n., adj.	seventy
bām	بام	m.s.	n.	roof, housetop
brek ke'dəl	برېک کېدل		comp. v.i.	to brake
ba'zār	بازار	m.s.	n.	bazaar, market
pan'zos	پنځوس		n., adj.	fifty
prot	پروت	m.	adj., v.	located, situated, lying down, flat
pra'ta / pra'te	پرته / پرتې	f.		
tā	تا	m., f.	obj. pro.	you
taβe'dəl	تاوېدل		v.i.	to turn, to revolve, to rotate
tas'wir	تصویر	m.s.	n.	picture, portrait, image, painting
tləl	تلل		v.i.	to go
ṭo'pəy	ټوپۍ	f.s.	n.	cap, hat
ǰā'ru ka'wəl	جارُو کول		comp. v.t.	to sweep
zə če	څه چې		ph.	let's
čā	چا		obj., q.	whom
tse'ra	څېره	f.	n.	face; covering
xa'bare ka'wəl	خبرې کول		comp. v.t.	to talk, to chat
xob ka'wəl	خوب کول		comp. v.t.	to sleep
xog / xwā'gə	خوږ / خواږهٔ	m.	adj.	sweet
xwa'ga / xwa'ge	خوږه / خوږې	f.		

xug	خوږ	*m.*	*n., adj.*	pain, ache, illness; injured, hurt
də	د		*prep.*	of, from
də čā	د چا	*m., f.*	*poss. pro.*	whose
də dwi	د دوئ	*m., f.*	*poss. pro.*	their, theirs (near)
də də	د دهٔ	*m.s.*	*poss. pro.*	his (near)
də de	د دې	*f.s.*	*poss. pro.*	hers (near)
də haɣˈwi	د هغوئ	*m., f.*	*poss. pro.*	their, theirs (far)
də haˈɣə	د هغهٔ	*m.s.*	*poss. pro.*	his (far)
də haˈɣe	د هغې	*f.s.*	*poss. pro.*	hers (far)
daˈru	دارُو	*m.*	*n.*	medicine, drug
dasˈtur	دستور	*m.*	*n.*	culture, custom
dwa zaˈra	دوه زره		*n., adj.*	two thousand
dwa saˈwa	دوه سوه		*n., adj.*	two hundred
də	دهٔ	*m.s.*	*obj. pro.*	him (near)
de	دې	*f.s.*	*obj. pro.*	her (near)
rɪšˈka	ریشکه [ریکشا]	*f.s.*	*n.*	rickshaw
zər	زر		*n., adj.*	a thousand
saˈbəq	سبق	*m.s.*	*n.*	lesson
sɪl	سل		*n., adj.*	one hundred
ˈsida	سیده		*adj.*	straight, forward
špeˈtə	شپیتهٔ		*n., adj.*	sixty
šer	شِعر	*m.s.*	*n.*	poem
xi	ښی		*adj.*	right (direction)
ˈsehen	صحن	*m.*	*n.*	courtyard, yard
surat	صُورَت	*m.*	*n.*	image
taˈraf	طرف	*m.s.*	*n.*	side, direction
fārˈsi	فارسی		*n.*	Farsi language

kaˈmis / kamiˈsuna	قمیص [کمیس] / قمیصونه [کمیسونه]	*m.*	*n.*	shirt
kaˈpṛa	کپړه	*f.s.*	*n.*	cloth
kəm	کم	*m.*	*adj*	less, few, insufficient
ˈkəma / ˈkəme	کمه / کمې	*f.*		
kuˈtsa / kuˈtse	کوڅه / کوڅې	*f.*	*n.*	street
kuzaˈwəl	کُوزول		*comp. v.t.*	to make or cause (someone or thing) to descend or come down
kog / kāˈgə	کوږ / کاږهٔ	*m.*	*adj.*	bent, crooked
kaˈga	کږه	*f.*		
kaˈwəl	کول		*v.t.*	to do
gaˈṛəy	ګړۍ	*f.s.*	*n.*	watch
gəs	ګس / ګڅ		*adj.*	left
ˈlobe kaˈwəl	لوبې کول		*comp. v.t.*	to play
ˈluxey / ˈluxi	لوښے / لوښی	*m.*	*n.*	pot, utensil, vessel
lund / lāmˈdə	لوند / لامدهٔ	*m.*	*adj.*	wet, moist
lamˈda / lamˈde	لمده / لمدې	*f.*		
mā	ما	*m., f.*	*obj. pro.*	me
munaˈsıb	مُناسب	*m.*	*adj.*	proper, appropriate
nā-ˈǰoṛa	ناجوړه	*m., f.*	*adj.*	ill, sick
nā-ˈroɣa	ناروغه	*m., f.*	*adj.*	sick, ill, unhealthy, diseased
noˈkər	نوکر	*m.s.*	*n.*	servant
ˈnawi	نوی		*n., adj.*	ninety
wāsˈkaṭ	واسکټ	*m.s.*	*n.*	vest, waistcoat
odreˈdəl	ودرېدل		*v.i.*	to stop, to stand, to wait
waˈda kaˈwəl	وعده کول		*v.t.*	to promise
haˈɣə	هغهٔ	*m.s.*	*obj. pro.*	him (far)
haˈɣe	هغې	*f.s.*	*obj. pro.*	her (far)
yunıwersıˈṭi	یونیورسټی	*f.*	*n.*	university

āˈtəm saˈbəq اتم سبق

Lesson Eight

Dialogue eight: Ladies 'chit-chat' گپ شپ

L: ˈxore, zə xəˈfa yım. Sister, I am discouraged.	خوري زۀ خفه يم.
H: ˈtsənga ˈxore? How come, sister?	څنګه خوري؟
L: pa pəxˈto ke xə taraˈqi nə kaˈwəm. I am not making good progress in Pukhto.	په پښتو کښې ښۀ ترقی نۀ کوم.
H: pa rıšˈtya? Really?	په ريشتيا؟
L: pa kor ke zəˈmā ḍer kār dey. I have a lot of work at home.	په کور کښې زما ډېر کار دے.
H: zəˈmā həm. Me too.	زما هم.
L: če pəxˈto ızˈda kaˈwəm, zə ˈstəṛe ˈkegəm. When I learn Pukhto I become tired.	چې پښتو زده کوم، زۀ ستړې کېږم.
H: zə poˈhigəm. *or* mā ta ˈpata da. I understand.	زۀ پوهېږم. (يا) اؤ ما ته پته ده.
L: dā waxt zəˈmā dəˈpāra be-ˈxwanda dey. This is a joyless time for me.	دا وخت زما د پاره بې خونده دے.
H: ˈmə-xəfa ˈkega. Don't be sad.	مۀ خفه کېږه.
L: xoˈdey pāk zəˈmā maˈdəd kaˈwi, če koˈšiš kaˈwəm. God helps me when I try.	خُدائ پاک زما مدد کوی چې کوشش کوم.
H: deṛa xə da. xoˈdey raˈhim dey. That's good. God is merciful.	ډېره ښۀ ده. خُدائ رحيم دے.
L: akˈsər zəˈmā xwā la rāˈza! Come to visit me often!	اکثر زما خوا له راځه!

Men's *gəpˈšəp* with a shopkeeper

L: kār de ˈtsənga raˈwān dey? How is your business going?	کار دې څنګه روان دے؟
H: də ālˈlā ˈfəzəl dey guzaˈra ˈkigi. By the grace of God it's OK.	د الله فضل دے ګُزاره کېږی.
L: dā ˈstāso xpəl kār dey? Is it your own business?	دا ستاسو خپل کار دے؟
H: na ǰi, zə noˈkər yım. No sir, I'm an employee. də gul mohˈmad kār dey. It's Gul Muhammad's business.	نه جی، زهٔ نوکر یم. د ګُل محمد کار دے.
L: stā dyāˈṛi ˈtsumra da? How much is your daily wage?	ستا دیاړی څومره ده؟
H: ˈyara ˈdwa saˈwa ruˈpəy rākaˈwi. Oh friend, he's paying me two hundred rupees.	یره دوه سوه روپۍ راکوی.
L: zə pəxˈto ızˈda kaˈwəl ɣwāˈṛəm. I want to learn Pukhto.	زهٔ پښتو زده کول غواړم.
kə ˈstāso ıtaˈrāz nə wi, no zə ba ˈdəlta gəpˈšəp la rāˈzəm. If you don't object, then I'll come here to chat with you.	کهٔ ستاسو اعتراض نهٔ وی، نو زهٔ به دلته ګپ شپ له راځم.
H: ˈhits xaˈbara nə da, ˈstāso če ˈkəla mərˈzi wi, rātˈley šəy. It's no problem, whenever you wish you can come.	هیڅ خبره نهٔ ده، ستاسو چې کله مرضی وی، راتلے شئ.
L: ˈḍera merabāˈni, xo byā həm ˈtāso mā ta ṭaym ˈrākṛəy. zə ˈstāso kār xarābaˈwəl ˈnə- ɣwāṛəm. Many thanks, but still give me a time. I don't want to disturb your business.	ډیره مِهربانی، خو بیا هم تاسو ما ته ټیم راکړئ. زهٔ ستاسو کار خرابول نهٔ غواړم.
H: xa, no də ˈdwəo baˈǰo na tər dreo baˈǰo ˈpore zə uzˈgār yım. Fine, from two o'clock up to three o'clock I'm free.	ښه، نو د دوؤ بجو نه تر دریو بجو پورې زهٔ وزګار یم.

Pronunciation drill

Contrasting / **k** / ک with / **x** / ښ and خ

dey kār ta ra'wān dey.	He is going to work.	دے کار ته روان دے.
dey xār ta ra'wān dey.	He is going to the city.	دے ښار ته روان دے.
zmung kor os pa 'kəli ke dey.	Our house is now in the village.	زمونږ کور اوس په کلی کښې دے.
zmung xor os pa 'kəli ke da.	Our sister is now in the village.	زمونږ خور اوس په کلی کښې ده.
tə kāl 'olika!	Write 'kaal'!	تهٔ کال ولیکه!
tə xāl 'olika!	Write 'khaal'!	تهٔ خال ولیکه!

There are several words where these sounds come close to each other in the same word and need careful practice to say well. For example:

'xkwəle ښکُلې

'maxke مخکښې

The preposition *də* 'of' with masculine nouns and adjectives

The preposition *də* (د) denotes belonging to.

Possessive noun	Subject	Adjective	Verb	
də mā'lək	kor	luy	dey.	د ملک کور لوئ دے. The chief's house is big.
də sa'ṛi	ās	tez	dey.	د سړی اس تېز دے. The man's horse is fast.
də ḍāk'ṭər	zwe	ux'yār	dey.	د ډاکټر زوئ هوښیار دے. The doctor's son is wise.
də sṭu'danṭ	ki'tāb	lənḍ	dey.	د سټوډنټ کتاب لنډ دے. The student's book is short.
də sṭu'danṭāno	sa'bəq	ā'sān	dey.	د سټوډنټانو سبق آسان دے. The students' lesson is easy.
də us'tāz	kār	grān	dey.	د اُستاذ کار گران دے. The teacher's work is hard.
də mo'ṭər	mā'lık	bu'ḍā	dey.	د موټر مالک بوډا دے. The owner of the car is old.

də kor'uno	mā'lɪk	mal'dār	dey.	د کورونو مالک مالدار دے. The owner of the houses is rich.
də māšu'māno	plār	bi'mār	dey.	د ماشُومانو پلار بيمار دے. The children's father is sick.
də klərk	af'sər	ɣaṭ	dey.	د کلرک افسر غټ دے. The clerk's boss is fat.
də pəxta'no	ɣe'rət	məša'hur	dey.	د پښتنو غيرت مشهُور دے. The bravery of Pukhtuns is famous.
də šā'hɪd	mā'mā	ɣaṭ	dey.	د شاهد ماما غټ دے. Shahid's uncle is fat.

NOTE:

The possessive preposition *də* (د) 'of' precedes the noun it modifies. It usually comes first in the sentence.

The oblique case (inflection)

1. Nouns are inflected into the oblique case when they are preceded by a preposition and/or followed by a postposition. When such a noun is the object of a pre- or postposition, the inflection that occurs is in addition to the inflection for number and gender, as in the following example and the chart below (cf. Lesson 3):

   mung pa de kor'uno ke 'osu. We are living in these houses. مُونږ په دې کورونو کښې اوسو.

2. Nouns in the possessive case are also considered to be in the oblique case because they are preceded by də (د). The three most common ways masculine nouns are inflected are shown below:

	Animate		Inanimate	
	Direct	**Oblique**	**Direct**	**Oblique**
m.s.	ha'lək هلک	ha'lək هلک	kor کور	kor کور
m.pl.	haləK-ān هلکان	halək-ān-o هلکانو	kor-una کورونه	kor-uno کورونو
m.s.	saṛ-ey سړے	saṛ-i سړی		
m.pl.	saṛ-i سړی	saṛ-o سړو		

3. Adjectives are only in the oblique case (i.e. inflected) if they precede a noun in the oblique case. Compare the first sentence – which is NOT in the oblique case, because it follows the subject noun – with the second one which uses the oblique case.

də mo'ṭəruno mā'lık bu'ḍā dey.	The owner of the cars is old.	د موټرونو مالک بوډا دے.
də zaṛo moṭəruno mā'lık bu'ḍā dey.	The owner of the old cars is old.	د زړو موټرونو مالک بوډا دے.

Observe how the adjectives below are declined in the oblique case:

	Direct		Oblique		Direct		Oblique	
m.s.	spin	سپین	spin	سپین	'stəṛ-ey	ستړے	'stəṛ-i	ستړی
m.pl.	spin	سپین	'spin-o	سپینو	'stəṛ-i	ستړی	'stəṛ-o	ستړو
m.s.	zoṛ	زوړ	zā'ṛ-ə	زاړهٔ	sur	سُور	srə	سرهٔ
m.pl.	zā'ṛ-ə	زاړه	zā'ṛ-o	زړو	srə	سرهٔ	sro	سرو

4. The demonstrative pronouns are also inflected in the oblique case. The inflection occurs in both prepositional phrases and noun phrases in the possessive case. For example,

pa de ǰeb ke	in this pocket	په دې جېب کښې
pa ha'ɣo me'zuno 'bānde	on those tables	په هغو مېزونو باندې
də de sa'ṛi	of this man	د دې سړی
də 'daɣo sa'ṛo	of these men	د دغو سړو

Pronouns in the oblique case

Singular	Direct	Oblique	Plural	Direct	Oblique
this	dā دا	de دې	these	dā دا	de دې
this	'daɣa دغه	'daɣe دغې	these	'daɣa دغه	'daɣo دغو
that	'haɣa هغه	'haɣe هغې	those	'haɣa هغه	'haɣo هغو

Masculine nouns inflected in the oblique case

1. Masculine nouns ending in a consonant are not inflected in the oblique case:

də 'haɣa ha'lək ma'ṇa šta?	Does that boy have an apple?	د هغه هلک مڼه شته؟
də 'haɣa ha'lək ma'ṇa pa de tā'li ke da.	That boy's apple is in the dish.	د هغه هلک مڼه په دې تالی کښې ده.

ˈhaɣa mazˈdur dəlta kār kəy.	That worker works here.	هغه مزدُور دلته کار کوي.
də ˈhaɣa mazˈdur nek pa de dəfˈtər ke kār kawi.	That worker's boss works in this office.	د هغه مزدُور نېک په دې دفتر کښې کار کوي.
ɣaṭ baˈkəs mā saˈra dey.	The big case is with me.	غټ بکس ما سره دے.
də ɣaṭ baˈkəs čāˈbi pa de mez ˈbānde da.	The big case's key is on this table.	د غټ بکس چابی په دې مېز باندې ده.

2. Masculine singular nouns which end in a consonant add the plural suffix / -ān / ان- plus the vowel / -o / و- in the oblique case:

də haləˈkāno saˈra bāl šta?	Do the boys have a ball?	د هلکانو سره بال شته؟
də haləˈkāno bāl xaˈrāb dey.	The boys' ball is bad.	د هلکانو بال خراب دے.
də mariˈzāno ḍākˈṭər šta?	Do these patients have a doctor?	د مریضانو ډاکټر شته؟
də mariˈzāno ḍākˈṭər qāˈbɪl dey.	The patients' doctor is skilled.	د مریضانو ډاکټر قابِل دے.

3. The final / -a / ه- in the masculine plural suffix / -una / ونه- is declined in the oblique case to / -uno / ونو- :

zmung korˈuna ˈhalta di.	Our houses are there.	زمُونږ کورونه هلته دی.
mung pa de korˈuno ke ˈosu.	We are living in these houses.	مُونږ په دې کورونو کښې اوسو.

4. Masculine singular nouns and adjectives ending in / -ey / ے- are declined to / -i / ی- in the oblique case:

ˈdaɣa saˈṛey ɣerətˈmənd dey.	This man has *ghairat.*	دغه سړے غیرتمند دے.
də ˈdaɣe saˈṛi ɣeˈrət zyāt dey.	This man's *ghairat* is great.	د دغې سړی غیرت زیات دے.

5. Masculine plural nouns and adjectives ending in / -i / ی- are declined to / -o / و- in the oblique case:

ˈhaɣa saˈṛi də ṭoˈpəy di.	These men are from Topi.	هغه سړی د ټوپی دی.
də saˈṛo beˈguna pa moˈṭər ke di.	The men's bags are in the car.	د سړو بیگونه په موټر کښې دی.

haɣwi zə'mā də mal'gəro melmā'nə di.	They are my friends' guests.	هغوی زما د ملگرو مېلمانهٔ دی.
zmung pa mal'gəro ke yo amrika'ney həm šta.	Among our friends there is also an American.	زمونږ په ملگرو کښې يو امريکنے هم شته.

NOTE:
ghairat (غيرت *ɣe'rət*) is a central idea in Pukhtun culture. It has no direct English equivalent, but is close to the idea of jealous pride, zeal and honour.

Fun with animals

☝ Apart from sitting with your helper and this book, it is good to be out and about using new words and phrases. Photocopies of pictures are a great conversation starter, and will also allow you to control the talk in the area you are studying. Photocopy the following pages and find out about these animals from your friends.

Here are some useful phrases to memorise:

de zanā'war ta tsə 'waye?	What is this animal called?	دې ځناور ته څهٔ وائي؟
ḍero ta tsə 'waye?	What are many called?	ډېرو ته څهٔ وائي؟
xəze ta tsə 'waye?	What are females called?	ښځې ته څهٔ وائي؟
nar ta tsu 'waye?	What are males called?	نر ته څهٔ وائي؟
wa'ṛuke ta tsə 'waye?	What are the young called?	وړوکي ته څهٔ وائي؟
wa'ṛuke xəze (nar) ta tsə 'waye?	What are young females (males) called?	وړوکي ښځې (نر) ته څهٔ وائي؟
dā zanā'war 'tsənga ā'wāz kawi?	What noise does this animal make?	دا ځناور څنگه آواز کوی؟

Intransitive verbs

As mentioned in Lesson Seven, there are two kinds of verbs in Pukhto: transitive and intransitive. (Transitive verbs are 'doing' verbs, for example 'to eat'.)

Intransitive verbs are verbs that do not act on anyone or anything. For example, to understand, to sleep, to be born, to start out, to wait, to smile, to arrive, to leave, to leak, etc.

The distinction between transitive and intransitive verbs is very important in Pukhto.

The intransitive verb *tləl* 'to go' and the postposition *ta* 'to' تلل، ته

Subject	Adverb	Noun	Post-position	Verb	
tə	os	kor	ta	ze?	تهٔ اوس کور ته ځې؟ Are you going home now?
na,	os	xār	ta	zəm.	نه، اوس ښار ته ځم. No, I'm going to the city.
stā wror	tsə waxt	čārsa'de	ta	zi?	ستا ورور څهٔ وخت چارسدې ته ځی؟ When is your brother going to Charsadda?
zə'mā wror	nən	čārsa'de	ta	zi.	زما ورور نن چارسدې ته ځی. My brother is going to Charsadda today.
tə	nən špa	sɪne'mā	ta	ze?	تهٔ نن شپه سنيما ته ځې؟ Are you going to the cinema tonight?
na,	nən špa	ba'zār	ta	zəm	نه، نن شپه بازار ته ځم. No, I'm going to the market tonight.

Subject	Adverb	Noun	Post-position	Verb	
ˈtāso	saˈbā	ˈčerta		zəy?	تاسو صبا چرته ځئ؟ Where are you going tomorrow?
	saˈbā	skul	ta	zu.	صبا سکُول ته ځُو. We are going to school tomorrow.
haləˈkān	tsə waxt	ˈkəli	ta	zi?	هلکان څۀ وخت کلي ته ځي؟ When are the boys going to the village?
	saˈbā də špe ba	ˈhalta		zi.	صبا د شپې به هلته ځي. They are going there tomorrow night.

Two forms of intransitive verbs

Many intransitive verbs have two infinitives. For example, 'to understand': *poˈhe šwəl* (پوئ شول) and *poheˈdəl* (پوهېدل). The verb *pohe šwəl* (پوئ شول) is from the root *šwəl* (شول) and is 'weaker' than *poheˈdəl* (پوهېدل) which is from the root *kedəl* (کېدل).

Many other verbs appear in two forms like this. Some examples are:

	'Strong' form		'Weak' form	
to be(come) ready	tayāreˈdəl	تيارېدل	taˈyār šwəl	تيار شول
to get down	kuzeˈdəl	کُوزېدل	ˈkuz šwəl	کُوز شول
to go to sleep	uˈdə keˈdəl	اُودۀ کېدل	uˈdə šwəl	اُودۀ شول
to be broken	māteˈdəl	ماتېدل	māt šwəl	مات شول
to be known	māˈlumeˈdəl	معلومېدل	māˈlum šwəl	معلُوم شول
to be born	peˈdā keˈdəl	پيدا کېدل	peˈdā šwəl	پيدا شول
to start out	raˈwāneˈdəl	روانېدل	raˈwān šwəl	روان شول
to be(come) lit	baleˈdəl	بلېدل	bal šwəl	بل شول

NOTES:

1. The distinction between the two forms is particularly important in past tenses.
2. Different forms of the same verb are also used in the present, future and imperative tenses. The 'strong' form is used for events that will definitely happen.

3. The verb 'to go' is an irregular intransitive verb, and has two different roots: *tləl* (تلل) and *'lāṛəl* (لاړل). Of these, *tləl* (تلل) is stronger and is changed to *zəm* (ځم), *zi* (ځی), *ze* (ځي) in the present and future tenses. *'lāṛəl* (لاړل) is weaker and implies some doubt that action will take place.

4. Notice that nouns preceding postpositions, for example *ta* (ته) are in the oblique case. *'kəley* (کلے) is inflected to *'kəli ta* (کلی ته), etc.

The intransitive verb *rāt'ləl* 'to come' راتلل

dā 'hara wrəz de ba'zār ta rā-'zi?	Does she come to this market every day?	دا هره ورځ دي بازار ته راځی؟
na, 'hara wrəz 'dəlta nə-rā'zi.	No, she doesn't come here every day.	نه، هره ورځ دلته نهٔ راځی.
'tāso 'hara špa de ǰu'māt ta rā-'zəy?	Do you come to this mosque every night?	تاسو هره شپه دي جُماعت ته راځئ؟
āw, 'hara špa 'dəlta rā-'zu.	Yes, we come here every night.	آو، هره شپه دلته را ځُو.
stā lur tsə waxt kor ta rā-'zi?	When does your daughter come home?	ستا لُور څهٔ وخت کور ته راځی؟
ha'ɣa har sa'har kor ta rā-'zi.	She comes home every morning.	هغه هر سحر کور ته راځی.
ha'ɣa har kāl de 'kəli ta rā-'zi?	Does she come to this village every year?	هغه هر کال دي کلی ته راځی؟
na, 'hara myāšt 'dəlta rā-'zi.	No, she comes here every month.	نه، هره میاشت دلته راځی.
dā ǰɪ'nəy har mā'xām de haspa'tāl ta rā-'zi?	Does this girl come to this hospital every evening?	دا جینۍ هر ماښام دي هسپتال ته راځی؟

NOTES:

1. The prefix / *rā-* / -را indicates movement towards the speaker and transforms the verb *tləl* (تلل) 'to go' to *rāt'ləl* (راتلل) 'to come'.
2. The adjective 'every' may be masculine (*har* هر) or feminine (*'hara* هره) depending on the gender of the time word it is modifying.
3. Both *wrəz* (ورځ) and *myāšt* (میاشت) are feminine, and are exceptions to the gender rules for nouns ending in consonants.

4. *da* (ده) is inflected to *de* (دې) if it precedes the postposition *ta* (ته) as in *de ba'zār ta* (دې بازار ته).
5. It may also be modified by the prefix / *dar-* / -در which indicates a movement towards you; and the prefix / *war-* / -ور which indicates movement towards a third person or place. For example,
   rātləm (راتلم) – coming to me
   dartləm (درتلم) – coming to you
   wartləm (ورتلم) – going to them

Cover up the script and phonetics and see if you can say these sentences.

'halta lāṛ ša!	Go over there!	هلته لاړ شه!
dar-'zəm.	I am coming to you.	درځم.
de xār ta war-'zi	He is going to the city.	دے ښار ته ورځی.
'rā-ša!	Come here!	راشه!
dar-'zi.	He is coming to you.	درځی.

The preposition – postposition *də____ də'pāra* 'for' د ___ د پاره

dey də čā də'pāra kār kəy?	Who does he work for?	دے د چا د پاره کار کوی؟
dey mā də'pāra kār kəy.	He works for me.	دے ما د پاره کار کوی.
dā də tsə də'pāra zyā'rət ta zi?	What is she going to the shrine for?	دا د څۀ د پاره زيارت ته ځی؟
dā də do'ə də'pāra 'halta zi.	She is going there for prayer.	دا د دعا د پاره هلته ځی.
ǰa'mal xān də tsə də'pāra du'kān ta zi?	What is Jamal Khan going to the shop for?	جمال خان د څۀ د پاره دُوکان ته ځی؟
ha'ya də dəwa'i də'pāra 'halta zi.	He is going there for medicine.	هغه د دوائی د پاره هلته ځی.
tə də tsə də'pāra rā'ze?	What are you coming here for?	تۀ د څۀ د پاره راځې؟
zə də sa'bəq də'pāra 'dəlta rā'zum.	I'm coming here for a lesson.	زۀ د سبق د پاره دلته راځم.

NOTES:

1. *də* (د) is often dropped in daily conversation or altered to *la* (له). So the last sentence becomes *sa'bəq la rā'zum* (سبق له راځم) in everyday talk.

Nouns preceding *də'pāra* (د پاره) are in the oblique case. For example in the second sentence above: *dey mā də'pāra kār kəy* (دے ما د پاره کار کوی).

Comprehension drill: Learning to obey commands

Listen to the commands and do the action!

ˈo-drega!	Stand up!	ودرېږه!
ˈwāxla!	Take it!	واخله!
ˈkena!	Sit down	کښېنه!
ˈkeda!	Put down!	کېده!
ˈrāša!	Come here!	راشه!
ˈo-ska!	Drink!	وڅکه!
ˈlāṛ-ša!	Go!	لاړ شه!
ˈo-xora!	Eat!	وخوره!
xi taˈraf-ta ˈlāṛ-ša!	Go to the right!	ښی طرف ته لاړ شه!
gəs taˈraf-ta ˈlāṛ-ša!	Go to the left!	ګڅ طرف ته لاړ شه!
ˈšāta rāˈogarza!	Turn around!	شاته راؤګرځه!
ˈšāta za!	Go back!	شاته ځه!
ˈmaxke ˈrāša!	Come forward!	مخکښې راشه!

NOTE:
Studies have shown that new words introduced during a drill are more likely to be remembered if you really follow the commands with enthusiasm. Resist the temptation to simply repeat the commands. Do the actions as fast as possible. Have fun and make a game of it.

Memorising moment

mataˈluna

اول وخوره دَ ځان غوښے بیا وخوره دَ ښکار غوښے.

āˈwal ˈoxora də zān ˈɣwaxey byā ˈoxora də xkār ˈɣwaxey.
First eat the meat of yourself then eat the meat of the hunt.

دې ته به دَ چا پلار ټينګ شي!

de ta ba də čā plār ṭing ši!

Whose father can resist it!

هر څۀ ځي خو عادت نۀ ځي.

har tsə zi xo aˈdət nə zi.

Everything leaves but not a habit.

Rahman Baba[7]

په ظاهر لباس غلط د سړی مۀ شه

مينځ يې ګوره له چغزي او له مټاکه.

pa zaˈhɪr lɪˈbās ɣaˈlat də saˈṛi mə ša

menz ye ˈgora la čəɣˈze āw la məˈṭāka.

Do not be fooled by the outer appearance of a man,

Look in the centre to see whether he is soft or hard.

Exercises for Lesson Eight

1. Make sentences in the possessive case from the following pairs of words. For example:

dā də tālɪˈbɪləm almāˈrəy da. This is the student's bookcase. دا د طالبعلم الماریٔ ده.

a. mariˈzān kamˈra ________ مريضان کمره

b. trə duˈkān ________ ترۀ دُوکان

c. mašuˈmān bāl ________ ماشُومان بال

d. plāˈrān mašuˈmān ________ پلاران ماشُومان

e. ˈwruṇa ˈxwende ________ ورُونړه خوېندې

[7] The most popular Pukhtun poet, Rahman Baba, lived near Peshawar during the Mughal era. Couplets of his Sufi and wisdom poetry still find proverbial use in Khyber Pukhtunkhwa. When learning his poetry work on trying to get the rhythm and rhyme of the couplets.

f. ḍākta'rān dəf'tər ڈاکټران دفتر

g. spey xā'wənd سپے خاوند

2. Answer the following question by using a statement plus the time words listed below:

stā wror tsə waxt mıngo're ta zi?	When is your brother going to Mingora?	ستا ورور څۀ وخت مینګورې ته ځی؟

a.	nən	نن
b.	sa'bā	صبا
c.	mā'xām	ماښام
d.	sa'har	سحر
e.	sa'bā špa	صبا شپه
f.	nən sa'har	نن سحر
g.	sa'bā sa'har	صبا سحر
h.	māspa'xin	ماسپښین

Vocabulary for Lesson Eight

āˈsān	آسان	m.	adj.	easy
āˈsāna / āˈsāne	آسانه / آساني	f.		
āˈwāz	آواز	m.	n.	sound; voice, noise
ıtaˈrāz	اعتراض	m.	n.	objection, protest
afˈsər	افسر	m.	n.	boss, officer
akˈsər	اکثر	m.	adj.	usually, often
amrikaˈney	امریکنے		adj.	American
bāl	بال	m.s.	n.	ball
baˈǰa	بجه	f.	n.	o'clock, hour
baleˈdəl	بلیدل		v.i.	to be alight, to burn,
be ˈxwanda	بي خونده	f.	adj.	joyless, tasteless
beg / beˈguna	بیګ / بیګونه	m.	n.	bag
biˈmār	بیمار	m.	adj.	sick
biˈmāra / biˈmāre	بیماره / بیماري	f.		
pāk	پاک	m.	adj.	pure, holy, clean
ˈpāka / ˈpāke	پاکه / پاکي	f.		
peˈdā keˈdəl	پیدا کېدل		comp. v.i.	to be born; to be found; to sprout
tāˈli	تالی	f.s.	n.	dish
taraˈqi kaˈwəl	ترقی کول		comp. v.t.	to progress, to advance
tez	تېز	m.	adj.	fast, strong, quick
ˈteza / ˈteze	تېزه / تېزي	f.		
ṭaym	ټیم	m.s.	n.	time
tayāreˈdəl	تیارېدل		v.i.	to be(come) prepared, to be(come) ready, to be made
ǰi	جی		n.	sir
zanāˈwar	ځناور	m.	n.	animal

čā'bi	چابی	*f.s.*	*n.*	key
xpəl	خپل	*m.*	*adj.* *n.*	own; relative
xarāba'wəl	خرابول		*v.*	to destroy, to ruin, to wreck, to spoil; to disturb
də'pāra	د پاره		*post.*	for
do'ə [də'wa *or* du'a]	دعا	*f.s.*	*n.*	prayer, benediction
dəwa'i	دوائی	*f.pl.*	*n.*	medicine, drug
dyā'ṛi	دیاړی	*f.s*	*n.*	daily wage
ra'him	رحیم	*m.*	*adj.*	merciful
ra'wāne'dəl	روانېدل		*comp. v.i.*	to start out, to start moving; to go, to flow
rɪš'tya	ریشتیا	*f.s.*	*n.*	real, true
zyāt	زیات	*m.*	*adv.*	much, more, many, most, great, excess
zyā'rət	زیارت	*m.*	*n.*	shrine
'stəṛe ke'dəl	ستړی کېدل		*comp. v.i.*	to become tired
sa'har	سحر	*m.*	*n.*	morning
sɪne'mā	سنیما	*f.*	*n.*	cinema
'šāta	شاته		*prep.*	back, backwards, to the rear
sa'bā	صبا		*adv.*	tomorrow
ɣe'rət	غیرت	*m.*	*n.*	zeal, honour, pride
klərk	کلرک	*m.*	*n.*	clerk
kuze'dəl	کُوزېدل		*v.i.*	to get down, to get off
ko'šiš ka'wəl	کوشش کول		*comp. v.t.*	to try, to attempt
gəp'šəp	گپ شپ	*m.*	*n.*	chit chat
guza'ra ke'dəl	گُزاره کېدل		*comp. v.i.*	to make do, to get by, to be barely adequate
la'rəl	لرل		*v.i.*	to have, to possess

māte'dəl	ماتېدل		v.i.	to be broken, to break (itself); to be defeated
māspa'xin	ماسپښين	m.s.	n.	afternoon; afternoon prayers
mā'xām	ماښام	m.s.	n.	evening, late afternoon
mā'mā	ماما	m.	n.	uncle (maternal)
mā'lık	مالِک	m.	n.	owner, landlord; Lord
'maxke	مخکښې		prep.	forward, in front of
mər'zi	مرضی	f.s.	n.	wish, desire, choice
ma'riz / mari'zān	مریض / مریضان	m.	n.	patient (ill)
mar'iza / mari'zāne	مریضه / مریضانې	f.		
məša'hur	مشهُور	m.	adj.	famous, renowned, well-known
mālume'dəl	معلومېدل		v.i	to be known, to find out, to become aware of
myāšt	میاشت	f.s.	n.	month
nar	نر	m.	adj.	male, masculine
nən	نن	f.s.	adv.	today
nən špa	نن شپه	f.s.	adv.	tonight
nek	نېک	m.	n.	boss
waxt	وخت	m.	n.	time, season
wa'ṛukey	وړُوکے	m.s.	n., adj	(the) young, small
uz'gār	وزګار	m.	adj.	free, at leisure, unoccupied
uz'gāra / uz'gāre	وزګاره / وزګارې	f.		
har	هر	m.	adj.	every, each, any
'hara / 'hare	هره / هرې	f.		
'hara wrəz	هره ورځ		adj.	daily, every day
haspa'tāl	هسپتال	m.	n.	hospital
həm	هم		adv.	also, too

nəˈhəm saˈbəq نهم سبق

Lesson Nine

Dialogue nine: Multiplying language learning

L. dā tsə di? What is this?	دا څۀ دی؟
H. dā lānˈgrəy da. It is a mortar.	دا لنګرئ ده.
L. dā də tsə dəˈpāra paˈkār rāˈzi? What is it needed for?	دا د څۀ د پاره پکار راځی؟
H. dā də lāˈči mātaˈwəlo āw də čəṭˈnəy ǰoṛaˈwəlo dəˈpāra paˈkār rāˈzi. This is needed for crushing cardamom and making chutney.	دا د لاچی ماتولو او د چټنۍ جوړولو د پاره پکار راځی.
L. dā də kəm zay ˈǰoṛa da? Where is it made?	دا د کُوم ځائ جوړه ده؟
H. dā də lāˈhor ˈǰoṛa da. It's made in Lahore.	دا د لاهور جوړه ده.
L. dā də tsə na ˈǰoṛa da? What is it made of?	دا د څۀ نه جوړه ده؟
H. dā də gaˈṭe na ˈǰoṛa da. It's made of stone.	دا د ګټې نه جوړه ده.
L. čəṭˈni tsə šey dey? What is chutney?	چټنی څۀ شے دے؟
H. čəṭˈni də xwaˈrāk siz dey, āw ˈxalak ye də hazˈme dəˈpāra xoˈri. Chutney is a kind of food and people eat it for digestion. ˈḍera trasˈkona wi. It's very tasty.	چټنی د خوراک څیز دے، او خلق يې د هضمې د پاره خوری. ډېره ترسکُونه وی.

L.	pa de čəṭ'ni 'tsənga ǰo'ṛigi? How is chutney made (*lit.* 'made by it')?	په دي چټنی څنګه جوړیږی؟

NOTE:

☝ Memorise a few of these learners' questions and take a small recorder to your friend's house. Record a few replies. When you get home transcribe the answers in phonetics and then get your helper to explain the answers to you. Try to do this weekly with new topics.

You might get a reply like this from the last question in the Dialogue above:

ā'wal ba marča'key rā'wāxle.	First you will bring some peppers.	اول به مرچکے راواخلي.
āw pa de ke ba ye 'kegde.	And you will put them in it.	او په دي کښي به يي کيږدي.
byā ba ye pa ča'ṭu ke 'oṭəke.	Then you will hit them with a pestle.	بيا به يي په چټو کښي وټکي.
byā ba pa ke ṭamā'ṭər 'wāčawe.	Then you will put tomatoes in it.	بيا به په کښي ټماټر واچوي.
āw ha'ɣa həm kəṭ kṛa.	And grind them also.	او هغه هم کټ کړه.
ləg sāt pas ba čəṭ'ni ta'yāra wi.	A little time later chutney will be ready.	لږ ساعت پس به چټنی تياره وی.

L.	dā kār tsok ka'wi? Who does this work?	دا کار څوک کوی؟
H.	dā də zanā'no kār dey. It is ladies' work.	دا د زنانوو کار دے.

Here are two useful phrases to prompt people to say things for the recorder:

byā 'owaya!	Say it again!	بيا ووايه!
dā ǰa'wāb ba pa ṭep 'owaye?	Will you put that reply on tape?	دا جواب به په ټيپ ووائي؟

NOTE:

The word *ṭep* (ټيپ) is used of all forms of recording devices from audio cassettes to digital devices like MP3s.

Pronunciation drill

Focus on / ɣ / غ :

In this drill pay special attention to the / ɣ / غ sound.

də 'haɣa ɣaṭ ha'lək 'ɣaṭa 'ɣwaxa 'xwaxa da.	That fat boy likes beef.	د هغه غټ هلک غټه غوښه خوښه ده.

☝ Ask your helper to correct your pronunciation. Keep drilling until you have the same rhythm and pronunciation.

Try this tongue twister:

چې غل غلا کوله نو غلې نوکرې په غُسلخانه کښې غوښې او غلې خوړې.

če ɣəl ɣlā ka'wəla no ɣle no'kəre pa ɣosalxā'na ke 'ɣwaxe āw ɣa'le xwa'ṛe.

When the thief was stealing, the silent servant was eating meat and food in the bathroom.

The preposition *də* 'of' with feminine nouns and adjectives

Possessive noun	Subject	Adjective	Verb	
də ǰɪ'nəy	mor	'xkwəle	da.	د جینۍ مور ښکُلې ده. The girl's mother is beautiful.
də spog'məy	ra'ṇā	'teza	da.	د سپوږمۍ رڼا تېزه ده. The light of the moon is bright.
də 'wəne	'pāṇe	šne	di.	د ونې پاڼې شنې دي. The leaves of the tree are green.
də pəxtā'no	ha'yā	məša'hura	da.	د پښتنو حیا مشهُوره ده. The *haya* of Pukhtuns is famous.

NOTE:
haya (حیا *ha'yā*), like *ghairat*, has no exact English equivalent; and also, like *ghairat*, it has great cultural significance. *haya* includes the idea of modesty, respectful behaviour and the seclusion of women from public view.

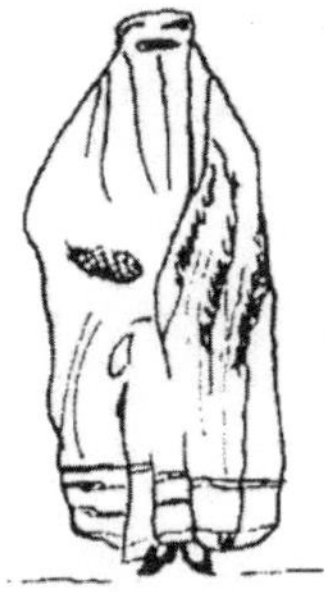

Feminine nouns and adjectives in the oblique case

1. Feminine singular nouns and adjectives ending in / -a / ـه- are inflected to / -e / ې - in the oblique case, while their plural forms are inflected from / -e / ې - to / -o / و - ; nouns and adjectives ending in / -əy / ۍ - are inflected to / -o / و - in the plural form only. See the following examples:

Nouns

	Direct		Oblique		Direct		Oblique	
f.s.	spəy	سپۍ	spəy	سپۍ	'xəza	ښځه	'xəze	ښځې
f.pl.	spəy	سپۍ	spəyo	سپيو	'xəze	ښځې	'xəzo	ښځو

Adjectives

	Direct		Oblique		Direct		Oblique	
f.s.	spina	سپينه	'spine	سپيني	'stəṛe	ستړي	'stəṛe	ستړي
f.pl.	'spine	سپيني	'spino	سپينو	'stəṛe	ستړي	'stəṛ-o	ستړو
f.s.	na'rəy	نرۍ	na'rəy	نرۍ				
f.pl.	na'rəy	نرۍ	na'ro	نرو				

dā za'ṛa 'wəna da.	This is an old tree.	دا زړه ونه ده.
də za'ṛe 'wəne me'wa xwa'ga da.	The old tree's fruit is sweet.	د زړې ونې مېوه خوږه ده.
'haɣa 'məšre 'xəze haspa'tāl ta zi.	Those old ladies are going to the hospital.	هغه مشرې ښځې هسپتال ته ځي.
haɣ'wi ha'ɣo 'məšro 'xəzo sa'ra 'xār ta zi.	They are going to the city with those old ladies.	هغوی هغو مشرو ښځو سره ښار ته ځي.
'haɣa zmung 'spina 'čərga da.	That is our white hen.	هغه زمونږ سپينه چرګه ده.
'haɣa zmung də 'spine 'čərge a'gəy da.	That is our white hen's egg.	هغه زمونږ د سپينې چرګې اګۍ ده.
də xandā'ne tsa'lor 'čərge di.	Khandana has four hens.	د خندانې څلور چرګې دي.
də tsa'loro 'čərgo a'gəy 'ɣaṭe di.	The eggs of the four hens are large.	د څلورو چرګو اګۍ غټې دي.

2. Feminine singular nouns and adjectives ending in the suffix / -e / ې- are not inflected in the oblique case, while their plural is inflected to / -o / و -.

zə'mā mal'gəre 'wəge da.	My (female) friend is hungry.	زما ملګرې وږې ده.
dā mo'ṭər zə'mā də mal'gəro dey.	This car belongs to my friends.	دا موټر زما د ملګرو دے.
də de tālıbıl'māne 'stəṛe di.	Her (female) students are tired.	د دې طالبعلمانې ستړې دي.
də 'stəṛo tālıbıl'māno us'tāza həm 'stəṛe da.	The tired students' teacher is also tired.	د ستړو طالبعلمانو اُستاذه هم ستړې ده.

NOTE:

In the oblique case, numbers two through to ten change with the addition of the suffix / -o / (و-); and *yo* (یو) changes to *'yəwe* (یوې). For example:

də 'yəwe 'xəze	one woman's	د یوې ښځې
də 'dreo 'čərgo	three hens'	د درېو چرګو
də 'ləso ustā'zāno	ten teachers'	د لسو اُستاذانو

The transitive verbs *xo'ṛəl* 'to eat' and *skəl* 'to drink' خوړل، څښل

1. *xo'ṛəl* – to eat, to consume

tə sa'hār 'ḍera ḍo'ḍəy xo're?	Do you eat a lot of food in the morning?	ته سحر ډېره ډوډۍ خورې؟
na, sa'hār bas 'yəwa parā'ṭa xo'rəm.	No, in the morning I eat just a single *paratha*.	نه، سحر بس یوه پراټه خورم.
'stāso mal'gəri 'ɣwaxa xo'ri?	Do your friends eat meat?	ستاسو ملګري غوښه خوري؟
na, hay'wi 'ɣwaxa 'nə-xori.	No, they don't eat meat.	نه، هغوی غوښه نه خوري.
də špe tsə waxt ḍo'ḍəy xo'rəy?	When do you eat food at night?	د شپې څه وخت ډوډۍ خورئ؟
mung ā'tə ba'ǰe ḍo'ḍəy xo'ru.	We eat food at eight o'clock.	مونږ اته بجې ډوډۍ خورُو.
ha'ɣa 'wriǰe 'hits-kəla 'nə-xori?	Does she never eat rice?	هغه وريژې هيڅ کله نه خوري؟
na, ha'ɣa 'sıraf alu'gān xo'ri.	No, she only eats potatoes.	نه، هغه صرف آلُوګان خوري.

2. *skəl* – to drink, to smoke

tə də špe čay ske?	Do you drink tea at night?	ته د شپې چائې څښې؟
āw, də špe ka'wa skəm.	Yes, I drink green tea at night.	آو، د شپې قهوه څښم.
'tāso mā sa'ra čay skəy?	Will you drink tea with me?	تاسو ما سره چائې څښئ؟
merabā'ni, 'sıraf u'bə skəm.	Thanks, I just drink water.	مِهرباني، صرف اوبهٔ څکم.
'tāso ba tsə skəy, 'tore čay kə ka'wa?	What will you drink, black tea or green tea?	تاسو به څهٔ څښئ تورې چائې کهٔ قهوه؟

xer, ˈtore čay ba ˈsku.	Fine, I'll drink black tea.	خیر، تورې چائې به څښُو.
dey pa ˈyəwa wrəz ke ˈtsumra sɪgˈreṭe ski?	How many cigarettes does he smoke a day?	دے په یوه ورځ کښې څومره سګرټې څښی؟

NOTE:

kawa is green tea. It is a favourite in Khyber Pukhtunkhwa.

Ask your language helper to show you the art of preparing *kawa* and have some together.

The preposition *də* ____ *na* 'from' د ____ نه

stā plār də kəm zay na pa ṭeleˈfun xaˈbare kaˈwi?	Where is your father calling from on the phone?	ستا پلار د کُوم ځائ نه په ټیلیفون خبرې کوی؟
haˈɣa də ṭānk na xaˈbare kəy.	He is calling from Tank.	هغه د ټانک نه خبرې کوی.
stā zwe tsə waxt də skul na kor ta rāˈzi?	What time does your son come home from school?	ستا زوئ څهٔ وخت د سکُول نه کور ته راځی؟
haˈɣa dā waxt də skul na rāˈzi.	He comes from school at this time.	هغه دا وخت د سکُول نه راځی.
stā malˈgərey də ˈkəm məlk na ˈdəlta rāˈzi?	Which country does your friend come here from?	ستا ملګرے د کُوم ملک نه دلته راځی؟
haˈɣa də ɪnglɪˈstān na rāˈzi.	He comes from England.	هغه د اِنګلستان نه راځی.

The interrogatives *kəm* 'which' and *kəm yo* 'which one' کُوم، کُوم یو

kəm saˈṛey ḍer kār kaˈwi?	Which man works a lot?	کُوم سړے ډېر کار کوی؟
kəm haˈlək wrāˈney kaˈwi?	Which boy is naughty?	کُوم هلک ورانے کوی؟
ˈkəma ˈxəza ḍākˈṭəra da?	Which woman is a doctor?	کُومه ښځه ډاکټره ده؟
ˈkəma ǰɪˈnəy xə paxˈley kaˈwi?	Which of the girls cooks well?	کُومه جینئ ښهٔ پخلے کوی؟
kəm yo ḍer wrān dey?	Which one is really naughty?	کُوم یو ډېر وران دے؟
ˈkəma ˈyəwa ǰoˈṛa ˈɣwāṛe?	Which pair do you want?	کُومه یوه جوړه غواړې؟

Comprehension drill: More commands to obey

☝ Try to obey the following commands as fast as possible. Have your helper mix up the order.

ˈkuz- ša!	Get down!	کُوز شه!
ˈo-xeǰa!	Climb in!	وخېژه!
dəˈnəna ˈlāṛša!	Go in!	دننه لاړ شه!
ˈhalta ˈo-drega!	Stop there!	هلته ودرېږه!
ˈsəmla!	Lie down!	څمله!
ˈpāsa!	Stand up!	پاڅه!
ˈlāṛša!	Go away!	لاړشه!

Now add these to the commands found in Lesson Eight: Learning to obey commands, and practice them in the same way.

Memorising moment

mataˈluna

چرګه زما یې او اګۍ دَ بل کره اچوې.

ˈčerga zəˈmā ye āw aˈgəy də bəl ˈkara āčaˈwi.

You are my hen and lay eggs in someone else's house.

ته پردو غمونو وخوړې.

tə praˈdo ɣəmˈuno ˈoxoṛe.

Someone else's sorrows consumed you.

د رحمان وېنا به هله در په یاد شي،

چې دې یو دېوال ته مخ بل ته دې شا شي.

də rahˈmān weˈnā ba ala dar pa yād ši,

če de yo diˈwāl ta məx bəl ta de šā ši.

You will remember Rahman's advice,

When one wall is in front of you and one behind.

Exercises for Lesson Nine

1. Make sentences in the possessive case from the following pairs of words.

   a. ˈǰɪˈnəy, kiˈtāb ________________ جینۍ، کتاب

   b. māˈšuma, mor ________________ ماشُومه، مور

   c. haˈlək, tsaˈpləy ________________ هلک، څپلۍ

   d. ḍākˈṭəra, lur ________________ ډاکټره، لُور

   e. saˈṛi, kār ________________ سړی، کار

   f. ˈwəna, ˈpāṇe ________________ ونه، پاڼې

   g. ˈxwende, wror ________________ خوېندې، ورور

2. Fill in the blanks in the following sentences with the present tense form of the infinitive listed at the end of the sentence.

   a. mung də de saˈra xār ta ________________. — tləl

   مُونږ د دې سره ښار ته ________________. — تلل

   b. zə špəg ˈbaǰe ḍoˈḍəy ________________. — xoˈṛəl

   زهٔ شپږ بجې ډوډۍ ________________. — خوړل

   c. dā ˈhits čay nə ________________ yaˈwāze uˈbə. — skəl

   دا هیڅ چائې نهٔ ________________ یواځې اوبهٔ. — څښل

   d. dey ˈhara wrəz pa ṭeleˈfun xaˈbare ________________. — kaˈwəl

   دے هره ورځ په ټیلیفون خبرې ________________. — کول

   e. ˈtāso tsə waxt zmung kor ta ________________. — rātˈləl

   تاسو څهٔ وخت زمُونږ کور ته ________________. — راتلل

   f. zəˈmā malˈgərey məṛ ________________. — keˈdəl

   زما ملګرے مړ ________________. — کېدل

   g. zmung māšuˈmān os uˈdə ________________. — keˈdəl

   زمُونږ ماشُومان اوس اُودهٔ ________________. — کېدل

3. Say the following sentences and alter the numbers and pronouns:

   I am the brother of seven sisters. — زهٔ د اوؤ خوېندو ورور یم.

I am the father of twelve children.	زۀ د دولسو بچو پلار یم.
I am the husband of four wives.	زۀ د څلورو ښځو خاوند یم.

Finding out more about things and activities

☝ You can multiply language learning easily using pictures. The following pages can be photocopied and taken with you. Each picture can be a trigger for conversation. Record some of the responses and analyse them later with your helper. You can also use the illustrations in *Picture It in Dari and Pashto* to generate more conversations with your helper.

1. Some useful phrases to find out about things are:

de ta pəx'to ke tsə 'waye?	What is this called in Pukhto?	دې ته پښتو کښې څۀ وائي؟
dā __ də 'tsə pa'kār rā'zi?	What is ___ used for?	دا ___ د څۀ پکار راځي؟
tə pa 'xpəla ___ ɪstemāla'wəley še?	Do you know how to use a ___?	تۀ په خپله ___ استعمالولے شې؟
dā ___ grān dey? / 'grāna da?	Is ___ expensive?	دا ___ ګران دے / ګرانه ده؟
___ tsok ɪstemāla'wi?	Who uses a ___?	___ څوک استعمالوي؟

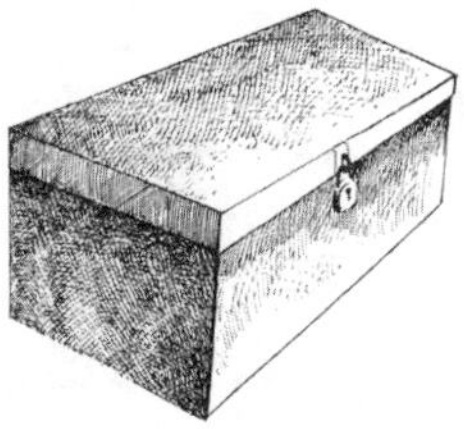

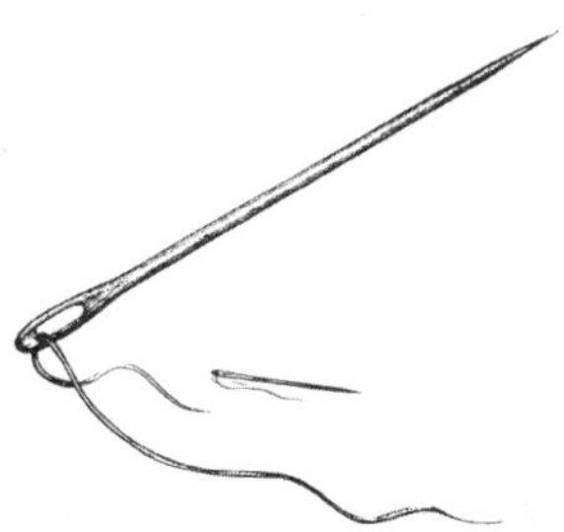

____

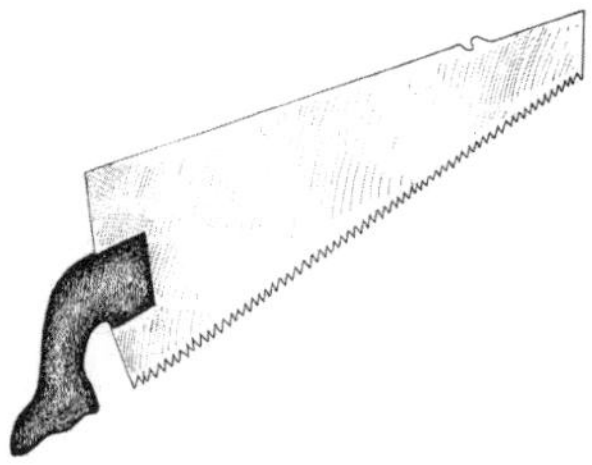

____

____

____

2. Some useful phrases to explore activities:

haˈɣa tsə kaˈwi?	What is he doing?	هغه څۀ کوی؟
tə dā kār ˈtsənga kawe?	How do you do this work?	تۀ دا کار څنګه کوې؟
mā ta dā kār kaˈwəl ˈoxāya.	Show me how to do this work.	ما ته دا کار کول وښايه.
de kār ta tsə ˈwaye?	What is this job called?	دې کار ته څۀ وائې؟

NOTE:
It is best to keep on using the name of a new thing in your questions. The more you use it, the more it 'sticks' in your memory.

Vocabulary for Lesson Nine

āča'wəl	اچول		v.t.	to put in, to add; to put on clothes; to lay (eggs)
ɪstemāla'wəl	استعمالول		comp. v.t.	to use
a'gəy	اگۍ	f.s.	n.	egg
ɪnglɪ'stān	انګلستان	m.s.	n.	England
pāsa'wəl	پاڅول		v.t.	to waken, to raise, to cause to rise, to get up
'pāṇa	پاڼه	f.s.	n.	leaf; sheet of paper, page
pax'ley ka'wəl	پخلے کول		comp. v.t.	to cook
parā'ṭa	پراټه	f.s.	n.	*paratha*
pas	پس		prep.	after, later
tras'kona	ترسکُونه	f.	adj.	tasty
ṭamā'ṭər	ټماټر	m.	n.	tomato
ṭep	ټيپ	m.s.	n.	tape, digital recorder
ṭele'fun	ټيليفون	m.	n.	telephone
ǰa'wāb	جواب	m.s.	n.	answer, reply
ǰoṛa'wəl	جوړول		comp. v.t.	to make, to build, to repair, to fix, to mend, to recover
ǰo'ṛa	جوړه	f.s.	n.	pair
čəṭ'ni	چټني	f.	n.	chutney
čaṭo 'kāṇey	چټو کاڼے	m.	n.	pestle
skəl	څښل		v.t.	to drink; to smoke
tsəmlā'stəl [səmlā'stəl]	څملاستل [سملاستل]		v.i.	to sleep, to lie (down)
siz	څيز	m.s.	n.	thing, object, matter, substance
ha'yā	حيا	f.s.	n.	modesty, respectful behaviour
'xalak	خلق	m.s.	n.	people
xwa'rāk [xorak]	خوراک	m.	n.	food

xwarak ka'wəl	خوراک کول		*comp. v.t.*	to eat
rāw'ṛəl	راوړل		*v.t.*	to bring (inanimate objects)
ra'ṇā	رڼا	*f.s.*	*n.*	light
sāt	ساعت	*m.s.*	*n.*	watch; hour
spog'məy	سپوږمۍ	*f.s.*	*n.*	moon
sıg'reṭe	سګرټې	*f.pl.*	*n.*	cigarettes
xo'dəl	ښودل		*v.t.*	to show, to teach
'sıraf	صرف		*adv, adj.*	only
ka'wa	قهوه	*f.*	*n.*	green tea
kəṭ ka'wəl	کټ کول		*v.t.*	to cut, to slice, to chop
ga'ṭa	ګټه	*f.s.*	*n.*	rock, stone
lā'či	لاچي	*f.*	*n.*	cardamom
lān'grəy	لنګرۍ	*f.*	*n.*	mortar
māta'wəl	ماتول		*comp. v.t.*	to break, to crush
marča'key	مرچکے	*m.s.*	*n.*	chilli pepper
məlk / məl'kuna	ملک / ملکُونه	*m.*	*n.*	country
me'wa	مېوه	*f.s.*	*n.*	fruit
wrā'ney ka'wəl	ورانے کول		*comp. v.t.*	to ruin, to spoil; to disobey
'hazm	هضم	*m.s.*	*n.*	digestion
'hits-kəla	هیڅ کله		*adv.*	never

lə'səm sa'bəq لسم سبق

Lesson Ten

Dialogue ten: Talking about religion

H: tə musal'mān 'šɪβey ye? Have you become a Muslim?	تهٔ مُسلمان شوے يې؟
L: zə yo xā'lɪq mā'lɪk rā'zɪq xo'dey ma'nəm. I believe in one creator, Lord, sustainer God. yo xə musal'mān ba tāso 'tsənga 'pejanəy? How would you recognise a good Muslim?	زهٔ يو خالِق، مالِک، رازِق خُدائ منم. يو ښهٔ مُسلمان به تاسو څنګه پيژنئ؟
H: ha'ɣa ba pin'zə 'waxta munz ka'wi. He would do prayers five times. āw ɣa'lat kār ba nə ka'wi. And he will not do wrong things.	هغه به پينځهٔ وخته مُونځ کوی. او غلط کار به نهٔ کوی.
L: tā haǰ 'kəṛey dey? Have you done the pilgrimage?	تا حج کړے دے؟
H: na, mā haǰ 'nə-dey 'kəṛey. No, I haven't done the pilgrimage.	نه، ما حج نهٔ دے کړے.
L: xa, dā rā'ta 'owaya če 'tsumra āsmā'ni kitā'buna di? Fine, tell me how many heavenly books there are?	ښه، دا راته ووايه چې څومره آسمانی کتابونه دی؟
H: tsa'lor āsmā'ni kita'buna di: qu'rān ša'rif, ɪn'ǰil ša'rif, za'bur ša'rif āw to'rāt ša'rif. There are four heavenly books: the Holy Quran, The Holy Gospel, the Holy Psalms and the Holy Torat.	څلور آسمانی کتابونه دی: قُرآن شريف، اِنجيل شريف، زبُور شريف او تورات شَريف.
L: tə dā kitā'buna 'waye? Do you read these books?	تهٔ دا کتابونه وائی؟
H: na, ṭol 'nə-wayəm. qu'rān ša'rif me wa'yəley dey. No, I don't read them all. I have read the Holy Quran.	نه، ټول نهٔ وايم. قُرآن شريف مې وئيلے دے.

Pronunciation drill

Focus on / ṛ / ړ

ṛund sa'ṛey la'ṛəm 'učičo āw məṛ šo. ړُوند سړے لړم وچيچو او مړ شو.

☝ Practice this sentence with your helper.

Non-emphatic possessive pronouns

Person	Singular			Plural		
1st	my	me	مې	our	mo	مو
2nd	your	de	دې	your (plural & polite singular)	mo	مو
3rd	his, her, its	ye	يې	theirs	ye	يې

NOTES:

1. These possessive pronouns are interchangeable with the possesive pronouns (*zə'mā* زما, *stā* ستا, etc.) already introduced (see Lesson 7: Possessive pronouns).

2. Possessive pronouns generally follow the noun they modify. For example, the sentence "My son is coming home" could be said as:

   zə'mā zwe kor ta rā'zi. زما زوئ کور ته راځي.

   zwe me kor ta rā'zi. زوئ مې کور ته راځي.

3. *mo* (مو) includes the meaning 'we', 'us' and 'you'. For example:

šor mo ḍer zyāt təngaʼwi	The noise disturbs us a lot.	شور مو ډېر زيات تنګوي.
da mo 'tsənga pox 'kəṛey dey?	How did you cook it?	دا مو څنګه پوخ کړے دے؟

4. *mo* (مو) can be used to address a person of higher rank.

Non-emphatic possessive pronouns in sentences

zəˈmā trə də warˈsək na nən rāˈzi.	My uncle is coming from Warsak today.	زما ترۀ د ورسک نه نن راځي.
trə me də warˈsək na nən rāˈzi.		ترۀ مې د ورسک نه نن راځي.
zmung xor halˈwa xoˈri.	Our sister is eating pudding.	زمُونږ خور حلوا خوري.
xor mo halˈwa xoˈri.		خور مو حلوا خوري.
stā plār pa kārxāˈna ke kār kaˈwi?	Does your father work in a factory?	ستا پلار په کارخانه کښې کار کوي؟
plār mo pa kārxāˈna ke kār kaˈwi?		پلار مو په کارخانه کښې کار کوي؟
ˈstāso ḍoˈḍəy ˈḍera məziˈdāra da.	Your food is very delicious.	ستاسو ډوډۍ ډېره مزېداره ده.
ḍoˈḍəy mo ˈḍera məziˈdāra da.		ډوډۍ مو ډېره مزېداره ده.
də de mor buˈḍəy da.	Her mother is old.	د دې مور بُوډۍ ده.
mor ye buˈḍəy da.		مور يې بُوډۍ ده.
də haˈɣwi kor ˈhalta dey.	Their house is there.	د هغوی کور هلته دے.
kor ye ˈhalta dey.		کور يې هلته دے.

Practice interchanging the possessive adjectives in similar sentences.

Possessive pronouns used with *paˈkār* to signal need پکار

stā ˈhaɣa qaˈləm paˈkār dey?	Do you need that pen?	ستا هغه قلم پکار دے؟
ˈhaɣa qaˈləm de paˈkār dey?		هغه قلم دې پکار دے؟
zəˈmā dre sre kāpˈyāne paˈkār di.	I need three red notebooks.	زما درې سرې کاپيانې پکار دی.
dre sre kāpˈyāne me paˈkār di.		درې سرې کاپيانې مې پکار دی.
də haˈɣə tsə šey paˈkār dey?	What does he need?	د هغۀ څۀ شے پکار دے؟
tsə šey ye paˈkār dey?		څۀ شے يې پکار دے؟
ˈstāso dā tsaˈpləy paˈkār ˈnə-di?	Don't you need these sandals?	ستاسو دا څپلۍ پکار نۀ دی؟
dā tsaˈpləy mo paˈkār nə-di.	We did not need these sandals.	دا څپلۍ مو پکار نۀ دی.
zmung os ˈhits šey paˈkār nə-dey.	We don't need anything now.	زمُونږ اوس هېڅ شے پکار نۀ دے.
os mo ˈhits šey paˈkār nə-dey.		اوس مو هېڅ شے پکار نۀ دے.

də haɣ'wi ḍo'ḍəy pa'kār da.	They need food.	د هغوی ډوډۍ پکار ده.
ḍo'ḍəy ye pa'kār da.		ډوډۍ يې پکار ده.

Fifteen common transitive verbs in the present tense

1. *āɣos'təl* – 'to wear', 'to put on' Present tense verb stem – *aɣond* اغوستل، اغوند

nən ha'wā 'ḍera 'yəxa da. tsə 'āɣonde?	Today the air is very cold. What are you wearing?	نن هوا ډېره يخه ده. څهٔ اغوندې؟
zə yo drund koṭ 'āɣondəm.	I am wearing a heavy coat.	زهٔ يو درُوند کوټ اغوندم.
ha'ɣa 'newe ǰā'me 'āɣondi.	He is wearing a new shalwar kamis.	هغه نوې جامې اغوندی.

2. *āwre'dəl* – 'to hear', 'to listen' Present tense verb stem – *āwr* اورېدل، اور

'tāso xab'runa 'āwrəy?	Do you listen to the news?	تاسو خبرُونه اورئ؟
mung 'hara špa xab'runa 'āwru.	We listen to the news every night.	مُونږ هره شپه خبرُونه اورو.
ha'ɣa də pəx'to san'dəre 'āwri?	Is he listening to Pukhto music?	هغه د پښتو سندرې اوری؟
na, ha'ɣa nə-āwri.	No, he isn't listening.	نه، هغه نهٔ اوری.

NOTE:
Verbs ending in / -edəl / (يدل- or ېدل-) are usually intransitive; *āwre'dəl* (اورېدل) is an exception.

3. *āxɪs'təl* – 'to buy', 'to take' Present tense verb stem – *āxl* اخستل، اخل

xānsa'ma mo 'hara wrəz də ba'zār na sodā 'āxli?	Does your cook buy goods from the bazaar daily?	خانسامه مو هره ورځ د بازار نه سودا اخلی؟
na, 'hara wrəz sodā 'nə-āxli.	No, he does not buy goods every day.	نه، هره ورځ سودا نهٔ اخلی.
tə də ha'ɣə na tsə 'āxle?	What are you taking from him?	تهٔ د هغهٔ نه څهٔ اخلې؟
də ha'ɣə na yo xə ki'tāb 'āxləm.	I'm getting a good book from him.	د هغهٔ نه يو ښهٔ کتاب اخلم.

4. *bot'ləl* – 'to take' (people / animals) Present tense verb stem – *boz* بوتلل، بوز

tsə waxt ha'ɣa ḍāk'ṭər ta bo'ze?	At what time are you taking him to the doctor?	څهٔ وخت هغه ډاکټر ته بوځې؟
os ye bo'zəm.	I'm taking him now.	اوس يې بوځم.
ḍre'wər dā 'xəza həm dəf'tər ta bo'zi?	Is the driver also taking this woman to the office?	ډرائيور دا ښځه هم دفتر ته بوځی؟
na, nə-ye bo'zi.	No, he's not taking her.	نه، نهٔ يې بوځی.

NOTES:

1. *bot'ləl* (بوتلل) is only used for taking or carrying people and animals (i.e. animate objects).
2. In contrast, the verb *o'ṛəl* (وړل) is used with inanimate objects. For example:

zə xat ḍākxā'ne ta 'yosəm?	Can I take a letter to the Post Office?	زهٔ خط ډاکخانې ته يوسم؟

5. *gan'ḍəl* – 'to sew', 'to mend' Present tense verb stem – *ganḍ* ګنډل، ګنډ

tə tsə waxt zə'mā ka'mis gan'ḍe?	When are you sewing my shirt?	تهٔ څهٔ وخت زما قميص ګنډې؟
os ye gan'ḍəm.	I'm sewing it now.	اوس يې ګنډم.
ha'ɣa os tsə gan'ḍi?	What is she sewing now?	هغه اوس څهٔ ګنډی؟
ha'ɣa 'newe ǰā'me gan'ḍi.	She is sewing new clothes.	هغه نوې جامې ګنډی.

6. *ɣox'təl* – 'to want, to ask (for)' Present tense verb stem – *ɣwaṛ* غوښتل، غوړ

ha'ɣa zə'mā na tsə 'ɣwaṛi?	What does she want from me?	هغه زما نه څهٔ غواړی؟
stā na 'ləge pe'se 'ɣwaṛi.	She wants a little money from you.	ستا نه لږې پيسې غواړی.
'tāso tsə 'ɣwaṛəy?	What do you want?	تاسو څهٔ غواړئ؟
merabā'ni, 'hits 'nə-'ɣwaṛəm.	Thanks, I don't want a thing.	مِهربانی، هيڅ نهٔ غواړم.

7. *li'dəl* – 'to see', 'to visit' Present tense verb stem – *win* ليدل، وين

'tāso 'haya sa'ṛey 'winəy?	Do you see that man?	تاسو هغه سړے وينئ؟

na, zə ye də de zay na ˈnə-winəm.	No, I don't see him from here.	نه، زۀ يې د دې ځائ نه نۀ وينم.
ˈhara wrəz xpəl malˈgərey ˈwine?	Do you see your friend daily?	هره ورځ خپل ملګرے وينې؟
na, ˈkəla ˈkəla ye ˈwinəm.	No, I see him now and again.	نه، کله کله يې وينم.

8. *liˈkəl* – 'to write' Present tense verb stem – *lik* ليکل، ليک

tsok ˈḍere məziˈdāre qiˈse ˈliki?	Who writes very enjoyable stories?	څوک ډېرې مزېدارې قيصې ليکى؟
ahˈmad ˈliki.	Ahmad writes.	احمد ليکى.
dā mazˈmun də čā dəˈpāra ˈlike?	Who are you writing this essay for?	دا مضمُون د چا د پاره ليکې؟
də klās dəˈpāra ye ˈlikəm.	I'm writing it for class.	د کلاس د پاره يې ليکم.

9. *losˈtəl* (or *lawasˈtəl*) – 'to read' Present tense verb stem – *lu* لوستل، لو

tə urˈdu losˈtəle še?	Can you read Urdu?	تۀ اُردو لوستلے شې؟
tə saˈhar tsə luˈəle?	What do you read in the morning?	تۀ سحر څۀ لولې؟
zə saˈhar quˈrāne pāk luˈələm.	I read the Holy Quran in the morning.	زۀ سحر قُرآن پاک لولم.
ˈtāso ˈḍere rəsāˈle luˈələy?	Do you read a lot of magazines?	تاسو ډېرې رسالې لولئ؟
na, ˈhara wrəz āxˈbār luˈəlu.	No, we read the newspapers daily.	نه، هره ورځ اخبار لولو.

NOTE:

In common speech *ˈwayəm* (وايم) is often used in place of *losˈtəl* (لوستل).
In special cases *liˈdəl* (ليدل) is also used to mean 'to read'.

10. *winˈzəl* – 'to wash' Present tense verb stem – *winz* وينځل، وينځ

ˈxəza de ˈhara wrəz yaˈwāze ˈluxi ˈwinzi?	Does your wife wash the dishes herself every day?	ښځه دې هره ورځ يواځې لوښى وينځى؟
āw, ˈwəle zə warsaˈra ˈwinzəm tsə?	Yes, why, should I wash with her?	آو، ولې زۀ ورسره وينځم څۀ؟

tə 'hara haf'ta ǰā'me 'winze?	Do you wash clothes every week?	تهٔ هره هفته جامې وينځې؟
āw, 'hara haf'ta 'winzəm.	Yes, I wash them every week.	آو، هره هفته وينځم.
ḍo'ḍəy na 'maxke zə lās 'winzəm.	I wash my hands before (eating) food.	ډوډۍ نه مخکښې زهٔ لاس وينځم.

NOTES:

1. *win'zəl* (وينځل) is used to describe washing hands and feet only, and not for the whole body (when *lambəl* لمبل is used).
2. Washing clothes and dishes is definitely *xəzo kār* (ښځو کار – a woman's job) amongst traditional Pukhtun families, even when women are sick.

11. *peǰan'dəḷ* – 'to know', 'to recognise' Present tense verb stem – *peǰan* پېژندل، پېژن

tə ha'sən 'peǰane?	Do you know Hassan?	تهٔ حسن پېژنې؟
āw, 'peǰanəm ye.	Yes, I know him.	آو، پېژنم يې.
xə'fa 'nə-šəy, zə 'tāso 'nə-peǰanəm.	Don't be upset, I don't know you.	خفه نهٔ شئ، زهٔ تاسو نهٔ پېژنم.
'tāso xə mo'ṭər 'peǰanəy?	Can you recognise a good car?	تاسو ښهٔ موټر پېژنئ؟
āw, mung 'peǰanu.	Yes, we can recognise (one).	آو، مُونږ پېژنُو.
hay'wi haqi'qət 'peǰani?	Do they know truth?	هغوی حقيقت پېژنی؟
zə de 'peǰanəm, xo num de 'rāna 'her šo.	I know you, but I've forgotten your name.	زهٔ دې پېژنم، خو نُوم دې رانه هېر شو.

NOTE:

The verb *pohe'dəl* (پوهېدل) means 'to know or understand something', while *peǰan'dəl* (پېژندل) means 'to know someone'.

12. *rāwəs'təl* – 'to bring' (animate objects) راوستل، راول

Present tense verb stem – *rāwəl*

'tāso 'hara wrəz ha'ɣa də dəf'tər na kor ta 'rāwələy?	Do you bring her home from the office daily?	تاسو هره ورځ هغه د دفتر نه کور ته راولئ؟
āw, 'hara wrəz ye 'rāwələm.	Yes, I bring her every day.	آو، هره ورځ يې راولم.

ˈrɪška ba de tsə waxt ˈdəlta ˈrāwəli?	When will the rickshaw bring you here?	رکشه به دې څۀ وخت دلته راولی؟
haˈɣa ba me beˈgāla ˈdəlta ˈrāwəli.	He will bring me here tonight.	هغه به مې بېګاله دلته راولی.

13. *rāwˈṛəl* – 'to bring' (inanimate objects) راوړل، راوړ

Present tense verb stem – *rāwṛ*

noˈkər de ˈtso ˈbaǰe də baˈzār na ḍoˈḍəy rāwˈṛi?	When does your servant bring bread from the bazaar?	نوکر دې څو بجې د بازار نه ډوډۍ راوړی؟
āˈtə ˈbaǰe rāwˈṛi.	He brings it at eight o'clock.	اتۀ بجې راوړی.
mung la tsok čay rāwˈṛi?	Who brings us tea?	مُونږ له څوک چائې راوړی؟
lur me rāwˈṛi.	My daughter brings it.	لُور مې راوړی.

14. *waˈyəl* – 'to say', 'to tell', 'to read', 'to study' وئيل، وائ

Present tense verb stem – *way*

tə tsə šey ˈwaye?	What are you reading?	تۀ څۀ شے وائې؟
ˈyəwa qiˈsa pa ɪnˈǰil šaˈrif ke ˈwayəm.	I am reading a story in the Holy Injil.	يوه قيصه په اِنجيل شريف کښې وايم.
tsə ˈwaye?	What are you saying?	څۀ وائې؟
ˈwayəm mā saˈra čay skəy?	I'm saying "Will you drink tea with me?"	وايم ما سره چائې څکئ؟
zə saˈbəq ˈwayəm.	I am studying a lesson.	زۀ سبق وايم.

15. *oˈṛəl* – 'to take' (inanimate objects) Present tense verb stem – *oṛ* وړل، وړ

tə nən zəˈmā kiˈtāb oˈṛe?	Are you taking my book today?	تۀ نن زما کتاب وړې؟
āw, nən stā kiˈtāb oˈṛəm.	Yes, I'm taking your book today.	آو، نن ستا کتاب وړم.
haˈɣa dā kaɣazˈuna dəfˈtər ta oˈṛi.	Is she taking these papers to the office?	هغه دا کاغذُونه دفتر ته وړی؟
na, nə-ye oˈṛi.	No, she is not taking them.	نه، نۀ يې وړی.

Memorising moment

mata'luna

پهٔ خوله خوږه او پهٔ زړهٔ کښې کږه.

pa xo'la xwa'ga, āw pa zṛə ke ka'ga.

Sweet mouth, but crooked heart.

چې دَ خُدایٔ پهٔ چا نظر شی تورے خاورې ورته زر شی.

če də xo'dey pa čā nə'zər ši 'torey 'xāwre war-ta zər ši.

Black soil becomes gold for the one whom God looks at with favour.

Rahman Baba

زهٔ رحمان چې غشے ولم خطا نهٔ ځی.

پهٔ بغداد کښې مې کامِل کامِل پیران شته.

zə rah'mān če 'ɣəšey 'waləm xa'tā nə zi.

pa baɣ'dād ke me kā'mıl kā'mıl pi'rān šta.

I, Rahman don't miss when I shoot an arrow.

In Baghdad there are perfect, perfect *pirs*.[8]

Tell a joke

☝ Have your language helper work with you so you can tell this joke. Then go out and use it.

زما یو دوست وو. هغهٔ وادهٔ نهٔ وو کړے او د خپل ورور پهٔ کور کښې اوسېدو. یوه ورځ پېښور ته راغے؛ پهٔ هوټل کښې یې ډوډۍ خوړله. چې ډوډۍ یې وکتلې نو ټولې سوزېدلې وې. بېره ته یې آواز ورکړو "دېخوا راشه!" "څهٔ پکار دی؟" "زهٔ باورچی خانې ته زم." "څهٔ د پاره؟ ما ته حکم کوئ چې څهٔ پکار وی، زهٔ به راوړم!" "نه! زهٔ پهٔ خپله کتل غوارم چې دا ډوډۍ زما ورندار خو نهٔ دی پخې کړې."

[8] A *pir* is a saint or religious guide. *xa'tā nə zi* (خطا نهٔ ځی), translated 'to miss', means literally, 'to not make a mistake'.

zəˈmā yo dost wo. haˈɣa wāˈdə ˈnə wo ˈkəṛey āw də xpəḷ wror pa kor ke oseˈdo. ˈyəwa wrəz pexaˈwar ta ˈrāɣey; pa hoˈṭəl ke ye ḍoˈḍəy xoˈṛəla. če ḍoˈḍəy ye ˈokatəle no ˈṭole swəzeˈdəle we. beˈrə ta ye āˈwāz ˈwarkṛo, "ˈdexwā ˈrāša!" "tsə paˈkār di?" "zə ˈbāwarči xāˈne tə zəm." "tsə dəˈpāra? mā ta ˈhokəm kaˈwəy če tsə paˈkār wi, zə ba ˈrāwṛəm!" "na! zə pa ˈxpəla kaˈtəl ˈɣwārəm če dā ḍoˈḍəy zəˈmā wranˈdār xo ˈnə-di ˈpaxe ˈkəṛe."[9]

Exercise for Lesson Ten

1. Fill in the blanks in the following sentences with the correct form of the verb shown.

a.	haˈɣa nən ǰāˈme ________________.	winˈzəl
	هغه نن جامې ________________.	وینځل
b.	mung la də saˈra xabˈruna ________________.	kaˈtəl
	مُونږ له دهٔ سره خبرُونه ________________.	کتل
c.	hayˈwi ˈhara wrəz xabˈruna ________________.	āwreˈdəl
	هغوی هره ورځ خبرُونه ________________.	اورېدل
d.	ˈtə haˈsən āw gul makəy ________________.	peǰanˈdəl
	تهٔ حسن او ګُل مکی ________________.	پېژندل
e.	ˈtāso ˈhara špa yo ˈnewey kiˈtāb ________________.	losˈtəl
	تاسو هره شپه یو نوے کتاب ________________.	لوستل
f.	ḍreˈwər mung dəfˈtər ta ________________.	botˈləl
	ډرائیور مُونږ دفتر ته ________________.	بوتلل
g.	ˈtāso tsə šey ________________.	ɣoxˈtəl
	تاسو څهٔ شے ________________.	غوښتل
h.	tə ˈhara špa zəˈmā malˈgərey ________________.	liˈdəl
	تهٔ هره شپه زما ملګرے ________________.	لیدل

[9] The English translation is given at the end of the Lesson. Use it to check your translation / comprehension.

i. ˈtāso ˈhaɣa kor _________________.		āxɪsˈtəl
تاسو هغه کور _________________.		اخستل
j. dwi nən ˈnewey māl zəˈmā duˈkān ta _________________.		rāwˈṛəl
دوئ نن نوے مال زما دُوکان ته _________________.		راوړل

2. Make meaningful questions and answers from the following pairs of words and then make similar sentences on your own.

a. ǰaˈme winˈzəl Q. .... جامې وینځل

A. ....

b. sanˈdəre āwreˈdəl Q. .... سندرې اورېدل

A. ....

c. axˈbār losˈtəl Q. .... اخبار لوستل

A. ....

d. kapˈṛa ganˈḍəl Q. .... کپړه ګنډل

A. ....

e. sodā āxɪsˈtəl Q. .... سودا اخستل

A. ....

f. māˈšum botˈləl Q. .... ماشُوم بوتلل

A. ....

g. qiˈsa liˈkəl Q. .... قیصه لیکل

A. ....

h. ˈluxi winˈzəl Q. .... لوښی وینځل

A. ....

Vocabulary for Lesson Ten

āsmā'ni	آسمانی	*f.*	*adj.*	heavenly; blue colour
āx'bār	اخبار	*m.s.*	*n.*	newspaper
āɣos'təl	اغوستل		*v.t.*	to wear, to put on
ɪn'ǰil ša'rif	اِنجیل شریف	*m.s.*	*n.*	Holy Gospel
āwre'dəl	اورېدل		*v.t.*	to hear, to listen
bot'ləl	بوتلل		*v.t.*	to take (animate objects)
be'gā	بېگا		*adv.*	last night
be'gāla	بېگاله		*adv.*	tonight
pa'kār	پکار		*prep. ph.*	need
peǰan'dəl	پېژندل		*v.t.*	to know, to recognise, to identify, to be acquainted with
tanga'wəl	تنگول		*v.t.*	to disturb, to annoy
to'rāt ša'riʃ	تورات شریف	*m.s.*	*n.*	Holy Pentateuch, Holy Torah
či'čəl	چیچل		*v.t.*	to bite, to sting
haǰ	حج	*m.s.*	*n.*	pilgrimage to Makkah
haqi'qət	حقیقت	*m.s.*	*n.*	truth, reality, fact
hal'wa	حلوا	*f.s.*	*n.*	pudding
xā'lɪq	خالِق	*m.s.*	*n.*	creator, originator, maker
xab'runa	خبرُونه		*n.*	news
xat / xa'tuna	خط / خطُونه	*m.*	*n.*	letter
dost / dos'tān	دوست / دوستان	*m., f.*	*n.*	friend
de	دې	*m., f.*	*poss. pro.*	your
ḍākxā'na	ډاکخانه	*f.s.*	*n.*	post office
ḍre'wər	ډرائیور	*m.s.*	*n.*	driver
rā'zɪq	رازِق	*m.*	*n.*	the provider, the sustainer
rāw'ṛəl	راوړل		*v.t.*	to bring (inanimate objects)

rāwəsˈtəl	راوستل		*v.t.*	to bring (animate objects)
rəsāˈle	رسالې	*f.*	*n.*	magazine
zaˈbur šaˈrif	زبُور شریف	*m.s.*	*n.*	Holy Psalms
sanˈdəre	سندرې		*n.*	music
sodā	سودا	*f.*	*n.*	goods, provisions, groceries
swazeˈdəl	سوزیدل		*v.i.*	to be burning
šor	شور	*m.*	*n.*	noise, din, 'racket', 'hubbub'
ɣaˈlat	غلط	*m.*	*adj.*	wrong, false, mistaken
ɣoxˈtəl	غوښتل		*v.t.*	to want, to ask (for), to request; to demand
quˈrān šaˈrif	قُرآن شریف	*m.s.*	*n.*	Holy Quran
qiˈsa / qiˈse	قیصه / قیصې	*f.*	*n.*	story
kāˈpi / kāpˈyāne	کاپی / کاپیانې	*f.*	*n.*	notebook
kārxāˈna	کارخانه	*f.s.*	*n.*	factory
kaˈtəl	کتل		*v.t.*	to look at, to see, to watch, to examine
ˈkəla ˈkəla	کله کله		*adv.*	sometimes, now and again
koṭ	کوټ	*m.s.*	*n.*	coat
ganˈḍəl	ګنډل		*v.t.*	to sew, to mend
losˈtəl [lawasˈtəl]	لوستل		*v.t.*	to read
liˈdəl	لیدل		*v.t.*	to see, to visit; to read
liˈkəl	لیکل		*v.t.*	to write
mazˈmun	مضمُون	*m.*	*n.*	essay, article; subject
maˈnəl	منل		*v.t.*	to accept, to obey, to agree; to believe
mo	مو	*m., f.*	*poss. pro.*	our, your (plural and polite singular), we, us, you
munz kaˈwəl	مُونځ کول		*v.t.*	to recite prayers
me	مې	*m., f.*	*poss. pro.*	my

wranˈdār	ورندار	*f.*	*n.*	sister-in-law (brother's wife)
oˈṛəl	وړل		*v.t.*	to take (inanimate objects)
winˈzəl	وينځل		*v.t.*	to wash
waˈyəl	وئيل		*v.t.*	to say, to talk; to read, to study
ˈhara hafˈta	هره هفته		*adv.*	weekly, every week
haˈwā	هوا	*f.*	*n.*	air, weather
hoˈṭəl	هوټل	*m.s.*	*n.*	hotel, restaurant
hereˈdəl	هېرېدل		*v.i.*	to forget
ˈyəxa	يخه	*f.*	*adj.*	cold
ye	يې	*m., f.*	*poss. pro.* *pro.*	his, hers, its, theirs; he, her, it, they

Translation of the joke

I had a friend. He was not married and lived with his brother. One day he came to Peshawar and ate bread in a restaurant. When he saw the bread, every piece was burned. He called to the waiter, "Come here!" "What do you want?" "I want to go into the kitchen." "What for? Tell me what you want and I will bring it for you." "No! I want to see for myself if my sister-in-law made this bread."

yolə'səm sa'bəq یوولسم سبق

Lesson Eleven

Dialogue eleven: Buying cloth

L: də ǰa'mo də'pāra ka'pṛa šta? Do you have cloth for clothes?	د جامو د پاره کپړه شته؟
H: dā 'ṭola ka'pṛa də ǰa'mo də'pāra da. All of the cloth is for clothes.	دا ټوله کپړه د جامو د پاره ده.
L: dā māl pākıstā'ney dey, āw kə bara'ney dey? Are these goods from Pakistan or from overseas?	دا مال پاکِستانے دے، او کۀ بهرنے دے؟
H: dā bara'ney dey, 'haɣa nor pākıstā'ni di. This is foreign, these others are Pakistani.	دا بهرنے دے، هغه نور پاکِستانی دی.
L: yo xə rang me pa'kār dey. I need a good colour.	یو ښۀ رنګ مې پکار دے.
H: dā ṭol xə ran'guna di. These are all good colours. asmā'ni rang sa'hi dey. Blue colour is good.	دا ټول ښۀ رنګونه دی. آسمانی رنګ صحیح دے.
L: āw, xo dā ka'pṛa 'ḍera ḍa'bəla 'xkāri. Yes, but that cloth looks very thick. 'ləga na'rəy 'ništa? Don't you have anything thinner?	آو، خو دا کپړه ډېره ډبله ښکاری. لږه نرۍ نشته؟
H: na, xo dā 'ṭole də 'oṛi də'pāra di. No, but all of these are for summer.	نه، خو دا ټولې د اوړی د پاره دی.
L: ǰo'ṛa ba də 'tso 'gəzo-na 'ǰoṛa ši? How many yards will it take to make a suit from it?	جوړه به د څو ګزو نه جوړه شی؟
H: stā ǰo'ra ba də u'wo 'gəzo-na 'ǰoṛa ši. It will take seven yards to make a suit for you.	ستا جوړه به د اوو ګزو نه جوړه شی.
L: tso šwe? How much?	څو شوې؟
H: špəg sa'wa ru'pəy. Six hundred rupees.	شپږ سوه روپۍ.
L: u'wə 'gəza 'rāka! Give me seven yards!	اووۀ ګزۀ راکه!

Pronunciation drill

1. Contrasting / l / ل and / ṛ / ړ

dā lund dey.	This is wet.	دا لوند دے.
dā ṛund dey.	This is a blind person.	دا ړُوند دے.
lamdə'wəl xə kār nə-dey.	It is not good to be wet.	لمدول ښهٔ کار نهٔ دے.
ṛanda'wəl xə kār nə-dey.	It is not good to be blind.	ړندول ښهٔ کار نهٔ دے.
dey dā ta'li.	He is weighing it.	دے دا تلی.
dey dā ta'ṛi.	He is tying it.	دے دا تړی.

2. Constrasting / **ey** / ے and / **əy** / ۍ

da'ɣa spey na'rey dey.	That dog is skinny.	دغه سپے نرے دے.
da'ɣa spəy na'rəy da.	That bitch (female dog) is skinny.	دغه سپۍ نرۍ ده.
ha'ɣa zə'mā nwa'sey dey.	That is my grandson.	هغه زما نوسے دے.
ha'ɣa zə'mā nwa'səy da.	That is my granddaughter.	هغه زما نوسۍ ده.
ha'ɣa paxwā'ney ǰermā'ney dey.	He is an old German.	هغه پخوانے جرمنے دے.
ha'ɣa paxwā'nəy ǰermā'nəy da.	She is an old German.	هغه پخوانۍ جرمنۍ ده.

The directive pronouns: *rā-*, *dar-* and *war-* را-، در-، ور-

The prefix *rā-* (را-) indicates movement towards me, the speaker. The prefix *war-* (ور-) indicates movement towards a third person or place, and *dar-* (در-) indicates movement towards you.

rā-	را-	to me, to us
war-	ور-	to him, to her, to them
dar-	در-	to you

1. *rā-* (را-):

dey mā ta ki'tāb rā-ka'wi. He is giving the book to me. دے ما ته کتاب راکوی.

Here *mā* (ما) 'me' has the same meaning as *rā* (را), but appears in the modified form, such as when *zə* (زهٔ) changes to *mā* (ما). (See Note 2. under Object pronouns in Lesson 7).

2. *war-* (ور-):

dey war-ta ki'tāb war-ka'wi.	He is giving the book to him.	دے ورته کتاب ورکوی.

Note that *ha'ɣa* (هغه) changes to *war* (ور).

3. *dar-* (در-):

ha'ɣa tā ta ki'tāb dar-ka'wi.	He is giving the book to you.	هغه تا ته کتاب درکوی.

Note that *'tāso* (تاسو) changes to *tā* (تا).

Examples:

ha'ɣa rā-zi.	He is coming (here).	هغه راځی.
ha'ɣa dar-zi.	He is going (towards you).	هغه درځی.
ha'ɣa war-zi.	He is going (there).	هغه ورځی.
war-ša!	Go (to him, her, them)!	ورشه!
rā-ša!	Come (to me)!	راشه!

NOTE:

These pronouns may also be used instead of object pronouns in the oblique case. For example:

rā-sa'ra ze?	Are you going with me?	راسره ځې؟
āw, dar-sa'ra zəm.	Yes, I'm going with you.	آو، درسره ځم.
mung war-sa'ra zu.	We are going with them.	مُونږ ورسره ځُو.
tə rā'ta tsə rā-ka'we?	What are you giving to me?	تهٔ راته څۀ راکوې؟
zə dar-ta čay dar-ka'wəm.	I'm giving tea to you.	زهٔ درته چائې درکوم.
zə war-ta ki'tāb war-kawəm.	I'm giving a book to them.	زهٔ ورته کتاب ورکوم.

More examples:

tə mā ta pe'se rā-ka'we?	Are you giving me money?	تهٔ ما ته پیسې راکوې؟
na, zə tā ta ḍo'ḍəy dar-ka'wəm.	No, I'm giving you bread.	نه، زهٔ تا ته ډوډۍ درکوم.
dey ka'rim ta kā'ɣəz war-ka'wi?	Is he giving paper to Karim?	دے کریم ته کاغذ ورکوی؟
na, war-ta yo ki'tāb war-ka'wi.	No, he is giving him a book.	نه، ورته یو کتاب ورکوی.

ˈtāso nā-ˈǰoṛo ta tsə war-kaˈwəy?	What are you giving to the sick?	تاسو ناجوړو ته څۀ ورکوئ؟
mung war-ta dāˈru war-kaˈwu.	We are giving them medicine.	مُونږ ورته دارُو ورکوؤ.
zəˈmā zwi ta maˈṇa war-kaˈwe?	Are you giving an apple to my son?	زما زوئ ته منړه ورکوې؟
na, maˈṇa war-ta nə-war-kaˈwəm.	No, I'm not giving him an apple.	نه، منړه ورته نۀ ورکوم.
dey ba tsə waxt rā-ta peˈse rā-kaˈwi?	When will he give me the money?	دے به څۀ وخت راته پېسې راکوی؟
peˈse ba ˈdarta nə-dar-kaˈwi.	He won't give you the money.	پېسې به درته نۀ درکوی.

Directive pronouns with *-ka* 'give!' -که

Use the pictures below to practice these sentences, and in addition, add your own. Imagine that one person in the picture is *zə* (زۀ).

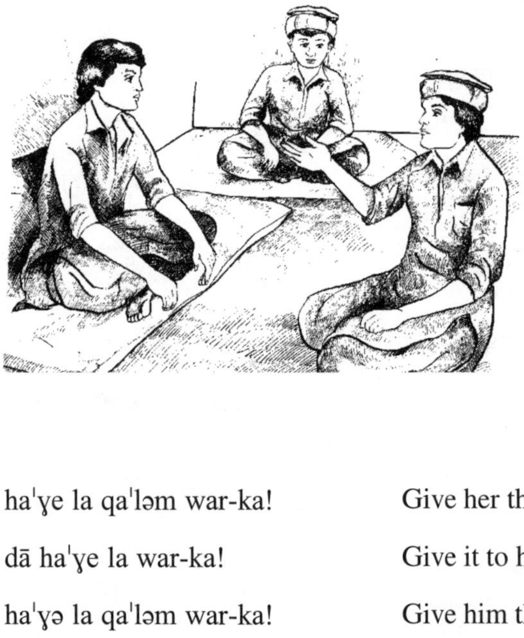

haˈɣe la qaˈləm war-ka!	Give her the pen!	هغې له قلم ورکه!
dā haˈɣe la war-ka!	Give it to her!	دا هغې له ورکه!
haˈɣə la qaˈləm war-ka!	Give him the pen!	هغۀ له قلم ورکه!
dā ˈmāla rā-ka!	Give it to me!	دا ماله راکه!
dā haɣˈwi la war-ka!	Give it to them!	دا هغوی له ورکه!
ˈmāla dwa kiˈlo rā-ka!	Give me two kilos!	ماله دوه کیلو راکه!

☝ Now practice the same drill with different objects around the room.

More practice with directive pronouns

tā la pe'se nə dar-kom, də la pe'se war-kom.	I'm not giving money to you, I'm giving it to him.	تا له پيسي نۀ درکوم، دۀ له پيسي ورکوم.
ki'tāb dar-sa'ra šta?	Do you have a book with you?	کتاب درسره شته؟
zə xpəl dost la war-kom āw tā la nə dar-kom.	I'm giving it to my friend and not to you.	زۀ خپل دوست له ورکوم او تا له نۀ درکوم.
kə zə'mā dost 'rāši, zə ba 'yəwa pukā'ṇəy 'war-la war-kom.	If my friend comes, I will give him a balloon.	کۀ زما دوست راشي زۀ به يوه پوقنړۍ ورله ورکوم.
mung 'war-la dəwa'i war-ka'wu.	We are giving him medicine.	مُونږ ورله دوائي ورکوو.

NOTE:
There is a slightly different use of the verb *kawəl* (کول) in the case of *tə* (تۀ) and *'tāso* (تاسو):

tə zə'mā zwi la ma'ṇa war-key?	Are you giving my son an apple?	تۀ زما زوئ له منړه ورکې؟
'tāso zə'mā zwi la ma'ṇa war-ka'wəy?	Are you giving my son an apple?	تاسو زما زوئ له منړه ورکوئ؟

Creating compound verbs from adjectives

or bal dey.	The fire is ablaze.	اور بل دے.
ha'ɣa or bal-a'wi.	He is lighting the fire.	هغه اور بلوی.
'haɣa war 'wəle band dey?	Why is that door shut?	هغه ور ولې بند دے؟
'haɣa war 'wəle band-a'we?	Why are you closing that door?	هغه ور ولې بندوې؟
stā mo'ṭər ǰoṛ šo?	Is your car fixed?	ستا موټر جوړ شو؟
stā mo'ṭər ǰoṛ-a'wəm.	I'm fixing your car.	ستا موټر جوړه وم.
lar'gi māt di.	The wood is broken.	لرگی مات دی.
ha'ɣa os lar'gi māt-a'wi.	He is breaking the wood now.	هغه اوس لرگی ماتوی.
də ha'ɣe ko'ṭa 'pāka da.	Her room is clean.	د هغې کوټه پاکه ده.
ha'ɣa ko'ṭa pāk-a'wi.	She is cleaning the room.	هغه کوټه پاکوی.
'ɣwaxa pa'xa da.	The meat is cooked.	غوښه پخه ده.
xānsā'ma 'ɣwaxa pax-a'wi.	The cook is cooking the meat.	خانسامه غوښه پخوی.

kıṛ'kəy ko'law di.	The windows are open.	کړکۍ کولاو دی.
zə kıṛ'kəy kolā'wəm.	I'm opening the windows.	زهٔ کړکۍ کولاوم.
os čay pa'xigi.	Tea is cooking now.	اوس چائې پخیږی.

NOTES:

1. Most adjectives can be combined with *kawəl* (کول) 'to do' to form compound transitive verbs. For example the feminine singular form of the adjective *pox* (پوخ) 'cooked' is *pa'xa* (پخه) and is combined to form the verb *pax-a'wəl* (پخول) 'to cook':

'tāso sāg pa u'bə ke paxa'wəy?	Do you cook spinach in water?	تاسو ساګ په اوبو کښې پخوئ؟
na, pa ɣwa'ṛo ke ye paxa'wu.	No, we cook it in oil.	نه، په غوړو کښې يې پخوُو.

2. Since most adjectives end in a consonant, the initial / k- / -ک in *kawəl* (کول) is dropped in the present tense:

Adjective			Compound transitive verbs		
bal	بل	ablaze, kindled	bal-a'wəl	بلول	to light, to turn on
band	بند	closed	band-a'wəl	بندول	to close, to shut
pāk	پاک	clean, tidy	pāk-a'wəl	پاکول	to clean
pox	پوخ	ripe, cooked	paxa-'wəl	پخول	to cook
ǰoṛ	جوړ	healthy, sound	ǰoṛ-a'wəl	جوړول	to build, to fix
sa'fā	صفا	clean, tidy	sa'fā ka'wəl	صفا کول	to clean
ko'law	کولاو	open	kolā-'wəl	کولاول	to open
māt	مات	broken	māt-a'wəl	ماتول	to break

3. Compound transitive verbs made from nouns ending in vowels usually retain the / k- / -ک:

is'tri ka'wəl	اِستری کول	to iron
ǰā'ru ka'wəl	جارُو کول	to sweep
xa'bare ka'wəl	خبري کول	to talk
'lobe ka'wəl	لوبي کول	to play
wā'də ka'wəl	وادهٔ کول	to marry

Exceptions include:

kār ka'wəl	کار کول	to work
xob ka'wəl	خوب کول	to sleep

4. Names of professions can also be combined with the auxillary verb *ka'wəl* (کول). In many cases a suffix / -i / ی- or / -ā / ا- is added to the noun:

Profession			Compound transitive verbs		
tar'kāṇ	ترکاڼ	carpenter	tarkā'ṇi ka'wəl	ترکاڼی کول	to do carpentry
ɣəl	غل	thief	ɣlā ka'wəl	غلا کول	to steal

5. The verb *ǰoṛ-a'wəl* (جوړول) 'to fix', 'to make', 'to repair' is also used in numerous ways:

tar'kāṇ stā də'pāra tsə ǰoṛa'wi?	What is the carpenter making for you?	ترکاڼ ستا د پاره څۀ جوړوی؟
tsə waxt xpəl wex'tə ǰoṛa'we?	When are you getting your hair cut?	څۀ وخت خپل وېښتۀ جوړوې؟
haɣ'wi čā də'pāra 'haɣa 'newey kor ǰoṛa'wi?	Who are they building that new house for?	هغوی چا د پاره هغه نوے کور جوړوی؟

The verb *wa'həl* 'to hit', 'to beat' وهل

dā halə'kān har waxt spi wa'hi.	These boys are hitting dogs all the time.	دا هلکان هر وخت سپی وهی.
'wəle 'hara wrəz mā wa'he?	Why do you hit me every day?	ولې هره ورځ ما وهې؟
dā 'hara špa pa xob ke 'čəɣe wa'hi.	She cries-out [i.e. shouts] in her sleep every night.	دا هره شپه په خوب کښې چغې وهی.
dey pa 'haɣa sind ke 'lāmbo wa'hi.	He is swimming in that river.	دے په هغه سيند کښې لامبو وهی.
fan'kār 'hara špa pa de ho'ṭəl ke ra'bāb wa'hi.	The musician plays *rabab* every night at this hotel.*	فنکار هره شپه په دې هوټل کښې رباب وهی.

* The *ra'bāb* (رباب) is a stringed instrument, popular with Pukhtuns.

The verb *niˈwəl* 'to catch', 'to take', 'to hold' نیول

də yo ˈnewey kor pa karāˈya niˈwəley dey.	He has rented a new house.	دهٔ یو نوے کور په کرایه نیولے دے.
musalmāˈnān har kal ˈyəwa myāšt roˈǰe ˈnisi.	Muslims take the fast for one month every year.	مسلمانان هر کال یوه میاشت روژې نیسی.
haɣˈwi pa ˈhaɣa sind ke luy maˈyān ˈnisi.	They are catching big fish in that river.	هغوی په هغه سیند کښې لوئ مهیان نیسی.
marˈɣəy niˈwəl xə xaˈbara nə da.	Catching birds is not a good thing.	مرغۍ نیول ښهٔ خبره نهٔ ده.
zəˈmā kiˈtāb ˈonisa, zə rāˈzəm.	Hold my book, I'm coming.	زما کتاب ونیسه زهٔ راځم.

How to say "I don't know"

mā ta ˈpata ˈništa.	I don't know (anything).	ما ته پته نشته.
ˈpata ˈnə-ləgi.	I don't know.	پته نهٔ لګی.

The emphatic adjective *xpəl* 'own' خپل

dā də čā kiˈtāb tā la dar-kaˈwi?	Whose book is she giving to you?	دا د چا کتاب تاله درکوی؟
dā xpəl kiˈtāb mā la rā-kaˈwi.	She is giving me her own book.	دا خپل کتاب ماله راکوی.
tə də čā ǰāˈme ˈāɣonde?	Whose clothes are you wearing?	تهٔ د چا جامې اغوندې؟
zə xpəle ǰāˈme ˈāɣondəm.	I'm wearing my own clothes.	زهٔ خپلې جامې اغوندم.
ˈtāso ˈyəwa qiˈsa čā ta ˈwayəy?	Who are you telling a story to?	تاسو یوه قیصه چاته وایئ؟
zə ye ˈxpəle lur ta ˈwayəm.	I'm reading it to my daughter.	زهٔ یې خپلې لُور ته وایم.
ˈtāso ˈyəwa qiˈsa čā ta kawəy?	Who are you telling a story to?	تاسو یوه قیصه چاته کوئ؟
zə ye ˈxpəle lur ta kaˈwəm.	I'm reading it to my daughter.	زهٔ یې خپلې لُور ته کوم.
dā kaˈmis də čā dəˈpāra ganˈḍe?	Whom are you sewing this shirt for?	دا قمیص د چا د پاره ګنډې؟
zə ye xpəl zān dəˈpāra ganˈḍum.	I'm sewing it for myself.	زهٔ یې خپل ځان د پاره ګنډم.

ha'ɣa də čā də'pāra par'de āw tolā'i ǰoṛa'wi?	Who is she making the curtains and mattresses for?	هغه د چا دپاره پردې او تولايئی جوړوی؟
də xpəle tror də'pāra ye ǰoṛa'wi.	She is making them for her aunt.	د خپلې ترور د پاره يې جوړوی.
tə os 'čerta ze?	Where are you going now?	تهٔ اوس چرته ځې؟
zə xpəl kor ta zəm.	I'm going to my house.	زهٔ خپل کور ته ځم.
ha'ɣa də čā se'kəl xarsa'wi?	Whose bicycle is he selling?	هغه د چا سائيکل خرڅوی؟
ha'ɣa xpəl se'kəl xarsa'wi.	He is selling his own bicycle.	هغه خپل سائيکل خرڅوی.
dā də čā də'pāra ḍo'ḍəy paxa'wi?	Whom is she cooking food for?	دا د چا د پاره ډوډۍ پخوی؟
də 'xpəlo māšu'māno də'pāra paxa'wi.	She is cooking for her own children.	د خپلو ماشُومانو د پاره پخوی.
dā ṭo'pəy stā 'xpəla da?	Is this hat your own?	دا ټوپۍ ستا خپله ده؟
āw, dā ṭo'pəy zə'mā 'xpəla da.	Yes, this is my own hat.	آو، دا ټوپۍ زما خپله ده.
hay'wi tsok di?	Who are they?	هغوی څوک دی؟
hay'wi zə'mā xpəl di.	They are my own (relatives).	هغوی زما خپل دی.

NOTES:

1. The same subject pronoun and possessive adjective cannot be used in the same sentence. *xpəl* (خپل) replaces the adjective.

2. Note the ungrammatical examples and corrections below:

Incorrect		Correct
zə zə'mā ki'tāb larəm. زهٔ زما کتاب لرم.	I have my book.	zə xpəl ki'tāb larəm. زهٔ خپل کتاب لرم.
tə stā kor ta ze? تهٔ ستا کور ته ځې؟	Are you going to your house?	tə xpəl kor ta ze? تهٔ خپل کور ته ځې؟
dey də 'də 'xəze sa'ra zi. دے د دهٔ ښځې سره ځی.	He is going with his wife.	dey 'xpəle 'xəze sa'ra zi. دے خپلې ښځې سره ځی.

3. *xpəl* (خپل) is inflected for number, gender and case. For example the phrase:

'xpəlo māšu'māno də'pāra   for your children   خپلو ماشُومانو د پاره

Memorising moment

mataˈluna

چې چرته اوسی په خوئی به دَ هغو شی.

če ˈčerta ˈosi pa ˈxuyi ba də haˈɣo ši.

Your manners will be the same as those you live with.

ښهٔ پوهېږم خو نهٔ پوهېږم.

xə poˈhegəm xo nə poˈhegəm.

I understand it well but don't understand it.

د ماشُوم په ژبه خپله مور پوهېږی.

də māˈšum pa ˈǰɪba ˈxpəla mor poˈhigi.

A mother knows the sound of her own child's voice.

Rahman Baba

سړیتوب څهٔ په دولت نهٔ دے رحمانه!

بت د سرو زرو کهٔ جوړ شی انسان نهٔ دے.

saṛiˈtob tsə pa doˈlət nə dey rahˈmāna!

but də sro ˈzəro kə ˈǰoṛ ši ɪnˈsān nə dey.

Manliness is not found in wealth, Rahman!

Even if an idol is made from gold, it is not human.

په یو قدم تر عرشه پورې رسی

ما لیدلے دے رفتار د درویشانو.

pa yo qaˈdəm tər ˈarša ˈpore ˈrasi

mā liˈdəley dey rɪfˈtār də darweˈšāno.

They reach God's throne in a single stride

I have witnessed the ways of Dervishes.

Comprehension drill: Learning location through commands

☝ Take a pen and quickly obey commands given by your helper without looking at your book!

qa'ləm xpəl sər də'pāsa 'onisa!	Hold the pen above your head!	قلم خپل سر د پاسه ونیسه!
xpəl qa'ləm də ki'tāb 'lande 'kegda!	Put your pen under the book!	خپل قلم د کتاب لاندي کېږده!
xpəl qa'ləm pa ki'tāb 'bānde 'kegda!	Put your pen on the book!	خپل قلم په کتاب باندي کېږده!
xpəl qa'ləm pa 'xpəla xwā ke 'onisa!	Put your pen by your side!	خپل قلم په خپله خوا کښي ونیسه!
xpəl qa'ləm də kā'ɣəz xwā ta 'kegda!	Put your pen next to the paper!	خپل قلم د کاغذ خواته کېږده!

Now add the directive pronouns *rā-* (را-), *dar-* (در-) and *war-* (ور-) to the commands. For example, "Put the pen next to her!", " ... next to me!", etc.

Exercises for Lesson Eleven

1. Substitute the following words for the underlined word in the sentence:

   ǰa'mo də'pāra ka'pṛe di? جامو د پاره کپړي دي؟

   a. ______________________ par'de پردي

   b. ______________________ bā'ləxt بالخت

   c. ______________________ tolā'i تولائی

2. Fill in the correct directional pronoun *rā-* (را-), *dar-* (در-) or *war-* (ور-) in the following sentences:

   a. dwi mung ta kitā'buna ________________ ka'wi.

   دوئ مونږ ته کتابونه ________________ کوی.

b. ha'lək malı'kāno ta alu'gān ________________ ka'wi.

هلک هلکانو ته آلُوګان ________________ کوی.

c. mung 'tāso ta yo pāw čay ________________ ka'wu.

مُونږ تاسو ته یو پاؤ چائې ________________ کوو.

d. plār me 'rāla pe'se ________________ ka'wi.

پلار مې راله پېسې ________________ کوی.

e. karim tā ta ḍo'ḍəy ________________ ka'wi.

کریم تا ته ډوډۍ ________________ کوی.

f. mung ta bṛəs'tən nə ________________ ka'wi.

مُونږ ته بړستن نۀ ________________ کوی.

3. Replace the object pronoun in the sentences below with the correct directional pronoun *rā-* (را-), *dar-* (در-) or *war-* (ور-) and adjust accordingly.

a. dey yo xat mā ta 'liki. — دے یو خط ما ته لیکی.

____

b. zə tā la 'yəwa ma'ṇa 'axləm. — زۀ تاله یوه مڼه اخلم.

____

c. mung 'tāso la ka'mis 'ganḍu. — مُونږ تاسو له قمیص ګنډو.

____

d. dey hay'wi na 'xəfa 'kigi. — دے هغوی نه خفه کیږی.

____

e. tə mung sa'ra kor ta ze? — تۀ مُونږ سره کورته ځې؟

____

Vocabulary for Lesson Eleven

or	اور	*m.*	*n.*	fire
ˈoṛey	اوړے	*m.*	*n.*	summer
baraˈney	بهرنے	*m.*	*adj.*	foreign
balaˈwəl	بلول		*comp. v.t.*	to light, to turn on
band	بند	*m.*	*adj.*	closed
ˈbanda / ˈbande	بنده / بندې	*f.*		
bandaˈwəl	بندول		*comp. v.t.*	to close, to shut, to lock, to turn off, to lock-up
pākaˈwəl	پاکول		*comp. v.t.*	to clean
paxaˈwəl	پخول		*comp. v.t.*	to cook
parˈda / parˈde	پرده / پردې	*f.*	*n.*	curtain, screen, drape, cover, veil;
			adv.	secrecy, privacy, modesty
pox / pāˈxə	پوخ / پاخهٔ	*m.*	*adj.*	ripe, cooked, baked; dark
paˈxa / paˈxe	پخه / پخې	*f.*		
pukāˈṇəy	پُوقنړۍ	*f.*	*n.*	balloon
tarkāˈṇi kaˈwəl	ترکاڼي کول		*comp. v.t.*	to do carpentry
taˈṛəl	تړل		*v.t.*	to tie, to bind, to wrap, to close
taˈləl	تلل		*v.t.*	to weigh
tolāˈi	تولاۍ / تولائی	*f.*	*n.*	mattress, *toshak*
ǰermāˈney	جرمنے	*m.*	*n.*	a German person
ǰermāˈnəy	جرمنۍ	*f.*		
ǰoˈṛa	جوړه	*f.s.*	*n.*	suit of clothes
zān	ځان	*m.*	*n., pro.*	self
ˈčəɣe waˈhəl	چغې وهل		*comp. v.t.*	to cry out, to scream, to shout
xarsaˈwəl	خرڅول		*v.t.*	to sell, to spend
xob kaˈwəl	خوب کول		*comp. v.t.*	to sleep

dəˈpāsa	د پاسه		*post.*	above, up, over
dar-	در-		*dir. pro.*	to you
ḍaˈbəl	ډبل	*m.*	*adj.*	thick, heavy
ḍaˈbəla / ḍaˈbəle	ډبله / ډبلې	*f.*		
rā-	را-		*dir. pro.*	to me, to us
raˈbāb	رباب	*m.*	*n.*	*rabab*
roˈǰa niˈwəl	روژه نيول		*comp. v.t.*	to fast
sāg	ساګ	*m.*	*n.*	spinach
seˈkəl	سائيکل	*m.s.*	*n.*	bicycle
sind	سيند	*m.s.*	*n.*	river
saˈhi	صحيح		*adj.*	right, true, OK
saˈfā kaˈwəl	صفا کول		*comp. v.t.*	to clean
ɣlā kaˈwəl	غلا کول		*comp. v.t.*	to steal
ɣwaˈṛi	غوړي	*m.pl.*	*n.*	cooking oil
fanˈkār	فنکار	*m.s.*	*n.*	musician
karāˈya	کرايه	*f.s.*	*n.*	rent, fare, hire
koˈṭa / koˈṭe	کوټه / کوټې	*f.*	*n.*	room
koˈlaw	کولاو	*m., f.*	*adj.*	open
kolāˈwəl	کولاول		*comp. v.t.*	to open
kexoˈdəl	کېښودل		*v.t.*	to put, to place
gaz	ګز	*m.s.*	*n.*	a yard (measure)
ˈlāmbo waˈhəl	لامبو وهل		*comp. v.t.*	to swim
larˈgey / larˈgi	لرګے / لرګي	*m.*	*n.*	wood
mātaˈwəl	ماتول		*comp. v.t.*	to break, to crush
māl	مال	*m.*	*n.*	property, goods, merchandise
marˈɣəy	مرغۍ	*f.*	*n.*	bird
maˈyān niˈwəl	مهيان نيول		*comp. v.t.*	to catch fish

nwaˈsəy	نوسئ [نمسۍ]	*f.*	*n.*	granddaughter
nwaˈsey	نوسے	*m.*	*n.*	grandson
niˈwəl	نیول		*v.t.*	to catch, to take, to hold
war-	ور-		*dir. pro.*	to him, to her, to them
waˈhəl	وهل		*v.t.*	to beat, to hit, to strike; to play a musical instrument
wexˈtə	وېښتهٔ	*m.*	*n.*	hair
wexˈtə ǰoṛaˈwəl	وېښتهٔ جوړول		*comp. v.t.*	to have a hair cut

doləˈsəm saˈbəq دولسم سبق

Lesson Twelve

Dialogue twelve: Ladies visiting a newborn

L: ˈāsalām aˈlekum! mubaˈrak ša! Peace be on you! Congratulations! ˈstāso ˈkara haˈlək ˈšɪβey dey. A male child has come in your house.	اسلام علیکم! مُبارک شه! ستاسو کره هلک شوے دے.
H: xoˈdey de ˈobaxa. xoˈšāla ˈosi! May God forgive you. Be happy!	خُدائ دې وبخښه. خوشحاله اوسی!
L: kaˈkey kəm dey? Where is the boy?	ککے کُوم دے؟
H: uˈdə dey. He's asleep.	اُودهٔ دے.

NOTE:

Much tradition surrounds the birth of sons. (This dialogue is just the start of your investigation into this aspect of the culture.) Congratulations are due to all in the household. Observe that the conversation above ended with an excuse to stop you from seeing the newborn. This is to prevent the 'evil eye'. If you are allowed to see him, then a conversation similar to the one below may take place. The first statement (below) is accompanied with a spitting of air rather like spitting an imaginary orange pip.

L: maˈšāˈlā! ḍer ˈxkwəley māˈšum dey. Thanks be to God! He's a pretty boy.	ماشاءالله! ډیر ښکُلے ماشُوم دے.
H: xoˈdey dey luy kṛi! May God grow him up!	خُدائ دې لوئ کړی!
L: ˈtāso kəm yo num xwax ˈkəṛey dey? What name have you chosen for him?	تاسو کُوم یو نُوم خوښ کړے دے؟
H: lā yo num mo həm nə-dey xwax ˈkəṛey, xo ˈkəšar trə ye war-ta sād ˈwayi. We haven't even chosen a name for him yet, but his youngest uncle calls him Saad.	لا یو نُوم مو هم نهٔ دے خوښ کړے، خو کشر ترهٔ یې ورته سعد وائی.
L: mor ye ˈtsənga da? How is his mother?	مور یې څنګه ده؟
H: xə da. She's fine.	ښهٔ ده.

NOTE:

A few rupees are put in the infant's hand without comment, leading to the following dialogue:

H: na, dā ḍere di, dā mə-kawa! No, it's too much, don't do it!	نه، دا ډېري دی، دا مهٔ کوه!
L: stā pa'ke tsə di? dā xo zə'mā āw də sād pa menz ke mamı'la da. What is it to you? This is an issue between me and Saad.	ستا پکښې څهٔ دی؟ دا خو زما او د سعد په مینځ کښې معامله ده.
H: 'ogora, ha'ɣə xo pe'se 'wāxıste! Look, he's taken the money!	وګوره، هغهٔ خو پېسې واخستې!

کرایه دار مالک ته:

"ستا دا کور ټول څاڅي بېګا مې ټول
چرګان مړهٔ شُو."

مالک کرایه دار ته:

"بطَخې اوساته."

karāya'dār mā'lik ta:

"stā dā kor ṭol 'sāsi be'gā me
ṭol čər'gān mṛə šo."

mā'lik karāya'dār ta:

"bat'e 'osāta."

☝ The English translation of this joke is at the end of the Lesson. Use it to check your comprehension.

Renting a house

L: xwao'šā ke də karā'ya ko'runa šta? Are there any houses for rent around here?	خواؤشا کښې د کرایه کورونه شته؟
H: āw, 'dəlta yo kor šta. Yes, one house is here.	آو، دلته یو کور شته.
L: dā kor 'stāso dey? Is this house yours?	دا کور ستاسو دے؟
H: na, zə tsoki'dār yım. No, I am a watchman.	نه، زهٔ څوکیدار یم.

L: dā kor xā'li dey? Is this house empty?	دا کور خالي دے؟
H: āw, xā'li dey. Yes, it's empty.	آو، خالي دے.
L: u'bə pa'ke šta? Does it have water?	اوبۀ په کښې شته؟
H: āw, xpəl ku'ey pa'ke dey. Yes, it has its own well.	آو، خپل کُوهے په کښې دے.
L: tso kam're pa'ke di? How many rooms are in it?	څو کمرې په کښې دي؟
H: pin'zə kam're āw dwa ɣosalxā'ne di pa'ke. It has five rooms and two bathrooms in it.	پينځۀ کمرې او دوه غُسلخانې دي په کښې.
L: 'bāwarči xā'na 'tsənga da? How is it's kitchen?	باورچي خانه څنګه ده؟
H: rā'za, 'ogora! Come and look at it!	راځه، وګوره!
L: kor xo xə dey, xo karā'ya 'tsumra da? The house is good, but how much is the rent?	کور خو ښۀ دے، خو کرايه څومره ده؟
H: də 'myāšte tsal'wext zara ru'pəy di. Forty thousand rupees a month.	د مياشتې څلوېښت زره روپۍ دي.
L: dā ḍer grān dey! It is very expensive!	دا ډير ګران دے.
H: də kor mā'lık sa'ra xa'bare 'oka. Talk with the landlord about it.	د کور مالِک سره خبرې وکه.
L: də ha'ɣə də ṭele'fun nəm'bər tsə dey? What is his telephone number?	د هغۀ د ټيليفون نمبر څۀ دے؟
H: də ha'ɣə də ṭele'fun nəm'bər dā dey. This is his telephone number.	د هغۀ د ټيليفون نمبر دا دے.

Pronunciation drill

1. Illustrating / **wr** / ور

ha'ɣa me wror dey.	He is my brother.	هغه مې ورور دے.
ha'ɣa me wrā'rə dey.	He is my nephew.	هغه مې ورارۀ دے.
'wrusto byā 'rāša.	Come later.	وروستو بيا راشه.
os wrəz da.	It is daytime now.	اوس ورځ ده.
'wriǰe pa'xe di.	The rice is cooked.	وريژې پخې دي.

2. Illustrating / **š** / ش

špəg pišo'gāne 'dəlta šta.	There are six cats here.	شپږ پیشوګاني دلته شته.
'špāṛəs špe 'halta 'pāte šu.	We spent sixteen nights here.	شپاړس شپې هلته پاتې شُو.
špun'ki də špe pa seh'ra ke 'pāte šwəl.	The shepherds spent the night in the desert.	شپُونکی د شپې په صحرا کښې پاتې شول.

NOTE:

How is your pronunciation going? Try recording your voice in the blanks in one of your practice sessions. Then listen to how you sound speaking Pukhto. You may find it discouraging to do this, but it should be a stimulus to review the sounds at the start of the book all over again. Keep encouraging your helper to correct you. For words you continue to mispronounce, make your own drills.

Twelve intransitive verbs in the present tense

1. *odre'dəl* – 'to stop', 'to stand', 'to wait' ودرېدل

bəs 'dəlta o'drigi?	Does the bus stop here?	بس دلته ودرېږي؟
āw, 'hara gın'ṭa pas 'dəlta o'drigi.	Yes it stops here after every hour.	آو، هره ګینټه پس دلته ودرېږي.

2. *garze'dəl* – 'to walk', 'to go around' ګرځېدل

tə har sa'har 'čerta 'garze?	Where do you walk every morning?	ته هر سحر چرته ګرځې؟
zə har sa'har pa xār ke 'garzəm.	I go for a walk in the city every morning.	زهٔ هر سحر په ښار کښې ګرځم.
zə'mā ga'ṛəy nən 'nə-garzi.	My watch is not going today.	زما ګړی نن نهٔ ګرځي.
nən gā'ṇəy 'garzi?	Is the sugar press running today?	نن ګانړی ګرځي؟
pa 'kəli ke 'xəze ko'law məx 'nə-garzi.	In the village, ladies don't go around with uncovered faces.	په کلي کښې ښځې کولاؤ مخ نهٔ ګرځي.

3. *isāre'dəl* – 'to wait', 'to stay', 'to become late' ایساریدل

zə ba 'həlta isā'regəm.	I will wait over there.	زهٔ به هلته ایساریږم.
'wəle bas ba hame'ša isā'regi?	Will the bus always be late?	ولې بس به همیشه ایساریږي؟

taso ba zə'mā pa kor ke isā'regəy?	Will you (*pl.*) stay in my house?	تاسو به زما په کور کښې ایسارېږئ؟

4. *kenas'təl* – 'to sit (down)' کښېناستل

hafiza pa tolā'i 'bānde 'nāsta da kə pa farš?	Is Hafiza sitting on the mattress or on the floor?	خافظه په تولائ باندې ناسته ده او که په فرش؟
ha'ɣa pa farš 'bānde 'nāsta da.	She is sitting on the floor.	هغه په فرش باندې ناسته ده.

NOTE:

The ending *-təl* (تل-) usually signals a transitive verb, but exceptions include *kena'stəl* (کښېناستل), *nənawa'təl* (ننوتل), *wa'təl* (وتل) and *tsəmlā'stəl* (څملاستل), which are all intransitive.

5. *prewa'təl* – 'to fall', 'to drop', 'to drop down' پرېوتل

'haɣa ha'lək də xpəl sāy'kəl na pre'uzi.	That boy is falling off his bike.	هغه هلک د خپل سائیکل نه پرېوزی.
ki'tāb me də mez na pre'uzi.	My book is falling off the table.	کتاب مې د مېز نه پرېوزی.

6. *nənawa'təl* – 'to enter', 'to go in' ننوتل

'tāso skul ta nəna'uzəy?	Are you going in to the school?	تاسو سکُول ته ننوزئ؟
na, mung nə-nəna'uzu.	No, we are not going in.	نه، مُونږ نهٔ ننوزُو.
'wəle pa guṭ ke nəna'uze?	Why are you going into the corner?	ولې په ګوټ کښې ننوزې؟

7. *ose'dəl* – 'to live', 'to stay', 'to reside' اوسېدل

'tāso pa pexā'wər ke 'čerta o'segəy?	Where do you live in Peshawar?	تاسو په پېښور کښې چرته اوسېږئ؟
mung os pa ṭāwn ke o'segu.	We are now living in Town.[10]	مُونږ اوس په ټاؤن کښې اوسېږُو.

[10] (University) Town is a suburb of Peshawar.

stā xana'dān pa paṛači'nār ke o'sigi?	Does your family live in Parachinar?	ستا خاندان په پاړه چنار کښې اوسېږی؟
na, xana'dān me pa karā'čəy ḳe o'sigi.	No, my family lives in Karachi.	نه، خاندان مې په کراچۍ کښې اوسېږی.

8. *pāse'dəl* – 'to get up (from sleep)', 'to rise', 'to awaken' پاڅېدل

tə tsə waxt pāse?	When do you get up?	ته څه وخت پاڅې؟
sa'hār wax'ti 'pasəm.	I get up early in the morning.	سحر وختی پاڅم.

9. *pohe'dəl* – 'to know', 'to understand' پوهېدل

tə pa 'ṭola pəx'to po'hege?	Do you understand everything in Pukhto?	ته په ټوله پښتو پوهېږې؟
na, zə ləga ləga po'higəm.	No, I understand a tiny bit.	نه، زه لږه لږه پوهېږم.
dā pa sa'bəq xə po'higi?	Does she understand the lesson well?	دا په سبق ښه پوهېږی؟
na, tər 'osa 'pore xə nə-po'higi.	No, she doesn't understand it well yet.	نه، تر اوسه پورې ښه نه پوهېږی؟
tə pa li'kəlo 'bānde po'hege?	Can you write? (*Lit.* Do you know writing?)	ته په ليکلو باندې پوهېږې؟
āw, zə pa li'kəlo 'bānde po'higəm.	Yes, I can write. (*Lit.* Yes, I know how to write.)	آو، زه په ليکلو باندې پوهېږم.
tə pa ḍray'βıng po'hege?	Can you drive?	ته په ډرائيونګ پوهېږې؟

NOTE:
pohe'dəl (پوهېدل) is used for 'knowing about' a thing, or 'knowing how to do' something.

10. *rase'dəl* – 'to arrive', 'to reach' رسېدل

'tāso tsə waxt swā'be ta 'rasəy?	What time are you reaching Swabi?	تاسو څه وخت صوابۍ ته رسئ؟
mung nən špa 'halta 'rasu.	We are arriving there tonight.	مونږ نن شپه هلته رسُو.
lās de 'bələf ta ra'sigi?	Does your hand reach the bulb?	لاس دې بلف ته رسېږی؟

āw, lās me ra'sigi.	Yes, my hand reaches.	آو، لاس مي رسېږی.
də ha'ɣə lās tər ḍer 'lәre 'lәre 'pore 'rasi.	He is influential. (*Lit.* His hand reaches very far.)	د هغهٔ لاس تر ډېر لري لري پوري رسی.

11. *tsəmlā'stəl* – 'to lie (down)', 'to sleep' څملاستل

ab'dul 'čerta 'səmli?	Where is Abdul lying?	عبدل چرته څملی؟
ha'ɣa pa 'haɣa kaṭ ke 'səmli.	He is lying on that bed.	هغه به هغه کټ کښي څملی.

12. *wa'təl* – 'to exit', 'to leave' وتل

pa de 'myāšt ke də pākı'stān na 'uze?	Are you leaving Pakistan this month?	په دي مياشت کښي د پاکِستان نه وځي؟
na, zə 'hits-kəla də pākı'stān na 'nə-uzəm.	No, I am never leaving Pakistan.	نه، زهٔ هېڅ کله د پاکِستان نه نهٔ وځم.
ɣəl me də lās na 'uzi.	The thief slips from my hand.	غل مي د لاس نه وځی.

Present participle *-ing*

In Pukhto the present participle is made my adding / -o / و- to the verb stem:

tlo	going	تلو
rat'lo	coming	راتلو
ka'wəlo	doing	کولو

li'dəlo	seeing	ليدلو
wa'yəlo	saying	وئيلو

Now you can translate this well-known *ṭa'pa* (ټپه):

'mina pa tlo, rāt'lo zyā'tigi

'kəla rā'za, 'kəla ba zə dar'zəm ma'yena.

مينه په تلو، راتلو زياتيږی

کله راځه، کله به زهٔ درځم مئينه.

____

____

NOTE:
The *tappa* is one of the oldest forms of folk poetry in the region. They often have a romantic theme, and like Japanese haiku they conform to an exact pattern of syllables, with 9 in the first line and 13 in the second.

Using the present participle *-ing*

ˈmina pa tlo, rātˈlo zyāˈtigi.	Love increases with coming and going.	مینه په تلو، راتلو زیاتیږی.
ˈɪləm pa losˈto ˈɪzda ˈkigi.	Knowledge is learned by reading.	علم په لوستو زده کېږی.
kār pa kaˈwəlo xatˈmigi.	Work is finished by doing.	کار په کولو ختمیږی.
ˈǰɪba pa waˈyəlo ɪzˈda ˈkigi.	Language is learned by speaking.	ژبه په وئیلو زده کېږی.
zə də marˈɣo āˈwāz āwreˈdəlo dəˈpāra bāɣ ta zəm.	I'm off to the park, to listen to (*lit.* for listening to the) bird song.	زۀ د مرغو آواز اورېدلو د پاره باغ ته ځم.
haˈɣa zəˈmā maˈdəd kaˈwəlo dəˈpāra rāˈzi.	He is coming to help (*lit.* for helping) me.	هغه زما مدد کولو د پاره راځی.
zə haspaˈtāl ta də haˈɣə liˈdəlo dəˈpāra zəm.	I'm going to the hospital to see (*lit.* for seeing) him.	زۀ هسپتال ته د هغۀ ليدلو د پاره ځم.
ˈwəle pa pəxˈto waˈyəlo šarˈmege?	Why are you embarrassed about speaking Pukhto?	ولې په پښتو وئیلو شرمیږې؟

The infinitives: 'to come', 'to go', 'to do', 'to say', 'to see', 'to eat' and 'to help'

An infinitive is the base form of the verb.

tləl	to go	تلل
ratˈləl	to come	راتلل
xoˈṛəl	to eat, to consume	خوړل

kaˈwəl	to do	کول
liˈdəl	to see	لیدل
waˈyəl	to say	وئیل

Many verbs, which are found in English in the infinitive form, such as 'to eat' and 'to help', are found in Pukhto as compound verbs. See below for two examples out of a vast range of possibilities:

xoˈrāk kaˈwəl	to eat (food)	خوراک کول
maˈdəd kaˈwəl	to help	مدد کول

Using the infinitive

One use of the infinitive form is with the verb 'to want'. As in the following examples:

zə tləl ˈɣwāṛəm.	I want to go.	زۀ تلل غواړم.
zə xoˈrāk kaˈwəl ˈɣwāṛəm.	I want to eat.	زۀ خوراک کول غواړم.
zə stā maˈdəd kaˈwəl ˈɣwāṛəm.	I want to help you.	زۀ ستا مدد کول غواړم.

NOTE:

Now you can recognise the infinitive and the present participle. The two can sometimes get mixed up.

☝ What is the meaning of this sentence?

pa de hoˈṭəl ke, čay ˈskəlo saˈra gəp ləgaˈwəl zaruˈri di.

په دې هوټل کښې چائې څښلو سره ګپ لګول ضرُوری دی.

The prepositions *pa haq ke, pa bāˈra ke* and *ˈbānde* meaning 'about'

په حق کښې، په باره کښې، باندې

stā də elekˈšən pa haq ke tsə xyāl dey?	What do you think about the election?	ستا د اليکشن په حق کښې څۀ خيال دے؟
dwi də pəxtaˈno pa bāˈra ke tsə ˈliki?	What are they writing about Pukhtuns?	دوئ د پښتنو په باره کښې څۀ ليکى؟
dwi də pəxtaˈno pa dasˈtur ˈyane ˈrəsam āw riˈwāǰ ˈbānde kiˈtāb ˈliki.	They are writing a book about Pukhtun culture, that is, customs and traditions.	دوئ د پښتنو په دستور يعنې رسم او رِواج باندې کتاب ليکى.

Memorising moment

mataˈluna

مُفت شراب قاضى هم څښلى دى.

maft šaˈrāb qāˈzi həm ˈskəli di.

Even a judge has drunk free alcohol.

پیشو د خُدایٔ د پاره منږک نهٔ نیسی.

pi'šo də xo'dey də'pāra mən'gək 'nə-nisi.

A cat doesn't catch mice for God.

راتلل په اراده او تلل په اجازه.

rāt'ləl pa ırā'da, āw tləl pa eǰā'za.

Coming requires intention, going requires permission.

کارغهٔ د خارو ګرځېدل زده کول،

خپل ګرځېدل ترې هم هېر شو. اوس په ټوپُونو ځی.

kār'ɣə də xā'ro garze'dəl ız'da ka'wəl,

xpəl garze'dəl tre həm her šo. os pa ṭo'puno zi.

The crow was learning to walk like a myna bird,

and forgot his own way to walk. Now he goes in hops.

Exercises for Lesson Twelve

1. Fill in the blanks with the correct form of the verb listed:

a. 'tāso har ma'xām 'čerta __________________?	garze'dəl
تاسو هر ماښام چرته __________________؟	ګرځېدل
b. bas 'dəlta __________________?	odre'dəl
بس دلته __________________؟	ودرېدل
c. ki'tāb me la mez na __________________.	prewa'təl
کتاب مې له مېز نه __________________.	پرېوتل
d. tə pa 'ṭola pəx'to __________________?	pohe'dəl
تهٔ په ټوله پښتو __________________؟	پوهېدل

2. For the twelve verbs listed in this chapter, make up sentences in the present tense, in the infinitive and using the present participle.

odre'dəl *pr.t.* ودرېدل

inf.

pa.p.

kena'stəl *pr.t.* کښېناستل

inf.

pa.p.

ose'dəl *pr.t.* اوسېدل

inf.

pa.p.

tsəmlā'stəl *pr.t.* څملاستل

inf.

pa.p.

garze'dəl *pr.t.* ګرځېدل

inf.

pa.p.

prewa'təl *pr.t.* پرېوتل

inf.

pa.p.

pāse'dəl *pr.t.* پاڅېدل

inf.

pa.p.

raseˈdəl	*pr.t.*	رسېدل
	inf.	
	pa.p.	
isāreˈdəl	*pr.t.*	ایساریدل
	inf.	
	pa.p.	
nənawaˈtəl	*pr.t.*	ننوتل
	inf.	
	pa.p.	
poheˈdəl	*pr.t.*	پوهېدل
	inf.	
	pa.p.	
waˈtəl	*pr.t.*	وتل
	inf.	
	pa.p.	

Summary of verbs in the present tense

Infinitive			Present tense					
			I We		You You (*pl*)		He, She They	
to buy	āxɪs'təl	اخستل	'āxləm	اخلم	'āxle	اخلې	'āxli	اخلی
			'āxlu	اخلُو	'āxləy	اخلئ	'āxli	اخلی
to wear	āɣos'təl	اغوستل	'āɣondəm	اغوندم	'āɣonde	اغوندې	'āɣondi	اغوندی
			'āɣondu	اغوندُو	'āɣondəy	اغوندئ	'āɣondi	اغوندی
to hear	āwre'dəl	اورېدل	'āwrəm	آورم	'āwre	آورې	'āwri	آوری
			'āwru	آورُو	'āwrəy	آورئ	'āwri	آوری
to live (reside)	ose'dəl	اوسېدل	o'segəm	اوسېږم	o'sege	اوسېږې	o'sigi	اوسېږی
			o'segu	اوسېږُو	o'segəy	اوسېږئ	o'sigi	اوسېږی
to wait	isāre'dəl	ايسارېدل	isā'regəm	ايسارېږم	isā'rege	ايسارېږې	isā'rigi	ايسارېږی
			isā'regu	ايسارېږُو	isā'regəy	ايسارېږئ	isā'rigi	ايسارېږی
to take (animate)	bot'ləl	بوتلل	bo'zəm	بوځم	bo'ze	بوځې	bo'zi	بوځی
			bo'zu	بوځُو	bo'zəy	بوځئ	bo'zi	بوځی
to get up	pāse'dəl	پاڅېدل	'pāsəm	پاڅم	'pāse	پاڅې	'pāsi	پاڅی
			'pāsu	پاڅُو	'pāsəy	پاڅئ	'pāsi	پاڅی
to fall	prewa'təl	پرېوتل	pre'uzəm	پرېوزم	pre'uze	پرېوزې	pre'uzi	پرېوزی
			pre'uzu	پرېوزُو	pre'uzəy	پرېوزئ	pre'uzi	پرېوزی
to under-stand (know)	pohe'dəl	پوهېدل	po'higəm	پوهېږم	po'hege	پوهېږې	po'higi	پوهېږی
			po'higu	پوهېږُو	po'hegəy	پوهېږئ	po'higi	پوهېږی
to know (recognise)	peǰan'dəl	پېژندل	'peǰanəm	پېژنم	'peǰane	پېژنې	'peǰani	پېژنی
			'peǰanu	پېژنُو	'peǰanəy	پېژنئ	'peǰani	پېژنی
to go	tləl	تلل	zəm	ځم	ze	ځې	zi	ځی
			zu	ځُو	zəy	ځئ	zi	ځی
to drink	skəl	څښل	skəm	څښم	ske	څښې	ski	څښی
			sku	څښُو	skəy	څښئ	ski	څښی

Infinitive			Present tense					
			I, We		You, You (*pl.*)		He, She, They	
to lie (down)	tsəmlāˈstəl	ثملاستل	ˈtsəmləm ˈtsəmlu	ثملم ثملو	ˈtsəmle ˈtsəmləy	ثملې ثملئ	ˈtsəmli ˈtsəmli	ثملی ثملی
to eat	xoˈṛəl	خوړل	xoˈrəm xoˈru	خورم خورو	xoˈre xoˈrəy	خورې خورئ	xoˈri xoˈri	خوری خوری
to come	rātˈləl	راتلل	rāˈzəm rāˈzu	راځم راځو	rāˈze rāˈzəy	راځې راځئ	rāˈzi rāˈzi	راځی راځی
to bring (inanimate)	rāwˈṛəl	راوړل	rāwˈṛəm rāwˈṛu	راوړم راوړو	rāwˈṛe rāwˈṛəy	راوړې راوړئ	rāwˈṛi rāwˈṛi	راوړی راوړی
to bring (animate)	rāwəsˈtəl	راوستل	rāwəˈləm rāwəˈlu	راولم راولو	ˈrāwəle rāwəˈləy	راولې راولئ	rāwəˈli rāwəˈli	راولی راولی
to arrive	raseˈdəl	رسېدل	ˈrasəm[11] ˈrasu	رسېږم رسو	ˈrase ˈrasəy	رسې رسئ	ˈrasi ˈrasi	رسی رسی
to want	ɣoxˈtəl	غوښتل	ˈɣwāṛəm ˈɣwāṛu	غواړم غواړو	ˈɣwāṛe ˈɣwāṛəy	غواړې غواړئ	ˈɣwāṛi ˈɣwāṛi	غواړی غواړی
to do	kaˈwəl	کول	kaˈwəm kaˈwu	کوم کوو	kaˈwe kaˈwəy	کوې کوئ	kaˈwi kaˈwi	کوی کوی
to become	keˈdəl	کېدل	ˈkegəm ˈkegu	کېږم کېږو	ˈkege ˈkegəy	کېږې کېږئ	ˈkigi ˈkigi	کېږی کېږی
to sit	kenaˈstəl	کښېناستل	ˈkenəm ˈkenu	کښېنم کښېنو	ˈkene ˈkenəy	کښېنې کښېنئ	ˈkeni ˈkeni	کښېنی کښېنی
to walk	garzeˈdəl	ګرځېدل	ˈgarzəm ˈgarzu	ګرځم ګرځو	ˈgarze ˈgarzəy	ګرځې ګرځئ	ˈgarzi ˈgarzi	ګرځی ګرځی
to sew	ganˈḍəl	ګنډل	ˈganḍəm ˈganḍu	ګنډم ګنډو	ˈganḍe ˈganḍəy	ګنډې ګنډئ	ˈganḍi ˈganḍi	ګنډی ګنډی
to have	laˈrəl	لرل	ˈlarəm ˈlaru	لرم لرو	ˈlare ˈlarəy	لرې لرئ	ˈlari ˈlari	لری لری

[11] The phonetics reflect the spoken form of the verbs in this chart. The script gives the written form.

Infinitive			Present tense: I, We		Present tense: You, You (*pl.*)		Present tense: He, She, They	
to read	losˈtəl *or* lawasˈtəl	لوستل	luˈələm luˈəlu	لولم لولُو	luˈəle luˈələy	لولې لولئ	luˈəli luˈəli	لولی لولی
to see	liˈdəl	ليدل	ˈwinəm ˈwinu	وينم وينُو	ˈwine ˈwinəy	وينې وينئ	ˈwini ˈwini	وينی وينی
to write	liˈkəl	ليکل	ˈlikəm ˈliku	ليکم ليکُو	ˈlike ˈlikəy	ليکې ليکئ	ˈliki ˈliki	ليکی ليکی
to enter	nənawaˈtəl	ننوتل	nənaˈuzəm nənaˈuzu	ننوزم ننوزُو	nənaˈuze nənaˈuzəy	ننوزې ننوزئ	nənaˈuzi nənaˈuzi	ننوزی ننوزی
to catch	niˈwəl	نيول	ˈnisəm ˈnisu	نيسم نيسُو	ˈnise ˈnisəy	نيسې نيسئ	ˈnisi ˈnisi	نيسی نيسی
to go out	waˈtəl	وتل	ˈuzəm ˈuzu	وځم وځُو	ˈuze ˈuzəy	وځې وځئ	ˈuzi ˈuzi	وځی وځی
to stop	odreˈdəl	ودرېدل	oˈdregəm oˈdregu	ودرېږم ودرېږُو	oˈdrege oˈdregəy	ودرېږې ودرېږئ	oˈdrigi oˈdrigi	ودرېږی ودرېږی
to take (inanimate)	oˈṛəl	وړل	oˈṛəm oˈṛu	وړم وړُو	oˈṛe oˈṛəy	وړې وړئ	oˈṛi oˈṛi	وړی وړی
to hit	waˈhəl	وهل	waˈhəm waˈhu	وهم وهُو	waˈhe waˈhəy	وهې وهئ	waˈhi waˈhi	وهی وهی
to wash	winˈzəl	وينځل	ˈwinzəm ˈwinzu	وينځم وينځُو	ˈwinze ˈwinzəy	وينځې وينځئ	ˈwinzi ˈwinzi	وينځی وينځی

☝ To practice these verbs, have your helper make a simple sentence using vocabulary you already know. Then have him or her give you a pronoun. Now make a sentence using the new pronoun. Fluency will improve if you resist the temptation to use English. As you get better, go faster.

For example:

H: zə lās ˈwinzəm. / mung — زهٔ لاس وينځم. / مُونږ

L: mung lās ˈwinzu. — مُونږ لاس وينځُو.

Vocabulary for Lesson Twelve

elek'šən	الېکشن	*m.*	*n.*	election
isāre'dəl	ایسارېدل [حصارېدل]		*v.i.*	to wait, to stay, to become late
'bānde	باندي		*prep.*	about
'bāwarči xā'na	باورچی خانه	*f.s.*	*n.*	kitchen
bəs / bə'suna	بس / بسُونه	*m.*	*n.*	bus
'bata	بطحه [بته، بطخه]	*f.*	*n.*	duck
'bələf	بلف	*m.*	*n.*	light bulb
pāse'dəl	پاڅېدل		*v.i.*	to get up (from sleep), to rise, to awaken
prewa'təl	پرېوتل		*v.i.*	to fall (down)
pa'ke	پکښې [په کښې]		*adv.*	between; in
pa'law	پولاؤ	*m.*	*n.*	pulao [pilau, pilaf] (an Afghan-style rice dish)
pa bā'ra ke	په باره کښې		*prep.*	about
pa haq ke	په حق کښې		*prep.*	about
tər'osa	تر اوسه			yet, up to now
ṭa'pa / ṭa'pe	ټپه / ټپې		*n.*	*tappa* (poetic couplet)
sase'dəl	څڅېدل		*v.i.*	to drip, to leak
xā'li	خالی	*m., f.*	*adj.*	empty
xana'dān	خاندان	*m.*	*n.*	family, dynasty
xatme'dəl	ختمېدل		*v.i.*	to be ended, to be finished, to be completed
xwao'šā	خواؤشا		*adj.*	approximately, round about, nearby, around
xwaxa'wəl	خوښول		*v.t.*	to like, to choose
das'tur	دستور	*m.*	*n.*	custom, tradition
ḍray'βıng	ډرائیونګ		*n.*	driving
'rəsam	رسم	*m.s.*	*n.*	custom, tradition

rase'dəl	رسېدل		v.i.	to arrive, to reach
ri'wāǰ	رِواج	m.s.	n.	custom, tradition
ız'da ke'dəl	زده کېدل		v.i.	to be learned
'ǰıba	ژبه	f.s.	n.	language; tongue; pronunciation
šarme'dəl	شرمېدل		v.i.	to be shy, to be ashamed, to feel embarrassed or humiliated
seh'ra / sehera'gāne	صحرا / صحراګانې	f.	n.	desert
zaru'ri	ضرُوری	f.	adj.	necessary, essential, urgent, indispensable, important
'ıləm	علم	m.	n.	knowledge
ɣosalxā'na	غُسلخانه	f.s.	n.	bathroom
farš	فرش	m.s.	n.	floor
kaṭ	کټ	m.s.	n.	bed, cot
karāya'dār	کرايه دار	m.	n.	tenant
'kara	کره	f.	n.	house
'kəšar / kəša'rān	کشر / کشران	m.	adj.	younger
'kəšra/ 'kəšre	کشره / کشرې	f.		
ku'ey	کُوهے	m.s.	n.	well
gā'ṇəy	ګانړۍ	f.s.	n.	sugar mill
gəp ləga'wəl	ګپ لګول	m.	v.t.	to talk; to visit
garze'dəl	ګرځېدل		v.i.	to walk; to move, to turn; to spin, to rotate, to go around, to revolve
guṭ	ګوټ	m.s.	n.	corner
gın'ṭa	ګېنټه	f.s.	n.	hour
lwe'dəl	لوئېدل		v.t.	to grow, to become big
muba'rak	مُبارک	m.		congratulations
ma'dəd ka'wəl	مدد کول		comp. v.t.	to help, to assist

mamı'la	معامله	*f.s.*	*n.*	transaction, issue
menz	مینځ	*m.*	*n.*	between, amongst; middle, centre
'mina	مینه	*f.*	*n.*	love
ma'yena	مئینه	*f.*	*n.*	beloved
nənawa'təl	ننوتل		*v.i.*	to enter, to go in
wa'təl	وتل		*v.i.*	to go out, to exit, to leave, to emerge, to come out
odre'dəl	ودرېدل		*v.i.*	to stop, to stand, to wait
wrā'rə / wreruna	وراره / وربرونه	*m.*	*n.*	nephew (brother's son)
'wrusto	وروستو		*adj.*	later
har tsə	هر څهٔ		*pro.*	everything
hame'ša	همیشه		*adv.*	always
'yane	یعنې			that is [i.e.], in other words

Translation of the joke:

Tenant to Landlord: "Your whole house is leaking. Last night every one of my hens died."

Landlord to Tenant: "Keep ducks."

dyārlə'səm sa'bəq دیارلسم سبق

Lesson Thirteen

Dialogue Thirteen: Talking about the weather

A cloudy day

L: nən mo'səm xə dey. Today the weather is good.	نن موسم ښهٔ دے.
H: āw, də pa'run na xə dey. Yes, it's been good since yesterday.	آو، د پرُون نه ښهٔ دے.
L: wa'reze di. stā tsə xyāl dey, bā'rān ba 'oši? There are clouds. What do you think, will it rain?	وريځې دی. ستا څهٔ خيال دے باران به وشی؟
H: bā'rān sa'ra ba 'fəsəl nə xarā'bigi? Won't the rain spoil the crops?	باران سره به فصل نهٔ خرابيږی؟
L: na, kə ga'ləy o'nə-ši, no bā'rān ba 'fəsəl ta 'ḍera fāy'da warki. No, if it doesn't hail then rain will give great benefit to the crops.	نه، کهږلۍ ونهٔ شی، نو باران به فصل ته ډېره فائده ورکوی.
H: xer dey, də ga'ləy mo'səm nə-dey. Don't worry, it's not the season for hail.	خېر دے، د ږلۍ موسم نهٔ دے.

A hot day

L: nən gar'mi da! It's hot today!	نن گرمی ده!
H: 'yara 'ḍera gar'mi šwa. Friend, it's become very hot.	يره ډېره گرمی شوه.
L: āw kəna, də hāṛ myāšt da, nwar ḍer tez dey. Yes it is, it's the month of Har, the sun is very strong.	آو کنه، د هاړ مياشت ده، نمر ډېر تېز دے.
H: rum ku'lər dar 'kara šta? Do you have a room cooler in your house?	رُوم کُولر در کره شته؟
L: āw, par'oskāl me yo ā'xıstey wo. Yes, I had bought one last year.	آو، پروسکال مې يو اخستے وو.

H: kam'ra 'tsənga da? 'yəxa da? How is the room? Is it cold?	کمره څنګه ده؟ یخه ده؟
L: āw, kam'ra 'yəxa da. Yes, the room is cold.	آو، کمره یخه ده.
H: xo če bij'li 'lāṛaši, no byā ḍer bəd hā'lat ǰoṛ ši. But when the electricity goes then the situation becomes very bad.	خو چې بجلی لاړه شی نو بیا ډېر بد حالت جوړ شی.
L: loḍ 'šeḍing mo ḍer zyāt tənga'wi. Load-shedding disturbs us a lot.	لوډ شیډنګ مو ډېر زیات تنګوی.

NOTE:

The word for 'sun' [*nwar* (نمر)] has a traditional bookish way of being written in Pukhto that is pronounced in a different way than it is spelt. This is one of several words like this. Ask a friend what some of the others are.

Some useful vocabulary about the weather:

heavy rain	drund bā'rān (*or*) tez bā'rān	درُوند باران (یا) تېز باران
only a light shower	'ase mamu'li bā'rān	هسې معمُولی باران
only a light rain	'ase narey bā'rān	هسې نرے باران
wind blows	bād (*or*) ha'wā čəl'igi	باد (یا) هوا چلېږی
storm	to'fān	طوفان
snow	'wāwra	واوره
dew	'parxa	پرخه

NOTE:

Both *'gəram* (ګرم) and *yəx* (یخ) add an / -ī / ی- to agree with feminine nouns.

Masculine		Feminine	
'gəram dey	ګرم دے	gar'mi da	ګرمی ده
yəx dey	یخ دے	yəx'ni da	یخنی ده

Pronunciation drill

1. Illustrating / **rg** / رګ

yo 'zbərg saṛey pa gulberg ke čər'gān sāti.	A saintly man keeps chickens in Gulberg.	یو زبرګ سړے په ګُلبرګ کښې چرګان ساتی.
dwi 'kara ḍer čər'gān di.	They have a lot of chickens at their house.	دوئ کره ډېر چرګان دی.

2. Illustrating / **yā** / يا

byā de pyā'la rā'wəṛa?	Did you bring the cup again?	بيا دې پياله راوړه؟
amir ǰān rɪx'tyā 'wāyi.	Amir Jan is telling the truth.	امير جان رښتيا وائى.
zyāt kār 'mə-kawa!	Don't work too hard.	زيات كار مۀ كوه!

3. Practicing / **ɣ** / غ and / **x** / خ

☝ Work on this tongue twister with your helper. The goal is to say the phrase clearly.

نۀ غم او نۀ غُصه بس هر وخت خفه.

nə 'ɣəm āw nə ɣo'sa bas har waxt xə'fa.

Changing verbs to the passive voice

1. Transitive verbs in their infinitive forms are changed to the passive voice by the addition of the auxiliary verb *'kigi* (كيږى) [from the verb *ke'dəl* (كېدل)].

'haɣa ḍo'ḍəy xo'ṛəle 'kigi?	Is that bread being eaten?	هغه ډوډى، خوړلې كيږى؟
āw, wro wro xo'ṛəle 'kigi.	Yes, it is being eaten slowly.	آو، ورو ورو خوړلې كيږى.
zə'mā xat nən li'kəley 'kigi?	Is my letter being written today?	زما خط نن ليكلے كيږى؟
āw, nən stā xat li'kəley 'kigi.	Yes your letter is being written today.	آو، نن ستا خط ليكلے كيږى.
dā ki'tāb los'təley 'kigi?	Is this book being read?	دا كتاب لوستلے كيږى؟
na, dā 'hits-kəla nə-los'təley 'kigi.	No, it will never be read. (*Lit.* '... is never being read'.)	نه، دا هيڅ كله نۀ لوستلے كيږى.
ka'mis me nən gan'ḍəley 'kigi?	Is my shirt being sewn today?	قميص مې نن گنډلے كيږى؟

āw, nən gan'ḍəley 'kigi.	Yes, it is being sewn today.	آو ، نن ګنډلے کېږی.
ka'pṛe tsə waxt win'zəle 'kigi?	When are the clothes being washed?	کپړې څهٔ وخت وينځلې کېږی؟
os win'zəle 'kigi.	They are being washed now.	اوس وينځلې کېږی.
ṭıkı'ṭuna 'čerta war-ka'wəley 'kigi?	Where are the tickets being given out?	ټيکټونه چرته ورکولے کېږی؟
pa de du'kān ke war-ka'wəley 'kigi.	They are being given out in this shop.	په دې دُوکان کښې ورکولے کېږی.
mung li'dəley 'kegu.	We are being seen.	مُونږ ليدلے کېږُو.
'tāso wa'həley 'kegəy?	Are you being hit?	تاسو وهلے کېږئ؟

NOTES:

1. In the passive voice the recipient of the action is the subject of the sentence.
2. Unlike English, the agent is not mentioned. For example, the phrase 'the clothes are washed by Mary' becomes 'the clothes are washed' in Pukhto. The verb indicates a change in the state of the clothes, not who is performing the action.

2. Compound transitive verbs are made passive by substituting the present tense forms of *ka'wəl* (کول).

zə dā 'ɣwaxa nə pre-ka'wəm.	I am not going to cut this meat.	زهٔ دا غوښه نهٔ پرې کوم.
os dā 'ɣwaxa nə-pre-ka'wəle 'kigi.	This meat is not being cut now.	اوس دا غوښه نهٔ پرې کولې کېږی.
zə'mā ka'mis os is'tri ka'wi?	Is he ironing my shirt now?	زما قميص اوس اِستری کوی؟
āw, stā ka'mis os is'tri 'kigi.	Yes, your shirt is being ironed now.	آو ، ستا قميص اوس اِستری کېږی.

3. Verbs whose roots end in a consonant are made passive by adding / -igi / يږی - (from the verb *ke'dəl* [کېدل].)

mo'ṭər de ǰoṛa'wəm.	I am fixing your car.	موټر دې جوړوم.
mo'tər de ǰo'rigi?	Is your car being fixed?	موټر دې جوړيږی؟

ha'ɣa os lar'gi māta'wi.	He is cutting the wood now.	هغه اوس لرګی ماتوی.
lar'gi mā'tigi.	The wood is being broken.	لرګی ماتېږی.
xānsā'ma 'ɣwaxa paxa'wi.	The cook is cooking the meat.	خانسامه غوښه پخوی.
'ɣwaxa pa'xigi.	The meat is being cooked.	غوښه پخېږی.
nən sıp'yāke swaza'wəm.	I am burning dung-cakes today.	نن سپیاکي سوزوم.
stā sıp'yāke swa'zigi?	Are your dung-cakes burning?	ستا سپیاکي سوزېږی؟
lati'fa 'wriǰe tayāra'wi.	Latifa is preparing the rice.	لطیفه وریژي تیاروی.
'wriǰe tayā'rigi.	The rice is being made ready.	وریژي تیارېږی.
tə me'wa həm xarsa'we?	Do you also sell fruit?	تهٔ مېوه هم خرڅوي؟
pa de ba'zār ke me'wa həm xar'sigi?	Is fruit also being sold in this market?	په دي بازار کښي مېوه هم خرڅېږی؟

A comparison of active and passive infinitive forms

Active verbs			Passive verbs		
ıstemāl-a'wəl	استعمالول	to use	ıstemāl-e'dəl	استعمالېدل	to be used
pax-a'wəl	پخول	to cook	pax-e'dəl	پخېدل	to be cooked
ta'yār-a'wəl	تیارول	to prepare	tayār-e'dəl	تیارېدل	to be made
ǰoṛ-a'wəl	جوړول	to fix	ǰoṛ-e'dəl	جوړېدل	to become fixed
xars-a'wəl	خرڅول	to sell	xars-e'dəl	خرڅېدل	to be sold
zoṛ-a'wəl	زړول	to make old	zoṛ-e'dəl	زړېدل	to be old
māt-a'wəl	ماتول	to break	māt-e'dəl	ماتېدل	to become broken

Changing intransitive verbs into transitive verbs

zə də xob-na pā'segəm.	I am getting up from sleep.	زهٔ د خوب نه پاڅېږم.
zə ha'ɣə də xob-na pāsa'wəm.	I am waking him up from sleep.	زهٔ هغهٔ د خوب نه پاڅوم.
zwe de 'wəle ḍer šar'migi?	Why is your son being so shy?	زوئ دي ولې ډېر شرمېږی؟

ˈwəle ˈhaɣa haˈlək šarmaˈwi?	Why is he shaming that boy?	ولې هغه هلک شرموی؟
zəˈmā lur ˈudə ˈkigi.	My daughter is going to sleep.	زما لُور اُودهٔ کېږی.
zə ˈxpəla lur ˈudə kaˈwəm.	I am putting my daughter to sleep.	زهٔ خپله لُور اُودهٔ کوم.
zə la tā-na ˈxəfa ˈkegəm.	I am getting upset at you.	زهٔ له تانه خفه کېږم.
tə ˈwəle mā xəˈfa kaˈwe?	Why are you making me upset?	تهٔ ولې ما خفه کوې؟

The prepositions *pa šān*, *ˈɣwonde*, *ˈləka*, *ˈdāse* and *pa rang* 'like', 'as'

په شان، غوندې، لکه، داسې، په رنګ

tə zəˈmā pa šān ye.	You are like me.	تهٔ زما په شان يې.
zwe de zəˈmā də zwi pa šān dey.	Your son is like mine.	زوئ دې زما د زوئ په شان دے.
də de qaˈləm pa šān nor qalamˈuna šta?	Do you have other pens like this one?	د دې قلم په شان نور قلمُونه شته؟
spogˈməy də nwar ˈɣwonde nə da.	The moon is not like the sun.	سپوږمۍ د نمر غوندې نهٔ ده.
spey me ˈləka də šərˈməx dey.	My dog is like a wolf.	سپے مې لکه د شرمخ دے.
ˈləka də ˈwəgi azmaˈri ḍoˈḍəy xoˈri.	He eats food like a hungry lion.	لکه د وږی ازمری ډوډۍ خوری.
ˈləka də lewaˈni xaˈbare kaˈwi.	He talks like a madman.	لکه د لېونی خبرې کوی.
stā lur zəˈmā də lur pa šān da.	Your daughter is like mine.	ستا لُور زما د لُور په شان ده.
haˈɣa stā pa rang dey.	He is like you.	هغه ستا په رنګ دے.
stā adətˈuna zəˈmā pa šān di.	Your habits are like mine.	ستا عادتُونه زما په شان دی.
stā pa məlk ke həm ˈdāse yəxˈni šta?	Is it as cold as this in your country?	ستا په ملک کښې هم داسې يخنی شته؟
wriǰe ba ˈwarla ˈdāse paˈxe.	Make (*lit.* cook) the rice like this.	وريژې به ورله داسې پخې.

NOTE:

Both *pa šān* (په شان) and *pa rang* (په رنګ) can describe similarities in behaviour or physical appearance.

Comprehension drill: Learning colours

Arrange several objects of different colours around the room and have your teacher instruct you to do different things with the objects dependent on their colour. For example, put a yellow pencil in your pocket! Throw the red ball to me!

u'di	blue	اودی
āsmā'ni	blue	آسمانی
batingə'ṇi	purple	باتینگنړی
banjā'ni	purple	بانجانی
tor	black	تور
xəṛ	grey	خړ
zyəṛ	yellow	زیړ

spin	white	سپین
sur	red	سُور
šin	blue or green	شین
gāzə'ri	purple	گازری
gulā'bi	pink	گلابی
naswā'ri	brown	نسواری

Modifiers:

light	ka'ča	کچه	spək	سپک
dark	pox	پوخ	tək	تک

Memorising moment

Colours in different genders and number

	m.s.	*m.pl.*	*f.s.*	*f.pl.*
black	tor تور	tor تور	'tora توره	'tore توري
grey	xəṛ خړ	xəṛ خړ	xṛa خړه	xṛe خړي
yellow	zyəṛ زیړ	zyəṛ زیړ	'zyəṛa زیړه	'zyəṛe زیړي
white	spin سپین	spin سپین	'spina سپینه	'spine سپیني
red	sur سُور	srə سرهٔ	sra سره	sre سري
green / blue	šin شین	šnə شنهٔ	šna شنه	šne شني

mata'luna

سودم ته شين دے.

so'dəm ta šin dey.

It's clear towards Sodum.[12]

تور سپے خړ سپے دواړه سپی دی.

tor spey xəṛ spey, 'dwāṛa spi di.

Black dog, grey dog, both are dogs.

د ګیدړ د سلو کالو ژوند نه د زمری یوه ورځ ژوند ښهٔ دے.

də gi'dəṛ də 'səlo 'kālo ǰwənd na, də zma'ri 'yəwa wrəz ǰwənd xə dey.

One day of a lion's life is better than one hundred years of a jackal.

Rahman Baba

خوب خندا په بې غمۍ کېږی، رحمانه.
چې په زړهٔ یې د یار غم وی څهٔ به خوب څهٔ به خندا کهٔ؟

xob xan'dā pa be ɣə'məy 'kigi, rah'māna.

če pa zṛə ye də yār ɣəm wi, tsə ba xob tsə ba xan'dā ka?

Sleep and laughter is found where there is an absence of sorrow, Rahman.

Where there is sorrow for a friend in one's heart, how can one sleep or laugh?

[12] Sodum is a village near Mardan.

Exercise for Lesson Thirteen

1. Change the following active sentences into passive ones:

   a. mung nən ˈḍera sodā ˈnə-āxlu. مونږ نن ډېره سودا نۀ اخلُو.

   ---

   b. tə ˈhara hafˈta ˈhaɣa saˈṛey ˈwine? تۀ هره هفته هغه سړے وينې؟

   ---

   c. ˈtāso xpəl lās swazaˈwəy! تاسو خپل لاس سوزوئ!

   ---

   d. mez āw kurˈsəy nən ǰoṛaˈwəm. مېز او کُرسۍ نن جوړوم.

Vocabulary for Lesson Thirteen

ıstemāleˈdəl	اِستعمالېدل		*v.i.*	to be used
uˈdi	اودی	*f.*	*adj.*	blue
batingəˈṇi	باتینګنړی	*f.*	*adj.*	purple
bād	باد	*m.*	*n.*	wind, breeze, air
bāˈrān	باران	*m.s.*	*n.*	rain
banjāˈni	بانجانی	*f.*	*adj.*	purple
bıǰˈli	بجلی	*f.s.*	*n.*	electricity
paxeˈdəl	پخېدل		*v.i.*	to be cooked; to become ripe
ˈparxa	پرخه	*f.s.*	*n.*	dew
parˈoskāl	پروسکال		*adv.*	last year
paˈrun	پرُون		*n.*	yesterday
pa rang	په رنګ		*prep.*	like, as
pa šān	په شانِ		*prep.*	like, as
pyāˈla	پیاله	*f.s.*	*n.*	cup
tək	تک	*m.*	*adj.*	dark (used with colours)
ˈtəka / ˈtəke	تکه / تکې	*f.*		
taˈyāraˈwəl	تیارول		*v.t.*	to prepare, to make ready
tez	تېز	*m.*	*adj.*	bright; loud; rude, heavy
ˈteza / ˈteze	تېزه / تېزې	*f.*		
ˈṭıkıṭ / ṭıkıˈṭuna	ټیکټ / ټیکټُونه	*m.*	*n.*	ticket
ǰoṛeˈdəl	جوړېدل		*v.i.*	to be made, to be built; to become fixed; to become well
čəleˈdəl	چلېدل		*v.i.*	to blow, to be in motion; to function
hāˈlat	حالت	*m.*	*n.*	state, condition, situation
xarābeˈdəl	خرابېدل		*v.i.*	to go bad, to be decayed, to be spoiled, to be ruined
xarseˈdəl	خرڅېدل		*v.i.*	to be sold

xəṛ	خړ	*m.*	*adj.*	grey [gray]
xṛa / xṛe	خړه / خړې	*f.*		
xob	خوب	*m.*	*n.*	sleep
ˈdāse	داسې		*prep.*	such, like, as
rɪxˈtyā	رښتيا	*f.*	*n.*	truth, true
ˈzbərg	زبرگ	*m.*	*n.*	saintly
zoṛaˈwəl	زړول		*v.t.*	to make old
zoṛeˈdəl	زړېدل		*v.i.*	to be old
zmaˈrey [azmaˈrey]	زمرے [ازمرے، امزرے]	*m.s.*	*n.*	lion
zyəṛ	زيړ	*m.*	*adj.*	yellow
ˈzyəṛa / ˈzyəṛe	زيړه / زيړې	*f.*		
sɪpˈyāke	سپياکې	*f.pl.*	*n.*	dung-cakes
swazaˈwəl	سوزول		*v.t.*	to burn (something)
šərˈməx	شرمخ	*m.s.*	*n.*	wolf
toˈfān	طوفان	*m.s.*	*n.*	storm
aˈdət / adətˈuna	عادت / عادتُونه	*m.*	*n.*	habit
ˈɣwaxa	غوښه	*f.s.*	*n.*	meat
ˈɣwonde	غوندې		*prep.*	like, as
fāyˈda	فائده	*f.s.*	*n.*	profit, use, advantage, benefit
ˈfəsəl / fəsəlˈuna	فصل / فصلونه	*m.*	*n.*	crop
kaˈpṛe	کپړې	*f.pl.*	*n.*	clothes
kaˈča	کچه	*m., f.*	*adj.*	light; raw
kuˈlər	کُولر		*n.*	room cooler
gāzəˈri	گازری	*f.*	*adj.*	purple
garˈmi	گرمی	*f.s.*	*n.*	heat, hot weather
gulāˈbi	گلابی	*f.*	*adj.*	pink
gaˈləy	ږلۍ	*f.*	*n.*	hailstones

ˈləka	لکه		*prep.*	like, as
loḍ ˈšeḍing	لوډ شيډنګ	*m.s.*	*n.*	load-shedding
lewaˈney	لېونے	*m.s.*	*n.*	madman .
mərg	مرګ	*m.*	*n.*	death
mamuˈli	معمُولی	*f.*	*adj.*	ordinary, usual
moˈsəm	موسم	*m.s.*	*n.*	weather, season
naswāˈri	نسواری	*f.*	*adj.*	brown
nwar	نمر	*m.*	*n.*	sun
warkaˈwəl	ورکول		*v.t.*	to give (to someone)
ˈwāwra	واؤره	*f.*	*n.*	snow
wro	ورو		*adv.*	slowly, slow
waˈreze	وريځې	*f.pl.*	*n.*	clouds
haˈwā	هوا	*f.*	*n.*	air, wind
ˈyəx	يخ	*m.*	*adj.*	cold; ice
ˈyəxa / ˈyəxe	يخه / يخې	*f.*		

swārlə'səm sa'bəq څوارلسم سبق

Lesson Fourteen

Dialogue fourteen: Directions

To the Post Office

L: ba'xana 'ɣwāṛəm, ḍākxā'na čerta da? Excuse me, where is the Post Office?	بخښنه غواړم، ډاکخانه چرته ده؟
H: 'tāso pyā'da zəy? Are you going on foot?	تاسو پیاده ځئ؟
L: āw, kə 'ləre 'nə-wi. Yes, if it's not far.	آو، کۀ لرې نۀ وی.
H: məxā'məx lāṛ ša, no byā pa čok ke gəs lās ta tāw ša byā 'halta pox'təna 'oka. Go straight and then turn left at the intersection, then ask there.	مخامخ لاړ شه، نو بیا په چوک کښې ګڅ لاس ته تاؤ شه بیا هلته پښتنه وکه.
L: 'tsumra 'ləre da? How far is it?	څومره لرې ده؟
H: 'ḍera 'ləre xo nə da, niz'de da. It's not very far, it's close.	ډیره لرې خو نۀ ده، نزدې ده.

NOTE:

☝ Today, as you go out, make a point of asking several people for directions to places you already know and use this dialogue. You can practice giving directions by looking for confirmation of what you already know about the location you are heading for. For example:

zə ḍākxā'ne ta zəm. ā'wal xi ta'raf-ta tāw šəm – dā ṭik da?	زۀ ډاکخانې ته ځم. اول ښی طرف ته تاؤ شم – دا ټیک ده؟

I'm going to the post office. First I turn right – is that correct?

Directions to your own house

☝ Ask someone who knows your house to give directions to it. Then write them here in phonetics or script and learn them. Invite a friend over.

____

____

____

____

Pronunciation drill

1. Illustrating / **xk** / ښک

dā xkər dey.	This is a horn.	دا ښکر دے.
dey xkār ka'wi.	He is hunting.	دے ښکار کوی.
dey 'xpəla mā'šuma xkwəla'wi.	He is kissing his daughter.	دے خپله ماشومه ښکلوی.
tə 'xkwəley 'xkāre.	You are looking handsome.	تهٔ ښکلے ښکارې.

2. Contrasting / **ṇ** / ڼ and / **n** / ن

ma'ṇe xwaxa'wəm.	I like apples.	منړې خوښوم.
ra'ṇa 'xkāri.	The light is coming.	رنړا ښکاری.
dā ka'ṇa da kə na?	Is she deaf or not?	دا کنړه ده کهٔ نه؟
kārxā'na 'banda da.	The factory is closed.	کارخانه بنده ده.

Imperatives

1. The imperative relates to commands, orders, directions, requests and prohibitions. Imperatives are formed by dropping the / -əl / (ل-) ending from a verb and adding the appropriate ending (see the charts below for examples). For example *pohe'dəl* (پوهېدل) meaning 'to know, to understand' in the imperative becomes:

singular	po'heša!	You understand!	پوه شه!
polite singular and plural	po'hešəy!	You understand!	پوه شئ!

The plural subject marker / -əy / (ئ -) might indicate that you are talking to several people, or that you are being polite to one person. For example:

'tāso 'halta 'o-gar-zəy! You walk there! تاسو هلته وګرځئ!

2. / o- / (written as -و in the examples below) may precede the verb to signal the imperative mood. It indicates that the order must be carried out right away. Note the following examples:

dā ha'lək wa'ha!	Hit this boy! (any time you want)	دا هلک وهه!
dā ha'lək 'o-waha!	Hit this boy! (now)	دا هلک ووهه!
'hara wrəz 'yəwa gu'ləy xo'ra!	Eat one pill every day!	هره ورځ یوه ګولۍ خوره!
dā gu'ləy nən 'o-xora!	Eat this pill today! (now)	دا ګولۍ نن وخوره!

3. Compound verbs with *kaˈwəl* (کول) have *kawa* (کوه) as an ending to show an order that continues on for some time. It does not take an / o- / (و-) prefix in all cases. For example:

ˈmina kaˈwa!	Show love! (continuously)	مينه کوه!
ˈmina ˈoka!	Show love! (now)	مينه وکه!
uˈbə war-kaˈwa!	Water it! (continuously)	اوبۀ ورکوه!
uˈbə ˈwar-ka!	Water it! (now)	اوبۀ ورکه!

4. The negative form is shown by the prefix / mə- / (مۀ-) meaning 'don't' as in the following:

dā ˈmə-kawa!	Don't do that!	دا مۀ کوه!

A summary of the imperative forms of verbs

Infinitive		Positive 2nd pn.s	Positive 2nd pn.p	Negative 2nd pn.s	Negative 2nd pn.p
to put in	āčaˈwəl اچول	ˈwāčawa واچوه	ˈwāčawəy واچوئ	ˈmə-āčawa مۀ اچوه	ˈmə-āčawəy مۀ اچوئ
to buy	āxɪsˈtəl اخستل	ˈwāxla واخله	ˈwāxləy واخلئ	ˈmə-āxla مۀ اخله	ˈmə-āxləy مۀ اخلئ
to wear	āɣosˈtəl اغوستل	ˈwāɣonda واغونده	ˈwāɣondəy واغوندئ	ˈmə-āɣonda مۀ اغونده	ˈmə-āɣondəy مۀ اغوندئ
to hear	āwreˈdəl اورېدل	ˈwawra واوره	ˈwawrəy واورئ	ˈmə-āwra مۀ اوره	ˈmə-āwrəy مۀ اورئ
to live (reside)	oseˈdəl اوسېدل [وسيدل]	ˈosa اوسه	ˈosəy اوسئ	ˈmə-osa مۀ اوسه	ˈmə-osəy مۀ اوسئ
		ˈosega اوسېږه	ˈosegəy اوسېږئ	ˈmə-osega مۀ وسېږه	ˈmə-osegəy مۀ اوسېږئ
to forgive	baˈxəl بخښل	ˈobaxa وبخښه	ˈobaxəy وبخښئ	ˈmə-baxa مۀ بخښه	ˈmə-baxəy مۀ بخښئ
to take (animate)	botˈləl بوتلل	ˈboza بوزه	ˈbozəy بوزئ	ˈmə-boza مۀ بوزه	ˈmə-bozəy مۀ بوزئ

Infinitive		Positive 2nd pn.s	Positive 2nd pn.p	Negative 2nd pn.s	Negative 2nd pn.p
to get up	pāseˈdəl پاڅېدل	ˈpāsa پاڅه	ˈpāsəy پاڅئ	ˈmə-pāsa مهٔ پاڅه	ˈmə-pāsəy مهٔ پاڅئ
to know (understand)	poheˈdəl پوهېدل	poˈheša پوهه شه	poˈhešəy پوهه شئ	ˈmə-pohega مهٔ پوهېږه	mə-pohegəy مهٔ پوهېږئ
to know (recognise)	peǰanˈdəḷ پېژندل	ˈopeǰana وپېژنه	ˈopeǰanəy وپېژنئ	ˈmə-peǰana مهٔ پېژنه	ˈmə-peǰanəy مهٔ پېژنئ
to go	tləl تلل	za ځه ˈlāṛša لاړ شه	zəy ځئ ˈlāṛšəy لاړ شئ	ˈmə-za مهٔ ځه	ˈmə-zəy مهٔ ځئ
to weigh	taˈləl تلل	ˈotala وتله	ˈotaləy وتلئ	ˈmə-tala مهٔ تله	ˈmə-taləy مهٔ تلئ
to drink	skəl څکل [څښل]	ˈoska وڅښه	ˈoskəy وڅښئ	ˈmə-ska مهٔ څښه	ˈmə-skəy مهٔ څښئ
to lie (down)	tsəmlasˈtəl څملاستل	ˈtsəmla څمله	ˈtsəmləy څملئ	ˈmə-tsəmla مهٔ څمله	ˈmə-tsəmləy مهٔ څملئ
to talk	xaˈbare kaˈwəl خبرې کول	xaˈbəre kaˈwa خبرې کوه	xaˈbəre kaˈwəy خبرې کوئ	xaˈbəre ˈməkawa خبرې مهٔ کوه	xaˈbəre ˈməkawəy خبرې مهٔ کوئ
to climb	xaˈtəl ختل	ˈoxeǰa وخېژه	ˈoxeǰəy وخېژئ	ˈmə-xeǰa مهٔ خېژه	ˈmə-xeǰəy مهٔ خېژئ
to eat	xoˈṛəl خوړل	ˈoxora وخوره	ˈoxorəy وخورئ	ˈmə-xora مهٔ خوره	ˈmə-xorəy مهٔ خورئ
to come	ratˈləl راتلل	ˈrāša راځه	ˈrāšəy راځئ	ˈmə-rāza مهٔ راځه	ˈmə-rāzəy مهٔ راځئ
to bring (inanimate)	rāwˈṛəl راوړل	ˈrāwṛa راوړه	ˈrāwṛəy راوړئ	ˈmə-rāwṛa مهٔ راوړه	ˈmə-rāwṛəy مهٔ راوړئ
to bring (animate)	rāwəsˈtəl راوستل	ˈrāwəla راوله	ˈrāwələy راولئ	ˈmə-rāwəla مهٔ راوله	ˈmə-rāwələy مهٔ راولئ

Infinitive		Positive 2nd pn.s	Positive 2nd pn.p	Negative 2nd pn.s	Negative 2nd pn.p
to arrive	rase'dəl رسېدل	'orasa ورسه	'orasəy ورسئ	'mə-[wa]rasa مۀ [و]رسه	'mə-[wa]rasəy مۀ [و]رسئ
to look at	ka'təl کتل	'ogora وګوره	'ogorəy وګورئ	'mə-gora مۀ ګوره	'mə-gorəy مۀ ګورئ
to sow	ka'rəl کرل	'okara وکره	'okarəy وکرئ	'mə-kara مۀ کره	'mə-karəy مۀ کرئ
to do	ka'wəl کول	'oka وکړه	'okəy وکړئ	'mə-kawa مۀ کوه	'mə-kawəy مۀ کوئ
to become	ke'dəl کېدل	ša شه	šəy شئ	'mə-ša مۀ شه	'mə-šəy مۀ شئ
to put	kexo'dəl کېښودل	'kegda ['keda] کېږده	'kegdəy ['kedəy] کېږدئ	'mə-ɪgda ['mə-keda] مۀ کېږده	'mə-ɪgdəy ['mə-kedəy] مۀ کېږدئ
to sit	kenas'təl کښېناستل	'kena کښېنه	'kenəy کښېنئ	'mə-kena مۀ کښېنه	'mə-kenəy مۀ کښېنئ
to walk	garze'dəl ګرځېدل	'ogarza وګرځه	'ogarzəy وګرځئ	'mə-garza مۀ ګرځه	'mə-garzəy مۀ ګرځئ
to sew	gan'ḍəl ګنډل	'oganḍa وګنډه	'ogandəy وګنډئ	'mə-ganda مۀ ګنډه	'mə-gandəy مۀ ګنډئ
to turn on	ləga'wəl لګول	'oləgawa ولګوه	'oləgawəy ولګوئ	'mə-ləgawa مۀ لګوه	'mə-ləgawəy مۀ لګوئ
to read (to yourself)	los'təl [lawas'təl] لوستل	'olwəla ['olwula] ولوله	'olwələy ['olwuləy] ولولئ	'mə-lwəla ['mə-lwula] مۀ لوله	'mə-lwələy ['mə-lwuləy] مۀ لولئ
to send	le'gəl لېږل	'olega ولېږه	'olegəy ولېږئ	'mə-lega مۀ لېږه	'mə-legəy مۀ لېږئ
to see	li'dəl لیدل	'owina ووینه	'owinəy ووینئ	'mə-wina مۀ وینه	'mə-winəy مۀ وینئ
to write	li'kəl لیکل	'olika ولیکه	'olikəy ولیکئ	'mə-lika مۀ لیکه	'mə-likəy مۀ لیکئ

Infinitive		Positive 2nd pn.s	Positive 2nd pn.p	Negative 2nd pn.s	Negative 2nd pn.p
to enter	nənawaˈtəl ننوتل	nənˈuza ننوزه	nənˈuzəy ننوزئ	ˈmə-nənuza مهٔ ننوزه	ˈmə-nənuzəy مهٔ ننوزئ
to catch	niˈwəl نیول	ˈonisa ونیسه	ˈonisəy ونیسئ	ˈmə-nisa مهٔ نیسه	ˈmə-nisəy مهٔ نیسئ
to exit	waˈtəl وتل	ˈuza اوځه	ˈuzəy وځئ	ˈmə-uza مهٔ وځه	ˈmə-uzəy مهٔ وځئ
to stop	odreˈdəl ودرېدل	ˈodrega ودرېږه	ˈodregəy ودرېږئ	ˈmə-odrega مهٔ ودرېږه	ˈmə-odregəy مهٔ ودرېږئ
to take (inanimate)	oˈṛəl وړل	ˈyosa یوسه	ˈyosəy یوسئ	ˈmə-oṛa مهٔ وړه	ˈmə-oṛəy مهٔ وړئ
to hit	waˈhəl وهل	ˈowaha ووهه	ˈowahəy ووهئ	ˈmə-waha مهٔ وهه	ˈmə-wahəy مهٔ وهئ
to extract	wisˈtəl ویستل [وبنکل]	ˈobāsa وباسه	ˈobāsəy وباسئ	ˈmə-obāsa مهٔ وباسه	ˈmə-obāsəy مهٔ وباسئ
to say	waˈyəl وئیل [ویل]	ˈowaya ووایه	ˈowayəy ووایئ	ˈmə-waya مهٔ وایه	ˈmə-wayəy مهٔ وایئ
to wash	winˈzəl وینځل	ˈowinza ووینځه	ˈowinzəy ووینځئ	ˈmə-winza مهٔ وینځه	ˈmə-winzəy مهٔ وینځئ

NOTES:

1. As mentioned above, when a positive command in the imperative mood is given, the prefix / o- / (و-) precedes the present tense verb stem. With prohibitions the negative prefix / mə- / (مهٔ-) precedes the verb. There are, of course, exceptions to this rule as shown in the chart above. Note especially the differences in the positive and negative forms of the verbs *kaˈwəl* (کول), *keˈdəl* (کېدل), *ratˈləl* (راتلل) and *tləl* (تلل).

2. The imperative mood is always directed at 'you' in the second person singular *tə* (تهٔ) or the second person plural *ˈtāso* (تاسو), but these pronouns are generally omitted unless there is some ambiguity or the speaker wants to add emphasis to the command.

3. In the imperative mood, the second person singular subject marker for verbs is / -a / (ه-). This differs from its present tense subject marker / -e / (ې -). For example,

tə 'halta 'ogarza!	You turn there!	تهٔ هلته وګرځه!
tə 'halta garze?	Are you walking there?	تهٔ هلته ګرځې؟

4. The plural subject marker for both the imperative mood and the present tense is / -əy / (ئ -).

Intransitive verbs in the imperative mood

1. Regular intransitive verbs:

tə də ka'rim sa'ra 'mə-garza!	Don't you walk with Karim! (s.)	تهٔ د کريم سره مهٔ ګرځه!
də špe ya'wāze 'mə-garzəy!	Don't walk alone at night! (pl.)	د شپې يواځې مهٔ ګرځئ!
də špe ya'wāze 'mə-garza!	Don't walk alone at night! (s.)	د شپې يواځې مهٔ ګرځه!
'dəlta 'mə-odrega!	Don't stand here! (s.)	دلته مهٔ ودرېږه!
pa klās ke xa'bare 'mə-kawa!	Don't talk in class! (s.)	په کلاس کښې خبرې مهٔ کوه!

2. Compound intransitive verbs:

nən špa 'dəlta 'pāte ša!	Stay here tonight! (*s.*)	نن شپه دلته پاتې شه!
māšu'māno, u'də šəy!	Children, go to sleep! (*pl.*)	ماشُومانو، اُودهٔ شئ!
'xore, 'mə-ɣosa 'kega!	Sister, don't be angry! (*s.*)	خورې، مهٔ غُصه کېږه!
'wrora, 'mə-xəfa 'kega!	Brother, don't be upset! (*s.*)	وروره، مهٔ خفه کېږه!
'kākā, 'mə-xəfa 'kega!	Uncle, don't be sad! (*s.*)	کاکا، مهٔ خفه کېږه!

NOTES:

1. The last two sentences could be made more respectful by making the imperatives plural with / -əy / (ئ -).
2. Positive commands take the stem / š- / (ش-), negatives take / keg- / (کېږ-).
3. Suffixes added for calling someone are:
   / -a / (ه -) for masculine nouns: *wror-a* (وروره)
   / -e / (ې -) for feminine nouns: *xor-e* (خورې)
   / -o / (و -) for plural nouns: *māšu'mān-o* (ماشُومانو)
4. The intransitive verb *ke'dəl* (کېدل) 'to become' does not take the prefix / o- / (و-) in the imperative mood. The negative prefix / mə- / (مهٔ-) 'don't', however, is still used, but it is prefixed directly to the adjective or noun instead of the verb.

Transitive verbs in the imperative mood

1. Regular transitive verbs:

nən xat ˈolika!	Write a letter today!	نن خط وليکه!
pa āngreˈzəy ke ˈmə-likəy!	Don't write in English!	په انګرېزئ کښې مۀ ليکئ!
dā kaˈmis nən ˈoganda!	Sew this shirt today!	دا قميص نن وګنډه!
byā dā ǰāˈme ˈowinzəy!	Then wash these clothes!	بيا دا جامې ووينځئ!
os axˈbār ˈmə-gora!	Don't read the paper now!	اوس اخبار مۀ ګوره!

2. Compound transitive verbs:

a. The imperative forms of *kaˈwəl* (کول) when used with nouns:

zər zər kār kaˈwa!	Do your work quickly!	زر زر کار کوه!
dā kamisˈuna isˈtri ka!	Iron these shirts!	دا قميصُونه اِسترى که!
pa skul ke ǰaˈgəṛe ˈmə-kawa!	Don't fight in school!	په سکُول کښې جګړې مۀ کوه!
ˈteze xaˈbare ˈmə-kawəy!	Don't talk loudly! (*pl.*)	تېزې خبرې مۀ کوئ!
ˈučəte xaˈbare ˈmə-kawa!	Don't talk so loudly! (*s.*)	اُوچتې خبرې مۀ کوه!

b. Imperative forms of transitive verbs derived from adjectives:

war band ka!	Shut the door!	ور بند که!
merabāˈni ˈoka kıṛˈkəy ˈmə-bandawa.	Please don't shut the window.	مِهربانى وکه کړکۍ مۀ بنده وه.
kıṛˈkəy koˈlaw ka!	Open the window!	کړکۍ کولاو که!
war ˈmə-kolaw-awa!	Don't open the door!	ور مۀ کولاووه!
nən dā kurˈsəy ˈǰoṛe ka!	Fix these chairs today!	نن دا کُرسۍ جوړې که!
kıṛˈkəy ˈdəlta ˈmə-ǰoṛawəy!	Don't build the window here!	کړکۍ دلته مۀ جوړوئ!
nən də ɣarˈme ḍoˈḍəy dəˈpāra səbˈzi paˈxa ka.	Cook vegetables for the mid-day meal today.	نن د غرمې ډوډۍ د پاره سبزى پخه که.
dā ˈɣwaxa də māˈxām ḍoˈḍəy dəˈpāra ˈmə-paxawa.	Don't cook this meat for the evening meal.	دا غوښه د ماښام ډوډۍ د پاره مۀ پخوه.

NOTES:

1. The / k- / (ک-) from *ka'wəl* (کول) is retained in positive commands, but dropped for negative ones.
2. Adjectives are inflected according to the object's gender and number. See the regular example (make it), and the irregular example (cook it) below:

a. Make it!

m.s.	ǰoṛ ka!	جوړ که!
m.pl.	ǰoṛ ka!	جوړ که!
f.s.	ˈǰoṛa ka!	جوړه که!
f.pl.	ˈǰoṛe ka!	جوړې که!

Try making these sentences, covering up the right-hand side.

bed kaṭ کټ

Make a bed! (*m.s.*) kaṭ ǰoṛ ka! کټ جوړ که!

Make beds! (*m.pl.*) kaˈṭuna ǰoṛ ka! کټُونه جوړ که!

slingshot linˈda لینده

Make a slingshot! (*f.s.*) linˈda ˈǰoṛa ka! لینده جوړه که!

Make slingshots! (*f.pl.*) linˈde ˈǰoṛe ka! لیندې جوړې که!

tea čay چائې

Make tea! (*f.pl.*) čay ˈǰoṛe ka! چائې جوړې که!

b. Cook it!

m.s.	pox ka!	پوخ که!
m.pl.	pāˈxə ka!	پاخهٔ که!
f.s.	paˈxa ka!	پخه که!
f.pl.	paˈxe ka!	پخې که!

Now try making sentences with some foods of different genders.
Have your helper say the food and you tell him or her to cook it!

m.s.	ṭeˈpər	ټیپر

f.s. (never *pl.*)	ˈɣwaxa	غوښه	
f.s.	muˈləy	مُولی	
f.s.	ḍoˈḍəy	ډوډی	
f.s.	səbˈzi	سبزی	
f.s.	aˈgəy	اګی	
f.pl.	ˈwriǰe	وريژې	
f.s.	čay [če]	چائې	
f.pl.	pəy	پئ	
f.pl.	uˈbə	اوبهٔ	

3. While Pukhtuns tend to be more direct in giving commands than English speakers, there are a number of polite ways in which to express orders, requests and directions. The addition of *merabāˈni* (مهربانی) to the start of the sentence, as in the request "Please don't shut the window" is one such way.

Verbs commonly used in the imperative mood

baˈzār ta lāṛša āw čiˈni ˈwāxla!	Go to the bazaar and get sugar!	بازار ته لاړ شه او چینی واخله!
biˈmār ye, nən skul ta ˈmə-za!	You are sick, don't go to school today!	بیمار يې، نن سکُول ته مهٔ ځه!
nən xpəl kār ˈxatəm ka!	Finish your work today!	نن خپل کار ختم که!
biǰˈli ˈoləgawa!	Turn on the electricity!	بجلی ولګوه!
biǰˈli ˈbala-ka!	Turn on the electricity!	بجلی بله که!
paˈkey band ka!	Turn off the fan!	پکے بند که!
pa ˈgarmo uˈbo dā kaˈpṛe ˈmə-winza!	Don't wash these cloths in hot water!	په ګرمو اوبو دا کپړې مهٔ وینځه!
melmāˈnə pa beˈṭək ke kenawa!	Seat the guests in the *betuk*!	میلمانهٔ په بیټک کښې کښېنوه!
dā kiˈtāb dəfˈtər ta ˈyosa!	Take this book to the office!	دا کتاب دفتر ته یوسه!

merabā'ni 'oka, zə'mā salā'muna ha'ɣa ta 'o-rasawa!	Please give my salams to him!	مِهرباني وکه زما سلامُونه هغه ته ورسوه!
'ləre ša!	Go away!	لرې شه!
čəp ša!	Be quiet!	چپ شه!
'səbər 'oka!	Be patient!	صبر وکه!
bač ša!	Save yourself!	بچ شه!
'šāta ša!	Get to the back!	شاته شه!
'āxwā ša!	Go there!	اخوا شه!
šor 'mə-kawa!	Don't make a noise!	شور مۀ کوه!
'dexwā ša!	Come here!	دېخوا شه!
čay 'oska!	Drink tea!	چائې اوڅښه!
'mənḍe 'mə-waha!	Don't run!	منډې مۀ وهه!
ḍo'ḍəy 'oxora!	Eat the food!	ډوډۍ وخوره!

NOTE:
The *be'ṭək* (بېټهک) is the men's guest room.

Some polite expressions

'tāso 'kenəy!	Sit down!	تاسو کښېنئ!
xəfa 'nə-šəy, 'tāso ləg ınte'zār 'okəy.	Don't be upset, please wait a little bit.	خفه نۀ شئ، تاسو لږ اِنتظار وکئ.
rā'zəy! zə os 'čerta tləm, xo yo sāt də'pāra 'kenəy.	Come in! I was just going somewhere, but sit down for a little while.	راځئ! زۀ اوس چرته تلم خو يو ساعت د پاره کښېنئ.

NOTE:
The last sentence is useful if you were leaving to go somewhere else at the moment a guest arrives.

Comprehension drill: Asking and giving directions

Learn the common landmarks around your area that people use for direction-giving.

☝ Try practising the words in the following chart with your teacher. Start by talking about an area you are familiar with, then move to something that is less familiar. Use a picture or a map to help you.

to the right	xi lās ta	ښى لاس ته	it's this road	dā lār da	دا لار ده

mosque	ǰu'māt	جُماعت
to the left	gəs lās ta	ګڅ لاس ته
a river	dā sind dey	دا سیند دے
go straight	mə'xā-məx zəy	مخامخ ځئ
park, orchard, garden	bāɣ	باغ
straight	neɣ	نېغ
	'sida	سیده
shopping centre, plaza	'plāza	پلازه
go 100 paces	sɪl qa'dəma lāṛ ša	سل قدمه لاړ شه
it's a narrow street	'tanga ku'tsa da	تنګه کوڅه ده
turn	tāw ša	تاؤ شه
wide road	plən sa'ṛək	پلن سړک
down	'xkəta	ښکته
up	'bara	بره
pole (electricity, telephone, etc.)	stən	ستن
bridge	pul	پُل

Memorising moment

mata'luna

چې ځې ځې ابازو له به راځې.

če ze ze ābā'zo la ba rā'ze.

However far you go you will come back to Abazai.

هله به خبر شې چې تارو جبې له ورشې.

'ala ba xa'bər še če 'tāru 'ǰɪbe la 'warše.

When you go to Taru Jabba you will know what to do.[13]

خپل بد د ولو مینځ وی.

xpəl bəd də 'wəlo menz wi.

Your own weakness lies between the shoulder blades.

---

[13] Taru Jabba is a small town on the outskirts of Peshawar that was known for its bandits and robbers. There are many regional versions of this proverb. One of the most common is: هله به خبر شې چې تالو ژبې له ورشې. (God knows when your tongue sticks to your palate). Discuss with local friends which variant they use and what they understand by it.

نېکي برباد ګُناه لازم.

ne'ki bar'bād gu'nā lā'zim.

Goodness went in vain and I am blamed of sin.

چې په زړهٔ کښې دې څهٔ عېب نهٔ وی رحمانه

ښکُلې مخ ته په کتو کښې ګُناه نشته.

če pa zṛə ke de tsə eb nə wi rah'māna

'xkwəle məx ta pa ka'to ke gu'nā 'ništa

If there is no flaw in your heart Rahman,

Then it's no sin to look at a pretty face.

NOTE:

The verb form de (دې) is used in prayers to mean 'may'. For example,

May God forgive you! xo'dey de 'obaxa! خُدایٔ دې وبخښه!

Exercises for Lesson Fourteen

1. Complete these sentences with the correct imperative verb form:

a. tə ba'zār ta __________________.	tləl
تهٔ بازار ته __________________.	تلل
b. pa ba'zār ke 'mə __________________.	garze'dəl
په بازار کښې مهٔ __________________.	ګرځېدل
c. 'wriǰe __________________.	paxa'wəl
وریژې __________________.	پخول
d. kur'səy də'nəna __________________!	o'ṛəl
کُرسۍ دننه __________________!	وړل
e. 'luxi __________________!	win'zəl
لوښی __________________!	وینځل

2. Make a list of sequential commands to perform several common tasks you need done. Write them down, learn them and then try them out.

Vocabulary for Lesson Fourteen

ˈāxwā	اخوا		*adv.*	that way, over there
ɪnteˈzār	اِنتظار	*m.*	*n.*	waiting; expectation, anticipation
ɪnteˈzār kaˈwəl	اِنتظار کول	*m.*	*v.t.*	to wait
bač	بچ	*m.*	*n.*	saved
baˈxəl	بخښل		*v.t.*	to forgive, to pardon
baˈxana	بخښنه	*f.*	*n.*	pardon, forgiveness
ˈbara	بره		*adj.*	up
bandaˈwəl	بندول		*v.t.*	to close, to shut, to lock, to turn off, to lock-up
beˈṭək	بیټهک	*m.*	*n.*	guest room
poxˈtəna	پښتنه	*f.s.*	*n.*	question, inquiry
paˈkey	پکے	*m.s.*	*n.*	fan
ˈplāza	پلازه	*f.*	*n.*	shopping centre, plaza
pyāˈda	پیاده		*adj.*	on foot
taˈləl	تلل		*v.t.*	to weigh
ˈtanga	تنگه	*f.s.*	*adj.*	tight, narrow
ǰaˈgəṛa	جگړه	*f.*	*n.*	fight
čəp	چپ		*adj.*	silent, quiet
čok	چوک	*m.s.*	*n.*	intersection
xaˈtəl	ختل		*v.i.*	to climb, to mount, to board
ˈdexwā	دېخوا		*adv.*	this way, this direction
ḍākxāˈna	ډاکخانه	*f.s.*	*n.*	post office
zər	زر		*adv.*	soon, quickly, hurriedly
səbˈzi	سبزی	*m.s.*	*n.*	vegetables
stən / ˈstəne	ستن / ستني	*f.*	*n.*	needle, injection; pillar, pole (electricity, etc.)
saˈṛək / saṛəˈkuna	سړک / سړکُونه	*m.*	*n.*	road

salāˈmuna	سلامُونه	*m.pl.*	*n.*	greeting, salutation, regards
ˈšāta	شاته		*prep.*	at the back, towards the back
xkār kaˈwəl	ښکار کول		*v.t.*	to hunt
xkāreˈdəl	ښکارېدل		*v.i.*	to look like, to appear
ˈxkəta	ښکته		*adj.*	down
xkər	ښکر	*m.*	*n.*	horn
xkwəlaˈwəl	ښکلول		*v.t*	to kiss
ˈsəbər	صبر	*m.*	*n.*	patience, endurance
ɣarˈme	غرمې		*adj., n.*	midday, noon
qaˈdəm / qadəmˈuna	قدم / قدمُونه	*m.*	*n.*	step, pace
ˈkākā	کاکا	*m.*	*n.*	uncle (father's brother)
kaˈrəl	کرل		*v.t.*	to sow, to plant
kuˈtsa / kuˈtse	کوڅه / کوڅې	*f.*	*n.*	alley, street
kexoˈdəl	کېښودل		*v.t.*	to put, to place
lār / ˈlāre	لار / لارې	*f.*	*n.*	road, path, way
ˈləre	لرې		*adj.*	far, distant, far away, remote
ləgaˈwəl	لګول		*v.t.*	to connect, to affix; to turn on
leˈgəl	لېږل		*v.t.*	to send, to dispatch
linˈda	لینده	*f.s.*	*n.*	slingshot
guˈləy	ګولۍ	*f.*	*n.*	pill, tablet; bullet
məxāˈməx	مخامخ	*m.*	*adj.*	facing, opposite; straight ahead
ˈmənḍa waˈhəl	منډه وهل		*comp. v.t.*	to run
nizˈde	نژدې		*adj.*	near
neɣ	نېغ	*m.*	*adj.*	straight, stiff, upright, erect
wisˈtəl	ویستل [وښکل]		*v.t.*	to remove, to extract
yaˈwāze	یواځې		*adv.*	alone

pinzələ'səm sa'bəq	پينځلسم سبق

Lesson Fifteen

Dialogue fifteen: Public transportation

L:	dā 'gāḍey xār ta zi? Is this vehicle going to the city?	دا ګاډے ښار ته ځي؟
H:	na, nə zi. No, it's not going.	نه، نۀ ځي.
L:	də xār 'gāḍey də kəm zay na 'zi? Where does the city bus go from?	د ښار ګاډے د کُوم ځائ نه ځي؟
H:	ogora! də xār 'gāḍey 'halta 'odrigi. Look! The city bus stops over there.	وګوره! د ښار ګاډے هلته ودرېږي.
L:	ba'xana 'ɣwārəm, zə nāba'ləd yım, ṭawn ta kəm 'gāḍey zi? Excuse me, I don't know my way around, which bus goes to Town?	بخښنه غواړم، زۀ نا بلد يم، ټاون ته کُوم ګاډے ځي؟
H:	dəlta odrega, yo tso 'mınṭa pas ba 'rāši. Stand here, it will come in a few minutes.[14]	دلته ودرېږه، يوڅو مېنټه پس به راشي.
L:	xa, merabā'ni . OK, thanks.	ښه، مِهرباني.
L:	'xāra 'pore tsumra karā'ya da? How many rupees is it to the city?	ښاره پورې څومره کرايه ده؟
H:	'sıraf šıl ru'pəy. Only twenty rupees.	صرف شل روپۍ.
L:	kə ṭek'si ke kenəm no tso ru'pəy ba wāxli? If I go in a taxi, how much will it cost?	کۀ ټکسی کښې کښېنم نو څو روپۍ به واخلي؟
H:	āt'ya ru'pəy. Eighty rupees.	اتيا روپۍ.

☝ **Men:** Spend a day riding around on public transport in your area. Listen for the names of destinations called out by conductors. Work out the routes. Later, confirm your findings with your helper.

☝ **Ladies:** This week become an expert on rickshaws or whatever transport is appropriate for you where you are. Learn the names of the useful landmarks and roads that rickshaw drivers know for directions.

---

[14] Like many English loan words, the Pukhto word for 'minute' is not uniform. Different speakers use it in a variety of forms.

Pronunciation drill

How are you doing at remembering and pronouncing the names of your new friends correctly? Here are some common names to practice with your helper. Knowing the meanings may help you remember them too.

1. Ladies' names:

Gulnar Begum	gulnār begəm	گلنار بیگم
Gulnaz	gulnāz	گُلناز
Gul Sanga	gul sānga	گُل ښانگه
Chaman Gul	čaman gul	چمن گُل
Shabnam	šabnam	شبنم
Shama	šama	شمع
Noor Jahan	nur ǰahān	نُورجهان
Noreen Gul	norin gul	نورین گُل
Naseem Begum	nasim begəm	نسیم بیگم
Shamim Akhtar	šamim axtar	شمیم اختر
Sakena	sakina	سکینه
Salma	salmā	سلمیٰ
Saleha	sāleha	صالحه
Taira	tāira	طائره
Saira	sāira	سائره
Sajida	sāǰida	ساجده
Bagh Aram	bāɣ ārām	باغ آرام
Rabeya	rābiya	رابعه
Parween	parwin	پروین
Qamro Jan	qamro ǰān	قمروجان
Kalsom	kalsom	کلثوم
Saeda	saida	سعیده
Sherbano	šerbāno	شیربانو
Zinat	zinat	زینت
Zahida	zāhida	زاهده
Rukhsana	ruxsāna	رُخسَانه
Farkhanda	farxanda	فرخنده
Bibi Fozia	bibi fozia	بی بی فوزیه
Bibi Ruqaia	bibi ruqaia	بی بی رقیه

Bakhtawera	baxtawəra	بختوره
Bibi	bibi	بی بی
Bibi Taira	bibi tāira	بی بی طائره
Halema Bibi	halima bibi	حلیمه بی بی
Khudija Bibi	xudiǰa bibi	خدیجه بی بی
Bibi Fatema	bibi fātima	بی بی فاطمه
Maryam Naz	maryam nāz	مریم ناز
Sultana	sultāna	سُلطانه
Hajira	hāǰira	هاجِره
Dilshad	dilšād	دلشَاد
Taj Mahal	tāǰ mahal	تاج محل
Bakht Taja	baxt tāǰa	بخت تاجه
Taj Begum	taǰ begəm	تاج بیگم
Khandana	xāndāna	خندانه
Jamila	ǰamila	جمیله
Jahan Ara	ǰahān āra	جهان آرا
Bakht Zaiba	baxt zaiba	بخت زیبا
Noor Mahal	nur mahal	نُور محل
Rehana	rehāna	ریحانه
Sabira	sābira	صابره
Salima	salima	سلیمه
Shabana	šabāna	شبانه
Shagufta	šagufta	شگُفته
Farizada	farizada	فری زاده
Badri Jamala	badri ǰamāla	بدری جماله
Jam-e Shereen	ǰāmi šherin	جامِ شیرین
Yasmin	yāsmin	یاسمین

2. Men's names:

Zrwar Khan	zṛwar xān	زړۀ ورخان
Abdul Wali	abdul wali	عبدالولی
Imtiaz Ahmad	imtiaz ahmad	امتیاز احمد
Fazal Khaliq	fazal xāliq	فَضل خالق
Zyarat Gul	zyarāt gul	زیارت گَل
Taza Gul	tāza gul	تازه گُل
Juma Gul	ǰuma gul	جُمعه گُل
Hazrat Hussain	hazrat husain	حضرت حُسین
Habib ur Rahman	habib ur rahmān	حبیب الرحمان
Jabir Khan	ǰābir xān	جابِرخان
Faqir Khan	faqir xān	فقیر خان
Gulab Gul	gulāb gul	گلاب گُل
Khaista Rakhman	xāista raxmān	خائسته رخمان
Khurshid	xuršid	خورشید
Muhammad Rafiq	muhamad rafiq	محمد رفیق
Sadiq	sādiq	صادِق
Yaqub	yāqub	یعقوب
Yunas	yunas	یُونس
Zahur	zahur	ظهور
Daud	dāwud	داؤد
Tahir	tāhir	طاهر
Itbar Gul	itbār gul	اعتبار گُل
Inzar Gul	inzər gul	اینځر گُل
Khan Zada	xān zāda	خان زاده
Gul Zada	gul zāda	گُل زاده
Gul Farosh	gul faroš	گُل فروش
Mian Said Karim	mian said karim	میاه سید کریم
Khan Nawab	xān nawāb	خان نواب
Khan Bader	xān bādər	خان بهادر
Mian Said Ali	mian said ali	میاه سید علی
Bahroz	bahroz	بهروز

Dildar Shah	dildār šāh	دِلدار شاه
Amir Jan	amir ǰān	امیرجان
Janbaz	ǰanbāz	جانباز
Behram Khan	behrām xān	بهرام خان
Dolat Khan	dulat xān	دولت خان
Akbar Khan	akbar xān	اکبر خان
Zahid	zāhid	زاهِد
Fazal Hussain	fazal husain	فضل حسین
Fazal Wahid	fazal wāhid	فضل واحد
Shahid Ullah	šāhid ula	شاهدالله
Karim Ullah	karim ula	کریم الله
Zafar Ali	zafar ali	ظفر علی
Said Ullah	said ula	سید الله
Abdul Ghafur	abdul ɣafur	عبدُالغفور
Jamaludin	ǰamāludin	جمال الدین
Sardar Ali	sardār ali	سردار علی

Abdul Qayyum	abdul qayum	عبدالقيوم
Abdul Kabir	abdul kabir	عبدالكبير
Abdul Baqi	abdul bāqi	عبدالباقى
Umar Hayat	umar hayāt	عُمر حيات
Ehsan Elahi	ihsān ilāhi	احسان الٰهى
Fakhrudin	faxrudin	فخرالدين
Ghazi	ɣāzi	غازى
Qazi	qāzi	قاضى
Qamar Din	qamar din	قمر دين
Abdurrashid	abdurašid	عبدالرشيد
Karim Bakhash	karim baxaš	كريم بخش
Khuda Bakhash	xudā baxaš	خُدا بخش
Bakht Bedar	baxt bedār	بخت بيدار

The future tense

There are two forms of the future tense, each with a slightly different meaning. In everyday speech the difference is often ignored and the distinction is made by intonation of voice rather than verb forms.

1. Imperfective:

This implies a continuous action: 'I will be going, seeing, finishing', etc. The verb takes present endings and adds the participle *ba* (به). For example,

zə ba ha'ɣa sa'bā 'winəm.	I will be seeing him tomorrow.	زۀ به هغه صبا وينم.
tə ba sa'bā 'čerta ze?	Where will be you going tomorrow?	تۀ به صبا چرته ځې؟
zə ba də xpəl dost 'kara zəm.	I will be going to my friend's house.	زۀ به د خپل دوست کره ځم.
dey ba nən špa kār kawi?	Will he be working tonight?	دے به نن شپه کار کوى؟
āw, nən špa ba kār ka'wi.	Yes, he will be working tonight.	آو، نن شپه به کار کوى.
tə ba 'kəla kār šo'ro ke [kawe]?	When will you be starting work?	تۀ به کله کار شروع کې؟
dwa 'wrəze pas ba kār šo'ro kəm [kawəm].	I will be starting work after two days.	دوه ورځې پس به کار شروع کوم.
'kəla ba dā kār xlās ke?	When will you be finishing this work?	کله به دا کار خلاص کې؟
nən ba ye xlās kəm.	I will be finishing this today.	نن به يې خلاص کوم.

NOTE:

The verb ending *kəm* (کوم) is interchangeable with *kom* (کوم). The use of *kom* (کوم) adds more emphasis.

2. Perfective

In the perfective future tense the action is delimited or complete, that is, it is of short duration.

zə ba ha'ɣa 'o-winəm.	I will see him.	زهٔ به هغه ووینم.
zə ba ha'ɣa 'o-wahəm.	I will hit him.	زهٔ به هغه ووهم.

Transitive verbs in the perfective future

Many verbs add an / o- / (-و) prefix:

tə ba nən špa xa'tuna 'olike?	Will you write letters tonight?	تهٔ به نن شپه خطُونه ولیکې؟
āw, begāla ba ye 'likəm.	Yes, I will write them tonight.	آو، بېګاله به يې ولیکم.
dey ba sakāl[15] ɣə'nəm 'okari?	Will he sow wheat this year?	دے به سخکال غنم وکری؟
pa de hafta ke ba ha'ɣa 'owine?	Will you see him this week?	په دې هفته کښې به هغه ووینې؟
āw, 'o-ba ye 'winəm.	Yes, I will see him.	آو، وبه يې وینم.
'kəla ba war-ta xat 'olege?	When will you send him the letter?	کله به ورته خط ولیږې؟
sa'bā ba war-ta 'olegəm.	I will send the letter tomorrow.	صبا به ورته ولیږم.
nən ba ka'pṛe 'owinze?	Will you wash clothes today?	نن به کپړې ووینځې؟
na, nən ba o'nə winzəm.	No, I will not wash them today.	نه، نن به ونهٔ وینځم.
zə ba yo saṛey 'otəxta'wəm.	I will kidnap one man.	زهٔ به یو سړے وتښتوم.
zə ba stā gre'wān 'ošılawəm.	I will tear your shirt.	زهٔ به ستا ګریوان وشلوم.
zə ba dā 'loba 'ogaṭəm.	I will win this match.	زهٔ به دا لوبه وګټم.
'tāso ba dā 'loba o'nə-gaṭəy.	You will not win the match.	تاسو به دا لوبه ونهٔ ګټئ.
xor ba me or 'oləgawi.	My sister will light the fire.	خور به مې اور ولګوی.

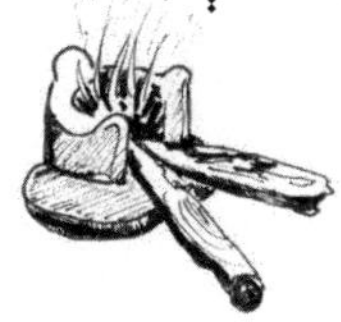

NOTE:

In everyday speech the / o- / (-و) prefix is sometimes dropped from sentences, this is especially so in the negative. For example,

zə ba dā ki'tāb o-nə-legəm. *or*	I will not send this book.	زهٔ به دا کتاب ونهٔ لیږم. (یا)
zə ba dā ki'tāb 'nə-legəm.		زهٔ به دا کتاب نهٔ لیږم.

---

[15] The / x / (خ) in the phrase سخکال (this year) is not pronounced, hence *sakāl*.

Some transitive verbs that take the / o- / (و-) prefix:

to send	āstaˈwəl	استول
to invite	baˈləl	بلل
to make flow	bayaˈwəl	بهیول
to inflate	paṛsaˈwəl	پړسول
to make shiny	pṛaqaˈwəl	پړقول
to kidnap	təxtaˈwəl	تښتول
to chase	zɣalaˈwəl	ځغلول
to hang	zwaṛandaˈwəl	ځوړندول
to drive	čəlaˈwəl	چلول
to send for	rābaˈləl	رابلل
to send (from here)	rāstaˈwəl	راستول
to shake	rapaˈwəl	رپول
to deliver	rasaˈwəl	رسول
to roll up	irɣaṛaˈwəl	رغړول
to humiliate	šarmaˈwəl	شرمول

to tear	šɪlaˈwəl	شلول
to want	ɣoxˈtəl	غوښتل
to look at	kaˈtəl	کتل
(present root is *gor-* گور-)		
to sow	kaˈrəl	کرل
to gain	gaˈṭəl	گټل
to take someone for a walk	garzaˈwəl	گرځول
to turn on	ləgaˈwəl	لگول
to send	leˈgəl	لېږل
to see	liˈdəl	لیدل
(present root is *win-* وین-)		
to write	liˈkəl	لیکل
to read	losˈtəl	لوستل
to wash	winˈzəl	وینځل
to boil	yešaˈwəl	یشول

Intransitive verbs in the perfective future tense

Here are some verbs that take the / o- / (و-) prefix:

to swell (up)	paṛseˈdəl	پړسېدل
to shine	pṛaqeˈdəl	پړقېدل
to run away	təxteˈdəl	تښتېدل
to drip	saseˈdəl	څڅېدل
to climb	xaˈtəl	ختل
to move	xwazeˈdəl	خوځېدل
to be scattered	xwareˈdəl	خورېدل
to shake	rapeˈdəl	رپېدل
to arrive	raseˈdəl	رسېدل
to roll along	irɣaṛeˈdəl	رغړېدل

to move	zɣaleˈdəl	زغلېدل
to be shy	šarmeˈdəl	شرمېدل
to be spread	ɣwaṛeˈdəl	غوړېدل
to be troubled	kaṛeˈdəl	کړېدل
to walk	garzeˈdəl	گرځېدل
to tremble	laṛzeˈdəḷ	لړزېدل
to be fixed	ləgeˈdəl	لگېدل
to tumble down	naṛeˈdəl	نړېدل
to enter	nənawaˈtəl	ننوتل
to be boiled	yešeˈdəl	یشېدل

Example sentences:

zə'mā xeta ba 'oparṣigi.	My stomach will swell up.	زما خېټه به وپړسيږي.
zmung čət ka'ča dey āw pa bā'rān ke ba 'osasi.	Our roof is poor quality and will leak in the rain.	زمونږ چت کچه دے او په باران کښې به وڅاڅي.
'haɣa siz če sa'fā ši, no 'o-ba pṛa'kigi.	The thing that is clean will shine.	هغه څيز چې صفا شي، نو وبه پړقيږي.

☝ Make more sentences from the list of verbs above.

____

____

____

____

The verb *šwəl* 'to become' in the future tense شول

1. In the perfective future the infinitive form for the verb *kedəl* (کېدل) 'to become' is *šwəl* (شول). The use of *šwəl* (شول) indicates a definite future tense. For example contrast:

ba 'xəfa 'kigi.	You will be upset	به خفه کيږې.
ba 'xəfa ši.	She will be upset.	به خفه شي.

The first sentence indicates a definite future action, whereas the second sentence communicates some doubt as to whether or not the action will take place.

2. The perfective verb stem for *šwəl* (شول) is / š / (ش) in the future tense. The verb endings are:

	singular		**plural**	
1st	šəm	شم	šu	شُو
2nd	še	شې	šəy	شئ
3rd	ši	شي	ši	شي

Example sentences:

ınšāl'la, ḍāk'ṭər ba še.	God willing, you will become a doctor.	انشاءالله، ډاکټر به شې.
ınšāl'la, šəm ba.	God willing, I will.	انشاءالله، شم به.

haɣ'wi ba zmung na 'xəfa ši?	Will they become upset with us?	هغوی به زمونږ نه خفه شی؟
na, 'xəfa ba nə-ši.	No, they won't get upset.	نه، خفه به نهٔ شی.
'tāso ba xo'šāla šəy?	Will you be happy?	تاسو به خوشحاله شئ؟
āw, xo'šāla ba šu.	Yes, we will be happy.	آو، خوشحاله به شو.
stā plār ba ǰoṛ ši?	Will your father be healed?	ستا پلار به جوړ شی؟
āw, ɪnšāl'la ǰoṛ ba ši.	Yes, God willing he will be healed.	آو، انشاءالله جوړ به شی.
ḍo'ḍəy ba os pa'xa ši?	Will the food be cooked now?	ډوډۍ به اوس پخه شی؟
āw, pa'xa ba ši.	Yes it will be cooked.	آو، پخه به شی.
čay ba os 'ǰoṛe ši.	Tea will be made now.	چائې به اوس جوړې شی.
zə'mā 'newe ga'ṛəy ba pe'dā ši?	Will my new watch be found?	زما نوې گړۍ به پیدا شی؟
'mə-xəfa kega, pe'dā ba ši.	Don't be upset, it will be found.	مهٔ خفه کېږه پیدا به شی.
nən ba zə'mā ka'pṛe is'tri ši?	Will my clothes be ironed today?	نن به زما کپړې اِستری شی؟
be 'ɣəma ša! is'tri ba ši.	Don't worry! They will be ironed.	بې غمه شه! اِستری به شی.

Intransitive verbs that do not take the / o- / prefix — و-

There are a number of verbs that do not take the / o- / (و-) prefix. These verbs often have two distinct roots. It may be helpful to think of them as 'strong' and 'weak' forms. Again the distinction may be ignored in everyday speech. For example

to understand:

'strong' form of the verb: *pohe'dəl* (پوهېدل) :

zə ba po'higəm.	I will understand. (Whenever you say it)	زهٔ به پوهېږم.

'weak' form of the verb: *po'he šwəl* (پوهه [پوئ] شول) :

zə ba ˈpoha šəm.	I may understand. (Some doubt)	زۀ به پوهه شم.

Some intransitive verbs that do not take the / o- / (-و) prefix in the perfective future are:

	'Strong' form		**'Weak' form**	
to go to sleep	u'də ke'dəl	اُودۀ کېدل	u'də šwəl	اُودۀ شول
to hide oneself	pəṭe'dəl	پټېدل	pəṭ šwəl	پټ شول
to be born	pe'dā ke'dəl	پېدا کېدل	pe'dā šwəl	پېدا شول
to be(come) ready	tayāre'dəl	تيارېدل	ta'yār šwəl	تيار شول
to start out	rawāne'dəl	روانېدل	ra'wān šwəl	روان شول
to appear	xkāre'dəl	ښکارېدل	xkā'ra šwəl	ښکاره شول
to get down	kuze'dəl	کُوزېدل	kuz šwəl	کُوز شول
to be broken	māte'dəl	ماتېدل	māt šwəl	مات شول
to be known	mālume'dəl	معلومېدل	mā'lum šwəl	معلُوم شول

☝ Generate some sentences with your helper using these verbs.

____

____

____

____

Transitive verbs that do not take the / o- / prefix in the future

1. As with intransitive verbs, these transitive verbs occur in 'strong' and 'weak' forms, and they have slightly different meanings in the future tenses. For example:

to cause to understand:

The perfective future *pohakṛəl* (پوهه کړل) implies strong force:

zə ba xpəl sṭu'danṭ 'poha kṛəm. [kəm][16]	I will make my student understand.	زۀ به خپل سټُوډنټ پوهه کړم [کم].

[16] In formal writing the letter / ṛ / (ړ) should always be present in the written form of the verbs *kṛi* (کړي), *kṛəm* (کړم), *kṛe* (کړې), etc, even though it is often omitted in everyday speech.

The imperfective future *po'he šwəl* (پوئ شول) is weaker:

zə ba xpəl tā'lıbıləm poha'wəm.	I will make my student understand (i.e. inform my student).	زهٔ به خپل طالبعلم پوهه وم.

NOTE:

ka'wəl (کول) and *kṛəl* (کړل) carry the same meaning.

2. There are verbs that do not normally take the / o- / (و-) prefix, but may add it before the verb ending. For example:

to ask *ta'pos ka'wəl*: تپوس کول

In the perfective future the / o- / (و-) prefix changes *ta'pos kṛəl* (تپوس کړل) to *ta'pos o'kṛəl* (تپوس وکړل). For example,

zə ba stā də plār na ta'pos o'kəm. ['okṛəm]	I will ask your father.	زهٔ به ستا د پلار نه تپوس وکم. [وکړم]

3. There are verbs that sometimes take the / o- / (و-) prefix to show that an action is limited and immediate, as in a one-off event. To show continuous action, the same verb uses a *ka'wəl* (کول) ending without the / o- / (و-) prefix. For example,

ha'ɣa ba nən špa kār oki?	Will he work tonight? (This night only)	هغه به نن شپه کار وکی؟
ha'ɣa ba nən špa kār kawi?	Will he be working tonight? (As usual)	هغه به نن شپه کار کوی؟

Some transitive verbs that do not take the / o- / (و-) prefix in the perfective future are:

	'Strong' form		'Weak' form	
to vomit	ul'ṭəy kṛəl	اُلټی کړل	ul'ṭəy ka'wəl	اُلټی کول
to cause to sleep	u'də kṛəl	اُودهٔ کړل	u'də ka'wəl	اُودهٔ کول
to cause to hide	pəṭ kṛəl	پټ کړل	pəta'wəl	پټول
to build, to mend, to cause to recover	ǰoṛ kṛəl	جوړ کړل	ǰoṛa'wəl	جوړول
to break (something)	māt kṛəl	مات کړل	māta'wəl	ماتول

Example sentences:

dā ba sakāl pa xār ke kār oki?	Will she work in the city this year?	دا به سخکال په ښار کښې کار وکی؟
āw, ˈo-ba ki.	Yes, she will.	آو، وبه کی.
tsə waxt ba ˈhalta xaˈbare oke?	What time will you speak there?	څهٔ وخت به هلته خبرې وکې؟
saˈbā na bəla wrəz ba ˈhalta xaˈbare okəm.	I shall speak there the day after tomorrow.	صبا نا بله روځ به هلته خبرې وکم.
tə ba də māˈxām ḍoˈḍəy dəˈpāra tsə paˈxə ke?	What will you cook for dinner?	تهٔ به د ماښام ډوډۍ د پاره څهٔ پاخهٔ کې؟
keˈdey ši če dāl paˈxə kṛəm.	I might cook lentils.	کېدے شی چې دال پاخهٔ کړم.
ˈtāso ba māˈxām wriǰe paˈxe kṛəy?	Will you cook rice tonight?	تاسو به ماښام وريژې پخې کړئ؟
na, māˈxām ba nə paxaˈwu.	No, we won't cook it tonight.	نه، ماښام به نهٔ پخوُو.
pa de moˈsəm ke ba haˈɣa tsə xarts ki?	What will he sell in this season?	په دې موسم کښې به هغه څهٔ خرڅ کی؟
pa de moˈsəm ke ba ānˈgur āw aˈnār xarts ki.	He will sell grapes and pomegranates in this season.	په دې موسم کښې به انگُور او انار خرڅ کړی.
tarˈkāṇ ba ˈkəla mez ǰoṛ ki?	When will the carpenter build the table?	ترکاڼ به کله مېز جوړ کړی؟
pa de hafta ke ba ǰoṛ nə-ki.	He won't make it this week.	په دې هفته کښې به جوړ نهٔ کی.
kurˈsəy ba ˈkəla ˈǰoṛa ke?	When will you fix the chair?	کُرسۍ به کله جوړه کې؟
āˈwal ba dā kurˈsəy ˈǰoṛa kəm, āw byā ba stā kurˈsəy ˈǰoṛa kəm.	First I will fix this chair, and then I will fix your chair.	اول به دا کُرسۍ جوړه کم، او بيا به ستا کُرسۍ جوړه کړم.
ˈkəla ba haˈɣa xpəl duˈkān band ki?	When will he close his shop?	کله به هغه خپل دُوکان بند کړی؟
haˈɣa ba āˈtə baˈǰe band ki.	He will close it at eight.	هغه به اتهٔ بجې بند کړی.

ˈkəla ba axˈbār ˈxatəm ke?	When will you finish the newspaper?	کله به اخبار ختم کړې؟
ləs ˈmɪnṭa pas ba ye ˈxatəm kəm.	I will finish it after ten minutes.	لس مېنټه پس به يې ختم کړم.

NOTES:

1. Verbal adjectives are inflected in agreement with the object.
2. The negative verb prefix nə- (نۀ) precedes the verb stem / k- / (-ک):

zə ba war koˈlaw kəm.	I will open the door.	زۀ به ور کولاؤ کم.
zə ba war koˈlaw nə-kəm.	I will not open the door.	زۀ به ور کولاؤ نۀ کم.

The future progressive tense *wi* وی

In the future tense the verb *wi* (وی) is used instead of *di* (دی) the third person singular and plural forms of the verb 'to be'. When *wi* (وی) is used in a sentence, it signals an existing continuous or habitual state of a person or thing, for example, the weather every year at springtime.

hayˈwi tsə waxt pa ˈkəli ke wi?	When are they usually in the village?	هغوی څۀ وخت په کلی کښې وی؟
hayˈwi ˈhɪčere pa ˈkəli ke ˈnə-wi.	They are never in the village.	هغوی هېچرې په کلی کښې نۀ وی.
seb rozāna pa dəfˈtər ke wi?	Is the boss in his office daily?	صيب روزانه په دفتر کښې وی؟
āw, də kār pa ˈwrəzo ke rozāˈna pa dəfˈtər ke wi.	Yes, he is in the office on every work day.	آو، د کار په ورځو کښې روزانه په دفتر کښې وی.
pa sparˈli ke moˈsəm tsənga wi?	What is the weather like during the spring?	په سپرلی کښې موسم څنګه وی؟
pa sparˈli ke nə garˈmi wi, nə yəxˈni.	In the spring, there is neither hot nor cold.	په سپرلی کښې نۀ ګرمی وی نۀ يخنی.
guˈluna ba srə wi?	Will the flowers be red?	ګُلُونه به سرۀ وی؟
haləˈkān ba dā waxt pa gronḍ ke wi?	Will the boys be at the sports ground at this time?	هلکان به دا وخت په ګراونډ کښې وی؟

NOTES:

1. The / w / (و) sound here is somewhere between a / v / and / w /.
2. *ba* (به) is added to *wi* (وی) to make the imperfective future tense.

Comprehension drill: Learning your way around

☝ Find a big map of your area. Take an imaginary trip with your finger, or give instructions for your helper to travel. Use the following words in your description, making complete sentences:

otrā'i	اترائی	downward slope
ban'duna	بندونه	dams
pul	پُل	bridge
čaṛā'i	چړائی	upward slope
zən'gəl	ځنګل	jungle
saṛək'una	سړکُونه	roads
sin'duna	سیندُونه	rivers
xār	ښار	city
sehera'gāne	صحراګاني	deserts
'ɣruna	غرُونه	mountains
qabi'le	قبيلې	tribes
'kəli	کلی	villages

Towns in Khyber Pukhtunkhwa

Learn the names of the principal towns. Pay special attention to those 'hard' sounds that occur in names like *malā'kanḍ* (ملاکنډ).

______________________________ ______________________________

______________________________ ______________________________

______________________________ ______________________________

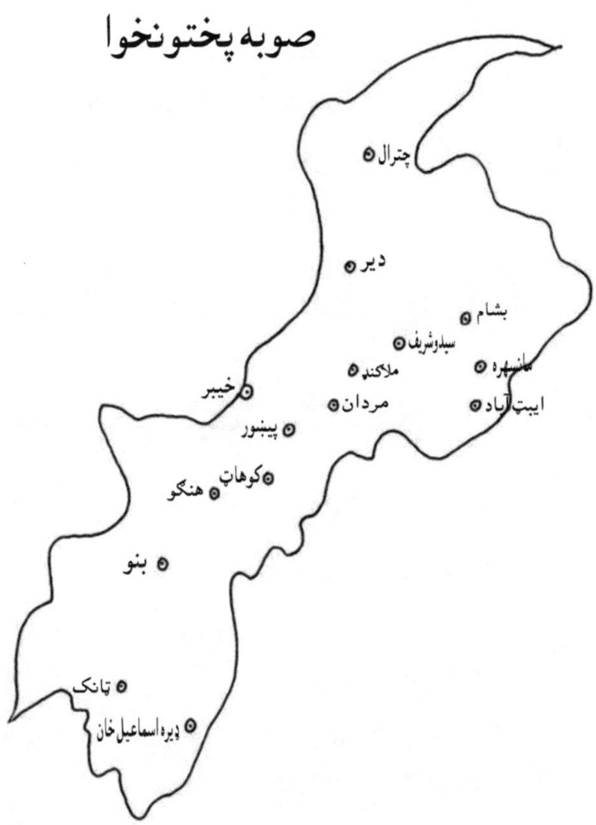

Memorising moment

mataˈluna

دې کښې به يې خېر وي.

de ke ba ye xer wi.

There will be good in it.

دَ پښتُون يوه خبره وي.

də pəxˈtun ˈyəwa xaˈbara wi.

Pukhtuns stick to their word.

شپه چې تېره شي، خبره هېره شي.

špa če ˈtera ši, xaˈbara ˈhera ši.

The night is gone, the talk is forgotten.

مهٔ کوه په ما وبه شي په تا .

mə kawa pa mā, ˈo-ba ši pa tā.

Don't do it to me, it will be done to you.

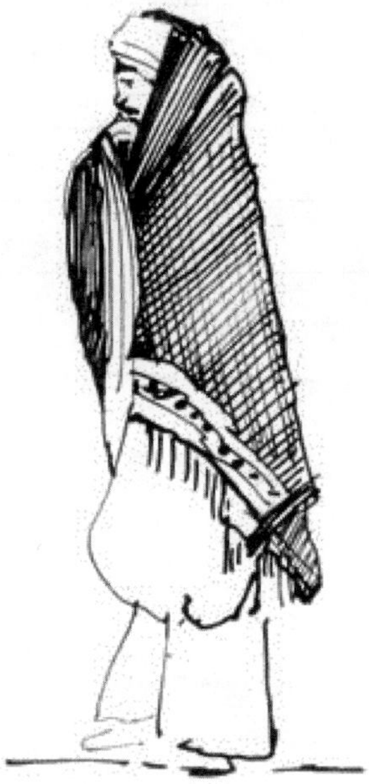

Rahman Baba *šer*

کر د گُلو کړه چې سيمه دې گُلزار شي.

اغزي مهٔ کره په پښو کښې به دې خار شي.

kar də guˈlo kṛa če siˈma de gulˈzār ši.

āɣˈzi mə ˈkara pa xpo ke ba de xār ši.

Grow flowers to make your surroundings blossom.

Don't sow thorns, they will become thorns in your feet.

چې الله درسره مل نۀ وی، رحمانه،
کۀ لښکرې درسره وی یک تنها یې.

če āl'lā dar-sa'ra məl 'nə wi, rah'māna,

kə lax'kəre dar-sa'ra wi, yek tan'hā ye.

If God is not your companion, Rahman,

Even if you have an army you are all alone.

Exercises for Lesson Fifteen

1. Change the following sentences into perfective future tense. For example:

zə de ta be'gāla yo xat likəm. — زۀ دې ته بېګاله یو خط لیکم.

Becomes

zə ba de ta be'gāla yo xat o-likəm. — زۀ به دې ته بېګاله یو خط ولیکم.

a. dā pa kor ke 'luxi 'winzi. — دا په کور کښې لوښی وینځی.

____

b. dey os mā sa'ra xa'bare nə-kawi. — دے اوس ما سره خبرې نۀ کوی.

____

c. ha'ɣa os lar'gi māta'wi. — هغه اوس لرګی ماتوی.

____

d. dey 'sıraf tā'za ke'le xartsa'wi. — دے صرف تازه کېلې خرڅوی.

____

e. tarˈkāṇ yo kurˈsəy ǰoṛaˈwi. ترکانړ یو کُرسۍ جوړوي.

f. zə beˈgāla haˈɣe saˈra kār kaˈwəm. زهٔ بېګاله هغې سره کار کوم.

g. kor ta ye ˈboze? کور ته يې بوځې؟

h. dey həm ḍoˈḍəy dəˈpāra ˈdəlta ˈrāwəle? دے هم ډوډۍ د پاره دلته راولې؟

i. zmung klās tsə waxt ˈšoro ˈkigi? زمُونږ کلاس څهٔ وخت شروع کېږي؟

j. zə pa pəxˈto poˈhigəm. زهٔ په پښتو پوهېږم.

2. Answer the following questions in full sentences.

a. dwi ba kor həm wāxli? دوئ به کور هم واخلی؟

b. tə ba haɣˈwi saˈra ˈkəli ta lāṛ še? تهٔ به هغوی سره کلی ته لاړ شې؟

c. māšuˈmān ba ˈdəlta ˈrāwəle? ماشُومان به دلته راولې؟

d. pa baˈzār ke ba ye xarts-ku? په بازار کښې به يې خرڅ کُو؟

e. kaˈrim ba xpəl kor ta ˈrāši? کريم به خپل کور ته راشی؟

Vocabulary for Lesson Fifteen

otrā'i	اترائی		*n.*	decline, downward slope
āsta'wəl	استول		*v.t.*	to send, to dispatch, to forward
ul'ṭəy ka'wəl	اُلټې کول		*v.t.*	to vomit
a'nār	انار	*m.*	*n.*	pomegranate
ınšāl'la	انشاءالله		*ph.*	God willing
u'də ka'wəl	اُودهٔ کول		*v.t.*	to put (someone) to bed, to make (someone) sleep
ba'ləl	بلل		*v.t.*	to invite, to call
band	بند	*m.s.*	*n.*	dam
ba	به		*ft.v.m.*	will, shall (when used with verbs indicates future tense)
baya'wəl	بهیول		*v.t.*	to make flow, to make run
pəṭa'wəl	پټول		*v.t.*	to hide; to steal
pəṭe'dəl	پټېدل		*v.i.*	to hide oneself, to become hidden, to be put away
paṛsa'wəl	پړسول		*v.t.*	to pump up, to inflate, to (make) swell
paṛse'dəl	پړسېدل		*v.i.*	to swell up, to be(come) swollen
pṛaqa'wəl	پړقول		*v.t.*	to make shiny, to polish
pṛaqe'dəl [pṛake'dəl]	پړقېدل [پړکیدل]		*v.i.*	to shine, to flash (e.g. lightning)
ta'pos ka'wəl	تپوس کول		*v.t.*	to ask, to inquire
təxta'wəl	تښتول		*v.t.*	to kidnap
təxte'dəl	تښتېدل		*v.i.*	to run away, to flee, to escape
ṭāwn	ټاؤن		*n.*	town
ṭek'si	ټکسی	*f.s.*		taxi
zɣala'wəl	څغلول [زغلول]		*v.t.*	to drive, to run, to chase
zən'gəl	ځنګل	*m.s.*	*n.*	jungle
zwaṛanda'wəl	ځوړندول		*v.t.*	to hang

čaṛā'i	چړائی		*n.*	incline, upward slope
čəla'wəl	چلول		*v.t.*	to drive, to operate, to make move
sase'dəl	څڅېدل		*v.i.*	to drip, to leak
xlās	خلاص	*m.*	*adj.*	open; finished; release
xwaze'dəl	خوځېدل		*v.i.*	to move
xware'dəl [ɣwaṛe'dəl]	خورېدل [غوړېدل]		*v.i.*	to be scattered, to be spread, to spread itself out
dāl	دال	*m.*	*n.*	lentils
rāba'ləl	رابلل		*v.t.*	to send for, to summon, to invite
rāsta'wəl	راستول		*v.t.*	to send from here
rapa'wəl	رپول		*v.t.*	to shake, to shiver, to tremble
rape'dəl	رپېدل		*v.i.*	to shake
rasa'wəl	رسول		*v.t.*	to deliver, to (cause to) reach, to supply, to provide
irɣaṛa'wəl	رغړول		*v.t.*	to roll up, to (make) roll
irɣaṛe'dəl	رغړېدل		*v.i.*	to roll along (by itself)
zɣale'dəl	زغلېدل		*v.i.*	to move along quickly, to run, to take flight
spar'ley	سپرلے	*m.*	*n.*	spring (season)
sakāl	سخکال		*adv.*	this year, the present year
šarma'wəl	شرمول		*v.t.*	to humiliate
šo'ro	شروع	*f.*	*n.*	beginning, start, commencement, outset
šɪla'wəl	شلول		*v.t.*	to tear (something), to rip
xkāre'dəl	ښکارېدل		*v.i.*	to appear, to look like
ɣwaṛe'dəl [xware'dəl]	غوړېدل [خورېدل]		*v.i.*	to be scattered, to be spread, to spread itself out
qabi'la	قبیله	*f.s.*	*n.*	tribe
ka'ča	کچه	*f.*	*adj.*	poor quality
kaṛe'dəl	کړېدل		*v.i.*	to be troubled, to suffer, to pine

ga'ṭəl	ګټل		*v.t.*	to gain, to win, to earn, to profit
gronḍ	ګراونډ	*m.*	*n.*	sports ground
garza'wəl	ګرځول		*v.t.*	to take someone for a walk
gre'wān [gre'bān]	ګرېوان [ګرېبان]	*m.*	*n.*	collar; shirt
laṛze'dəl	لړزېدل		*v.i.*	to shake
ləge'dəl	لګېدل		*v.i.*	to be fixed; to be lit
'loba	لوبه	*f.s.*	*n.*	play, game, match
mālume'dəl	معلومېدل		*v.i.*	to be known, to become aware of, to find out
'mɪnṭa ['mɪnaṭ]	مېنټه [منټ]		*n.*	minute
nāba'ləd	نا بلد		*adj.*	unacquainted, unfamiliar
naṛe'dəl	نړېدل		*v.i.*	to be demolished, to tumble down, to fall apart
yeša'wəl	يشول		*v.t.*	to boil (something)
yeše'dəl	يشېدل		*v.i.*	to boil (itself), to be boiled

špāṛlə'səm sa'bəq شپاړلسم سبق

Lesson Sixteen

Dialogue sixteen: Ladies finding out about cooking

L: ḍer 'xkwəley pa'law dey. dā mo 'tsənga pox 'kəṛey dey? This is very nice pulao. How did you (*pl.*) cook it? mā ta ye tari'qa 'oxāya. Teach me the method.	ډېر ښکُلے پولاؤ دے. دا مو څنګه پوخ کړے دے؟ ما ته يې طريقه وښايه.
H: ā'wal ba pa ɣwa'ṛo ke ṭamā'tər āw pyāz də 'garme masā'le sa'ra srə ke. byā ba pa'ke 'safā šɪβe 'wrije 'wāčawe. u'bə ba pa'ke 'wāčawe, āw byā ba ye 'oyašawe. če u'bə tsə waxt 'uče ši no 'wrije ba ta'yāre wi. First you will put tomatoes and onions in oil and fry with hot spices. Then you will put in the cleaned rice. You will then put in water and boil it. When the water is dry the rice will be ready.	اول به په غوړو کښې ټماټر او پياز د ګرمې مصالحې سره سرۀ کې. بيا به په کښې صفا شوې وريژې واچوې. اوبۀ به په کښې واچوې، او بيا به يې ووېشوې. چې اوبۀ څۀ وخت وچې شی نو وريژې به تيارې وی.
L: 'kəme masā'le ba pa'ke 'āčawəm? Which spices do I put in?	کُومې مصالحې به په کښې اچوم؟
H: ba'zār ke če 'kəma ta'yāra 'garma masā'la wi ha'ɣa pa'ke 'wāčawa. Put in whatever prepared hot spices are in the bazaar.	بازار کښې چې کُومه تياره ګرمه مصالحه وی هغه په کښې واچوه.
L: 'uga āw a'drək 'tāso kəṭ'wəy ke 'wəle ɪstemāla'wəy? Why are you using garlic and ginger in the curry?	اوږه او ادرک تاسو کټوۍ کښې ولې استعمالوئ؟
H: de sa'ra kəṭ'wəy xə 'kigi āw mazi'dara kigi. They make the curry good and tasty.	دې سره کټوئ ښۀ کېږی او مزېداره کېږی.
L: 'ɣwaxa də 'mexe zər pa'xigi āw kə də ɣwā? Does buffalo meat cook faster or cow's meat?	غوښه د مېښې زر پخېږی او کۀ د غوا؟
H: də 'mexe āw də ɣwā xa'bara nə da, 'ɣwaxa če də zwān sar'wi wi no zər pa'xigi. It is not a matter of whether it is buffalo or cow, if it is the meat of a young animal it will cook quickly.	د مېښې او د غوا خبره نۀ ده، غوښه چې د ځوان څاروی وی نو زر پخېږی.

NOTE:
sar'wi (خاروی) is a general term referring to domestic animals kept for meat or milk.

Men: Eating at a restaurant

L: haˈləka, tsə de pāxə kəṛi di? Lad, what have you cooked?	هلکه، څۀ دې پاخۀ کړی دی؟
H: čaˈṇa, ˈɣwaxa, sāg, paˈlaw, səbˈzi, čərg āw ˈtike. tsə ˈrawṛəm, seb? Chick peas, meat, spinach, pulao, vegetables, chicken and tikkas. What shall I bring, sir?	چنړه، غوښه، ساګ، پولاؤ، سبزی، چرګ او تیکې. څۀ راوړم، صیب؟
L: dā šān oka! yo kaˈṛəy tika ˈrāwṛa āw war saˈra sabˈzi həm ˈrāwṛa! Do like this, bring a karai tikka and with it bring vegetables! saˈlād āw čaka ba meˈlaw ši? Do you have salad and *chaka* [a yoghurt sauce]?	دا شان وکه! یو کړائ تیکه راوړه او ورسره سبزی هم راوړه! سلاد او چکه به مِلاؤ شی؟
H. bɪlˈkəl seb, be ˈɣəma šəy, har tsə ba meˈlaw ši. Absolutely sir, don't worry everything will be available.	بِلکل صیب، بې غمه شئ، هر څۀ به ملاؤ شی.

During the meal

L: rāša, xaˈbara wāwra! dwa roˈtəy ˈgarme ˈgarme ˈrāwṛa! Come here, listen! Bring two hot, hot breads!	راشه خبره واوره! دوه روټۍ ګرمې ګرمې راوړه!
H: dā ˈwāxləy ˈgarme rotəy. nor xo ǰi tsə nə di paˈkār? Take this hot bread. You don't need anything else?	دا واخلئ ګرمې روټۍ. نور خو جی څۀ نۀ دی پکار؟
L: na, merabāˈni, če paˈkār ši no āˈwāz ba ˈdarkom. No thanks, if I want something I will call.	نه، مِهربانی، چې پکار شی نو آواز به درکړم.

L: ˈḍere ˈxkwəle ˈtɪke we! dā ˈwāxla. panˈzos ruˈpəy stā ɪˈnām šo. ˈnime stā šwe, ˈnime də uˈstāz šwe. They were very good tikkas! Take this. Fifty rupees is your tip. Half for you, half for the cook.	ډېرې ښکُلې تیکې وې! دا واخله. پنځوس روپۍ ستا اِنعام شو. نیمې ستا شوې، نیمې د اُستاذ شوې.

L: ˈstāso xwaˈrāk zmung xwax šo. mung ba byā rāˈzu. We liked your food. We will come again.	ستاسو خوراک زمونږ خوښ شو. مونږ به بیا راځو.

☝ Take your helper out for a meal and practice this dialogue.

Pronunciation drill

Illustrating / **xr** / خر

xərˈkār ḍer xrə sāˈti.	The donkey-*wallah* keeps many donkeys.	خرکار ډېر خرهٔ ساتي.
ḍoˈḍəy pa xrap xrap ˈmə-xora!	Do not eat food noisily.	ډوډۍ په خرپ خرپ مهٔ خوره!
zə ˈxpəla ˈgira ˈxrayəm.	I am shaving my chin [*lit.* 'beard'].	زهٔ خپله ږیره خرایم.

NOTE:
xərˈkār (خرکار), translated 'donkey-*wallah*' is the man who keeps donkeys that are used to carry bricks in buiding sites, etc.

A tongue twister

Try this *maˈtəl*:

خر د خِد په خوراک څهٔ پوهېږي!

xər də xed pa xwaˈrāk tsə poˈhigi!

What does the donkey know about eating barley!

Introducing the subjunctive mood

1. Possibility:

Words that express possibility include *keˈdey ši* (کېدے شی) 'it is possible', *ˈšāˈɪd* (شاید) 'perhaps' and *ɪnšālˈla* (انشاءالله) 'God willing'.

keˈdey ši če haɣˈwi ˈhalta wi.	It is possible that they are there.	کېدے شی چې هغوی هلته وی.
keˈdey ši če zə ye māˈlum nə kəm.	It is possible that I will not find it.	کېدے شی چې زهٔ یې معلوم نهٔ کړم.

keˈdey ši če zə həm lāṛ šəm.	It is possible that I will also go.	کېدے شی چې زهٔ هم لاړ شم.
keˈdey ši če dey həm wəgey wi.	Perhaps he is also hungry	کېدے شی چې دے هم وږے وی.
šāˈɪd če zə nən haˈɣa ˈowinəm.	Maybe I will see him today.	شاید چې زهٔ نن هغه ووینم.
šāˈɪd če haˈɣa ba war-saˈra xaˈbare ˈoki.	Perhaps he will talk with them.	شاید چې هغه به ورسره خبرې وکی.
ɪnšālˈla, də ˈbəle ǰuˈme ˈpore ba zə waˈpas šɪβey yɪm.	God willing, I will have returned before next Friday.	انشاءالله د بلې جُمعې پورې به زهٔ واپس شوے یم.
ɪnšālˈla, bəl kāl ˈpore ba zə xə pəxˈto ɪzˈda kṛəm.	God willing, I will have learned good Pukhto by next year.	انشاءالله، بل کال پورې به زهٔ ښهٔ پښتو زده کړم.

NOTES:

1. The subjunctive mood indicates that there is some uncertainty of an event taking place. It is used to express possibilities, wishes, desires and obligations.
2. Verbs in the subjunctive mood follow the same pattern as those outlined in Lesson Fifteen (the perfective future). This includes the addition of the prefix / o- / (و-) to most regular verb root stems. The participle *ba* (به) is generally not used in the subjunctive.
3. Possibility words normally occupy the initial place in a sentence, followed by *če* (چې) 'that'.
4. The last phrase includes the pre- and postpositions *də _ ˈpore* (د _ پورې) 'up to', although often the *də* (د) is left out. Note some of its uses in the following examples:

də xār ˈpore tso ruˈpəy ˈāxli?	How many rupees does it take to get to the city?	د ښار پورې څو روپۍ اخلی؟
špəgo baǰo ˈpore ˈdəlta yɪm.	I'm here up to six o'clock.	شپږو بجو پورې دلته یم.
rātlunki kāl ˈpore ba tsə kaˈwe?	What will you do until next year?	راتلونکی کال پورې به څهٔ کوې؟

2. Necessity, responsibility:

pa'kār (پکار) 'have to', 'need to', 'should', *za'rur* (ضرُور) 'must', *lā'zım* (لازم) 'necessary', *maǰ'bur* (مجبُور) 'compelled to', 'forced to' and *xāma'xa* (خامخا) 'must'.

mung la də haɣ'wi ma'dəd ka'wəl pa'kār di.	We should help them.	مُونږ له د هغوی مدد کول پکار دی.
pa'kār di če rozā'na war'zıš okṛi.	It is necessary for him to exercise daily.	پکار دی چې روزانه ورزش وکړی.
pa'kār di če mašu'mān u'də ši.	The children ought to go to sleep.	پکار دی چې ماشُومان اُودهٔ شی.
tā ta pa'kār di če dā kār o-nə-ke.	You should not do that job.	تا ته پکار دی چې دا کار ونهٔ کړې.
mung la də šāhıd kor ta tləl pa'kār di.	We need to go to Shahid's house.	مُونږ له د شاهد کور ته تلل پکار دی.
'tāla xpəl 'kəli ta tləl pa'kār di.	You should go to your own village.	تاله خپل کلی ته تلل پکار دی.
tə za'rur haspa'tāl ta lāṛ ša!	You must go to the hospital.	تهٔ ضرُور هسپتال ته لاړ شه!
ha'ɣa ba za'rur nən pa kor ke wi.	She has to be in the house today.	هغه به ضرُور نن په کور کښې وی.
tə ba sa'bā za'rur rā'še.	You must come tomorrow.	تهٔ به صبا ضرُور راشې!
lā'zıma da če 'hara wrəz də re'ḍyo xab'runa 'wawru.	It is necessary for us to listen to the radio every day.	لاِزمه ده چه هره ورځ د ریډیو خبرُونه واورو.
lā'zıma da če nən də kor də'pāra sodā 'wāxlu.	It is necessary for us to buy groceries for the house today.	لاِزمه ده چه نن د کور د پاره سودا واخلُو.
ha'ɣa də maǰbu'rəy na 'dəlta 'pate 'kigi.	He is compelled to stay here.	هغه د مجبُورۍ نه دلته پاتې کیږی.
sa'bā xāma'xā ḍāk'ṭər ta lāṛšəy.	You must go to the doctor tomorrow.	صبا خامخا ډاکټر ته لاړ شئ.
tə xāma'xā ha'ɣa 'owina.	You must see him.	تهٔ خامخا هغه ووینه.

3. Wishes and desires:

u'mɪd la'təl (أُميد لرل) 'to hope', *šoq* (شوق) 'interest', 'desire', *xo'dey de 'oki* (خُدائ دي وکی) 'may God do it', *zṛə ke'dəl* (زړهٔ کېدل) 'to want' and *γox'təl* (غوښتل) ' want'.

zə u'mɪd la'rəm če ha'γa ba də ǰel na rā'xlās ši.	I hope he will be set free from jail.	زهٔ أُميد لرم چې هغه به د جېل نه راخلاص شی.
u'mɪd la're če zər ba kār pe'dā ke?	Do you hope to find work quickly?	أُميد لرې چې زر به کار پېدا کې؟
zə'mā zwe u'mɪd la'ri če xpəl ta'lim pa lan'dən ke pu'ra ki.	My son hopes to complete his education in London.	زما زوئ أُميد لری چې خپل تعليم په لندن کښې پُوره کړی.
zə'mā šoq dey če āngre'zi ɪz'da kəm.	It's my desire to learn English.	زما شوق دے چې انګرېزی زده کړم.
zə'mā šoq dey če dun'yā 'owinəm.	My desire is to see the world.	زما شوق دے چې دُنياووينم.
xo'dey de bā'rān 'oki!	May God make it rain!	خُدائ دې باران وکی!
xo'dey de 'okṛi če byā de 'owinu!	May God grant that we see you again!	خُدائ دې وکړی چې بيا دې ووينُو!
xo'dey de tāla də zṛə i'mān dar-kṛi!	May God give you belief of the heart!	خُدائ دې تا له د زړهٔ ايمان درکړی!
xo'dey de tā pa ɪmtɪ'hān ke pās ki!	May God grant that you pass the exam!	خُدائ دې تا په اِمتحان کښې پاس کی!
zṛə ta de tsə 'kigi?	What would you like?	زړهٔ ته دې څهٔ کېږی؟
ḍo'ḍəy ta me zṛə 'kigi.	I would like some food.	ډوډۍ ته مې زړهٔ کېږی.
čayo ta me zṛə 'kigi.	I would like tea.	چائو ته مې زړهٔ کېږی.
zə lāmbo wa'həl 'γwāṛəm.	I want to swim.	زهٔ لامبو وهل غواړم.
dā ḍer kār ka'wəl 'γwāṛi.	She wants to do a lot of work.	دا ډېر کار کول غواړی.

4. Questions and inquiries:

zə čā sa'ra xa'bare 'okəm?	Who should I talk with?	زهٔ چا سره خبرې وکم؟
tə mā'lɪk sa'ra xa'bare 'oka.	You should talk to the owner.	تهٔ مالِک سره خبرې وکه.
zə kor ta lāṛšəm kə dəf'tər ta?	Should I go to the house or to the office?	زهٔ کور ته لاړ شم کهٔ دفتر ته؟

ˈmāla kor ta tləl paˈkār di āw kə dəfˈtər ta?	Do I need to go to the house or to the office?	ما له کور ته تلل پکار دی او کهٔ دفتر ته؟
xāmaˈxā kor ta lāṛ ša.	You should definitely go to the house.	خامخا کور ته لاړ شه.
tsə ˈoxoru? kaˈbāb āw kə ˈwriǰe?	What should we eat? Kababs or rice?	څهٔ وخورُو؟ کباب او کهٔ وريژې؟
zə če kaˈbāb ˈoxoru.	Let's eat kababs.	څه چې کباب وخورُو.
ˈtsənga kiˈtāb ˈwāxlu?	What kind of book should we buy?	څنګه کتاب واخلُو؟
zə če də qiˈso kiˈtāb ˈwāxlu.	Let's buy a story book.	څه چې د قصو کتاب واخلُو.

5. Permission:

eǰāˈzət dey če ˈlāṛ šu?[17]	Is there permission for us to go?	اِجازت دے چې لاړ شو؟
eǰāˈzət dey če stā tasˈwir oˈbāsəm?	Is it OK that I take your picture?	اِجازت دے چې ستا تصوير اوباسم؟
mung ta də rātˈlo eǰāˈzət dey?	Do we have permission for coming?	مُونږ ته د راتلو اِجازت دے؟
stā moˈtər botˈley šəm?	May I take your car?	ستا موټر بوتلے شم؟
zə dəˈnəna rātˈley šəm?	May I come in?	زهٔ دننه راتلے شم؟

6. Exhortations and warnings:

koˈšiš kawa! (کوشش کوه!) 'try!', *xyāl kawa!* (خيال کوه!) 'be careful!', 'watch out!', *pām kawa!* (پام کوه!) 'be careful!', *xabarˈdār!* (خبردار!) 'beware!' and *mə-kawa!* (مهٔ کوه!) 'don't do it!'.

koˈšiš kawa če pa ımtıˈhān ke kamˈyāb še.	Try to be successful in the test.	کوشش کوه چې په اِمتحان کښې کامياب شې.
də ızˈda kaˈwəlo košiš kawa!	Try to learn!	د زده کولو کوشش کوه!
koˈšiš ˈoka če pinˈzo ˈbaǰo ˈpore ˈhalta ˈorase.	Try to reach there by five o'clock.	کوشش وکه چې پينځو بجو پورې هلته ورسې.

---

[17] In Pashto, a / -t / (ت-) is sometimes added to words of Arabic origin. Thus *eǰāˈza* (اِجازه) 'permission' becomes *eǰāˈzət* (اِجازت), *šariˈa* (شريعه) 'Islamic law' becomes *šariˈat* (شريعت), etc.

ko'šiš kawa če pa haspa'tāl ke ha'ɣa 'owine.	Try to see him at the hospital.	کوشش کوه چې په هسپتال کښې هغه ووينې.
xyāl kawa če xug nə-še!	Be careful not to get hurt!	خيال کوه چې خوږ نۀ شې!
xyāl ka'wa če pa čayo 'bānde 'xpəla 'ǰıba o-'nə-swaze!	Be careful your tongue is not burned by the tea!	خيال کوه چې په چايو باندې خپله ژبه ونۀ سوزوې!
xyāl kawa če do'ka dar-nə-ki!	Watch out that he doesn't trick you!	خيال کوه چې دوکه در نۀ کی!
xyāl ka'wa če spey tā o-'nə-xori!	Be careful the dog doesn't bite you!	خيال کوه چې سپے تا ونۀ خوری!
xyāl kawa če na'ša o-'nə ke!	Be careful not to take drugs!	خيال کوه چې نشه ونۀ کې!
pām kawa če mo'ṭər o-nə ǰanga'we!	Be careful not to crash the car!	پام کوه چې موټر ونۀ جنګوې!
'xabardār! 'halta mār dey.	Beware! There's a snake there.	خبردار! هلته مار دے.
mə-kawa! 'wrək še! xug ba še!	Don't do it! Get lost! You will be hurt!	مۀ کوه! ورک شې! خوږ به شې!

7. Conditional clauses:

kə _ *no* (کۀ _ نو) 'if __ then'.

kə dā rā-nə-ɣla, no zə ba lāṛ-šəm.	If she doesn't come, then I will go.	کۀ دا رانۀ غله نو زۀ به لاړ شم.
kə xə kār 'oke, no 'nore pe'se ba dar-kom.	If you do good work, then I will give you more money.	کۀ ښۀ کار وکې نو نورې پيسې به درکم.
kə ga'ṛəy de xa'rāba wi, no ba'dəla ye ka!	If your watch is bad, then replace it!	کۀ ګړۍ دې خرابه وی نو بدله يې که!
če yo zəl de na'ša 'oka byā ba tər 'mərga 'pore xlās 'nə-še.	If you take drugs one time then you will not be free until death.	چې يو ځل دې نشه وکړه بيا به تر مرګه پورې خلاص نۀ شې.
yāra, če dā məsə'la hal ši no ım'dād ba ḍer xo'šāla ši.	Friend, if this problem is solved then Imdad will be very happy.	ياره، چې دا مسئله حل شی نو امداد به ډېر خوشحاله شی.

Telephone talk

zə aš'raf sa'ra xa'bare ka'wəl 'ɣwāṛəm.	I want to talk with Ashraf.	زۀ اشرف سره خبرې کول غواړم.
zə də mar'dān na xa'bare ka'wəm.	I am calling from Mardan.	زۀ د مردان نه خبرې کوم.
tə aš'raf xa'bare ke tsə?	Is this Ashraf speaking?	تۀ اشرف خبرې کې څۀ؟
'tāso čā sa'ra xa'bare ka'wəl 'ɣwāṛəy?	Who do you want to talk to?	تاسو چا سره خبرې کول غواړئ؟
ləg ınte'zār 'okəy, zə ha'ɣa rā-'ɣwāṛəm.	Wait a little, I will get him.	لږ اِنتظار وکئ، زۀ هغه راغواړم.
zə'mā xa'bare 'āwre?	Can you hear me?	زما خبرې اورې؟
zə'mā ā'wāz dar-zi?	Is my voice reaching you?	زما آواز درځی؟
xo zə 'stāso ā'wāz nə-šəm awre'dey.	But I can't hear you.	خو زۀ ستاسو آواز نۀ شم اوریدے.
māfi ɣwāṛəm, māna ɣa'lat nəm'bər me'law šo.	Sorry, I dialled the wrong number.	معافی غواړم، مانه غلط نمبر ملاؤ شو.
ha'ɣə pa'run mā ta ṭele'fon 'kəṛey wo.	Yesterday he had telephoned me.	هغۀ پرُون ما ته ټیلیفون کړے وو.
ha'ɣa pa kor ke nə wo.	He was not at home.	هغه په کور کښې نۀ وو.
də xe'bər haspa'tāl də ṭele'fun nəm'bər tsə dey?	What is the telephone number for the Khyber Hospital?	د خیبر هسپتال د ټیلیفون نمبر څۀ دے؟

NOTE:

To say, *māna ɣa'lat nəm'bər me'law šo* (مانه غلط نمبر ملاؤ شو) literally means, 'I met a wrong number'. This way of talking, without admitting personal fault, is the norm in a culture which does not readily accept responsibility for error. For example, the excuse for breaking a cup is, *pyā'la māta šwa* (پیاله ماته شوه) 'the cup became broken'.

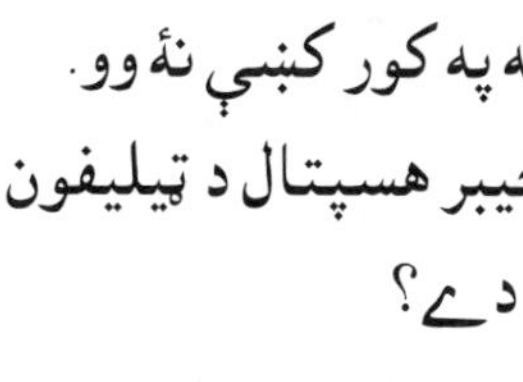

Memorising moment

mata'luna

عقل دَ بې عقلو نه زده کېږی.

'aqəl də be aqlo na ızda 'kigi.

Wisdom can be learned from fools.

دَ خیشکو نسوار دی، په وروستو زور کوی.

də xweško nas'wār di, pa 'wrusto zor ka'wi.

The *naswar* of Kheshko has its effects later.[18]

شاګرد ته ټول چلُونه ښایه، یو ترې پټ ساته.

šā'gərd ta ṭol čəl'una 'xāya, yo tre pəṭ sāta.

Teach a student everything, keep one thing hidden.

Rahman Baba

رحمان هسې بې وقُوف سوداګر نۀ دے
چې دَ دین متاع بدله په دینار کا.

rah'mān 'həse be wa'quf soda'gar nə dey
če də din mə'tā ba'dəla pa di'nār ka.
Rahman is not so stupid a merchant
As to exchange religion's wealth for money.

[18] *naswar* is a wad of tobacco placed under the front lip. Kheshko is a village near Nowshera.

Exercises for Lesson Sixteen

1. Role Play: Visit a restaurant or ask about cooking.

2. Make the following sentences negative:

   a. ke'dey ši hay'wi 'halta wi. — کېدے شي هغوی هلته وي.

   ____

   b. zə ba nən ha'ɣa 'owinəm. — زۀ به نن هغه ووينم.

   ____

   c. pa'kār dey če mašu'mān u'də ši. — پکار دے چې ماشُومان اُودۀ شي.

   ____

   d. tə ba sa'bā za'rur 'rāše. — تۀ به صبا ضرُور راشې.

   ____

   e. u'mɪd la'rəm če lur ye 'oši. — اُمید لرم چې لُور یې وشي.

   ____

3. Complete the following sentences with the appropriate subjunctive form of the verb:

a. ke'dey ši če war-sa'ra ________________.	xa'bare ka'wəl
کېدے شي چې ورسره ________________.	خبرې کول
b. tə za'rur haspa'tāl ta ________________.	tləl
تۀ ضرُور هسپتال ته ________________.	تلل
c. zə'mā šoq dey če dun'yā ________________.	li'dəl
زما شوق دے چې دُنیا ________________.	لیدل

4. Complete the following questions with the first person subjunctive form of the verb:

a.	kaˈbāb kə wriǰe ____________________________?	rāwˈṛəl
	کباب کۀ وریژې ________________؟	راوړل
b.	nən tsə šey _________________?	āɣosˈtəl
	نن څۀ شے _____________؟	اغوستل
c.	ˈdəlta xi lās ta _________________?	garzeˈdəl
	دلته ښی لاس ته _______________؟	ګرځېدل
d.	pa kuma lār _________________?	tləl
	په کُومه لار _____________؟	تلل

Vocabulary for Lesson Sixteen

aˈdrək	ادرک	*m.*	*n.*	ginger
ɪmtɪˈhān	امتحان	*m.*	*n.*	test, examination
uˈmɪd laˈrəl	اُمید لرل		*comp. v.i.*	to hope, to wish, to desire
ɪˈnām	اِنعام	*m.*	*n.*	prize, reward, tip
ˈuga	اوږه	*f.*	*n.*	garlic
baˈdəl	بدل	*m.*	*n.*	exchange; vengeance, retaliation
badlaˈwəl	بدلول		*v.t.*	to replace, to exchange
pās kaˈwəl	پاس کول		*comp. v.t.*	to pass an exam
pām kaˈwəl	پام کول		*comp. v.t.*	to be careful, to take heed
paˈkār	پکار		*adj. ph.*	have to, ought to, need to, should, necessary
ˈpore [də _ ˈpore]	پورې [د ــ پورې]		*prep.*	up to, until
paˈlaw	پولاؤ	*m.*	*n.*	pulao [pilau, pilaf] (an Afghan-style rice dish)
taˈlim	تعلیم	*m.*	*n.*	education, instruction
ˈtike	تیکې	*f.pl.*	*n.*	tikka
ǰuˈme [ǰuˈma]	جُمعې [جُمعه]	*f.*	*n.*	Friday
ǰangaˈwəl	جنګول		*v.t.*	to put to fight; to crash (a vehicle)
ǰangeˈdəl	جنګېدل		*v.i*	to fight; to quarrel
ǰel	جېل	*m.*	*n.*	jail [gaol]
zwān	ځوان	*m.*	*n., adj.*	young, youth, adolescent
čaka	چکه		*n.*	*chaka* (a yoghurt sauce)
čaˈṇa	چنړه	*f.*	*n.*	garbanzo beans, chick peas
sarˈwi	ښاروی	*m.*	*n.*	cattle, livestock
hal kaˈwəl	حل کول		*comp. vt.*	to solve; to dissolve
xāmaˈxā	خامخا		*adv.*	must, definitely

xabar'dār!	خبردار!		*v.*	beware, look out
xa'bara	خبره	*f.*	*n.*	word, talk
xo'dey de 'oki	خُدائ دې وکی		*ph.*	may God do it
xray'əl	خرايل		*v.t.*	to shave
xrap	خرپ		*adv.*	crunching
xər'kār	خرکار	*m.*	*n.*	donkey-*wallah*
xyāl ka'wəl	خيال کول		*comp. v.t.*	to take care, to take notice
dun'yā	دُنيا	*f.*	*n.*	world
do'ka	دوکه	*f.*	*n.*	deceit, cheating
rāt'lunkey	راتلُونکے	*m.*	*n., adj.*	coming, forthcoming, 'next'
re'ḍyo	رېډيو	*m.*	*n.*	radio
zṛə ke'dəl	زړۀ کېدل		*comp. v.i.*	to want, to desire
'ǰıba	ژبه	*f.s.*	*n.*	tongue
'gira	ږيره	*f.*	*n.*	beard
srə ka'wəl	سرۀ کول		*v.t.*	to fry
sa'lād	سلاد	*m.*	*n.*	salad
šā'ıd	شايد		*adv.*	perhaps, maybe, possibly
šoq	شوق	*m.*	*n.*	enthusiasm, interest, desire
za'rur	ضرُور		*adv.*	must, necessary
tari'qa	طريقه	*f.s.*	*n.*	way, manner, method
ɣox'təl	غوښتل		*v.t.*	to want, to ask (for), to request; to demand
kāl	کال	*m.*	*n.*	call
kəṭ'wəy	کتهوۍ	*f.*	*n.*	curry
ka'ṛey	کړهے	*m.*	*n.*	karai (a meat dish made in a small wok-like pot)
ko'šiš	کوشش	*m.*	*n.*	effort, endeavour, attempt
ke'dey ši	کېدے شی		*v. ph.*	it is possible, perhaps

lā'zım	لاژم	*m.*	*adj.*	necessary
la'zıma / la'zıme	لاژمه / لاژمي	*f.*		
maǰbur	مجبُور	*m.*	*adj.*	compelled to, forced to
maǰ'bura / maǰ'bure	مجبُوره / مجبُوري	*f.*		
masā'la	مساله [مصالحه]	*f.s.*	*n.*	spices (for cooking)
məsə'la	مسئله	*f.*	*n.*	problem, question, issue
mā'lum	معلُوم	*m.*	*adj.*	known, evident, obvious, apparent
mā'luma / mā'lume	معلُومه / معلومي	*f.*		
me'law	مِلاؤ		*adv.*	receiving, obtaining, meeting
'mexa	مېښه	*f.*	*n.*	water buffalo
na'ša	نشه	*f.*	*n.*	drugs
nim	نيم	*m.*	*n.*	half
'nima / 'nime	نيمه / نيمې	*f.*	*adj.*	
wa'pas	واپس		*adv.*	back again
uč	وچ	*m.*	*adj.*	dry, arid, parched, barren
'uča / 'uče	وچه / وچې	*f.*		
war'zıš	ورزش	*m.*	*n.*	exercise
yāra	ياره		*n., adj*	friend; dear

uwələˈsəm saˈbəq اووۀ لسم سبق

Lesson Seventeen

Dialogue seventeen: Ladies' visit to the tailor

L: dā kaˈpṛa me rāˈwṛe da. I have brought this cloth. zə ˈɣwāṛəm če də ˈde na yo āˈlā kaˈmis ˈǰoṛ kṛəm. I wish to make a lovely kamis from it. xo ˈɣāṛa ba ˈwarla ˈdāse kaˈwe. But make the neck like this.	دا کپړه مې راوړې ده. زۀ غواړم چې د دې نه يو اعلیٰ قميص جوړ کړم. خو غاړه به ورله داسې کوې.
H: ˈtāso be ˈɣəma šəy, ˈḍera xwāˈri ba warsaˈra ˈokṛəm. Don't worry, I will work very hard on it. ˈdexwā ˈrāša če nāp de ˈwāxləm. Come here so I can take your measurements.	تاسو بې غمه شئ، ډېره خواری به ورسره وکړم. دېخوا راشه چې ناپ دې واخلم.
L: ˈḍera merabāˈni. ˈkəla ˈpore ba ˈǰoṛe ši? Thank you very much, when will it be ready?	ډېره مِهربانی کله پورې به جوړې شی؟
H: bas, ləs ˈwrəze pas ˈwarpas ˈrāšəy. OK, come after ten days.	بس، لس ورځې پس ورپسې راشئ.
L: nə, špəg ˈwrəze pas ba ˈwarpase ˈrāšəm. No, I will come back for it after six days.	نه، شپږ ورځې پس به ورپسې راشم.
H: da xo ba ˈḍera ˈgrāna ši, mā saˈra xo də ˈmaxke na kār ḍer dey. That will be very hard, I have a lot of work to do before it.	دا خو به ډېره ګرانه شی، ما سره خو د مخکښې نه کار ډېر دے.
L: xer dey, arˈǰənṭ kaˈpṛo ke ye ˈrāla ˈǰoṛe kṛa! That's OK, make it as a priority!	خېر دے، ارجنټ کپړو کښې يې راله جوړې کړه!
H: xə da če ˈtāso ˈdumra ɪsˈrār kaˈwəy, no byā warpaˈse pa dərˈšəm tāˈrix maziˈgər ṭaym ˈrašəy. OK, if you insist so much, come back on the 30th in the afternoon.	ښۀ ده چې تاسو دومره اِصرار کوئ، نو بيا ورپسې په دېرشم تاريخ مازيګر ټيم راشئ.

NOTE:

Another useful phrase is:

saˈbā ba de paˈse ˈrāšəm. I will come for it tomorrow. صبا به دې پسې راشم.

Men: Ordering a pair of sandals

L: kā'kā, sāy'dāre tsa'pləy ba 'rāla 'ǰoṛe kṛe āw kə na? Uncle, would you make a pair of sandals for me by order or not?	کاکا، سائیداري څپلۍ به راله جوړې کړې او کهٔ نه؟
H: 'wəle na seb, dāse tsa'pləy ba 'darta 'ǰoṛe kṛəm če yād ba sā'te! Why not sir, I will make shoes that you will remember!	ولې نه صېب، داسې څپلۍ به درته جوړې کړم چې یاد به ساتې!
L: xa, no nāp me 'wāxla. OK, then take my measurements.	ښه، نو ناپ مې واخله.
H: 'rāwṛa, xpa pa de kā'ɣaz 'keda. Put your foot on this paper.	راوړه، خپه په دې کاغذ کېده.
L: xo yo xyāl ba ka'we, če tsa'pləy maz'bute həm wi āw 'xkwəle həm. But take care that the shoes are strong and also good looking.	خو يو خيال به کوې، چې څپلۍ مضبُوطې هم وي او ښکُلې هم.
H: be 'ɣəma ša seb, zə ba 'darta čarsad'wāle tsa'pləy 'ǰore kəm. Don't worry, I will make Charsadda sandals for you.	بې غمه شه صېب، زهٔ به درته چارسد والې څپلۍ جوړې کړم.
L: āw če tsa'pləy pa rang 'tore wi. And the sandals should be black. zə'mā sre tsa'pləy 'nə-wi 'xwaxe. I don't like red sandals.	او چې څپلۍ په رنګ تورې وي. زما سرې څپلۍ نهٔ وي خوښې.
H: 'fikar məkawəy, čarsad'wāle tsa'pləy 'ṭole 'tore wi. Don't worry, all Charsadda sandals are black.	فکر مهٔ کوئ، چارسد والې څپلۍ ټولې تورې وي.
L: 'kəla 'pore ba ye 'rāta ta'yāre kṛe? When will you have them ready for me?	کله پورې به يې راته تيارې کړې؟
H: yo 'myāšt pas ye ta'pos 'okəy. You inquire after one month.	يو مياشت پس يې تپوس وکئ.
L: na yār, bas 'yəwa 'hafta ke 'rāta ta'yāre kṛa. No friend, just get it ready for me in one week.	نه يار، بس يوه هفته کښې راته تيارې کړه.

NOTE:

sā'i (سائ) is money paid in advance if goods are made to order. Hence *sāy'dāre* (سائیداري) means 'made to order'.

Pronunciation drill

☝ You have probably found that you are consistently getting some words corrected by helpful friends. Over this next week keep reminding everyone you talk to, to help you in pronunciation, and make a list of words you get wrong. Write them here and get your helper to drill you.

One good idea is to either draw pictures or take photographs of the things which you have trouble pronouncing. Take these pictures with you for practice. Try to avoid translation back to your mother tongue.

Some useful phrases are:

kəm la'fəz če zə sa'fā nə-šəm wa'γəley ha'γa ba 'rāta ṭik kṛe?	Will you correct any words I can't speak clearly?	کُوم لفظ چې زهٔ صفا نهٔ شم وئيلے هغه به راته ټيک کړې؟
dā ba tə 'tsənga sa'fā 'waye?	How do you say this clearly?	دا به تهٔ څنګه صفا وائې؟
tə zə'mā pa xa'bəro po'hege?	Do you understand my speech?	تهٔ زما په خبرو پوهېږې؟
zə'mā 'ǯıba ṭik da?	Is my pronunciation OK?	زما ژبه ټيک ده؟
'ḍera merabā'ni če tā mā ta dā ṭik kṛo!	Thanks for correcting it for me!	ډېره مِهربانی چې تا ما ته دا ټيک کَړو!

Inflection rules in present, future and imperative tenses

Before moving on to the past tenses in Lesson Eighteen, it is worthwhile summarising the inflections used so far.

Singular		**Plural**		**Inflected**	
plār	پلار	pla'rān	پلاران	pla'rāno	پلارانو
sa'ṛey	سړے	sa'ṛi	سړی	sa'ṛo	سړو
kam'ra	کمره	kam're	کمرې	kam'ro	کمرو
gul	ګُل	gul'una	ګُلونه	gul'uno	ګُلونو

☝ Cover the right-hand side and try to say these sentences. The inflections are underlined. Some sentences without inflections are included to clarify the rules.

1. Possession

dā xə kiˈtāb dey.	This is a good book.	دا ښهٔ کتاب دے.
dā də moˈmin kiˈtāb dey.	This is Momin's book.	دا د مومن کتاب دے.
dā xə kitaˈbuna di.	These are good books.	دا ښهٔ کتابونه دی.
də de kitaˈbuno qiˈmət tsə dey?	What is the price of these books?	د دې کتابونو قیمت څهٔ دے؟
də mālˈṭo darˈzən pa tso dey?	What is the cost of a dozen oranges?	د مالټو درزن په څو دے؟
də ɣwāˈgāno pəy xwāˈga di?	Is the cows' milk sweet?	د غواګانو پئ خوارهٔ دی؟
də mašuˈmāno plār məṛ dey.	The children's father is dead.	د ماشُومانو پلار مړ دے.
də kābəlˈyāno waˈtən āˈzād šo.	The Kabulis' country (Afghanistan) has become free.	د کابلیانو وطن آزاد شو.
də dukandarˈāno haṛˈtāl dey.	It is the shopkeepers' strike.	د دُوکاندارانو هړتال دے.
də angreˈzāno āxˈtar dey.	It is the English people's festival.	د انګریزانو اختر دے.

NOTE:
angrez (انګریز) is a general term for westerners.

2. To

zə gul la uˈbə war-kom.	I am giving water to the flower.	زهٔ ګُل له اوبهٔ ورکوم.
zə gulˈuno la uˈbə war-kom.	I am giving water to the flowers.	زهٔ ګُلُونو له اوبهٔ ورکوم.
mašuˈmāno ta ḍoˈḍəy warkəy!	Give food to the children!	ماشُومانو ته ډوډئ ورکئ!
mašuˈmān ɪslāmaˈbād ta zi.	The children are going to Islamabad.	ماشُومان اسلام آباد ته ځی.

3. Of

gulˈuna mə-šukaˈwa!	Don't pick the flowers!	ګُلُونه مهٔ شُوکوه!
də gulˈuno xyāl kawa!	Take care of the flowers!	د ګُلُونو خیال کوه!

4. With

də gul'uno sa'ra az'ɣi wi.	Flowers have thorns.	د ګُلُونو سره ازغي وي.
də mašu'māno sa'ra 'mina kawa!	Love the children!	د ماشُومانو سره مينه کوه!
də mašu'māno tsə kār nə wi.	With children there is no work.	د ماشُومانو څۀ کار نۀ وي.

5. On

pa kur'so 'bānde ga'dəy keda!	Put cushions on the chairs!	په کرسو باندې ګدۍ کېږده!
pa mez'uno 'bānde māl'ṭe di.	Oranges are on the tables.	په مېزونو باندې مالټې دي.
pa 'lāro 'bānde 'xəṭe di.	Mud is on the roads.	په لارو باندې خټې دي.
pa ustaz'āno 'bānde səx'ta da.	Teachers face hardship.	په اُستاذانو باندې سخته ده.

6. In

pa de kam'ro ke mā'rān di.	There are snakes in these rooms.	په دې کمرو کښې ماران دي.

Expressing the ability to do something *ka'wəley ši* کولے شی

tə də hay'wi ma'dəd ka'wəley še?	Can you help them?	تۀ د هغوی مدد کولے شې؟
āw, ka'wəley šəm.	Yes, I can.	آو، کولے شم.
ha'ɣa xə ḍo'ḍəy paxa'wəley ši?	Can she cook good food?	هغه ښۀ ډوډۍ پخولے شی؟
na, nə-ši paxa'wəley.	No, she can't.	نه، نۀ شی پخولے.
hay'wi sa'bā zə'mā kor ta nə-ši rāt'ley?	Can't they come to my house tomorrow?	هغوی صبا زما کور ته نۀ شی راتلے؟
rāt'ley ši.	They can come.	راتلے شی.
kə tə 'nə-še ka'wəley no zə ka'wəḷey šəm.	If you can't do it, I can.	کۀ تۀ نۀ شې کولے نو زۀ کولے شم.
tə ka'pṛa gan'ḍəley še?	Can you sew cloth?	تۀ کپړه ګنډلے شې؟
āw, gan'ḍəley šəm.	Yes, I can sew.	آو، ګنډلے شم.

mung sa'bā-na-'maxke dā sa'bəq nə-šu xlāsa'wəley!	We can't finish this lesson by tomorrow!	مُونږ صبا نه مخکښې دا سبق نهٔ شُو خلاصولے!
tə c.s.s ka'wəley še?	You can do the C.S.S.?	تهٔ سی- ایس-ایس کولے شې؟
āw, ka'wəley šəm.	Yes, I can.	آو، کولے شم.

NOTES:

1. Ability to do something is expressed by the past participle of the verb *šwəl* (شول). Only *šwəl* (شول) is inflected.
2. The negative verb marker often precedes both the participle and the auxilary verb *šwəl* (شول). For example, *nə-šəm ka'wəley* (نهٔ شم کولے).
3. C.S.S.: Civil Service Exam.

More examples of expressing ability

tə os xār ta tley še?	Are you able to go to the city now?	تهٔ اوس ښار ته تلے شې؟
na, 'nə-šəm tley.	No, I am not able to go.	نه، نهٔ شم تلے.
dā pəx'to həm wa'yəle ši?	Is she able to speak Pukhto too?	دا پښتو هم وئیلې شی؟
āw, dā wa'yəle ši.	Yes, she can.	آو، دا وئیلې شی.
zə də'nəna rāt'ley šəm?	Can I come in?	زهٔ دننه راتلے شم؟

NOTE:

In the above examples, gender is indicated by the verb endings *tləl* (تلل), *rat'ləl* (راتلل), and *wa'yəl* (وئیل). For example, *tley* (تلے) and *rāt'ley* (راتلے) are masculine, whereas *wa'yəle* (وئیلې) is feminine. This distinction can be difficult to hear.

☝ Practice it with your helper. More examples follow.

āw, rāt'ley šəy.	Yes, you can come in.	آو، راتلے شئ.
tə āh'məd ḍāk'ṭər la bot'ley še?	Can you take Ahmad to the doctor?	تهٔ احمد ډاکټر له بوتلے شې؟
nə-šəm bot'ley.	No, I can't take him.	نهٔ شم بوتلے.
zə nən ha'ɣa nə-šəm li'dey.	I can't see him today.	زهٔ نن هغه نهٔ شم لیدے.
zə nən dā kita'buna lāybre'rəy ta nə-šəm o'ṛəley.	I am not able to take these books to the library today.	زهٔ نن دا کتابونه لائبریرئ ته نهٔ شم اوړلے.

haˈɣa dā larˈgi mātaˈwəley ši.	He is able to break this wood.	هغه دا لرګی ماتولے شی.
haˈɣa ˈgāḍey čəlaˈwəley ši?	Can he drive a car?	هغه ګاډے چلولے شی؟
haˈɣa ˈlāmbo waˈhəley ši?	Can he swim?	هغه لامبو وهلے شی؟

Following the above pattern, continue practicing with other verbs that have previously been introduced. Have your helper say a verb and a noun, then construct a sentence using both.

Days of the week

ɪtˈwār	Sunday	اِتوار
pir	Monday	پیر
ˈnəhe	Tuesday	نهي
šoˈro	Wednesday	شورو
zyāˈrət	Thursday	زیارت
ǰuˈma	Friday	جُمعه
xāˈli	Saturday	خالی

NOTE:
In Khyber Pukhtunkhwa the Urdu names for the days of the week are widely used, in addition to Pukhto ones.

Use of days of the week in sentences

nən ˈkəma wrəz da?	What day is it today?	نن کُومه ورځ ده؟
nən šoˈro da.	Today is Wednesday.	نن شورو ده.
saˈbā ˈkəma wrəz da?	Which day is it tomorrow?	صبا کُومه ورځ ده؟
saˈbā zyāˈrət dey.	Tomorrow is Thursday.	صبا زیارت دے.
saˈbā na ˈbəla wrəz ba ˈkəma wrəz wi?	Which day will it be the day after tomorrow?	صبا نه بله ورځ به کُومه ورځ وی؟
saˈbā na ˈbəla wrəz ǰuˈma da.	The day after tomorrow is Friday.	صبا نه بله ورځ جُمعه ده.
xaˈli pa wrəz ba ˈčerta ze?	Where will you go on Saturday?	خالی په ورځ به چرته ځې؟
xaˈli pa wrəz ˈčerta ˈnə-zəm.	I'm not going anywhere on Saturday.	خالی په ورځ چرته نهٔ ځم.

dey hara wrəz pa kor ke wi?	Is he at home every day?	دے هره ورځ په کور کښې وی؟
na, ˈsɪraf də ǰuˈme pa wrəz kor ke wi.	No, he's only home on Friday.	نه، صرف د جُمعې په ورځ کور کښې وی.
də ǰuˈme pa wrəz čuˈṭi da?	Is it a holiday on Friday?	د جُمعې په ورځ چُټی ده؟
hara ǰuˈma čuˈṭi wi.	Every Friday is a holiday.	هره جُمعه چُټی وی.
zə ˈhits nə-kaˈwəm, uzˈgār yɪm, stā kor ta ba dar-zəm.	I am not doing anything, I'm free, I will come to your house.	زۀ هېڅ نۀ کوم، وزگار یم، ستا کور ته به درځم.
haˈɣa ba də rātˈlunki gul pa wrəz pɪnˈḍəy ta zi?	Will she go to Rawalpindi next Monday?	هغه به د راتلُونکی گُل په ورځ پینډۍ ته ځی؟
na, haˈɣa ba də ˈnəhe pa wrəz zi.	No, she will go on Tuesday.	نه، هغه به د نهې په ورځ ځی.
ˈyəwe ˈwrəze paˈse ˈbəla wrəz.	One day follows another.	یوې ورځې پسې بله ورځ.

NOTES:

1. The days are inflected when used with *də* (د) and *pa* (په).
2. In Pukhtun thought, the new day begins at sunset, so the name of the night is attached to the day that follows. If you want to invite someone over on Thursday night, ask him for Friday night, or you will have your guest arrive on Wednesday night! For example:

tə də pir pa špa tsə kaˈwe?	What are you doing Sunday night?	تۀ د پیر په شپه څۀ کوې؟

Negatives *hɪ-čerta* 'nowhere', *hits-kəla* 'never' [for people], *hɪ-čere* 'never' [for things] and *hɪ-čā* 'no one'. هېچرته، هېڅکله، هېچرې، هېچا

ˈhɪ-čerta ˈnə zu.	We are not going anywhere.	هېچرته نۀ ځُو.
zə ba ˈhits-kəla karāˈčəy ta ˈnə-zəm.	I will never go to Karachi.	زۀ به هېڅ کله کراچۍ ته نۀ ځم.
ˈhits-kəla ɣalaˈti ˈmə-kawəy!	Never make mistakes!	هېڅ کله غلطی مۀ کوئ!
zə ba ˈhɪ-čere guˈna oˈnə-kəm.	I will never sin (*lit.* 'do sin').	زۀ به هېچرې گُناه ونۀ کړم.
ˈhɪ-čā ta ˈmə-waya!	Don't tell anyone!	هېچا ته مۀ وایه!
ˈhɪ-čā ta nə dey māˈlum.	No one knows.	هېچا ته نۀ دے معلُوم.

Comprehension drill: Learning antonyms

We tend to want to write things down all the time, but this may not be too helpful in the long run. Try to conduct this drill entirely in Pukhto and not write anything down. Use it anytime you want to find out a new descriptive word.

Find two contrasting items that illustrate common descriptives such as sweet–bitter, hot–cold, clean–dirty, new–old, thin–thick, heavy–light, dull–sharp, etc.

A. Learning descriptives

Put some paired objects on a tray and ask these questions:

də de pa bā'ra ke tsə waye?	How would you describe this?	د دې په باره کښې څۀ وائې؟
dā _______ de.	This is _______.	دا ______ دې.
də _______ xɪ'lāf tsə 'ṭəkey dey?	What is the opposite word for _______?	د ______ خِلاف څۀ ټکے دے؟
də _______ xɪ'lāf _______ dey.	The opposite of _______ is _______.	د ______ خِلاف ______ دے.

B. Antonym soup

Put all the objects out on a tray and pick up the correct one when your helper describes it.

zə ba ḍer xo'šāla šəm kə tə 'yəwa 'loba mā sa'ra 'oke ...	I would be very happy if you would play a game with me ...	زۀ به ډېر خوشحاله شم کۀ تۀ يوه لوبه ما سره وکې ...
če zə pa ha'ɣe ke də pəx'to 'newi 'ṭɪki ɪz'da kəm.	so that from it I can learn new Pukhto words.	چې زۀ په هغې کښې د پښتو نوې ټکی زده کوم.
tə ba 'māla išā'ra 'rāke, zə ba 'goram če 'haɣa nišā'ni pa kəm siz ke da āw zə ba 'haɣa rā-učəta'wəm.	You will give me instructions, and I will look to see which object has that characteristic and pick it up.	تۀ به ماله اِشاره راکې، زۀ به ګورم چې هغه نشانی په کُوم څيز کښې ده او زۀ به هغه راوچتوم.

Memorising moment

mata'luna

کله کله سړے د شيطان هم منی.

'kəla 'kəla sa'ṛey də še'tān həm 'mani.

Sometimes a person should obey Satan.

یو خوا ډانګ دے بل خوا پړانګ دے.

yo xwā ḍang dey bəl xwā pṛāng dey.

On one side there is stick on the other side a leopard.

د ستړو ځای شهباز ګړه ده.

də ˈstəṛo zay šāˈbāz ˈgaṛa da.

The tired ones' place is Shabaz Gara.[19]

پردے جنګ نیم اختر دے.

praˈdey ǰang nim āxˈtar dey.

Other people's quarrels are half a festival.

حُجره نهٔ اخلم خو شپه په کښې تېروم.

huǰˈra ˈnə-axləm, xo špa paˈke teˈrəm.

I am not buying the *hujra*, but spending the night in it.

Exercises for Lesson Seventeen

1. Answer the following questions in both the positive and the negative:

   a. tə pəxˈto waˈyəley še? — تهٔ پښتو وئیلے شې؟

   ____

   ____

   b. haˈɣa kaˈwəley ši če xat ˈoliki? — هغه کولے شی چې خط ولیکی؟

   ____

   ____

   c. tə nən ǰāˈme winˈzəley še? — تهٔ نن جامې وینځلے شې؟

   ____

   ____

[19] Shabaz Gara is a famous village near Mardan.

d. zə os ba'zār ta tley šəm? زۀ اوس بازار ته تلے شم؟

e. ha'ɣwi ma'dəd ka'wəley ši? هغوی مدد کولے شی؟

2. Using the list below, discover the Pukhto for each word plus their opposites. Write them down in Pukhto script or phonetics. Find objects that illustrate these common descriptives, and then practice them according to the method found in the Comprehension drill for this Lesson (Learning antonyms).

big	thin
sharp	flat
rough	hot
dirty	alive
loose	heavy
soft	dark
fat	sweet
wide	uneven
wet	full
empty	fresh
shiny	sticky
hollow	whole

3. Find out how new words work. Use this exercise to start developing your own skills in Pukhto grammar.

☝ With a helper fill out the following chart in Pukhto (either script or phonetics). As far as possible just use Pukhto to do your investigation.

	Bitter	**Sweet**	**Sour**
m.s.			
m.pl.			
f.s.			
f.pl.			

Now pick some adjectives and match them with various items of food to test your ability to make sentences with them. Some to try are:.

sweet	seβ	سپو	(*m.*)	alu'ča	اُلوچه	(*f.*)
bitter	marča'key	مرچکے	(*m.*)	kare'la	کریله	(*f.*)
sour	nim'bu	نیمبو	(*m.*)	māl'ṭa	مالټه	(*f.*)

Vocabulary for Lesson Seventeen

āˈzād	آزاد	*m.*	*adj.*	free, independent; open
ɪtˈwār pa wrəz	اِتوار په ورځ	*f.*	*n.*	Sunday
āxˈtar	اختر	*m.*	*n.*	religious festival
arˈǰənṭ	ارجنټ		*adj.*	urgent, priority
azˈɣi	ازغی		*n.*	thorn
išāˈra	اِشاره	*f.s.*	*n.*	sign, signal, hint, allusion
ɪsˈrār kaˈwəl	اصرار کول		*comp. v.t.*	to insist, to persist
anˈgrez / angreˈzān	انګرېز / انګرېزان	*m.*	*n.*	westerner
ˈpase tləl	پسې تلل		*comp. v.i.*	to follow
pir pa wrəz	پیر په ورځ	*f.*	*n.*	Monday
tāˈrix	تاريخ	*m.s.*	*n.*	history
ǰume pa wrəz	جُمعې په ورځ	*f.*	*n.*	Friday
čuˈṭi	چُټی	*f.s.*	*n.*	holiday, leave, vacation
xāˈli pa wrəz	خالی په ورځ	*f.*	*n.*	Saturday
xɪˈlāf	خِلاف		*adj.*	opposite
xwāˈri kaˈwəl	خواری کول		*comp. v.t.*	to labour, to work hard, to toil
xoˈšāla	خوشحاله	*m., f.*	*adj.*	happy, glad
ˈdumra	دومره	*f.*	*adj., adv.*	so much, this much
rātˈlunkey	راتلُونکے	*m.*	*n., adj.*	coming, future, forthcoming
zyāˈrət pa wrəz	زيارت په ورځ	*f.*	*n.*	Thursday
ˈǰɪba	ژبه	*f.s.*	*n.*	pronunciation
sāyˈdāre	سائيدارې		*adj.*	made to order
səxˈta	سخته	*f.*	*n.*	hardship, privation
seβ	سېو	*m.*	*n.*	apple
šoˈro pa wrəz	شورو په ورځ	*f.*	*n.*	Wednesday
šukaˈwəl	شُوکول		*v.t.*	to pick (flowers, fruit); to snatch, to rob, to tear

ˈɣāṛa	غاړه	*f.s.*	*n.*	neck, throat; collar
ˈfɪkar kaˈwəl	فکر کول		*comp. v.t.*	to think, to care, to worry
qiˈmət	قیمت	*m.*	*n., adj.*	price, cost, value
kareˈla	کریله	*f.*	*n.*	*karela* (a bitter squash)
ˈkəla	کله		*adv.*	when
gaˈdəy	ګدۍ	*f.*	*n.*	cushion
guˈna	ګُناه	*f.s.*	*n.*	sin, fault
lāybreˈri	لائبریری		*n.*	library
ˈlafəz / lafˈsuna	لفظ / لفظُونه	*m.*	*n.*	word
maziˈgər	مازیګر	*m.*	*n.*	late afternoon
ˈmina kawəl	مینه کول		*comp. v.t.*	to love
nāp / nāˈpuna	ناپ / ناپُونه	*m.*	*n.*	measurement
nišāˈni	نشانی		*n.*	mark, sign, characteristic
ˈnəhe pa wrəz	نهې په ورځ	*f.*	*n.*	Tuesday
waˈtən	وطن	*m.s.*	*n.*	country, homeland
haṛˈtāl	هړتال	*m.s.*	*n.*	strike
ˈhɪ-čā	هیچا		*adv.*	no one, nobody
ˈhɪ-čerta	هیچرته		*adv.*	nowhere
ˈhɪ-čere	هیچرې		*adv.*	never (for things)
ˈhits-kəla	هیڅ کله		*adv.*	never (for people)
yād sāˈtəl	یاد ساتل		*comp. v.t.*	to remember, to memorise

atələˈsəm saˈbəq اتۀ لسم سبق

Lesson Eighteen

Dialogue eighteen: Questions about relatives

L: haˈɣə de tsə dey? What relation is he to you?	هغۀ دې څۀ دے؟
H: trə me dey. He is my uncle.	ترۀ مې دے.
L: trə tsə ta ˈwayi? What does uncle mean?	ترۀ څۀ ته وائی؟
H: trə ḍə plār wror ta ˈwayi. Uncle means father's brother.	ترۀ د پلار ورور ته وائی.
L: tə də haˈɣe tsə ˈkigi? What are you to her?	تۀ د هغې څۀ کیږې؟
H: zə də haˈɣe xor yım. I am her sister.	زۀ د هغې خور یم.
L: haˈɣə ta tsə num ˈaxle? What do you call him?	هغۀ ته څۀ نُوم اخلې؟
H: zə haˈɣə ta xānˈǰi ˈwayəm. I call him Khanji.	زۀ هغۀ ته خان جی وایم.
L: zə war-ta tsə ˈwayəm? What should I call him?	زۀ ورته څۀووایم؟
H: tə war-ta kākā ǰi ˈowaya. You should call him 'Uncle Sir'.	تۀ ورته کاکا جی ووایه.
H: tarˈbur me dey. He's my cousin.	تربُور مې دے.
L: dā stā saˈka də trə zwe dey? Is he your real first cousin?	دا ستا سکه د ترۀ زوئ دے؟
H: āw, saˈka də trə zwe me dey. Yes, he is my real first cousin.	آو، سکه د ترۀ زوئ مې دے.
L: tā na ˈməšar dey kə ˈkəšar? Is he older or younger than you?	تا نه مشر دے کۀ کشر؟
H: zəˈmā həmˈzoley dey. He is the same age as me.	زما همزولے دے.

NOTE:

Coming to grips with how families and relatives fit together is an important part of understanding Pukhtun culture. A useful introduction to family life is the anthropological study of Swat Pukhtuns by Charles Lindholm.[20]

Kinship terms

Paternal kinship chart

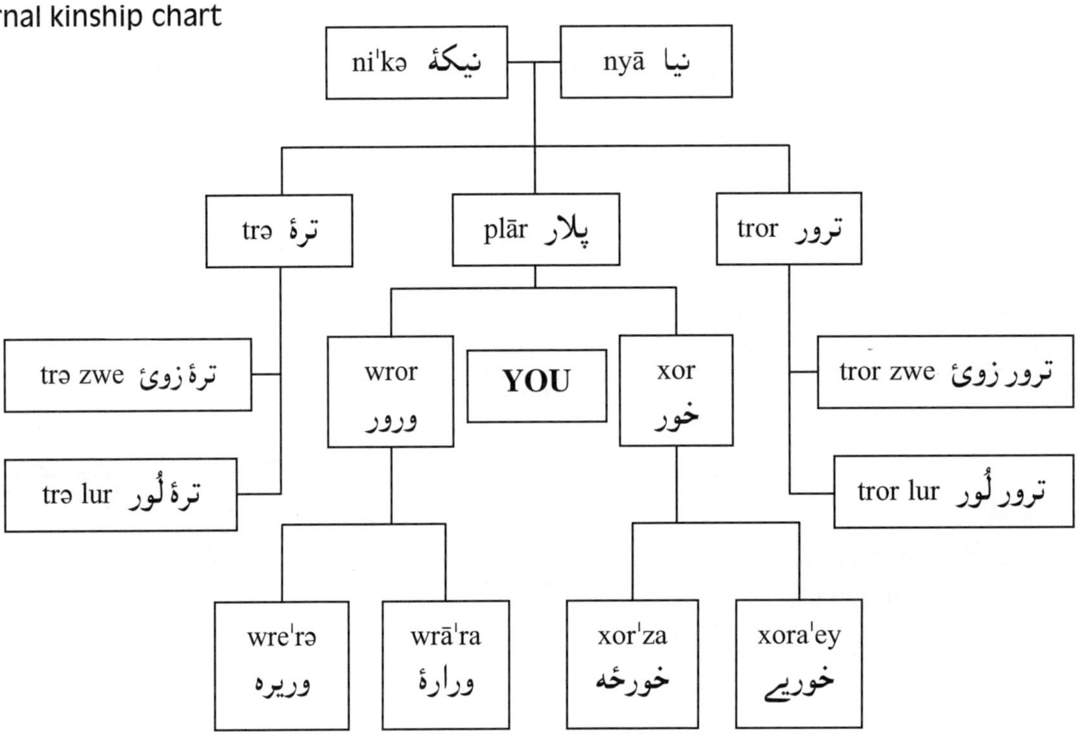

ni'kə نيکهٔ grandfather	nyā نيا grandmother	trə ترهٔ paternal uncle
tror ترور paternal aunt	plār پلار father	trə zwe ترهٔ زوئ uncle's son
tror zwe ترور زوئ aunt's son	trə lur ترهٔ لُور uncle's daughter	tror lur ترور لُور aunt's daughter
xora'ey خوريے sister's son	wre'ra وريره brother's daughter	wrā'rə وراره brother's son
xor'za خورځه sister's daughter		

[20] Lindholm, Charles. *Generosity and Jealousy.* Columbia University Press. 1982.

NOTE:
trə zwe (ترۀ زوئ) is also called *tar'bur* (تربُور); and *trə lur* (ترۀ لُور) may be *tər' la* (ترله).

In learning kinship terms it is a good idea to first ask what relationship someone is to your friend. After the reply see if you can correctly say what the reverse relationship is. The conversation might go like this:

ha'ɣa de tsə dey?	What's he to you?	هغه دي څۀ دے؟
trə me dey.	He's my uncle.	ترۀ مي دے.
no tə də ha'ɣə wrā'rə ye?	So you're his nephew?	نو تۀ د هغۀ وراره يې ؟

Maternal kinship chart

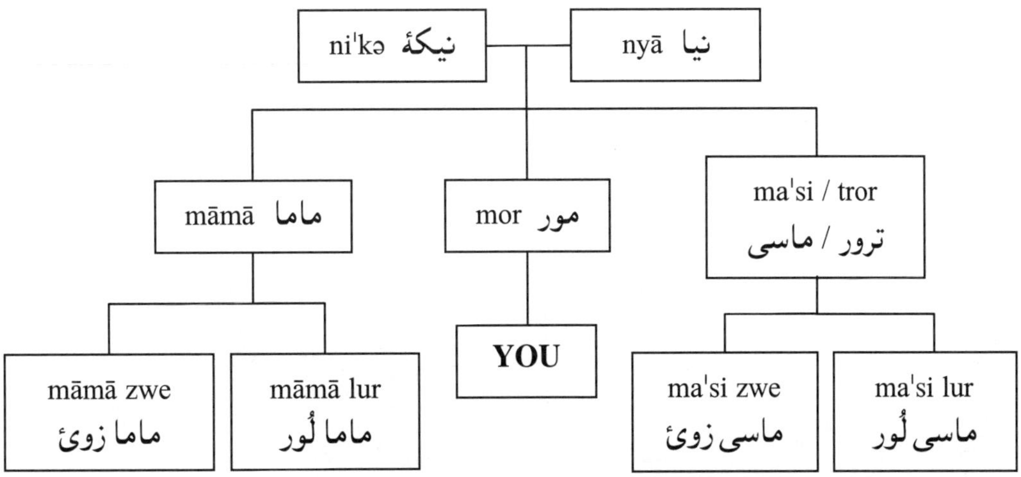

mor مور	mā'mā ماما	mā'si ماسی
mother	maternal uncle	maternal aunt

Kinship between inlaws

YOU represents a male in this chart

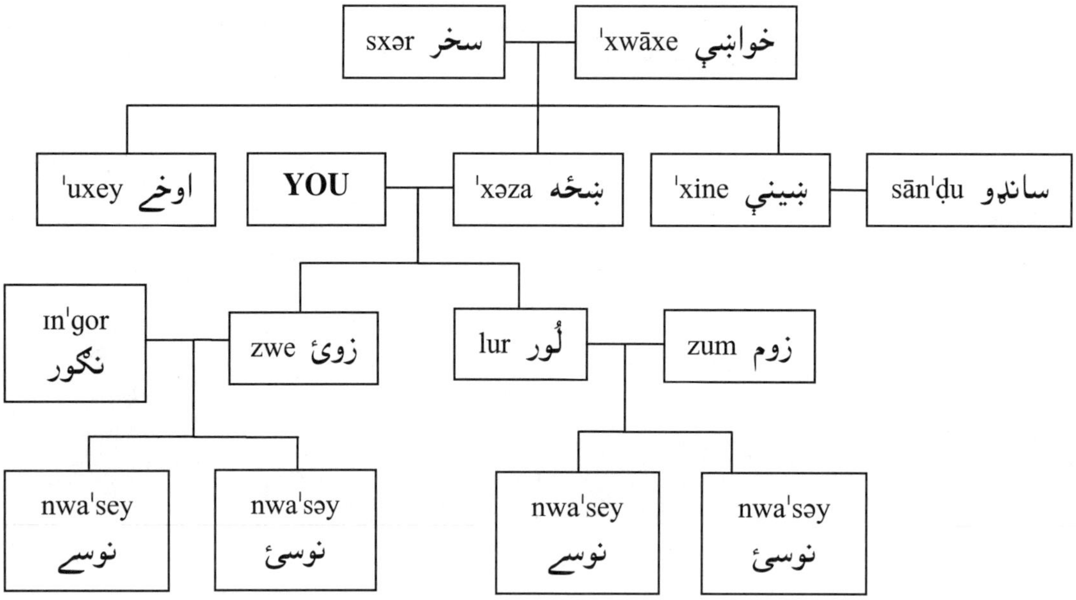

sxər سخر father-in-law	ˈxwāxe خوابنې mother-in-law	ˈuxey اوخے brother-in-law
ˈxine ښينې sister-in-law	ˈxəza ښځه wife	ɪnˈgor نګور daughter-in-law
zum زُوم son-in-law	nwaˈsey نوسے grandson	nwaˈsəy نوسئ granddaughter
sānˈḍu سانډُو sister-in-law's husband		

YOU represents a female in this chart

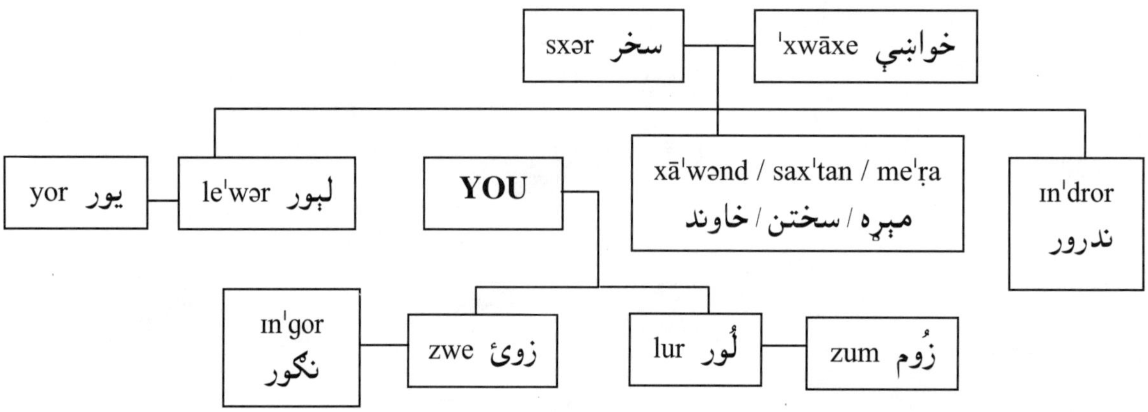

le'wər لېور brother-in-law	ɪn'dror ندرور sister-in-law	xā'wənd / sax'tan / me'ṛə خاوند / سختن / مېړهٔ husband
yor يور brother-in-law's wife		

Practicing kinship names

You might be wondering how to learn all these new kinship terms. One idea is to put together a collection of your own family pictures and develop a dialogue about each family member. Be aware that it is not appropriate for men to show pictures of females to Pukhtun men, so some creativity may be needed to avoid offense.

Pronunciation drill

Focus on / **q** / ق by practicing tongue twisters:

په قائره کښې عقلمند قاتِل د قانُون قابِل قاضی نه قلم وتښتولو.

pa qāy'ra ke aqəl'mənd qā'tɪl də qā'nun qā'bɪl qā'zi na qa'ləm 'otəxtawəlo.

In Cairo the clever assassin snatched the pen from the clever judge of law.

قاضی په قبر کښې هم د قدم، قلم، قسم قیصه کوله.

qā'zi pa 'qəbər ke həm də 'qadəm, qa'ləm, qa'səm qe'sa ka'wəla.

Even in the grave the judge was telling the tale of step, pen and oaths.

The past tense

Before starting the past tense it is helpful to be clear on the distinction between transitive and intransitive verbs. They operate in very different ways. Transitive verbs involve action on an object (he ate an apple, she hit me, etc.). Intransitive verbs have no object (I was walking, he was asleep, etc.). (See Lessons Seven and Eight.)

The simple past tense of the 'to be' verb

Person	Singular			Plural		
1st	wəm	I was	وم	wu	we were	وُو
2nd	we	you were	وې	wəy	you were	وئ
3rd m.	wo	he was	وو	wu	they were	وُو
3rd f.	wa	she was	وه	we	they were	وې

NOTE:

The 2nd person singular and 3rd person feminine plural are slightly different in pronunciation.

☝ Ask your helper to teach you this difference.

Examples of the past tense 'to be' verb in sentences

zə ḍāk'ṭər wəm.	I was a doctor.	زۀ ډاکټر وم.
mung ḍer xwā'gə dos'tān wu.	We were very sweet friends.	مُونږ ډېر خواږۀ دوستان وُو.
tə xə ha'lək we?	Were you a good boy?	تۀ ښۀ هلک وې؟
'tāso xə'fa nə-wəy?	Weren't you upset?	تاسو خفه نۀ وئ؟
ha'ɣa ḍer na'rey wo.	He was very skinny.	هغه ډېر نرے وو.
dā na'ǰoṛa wa.	She was sick.	دا ناجوړه وه.
ha'ɣa ḍer xo'šāla wo.	He was very happy.	هغه ډېر خوشحاله وو.
haɣ'wi 'ḍere 'xkwəle we.	They were very pretty. (*f.pl.*)	هغوی ډېرې ښکُلې وې.
'haɣa xə 'fɪləm nə-wo.	That was not a good film. (*m.s.*)	هغه ښۀ فلم نۀ وو.
'haɣa xə kita'buna wu.	Those were good books. (*m.pl.*)	هغه ښۀ کتابونه وُو.
'haɣa xə qi'sa wa.	That was a good story. (*f.s.*)	هغه ښۀ قيصه وه.
'haɣa xe qi'se we.	Those were good stories. (*f.pl.*)	هغه ښې قيصې وې.
rah'mān bābā ḍer luy ša'er wo.	Rahman Baba was a great poet. (*m.s.*)	رحمان بابا ډېر لوئ شاعر وو.

NOTE:

The bookish form of the 3rd person masculine plural is *wəl* (ول), but it is not used in normal speech.

Adverbs of time used in the past tense

ha'ɣa pəx'wā 'tsənga kāri'gər wo?	What kind of worker was he before?	هغه پخوا څنګه کاريګر وو؟
ha'ɣa ḍer mehna'ti wo.	He was very hard working.	هغه ډېر مِحنتی وو.
be'gā stā xor 'tsənga wa?	How was your sister last night?	بېګا ستا خور څنګه وه؟
'tera myāšt ke tə 'čerta we?	Where were you last month?	تېره مياشت کښې تهٔ چرته وې؟
zə pa swāt ke wəm.	I was in Swat.	زهٔ په سوات کښې وم.
pa 'tera haf'ta ke stā zā'mən 'čerta wu?	Where were your sons last week?	په تېره هفته کښې ستا زامن چرته وُو؟
pa 'tera haf'ta ke pa han'gu ke wu.	They were in Hangu last week.	په تېره هفته کښې په هنګُو کښې وُو.
'xəze parun pa kor ke we?	Were the women at home yesterday?	ښځې پرُون په کور کښې وې؟
na, hay'wi nə-we, də gāwən'ḍyāno pa kor ke we.	No, they were not, they were at the neighbours' house.	نه، هغوی نهٔ وې، د ګاونډيانو په کور کښې وې.
pa'rosa-kāl tə 'čerta we?	Where were you last year?	پروسکال ته چرته وې؟

NOTE:

The adjective *ter* (تېر) 'past' is used to modify the time words that point to the past, and like other adjectives it is inflected for number and gender.

Examples of the verb *šwəl* in past tense sentences شول

hay'wi mung ta ɣo'sa šu?	Did they become angry with us?	هغوی مُونږ ته غُصه شُو؟
na, ɣo'sa nə-šu.	No they didn't become angry.	نه، غُصه نهٔ شُو.
tə 'kəla xug šwe?	When did you get injured?	تهٔ کله خوږ شوې؟
zə 'yəwa haf'ta 'maxke xug šəm.	I got injured a week ago.	زهٔ يوه هفته مخکښې خوږ شوم.
tsə 'ošo? 'wəle ǰına'kəy 'dumra xo'šāla šwe?	What happened? Why have the girls become so happy?	څهٔ وشُو؟ ولې جينکۍ دومره خوشحاله شوې؟

ˈzəka če natiˈǰa ˈowata āw dwi pās šwe.	Because their results came out and they passed.	ځکه چې نتيجه ووته او دوئ پاس شوې.
tə beˈgā tsə waxt uˈda šwe?	When did you go to sleep last night?	ته بېګا څۀ وخت اُودۀ شوې؟
zə ləs ˈnime baˈǰe uˈda šəm.	I went to sleep at ten-thirty.	زۀ لس نيمې بجې اُودۀ شوم.
də xoˈdey pa ˈfəzəl saˈra kār ˈxatəm šo.	By the grace of God the job is finished.	د خُدائ په فضل سره کار ختم شو.

NOTE:

If you are British, take care with words like *beˈgā* (بېګا) that end in a long / -ā / ا- sound. It is a common mistake to add an / -r / (ر-) sound to the end of the word.

The use of *šwəl* to indicate the passive voice شول

1. Using *šwəl* with transitive verbs to form the passive voice

zəˈmā kaˈmis nən winˈzəley šo?	Was my shirt washed today?	زما قميص نن وينځلے شو؟
na, o-nə-winˈzəley šo.	No, it was not washed.	نه، ونۀ وينځلے شو.
xaˈtuna mo o-ˈnə-legəley šu?	Were your letters not sent?	خطُونه مو ونۀ لېږلے شُو ؟
āw, ˈolegəley šu.	Yes, they were sent.	آو، ولېږلے شُو.
ḍoˈḍəy tsə waxt xoṛəle šwa?	When was the food eaten?	ډوډۍ څۀ وخت خوړلې شوه؟
saˈhar waxti ˈoxoṛəle šwa.	It was eaten early this morning.	سحر وختى وخوړلې شوه.
zə paˈrun waˈhəley šwəm.	I was hit yesterday.	زۀ پرُون وهلے شوم.
tə beˈgā ˈolidey šwe?	Were you seen last night?	تۀ بېګا وليدے شوې؟
na, mā ḍer ıhtiˈyāt kaˈwu.	No, I was very careful.	نه، ما ډېر اِحتياط کوُو.
zə nə yım lidəley ˈšıβey.	I have not been seen.	زۀ نۀ يم ليدلے شوے.

NOTE:

The past tense form of *šwəl* (شول) is in agreement with the object in these sentences. For more details look at the next chapter, where transitive verbs in the past tense are dealt with.

2. The verb *šwəl* combined with nouns in the passive voice

pa'run bā'rān tsə waxt šo'ro šo?	When did the rain start yesterday?	پرُون باران څهٔ وخت شروع شو؟
taqri'bān ā'tə ba'je šo'ro šo.	It started about eight o'clock.	تقريباً اتهٔ بجې شروع شو.
kami'suna me is'tri šu?	Were my shirts ironed?	قميصُونه مې استرى شُو؟
na, is'tri nə-šu.	No, they were not ironed.	نه، اِسترى نهٔ شُو.
dā 'peɣla 'kəla wā'də šwa?	When did this girl get married?	دا پيغله کله وادهٔ شوه؟
'yəwa haf'ta 'maxke wā'də šwa.	She got married a week ago.	يوه هفته مخکښې وادهٔ شوه.
kam're ǰa'ru šwe?	Were the rooms swept?	کمرې جارُو شوې؟
āw, sa'har ǰa'ru šwe.	Yes, they were swept this morning.	آو، سحر جارُو شوې.
fɪl'muna 'okatəley šwəl?	Were the films watched?	فلمُونه وکتلے شول؟
na, biǰ'li nə-wa.	No, there was no electicity.	نه، بجلى نهٔ وه.

3. The use of *šwəl* with adjectives in the passive voice

stā moṭər 'kəla xarts šo?	When was your car sold?	ستا موټر کله خرڅ شو؟
'yəwa myašt 'maxke xarts šo.	It was sold a month earlier.	يوه مياشت مخکښې خرڅ شو.
ɣə'nəm tsə waxt lām'də šu?	When did the wheat become wet? *(m.pl.)*	غنم څهٔ وخت لامدهٔ شُو؟
be'gā lām'də šu.	It became wet last night.	بېګا لامدهٔ شُو.
pa wa'ṛuki ha'lək tsə 'ošo?	What happened to the small boy?	په وړُوکى هلک څهٔ وشُو؟
də ā'ǰəz xpa mā ta šwa.	The poor boy's foot was broken. *(f.s.)*	د عاجز خپه ما ته شوه.
kur'səy de 'kəla 'ǰoṛe šwe?	When were your chairs made? *(f.pl.)*	کُرسۍ دې کله جوړې شوې؟
dre 'wrəze 'maxke 'ǰoṛe šwe.	They were made three days ago.	درې ورځې مخکښې جوړې شوې.

NOTE:
The verbal adjectives are also inflected according to the number and gender of the subject.

See the following examples:

	Wet		Dry	
m.s	lund šo	لوند شو	uč šo	وچ شو
m.pl.	lām'də šu	لامدهٔ شُو	uč šu	وچ شُو
f.s.	lam'da šwa [lān'da šwa]	لمده شوه [لانده شوه]	'uča šwa	وچه شوه
f.pl.	lam'de šwe	لمدې شوې	'uče šwe	وچې شوې

	Cooked/Ripe		Dead	
m.s	pox šo	پوخ شو	məṛ šo	مړ شو
m.pl.	pa'xə šu	پاښهٔ شُو	mṛə šu	مړهٔ شُو
f.s.	pa'xa šwa	پخه شوه	mṛa šwa	مړه شوه
f.pl.	pa'xe šwe	پخې شوې	mṛe šwe	مړې شوې

čərg tsə waxt pox šo? — When was the chicken cooked? (*m.s.*) — چرګ څهٔ وخت پوخ شو؟

čer'gān tsə waxt pa'xə šu? — When were the chickens cooked? (*m.pl.*) — چرګان څهٔ وخت پاخهٔ شُو؟

ḍo'ḍəy tsə waxt pa'xa šwa? — When was the bread cooked? (*f.s.*) — ډوډۍ څهٔ وخت پخه شوه؟

wriǰe tsə waxt pa'xe šwe? — When was the rice cooked? (*f.pl.*) — وريژې څهٔ وخت پخې شوې؟

yo sa'ṛey nən məṛ šo. — A man died today. (*m.s.*) — يو سړے نن مړ شو.

dre sa'ṛi nən mṛə šu. — Three men died today. (*m.pl.*) — درې سړی نن مړهٔ شُو.

'yəwa 'xəza nən mṛa šwa. — One woman died today. (*f.s.*) — يوه ښځه نن مړهٔ شوه.

dre 'xəze nən mṛe šwe. — Three women died today. (*f.pl.*) — درې ښځې نن مړې شوې.

Comprehension drill: Inquiring about the time

tso baǰe di? — What time is it? — څو بجې دی؟

tsa'lor ba'ǰe di. — It's four o'clock. — څلور بجې دی.

stā pa ga'ṛəy ke tso ba'je di?	What's the time on your watch?	ستا په گړۍ کښې څو بجې دی؟
'doləs baǰe di.	It's twelve o'clock.	دولس بجې دی.
tsə waxt dey?	What time is it?	څهٔ وخت دے؟
špəg 'nime baǰe di.	It's six thirty.	شپږ نیمې بجې دی.
tsə waxt dey?	What time is it?	څهٔ وخت دے؟
pāw kəm pin'zə baǰe di.	It is quarter to five.	پاؤ کم پینځهٔ بجې دی.
tsə waxt dey?	What time is it?	څهٔ وخت دے؟
pāw 'bānde 'doləs baǰe di.	It is a quarter past twelve.	پاؤ باندې دولس بجې دی.
ləs 'mınṭa kəm tsa'lor baǰe di.	It is ten minutes to four.	لس مېنټه کم څلور بجې دی.
šıl də 'pāsa pin'zə baǰe di. (*or*)	It's twenty past five.	شل د پاسه پینځهٔ بجې دی. (یا)
šıl mın'ṭa də 'pāsa pin'zə baǰe di.		شل منټه د پاسه پینځهٔ بجې دی.
tsə waxt dey?	What time is it?	څهٔ وخت دے؟
'yəwa baǰa da.	It's one o'clock.	یوه بجه ده.

NOTE:

Remember to pay attention to the gender of 'one' (*yo* یو / *'yəwa* یوه)

☝ Use a clock or watch to practice asking or telling the time with your helper.

Memorising moment

mata'luna

پردے کټ تر نیمې شپې وی.

pra'dey kaṭ tar 'nime špe wi.

Someone else's bed is only good till half way through the night.

اولاد چې نیازبین شی نو نهٔ دَ دین شی او نهٔ دَ سادین شی.

āw'lād če nyāz'bin ši no nə də din ši āw nə də sā'din ši.

When a child is spoiled he becomes neither religious nor a labourer.

پردی نۀ خپلیږی.

pra'di nə xpəl'igi.

Outside folk never become relatives.

کۀ غر لوئ دے، خو په سر یې لار ده.

kə ɣar luy dey, xo pa sər ye lār da.

Even if the hill is big, there is a way to the top.

چې رښتیا راځی، دروغو به کلی وران کړی وی.

če rɪx'tyā rā'zi, da'roɣo ba 'kəli wrān kuṛī wi.

Before truth comes, lies will have ruined the villages.

Exercises for Lesson Eighteen

Change the following present tense questions into their simple past tense forms and answer the questions.

a. tə čerta 'pate 'kege? تۀ چرته پاتې کیږې؟

---

b. os bā'rān šoro 'kigi? اوس باران شروع کیږی؟

---

c. nən 'tāso pa dəf'tər ke yəy? نن تاسو په دفتر کښې یئ؟

---

d. tsa'pləy de xa'rābe di? څپلۍ دې خرابې دی؟

---

e. ha'ɣa ḍer xə sa'ṛey dey? هغه ډیر ښۀ سړے دے؟

---

f.	plār me na-ˈǰoṛa dey?	پلار مې ناجوړه دے؟
g.	ˈdaɣa baˈləxt šin dey?	دغه بالښت شين دے؟
h.	ˈhaɣa saˈṛey waˈṛukey dey?	هغه سړے وړُوکے دے؟
i.	ˈhaɣa moˈṭər ˈtsənga dey?	هغه موټر څنګه دے؟
j.	dey yo malˈdār māˈlɪk dey?	دے يو مالدار مالِک دے؟
k.	zəˈmā mor meraˈbāna da?	زما مور مِهربانه ده؟
l.	zəˈmā xor ˈməšra da?	زما خور مشره ده؟
m.	stā lur ˈḍera xāyˈsta da?	ستا لُور ډېره ښائسته ده؟

Vocabulary for Lesson Eighteen

ıhti'yāt ka'wəl	اِحتياط كول		comp. v.t.	to take care, to take precautions
'uxey	اوخے	m.	n.	brother-in-law (wife's brother)
bābā	بابا	m.	n.	father, respected elder
ba'ǰa	بجه	f.	n.	o'clock, hour
be'gā	بېگا		adv.	last night
pəx'wā	پخوا		adv.	before, in the past
'peɣla	پېغله	f.s.	n.	maiden, unmarried young woman
tar'bur	ترښور	m.	n.	cousin (paternal uncle's son)
tror / tror'yāne	ترور / ترورياني	f.	n.	paternal aunt
trə	ترهٔ	m.	n.	paternal uncle
taqri'bān	تقريباً		adv.	nearly, almost, about, approximately
'ter	تېر	m.	adj.	past, late
'zəka če	ځکه چي		conj.	because, since
xā'wənd	خاوند	m.s.	n.	husband; owner
'xwāxe	خواښي	f.	n.	mother-in-law
xor'za / xor'ze	خورځه / خورځي	f.	n.	niece (sister's daughter)
xora'ey	خوريے	m.	n.	nephew (sister's son)
zum	زُوم	m.	n.	son-in-law
sān'ḍu	ساندُو	m.	n.	sister-in-law's husband (wife's sister's husband)
sax'tan	سختن	m.	n.	husband
sxər / sxər'ān	سخر / سخران	m.	n.	father-in-law
sa'ka	سکه	m.	adj.	of full blood (relation)
ša'er / šae'rān	شاعر / شاعران	m.	n.	poet
ša'era / šae'rāne	شاعره / شاعراني	f.		

ˈxəza / ˈxəze	ښځه / ښځې	*f.*	*n.*	wife, married female, woman
ˈxine	ښينې	*f.*	*n.*	sister-in-law (wife's sister)
āˈǰəz	عاجز	*m.*	*n.*	weak, poor, humble, innocent
ˈfɪləm	فلم	*m.*	*n.*	film, movie
kāriˈgər	کاريګر	*m.*	*n.*	worker, labourer, craftsman
lund / lāmˈdə	لوند / لامدۀ	*m.*	*adj.*	wet, moist
lamˈda / lamˈde	لمده / لمدې	*f.*		
leˈwər / lewˈruna	لېور / لېورُونه	*m.*	*n.*	brother-in-law (husband's brother)
māˈsi	ماسی	*f.*	*n.*	maternal aunt
māˈmā	ماما	*m.*	*n.*	maternal uncle
mehnaˈti	مِحنتی		*adj.*	diligent, hardworking
ˈməšar / məšaˈrān	مَشر / مشران	*m.*	*adj.*	older
ˈməšra / ˈməšre	مشره / مشرې	*f.*		
mor / ˈmyende	مور / مياندې	*f.*	*n.*	mother
meˈṛə	مېړۀ	*m.*	*n.*	husband
ˈmɪnṭa [ˈmɪnaṭ]	مينټه [منټ]		*n.*	minute
natiˈǰa	نتيجه	*f.*	*n.*	result, conclusion, consequence
ɪnˈdror / ɪndrorˈyāne	ندرور / ندروريانې	*f.*	*n.*	sister-in-law (husband's sister)
ɪnˈgor / ɪngorˈyāne	نګور / نګوريانې	*f.*	*n.*	daughter-in-law
nwaˈsəy	نوسئ [نمسۍ]	*f.*	*n.*	granddaughter
nwaˈsey	نوسے	*m.*	*n.*	grandson
nyā / nyāˈgāne	نيا / نياګانې	*f.*	*n.*	grandmother
niˈkə / nikˈuna	نيکۀ / نيکونه	*m.*	*n.*	grandfather
uč	وچ	*m.*	*adj.*	dry, arid, parched, barren
ˈuča / ˈuče	وچه / وچې	*f.*		
wrāˈrə / wreruna	ورارۀ / ورېرُونه	*m.*	*n.*	nephew (brother's son)

wreˈra / wreˈre	وربره / وربري	*f.*	*n.*	niece (brother's daughter)
həmˈzoley	همزولے	*m.*	*adj.*	peer, same age
yor	يور			brother-in-law's wife

nulə'səm sa'bəq نُولسم سبق

Lesson Nineteen

Dialogue nineteen: Making the most of a monolingual situation

Language skills will quickly multiply when you use Pukhto to elicit more information. Here are some useful phrases to memorise that will allow you to get help from anyone.

L: tə mā ta də moxta'lıfo si'zuno nu'muna xo'dəley še? Can you tell me the names of different things?	تهٔ ما ته د مُختلفو خیزُونو نُومُونه ښودلے شې؟
L: tə ba mā ta də yo siz num 'oxaye, byā ba zə pa 'guta 'xāyım če tə 'tsənga num 'waxle. You tell me the name of something, then I will point to it when you say it.	تهٔ به ما ته د یو خیز نُوم وښایې، بیا به زهٔ په گوته ښایم چې تهٔ څنگه نُوم واخلې.
L: os mā ta 'newey num 'oxāya! Now teach me a new name!	اوس ما ته نوے نُوم وښایه!
L: tə mā ta də ba'dən anda'muno nu'muna xo'dəley še? Can you tell me the names of the parts of the body?	تهٔ ما ته د بدن د اندامُونو نُومُونه ښودلے شې؟
L: tə mā ta pəx'to ke šmer xo'dəley še? Can you teach me counting in Pukhto?	تهٔ ما ته پښتو کښې شمېر ښودلے شې؟
L: tə šmer 'owaya āw zə ba ye 'likəm. You say numbers and I will write them.	تهٔ شمېر ووایه او زهٔ به یې لیکم.
L: tə mā ta pəx'to ke hedā'yət rāka'wəley še? Can you give me some help with Pukhto?	تهٔ ما ته پښتو کښې هدایت راکولے شې؟
L: tə mā ta 'owaya āw zə ba ye ka'wəm. You tell me and I will do it.	تهٔ ما ته ووایه او زهٔ به یې کوم.
L: mā ta də sa'hi pəx'to ız'da ka'wəlo də'pāra də ḍer zyāt gar'dān zaru'rət dey. To learn correct Pukhto I need a lot of repetition.	ما ته د صحیح پښتو زده کولو د پاره د ډېر زیات گردان ضرُورت دے.

Pronunciation drill

Practice this tongue twister:

قاصد هره ورځ د قصاب نه قاضی له مُفت قیمه راوړی.

qā'sad 'hara wrəz də qa'sāb na qā'zi la maft qi'ma rāw'ṛi.

The judge's peon daily brings free mince from the butcher.

An intransitive verb in different tenses

pohe'dəl – 'to know', 'to understand' پوهېدل

Simple present and present continuous

Roots: *pohe'dəl* پوهېدل 'to understand' (strong)

I understand, I am understanding, etc.

1st s.	po'higəm	پوهېږم
2nd s.	po'hege	پوهېږې
3rd s.	po'higi	پوهېږی
1st pl.	po'higu	پوهېږُو
2nd pl.	po'hegəy	پوهېږئ
3rd pl.	po'higi	پوهېږی

'pwe šwəl پوی [پوهه] شول 'to understand' (weak)

I (just now) understand, I am (just now) understanding, etc.

1st s.	'pwc šwəm[21]	پوی [پوهه] شوم
2nd s.	'pwe šwe	پوی شوې
3rd m.s.	'pwe šo	پوی شو
3rd f.s.	'pwe šwa	پوی شوه
1st pl.	'pwe šu	پوی شُو
2nd pl.	'pwe šwəy	پوی شوئ
3rd m.pl	'pwe šwəl	پوی شول
3rd f.pl.	'pwe šwəle	پوی شولې

Future (strong)

I will understand, etc.

1st s.	ba po'higəm	به پوهېږم
2nd s.	ba po'hege	به پوهېږې
3rd s.	ba po'higi	به پوهېږی
1st pl.	ba po'higu	به پوهېږُو
2nd pl.	ba po'hegəy	به پوهېږئ
3rd pl.	ba po'higi	به پوهېږی

Future (weak)

I may understand, etc.

1st s.	ba 'pwe šəm	به پوی شم
2nd s.	ba 'pwe še	به پوی شې
3rd s.	ba 'pwe ši	به پوی شی
1st pl.	ba 'pwe šu	به پوی شُو
2nd pl.	ba 'pwe šəy	به پوی شئ
3rd pl.	ba 'pwe ši	به پوی شی

---

[21] Both versions of *'pwe šwəm* (پوی شوم and پوهه شوم) are commonly used. The difference in spelling does not affect pronunciation.

Roots: *pohe'dəl* پوهېدل 'to understand' (strong)

'pwe šwəl پوی [پوهه] شول 'to understand' (weak)

Imperative

Understand! (i.e. You must understand!)

2nd s.	'pwe ša	پوی شه
2nd pl.	'pwe šəy	پوی شئ

Past progressive/continuous

I was understanding, etc.

1st s.	pohe'dələm	پوهېدلم
2nd s.	pohe'dəle	پوهېدلې
3rd m.s.	pohe'dəlo	پوهېدلو
3rd f.s.	pohe'dəla	پوهېدله
1st pl.	pohe'dəlu	پوهېدلُو
2nd pl.	pohe'dələy	پوهېدلئ
3rd m.pl.	pohe'dəl	پوهېدل
3rd f.pl.	pohe'dəle	پوهېدلې

Simple past

I understood, etc.

1st s.	'pwe šwəm	پوی شوم
2nd s.	'pwe šwe	پوی شوې
3rd m.s.	'pwe šo	پوی شو
3rd f.s.	'pwe šwa	پوی شوه
1st pl.	'pwe šu	پوی شُو
2nd pl.	'pwe šəy	پوی شوئ
3rd m.pl.	'pwe šwu	پوی شُو
3rd f.pl.	'pwe šwəl	پوی شول

Past habitual

I used to understand, etc.

1st s.	ba pohe'dələm	به پوهېدلم
2nd s.	ba pohe'dəle	به پوهېدلې
3rd m.s.	ba pohe'dəlo	به پوهېدلو
3rd f.s.	ba pohe'dəla	به پوهېدله
1st pl.	ba pohe'dəlu	به پوهېدلُو
2nd pl.	ba pohe'dələy	به پوهېدلئ
3rd m.pl.	ba pohe'dəlo	به پوهېدلو
3rd f.pl.	ba pohe'dəle	به پوهېدلې

Present potential

I can understand, etc.

1st s.	pohe'de šəm	پوهېدے شم
2nd s.	pohe'de še	پوهېدے شې
3rd s.	pohe'de ši	پوهېدے شی
1st pl.	pohe'de šu	پوهېدے شُو
2nd pl.	pohe'dey šəy	پوهېدے شئ
3rd pl.	pohe'dey ši	پوهېدے شی

Roots: *pohe'dəl* پوهېدل 'to understand' (strong)

Past participle

	pohe'del	پوهېدل

'pwe šwəl پوى [پوهه] شول 'to understand' (weak)

Past participle

m.	'pwe 'šɪβey	پوى شوے
f.	'pwe 'šɪβe	پوى شوې
pl.	'pwe 'šɪβi	پوى شوى

Present perfect

I have understood, etc.

1st m.s.	'pwe 'šɪβey yɪm	پوى شوے يم
1st f.s.	'pwe 'šɪβe yɪm	پوى شوې يم
2nd m.s.	'pwe 'šɪβey ye	پوى شوے يې
2nd f.s.	'pwe 'šɪβe ye	پوى شوې يې
3rd m.s.	'pwe 'šɪβey dey	پوى شوے دے
3rd f.s.	'pwe 'šɪβe da	پوى شوې ده
1st pl.	'pwe 'šɪβi yu	پوى شوى يُو
2nd pl.	'pwe 'šɪβi yəy	پوى شوى يئ
3rd pl.	'pwe 'šɪβi di	پوى شوى دى

Past perfect

I had understood, etc.

1st m.s.	'pwe 'šɪβey wəm	پوى شوے وم
1st f.s.	'pwe 'šɪβe wəm	پوى شوې وم
2nd m.s.	'pwe 'šɪβey we	پوى شوے وې
2nd f.s.	'pwe 'šɪβe we	پوى شوې وې
3rd m.s.	'pwe 'šɪβey wo	پوى شوے وو
3rd f.s.	'pwe 'šɪβe wa	پوى شوې وه
1st pl.	'pwe 'šɪβi wu	پوى شوى وُو
2nd pl.	'pwe 'šɪβi wəy	پوى شوى وئ
3rd m.pl.	'pwe 'šɪβi wu	پوى شوى وُو
3rd f.pl.	'pwe 'šɪβe we	پوى شوې وې

Intransitive compound verbs

	ke'dəl	كېدل	**šwəl**	شول
to wait, to stay, to be late	isāre'dəl	ايسارېدل [حصارېدل]	isār šwəl	ايسار شول [حصار شول]
to go to sleep	u'də ke'dəl	اُودهٔ كېدل	u'də šwəl	اُودهٔ شول
to be destroyed	barbāde'dəl	بربادېدل	bar'bād šwəl	برباد شول
to hide oneself	pəṭe'dəl	پټېدل	pəṭ šwəl	پټ شول
to be born	pe'dā ke'dəl	پيدا كېدل	pe'dā šwəl	پيدا شول

to be known	peǰan'dey ke'dəl	پېژندے کېدل	peǰan'dey šwəl	پېژندے شول
to happen, to meet	pexe'dəl	پېښېدل	pex šwəl	پېښ شول
to pass by; to swallow	tere'dəl	تېرېدل	ter šwəl	تېر شول
to be spoiled	xarābe'dəl	خرابېدل	xa'rāb šwəl	خراب شول
to start out	rawāne'dəl	روانېدل	ra'wān šwəl	روان شول
to be injured	zax'mi ke'dəl	زخمی کېدل	zax'mi šwəl	زخمی شول
to be increased	zyāte'dəl	زیاتېدل	zyāt šwəl	زیات شول
to ride, to mount	sore'dəl	سورېدل	swā'rə šwəl	سوارۀ شول
to be shared	šarike'dəl	شریکېدل	šarik šwəl	شریک شول
to appear	xkāre'dəl	ښکارېدل	xkā'ra šwəl	ښکاره شول
to be decreased	kəme'dəl	کمېدل	kəm šwəl	کم شول
to get down	kuze'dəl	کُوزېدل	'kuz šwəl	کُوز شول
to be mixed	gəḍwəḍe'dəl	ګډوډ کېدل	gəḍwəḍ šwəl	ګډوډ شول
to be broken	māte'dəl	ماتېدل	māt šwəl	مات شول

Practice with these sentences:

zə də ha'ɣə pa xa'bara po'ha šəm.	I understood his talk.	زۀ د هغۀ په خبره پوهه شوم.
ha'ɣa zə'mā pa xa'bara po'he šwa.	She understood my talk.	هغه زما په خبره پوې شوه.
tə 'pohe šwe?	Did you understand?	تۀ پوې شوې؟
'māšey ye ter šo.	He swallowed a mosquito.	ماشے يې تېر شو.
sa'bəta špa u'da šəm.	I slept the whole night.	ثابته شپه اُودۀ شوم.
tə pa ās sor šwe?	Did you ride a horse?	ته په اس سور شوې؟
'bələf māt šo.	The light bulb broke.	بلف مات شو.
ha'ɣa rā-sa'ra na'sāpa melāw šo.	He suddenly met me.	هغه راسره ناڅاپه مِلاؤ شو.
pa sa'hi waxt ke rā-xkā'ra šwe.	You appeared just at the right time.	په صحيح وخت کښې راښکاره شوې.
māl'ṭe ṭole xa'rābe šwe.	The oranges were all spoilt.	مالټې ټولې خرابې شوې.
xār bar'bād šo.	The city is destroyed.	ښار برباد شو.

u'bə 'kəme šwe.	The water became less.	اوبهٔ کمې شوې.
ṭol qima'tuna zyāt šu.	All the prices increased.	ټول قيمتونه زيات شو.
'stərga ye xug šwa.	His eye was injured.	سترګه يې خوږ شوه.
špəg ka'sān ǰo'bəl šu.	Six people are injured.	شپږ کسان ژوبل شو.
xəze nar gəḍwəḍ šu.	Females and males [animals] were mixed up.	ښځې نر ګډوډ شُو.
dwa 'wrəze 'wrusto ǰoṛ šwəm.	I got well after two days.	دوه ورځې وروستو جوړ شوم.
ha'ɣa pa dəf'tər ke i'sār šo.	He stayed at the office.	هغه په دفتر کښې ايسار شو.
tə 'čerta pəṭ šwe?	Where were you hidden?	تهٔ چرته پټ شوې؟
zə də kaṭ 'lande pəṭ šəm.	I hid under the bed.	زهٔ د کټ لاندې پټ شوم.
xəze pa 'yəwa baǰa ra'wāne šwe.	The ladies started out at one o'clock.	ښځې په يوه بجه روانې شوې.
ha'lək pe'dā šo?	Was a boy born?	هلک پيدا شو؟
na, ǰɪ'nəy pe'dā šwa.	No, a girl was born.	نه، جينۍ پيدا شوه.

Regular intransitive verbs that take an / o- / prefix in the simple past tense

The verb *rase'dəl* (رسېدل) 'to arrive' provides a good example of a verb that takes the / o- / (و-) prefix in the simple past tense.

zə 'o-rasedəm.	I arrived.	زهٔ ورسېدم.
tə 'o-rasede.	You arrived.	تهٔ ورسېدې.
ha'ɣa 'o-rasedo.	He arrived.	هغه ورسېدو.
ha'ɣa 'o-raseda.	She arrived.	هغه ورسېده.
dā 'o-raseda.	She arrived.	دا ورسېده.
'tāso 'o-rasedəy.	You arrived.	تاسو ورسېدئ.
haɣ'wi 'o-rasedəl.	They (*m.pl.*) arrived.	هغوی ورسېدل.
dwi 'o-rasede.	They (*f.pl.*) arrived.	دوئ ورسېدې.

NOTES:

1. Like other verbs that imply direction, the directional prefixes are used:

stā 'xəza pa'run rā-'oraseda?	Did your wife arrive (here) yesterday?	ستا ښځه پرُون راورسېده؟
stā 'xəza pa'run war-'oraseda?	Did your wife arrive (there) yesterday?	ستا ښځه پرُون ورورسېده؟
stā 'xəza pa'run dar-'oraseda?	Did your wife reach you yesterday?	ستا ښځه پرُون درورسېده؟
hay'wi pa hefā'zət dar-'orasedəl?	Did they reach you safely?	هغوی په حفاظت درورسېدل؟

2. Notice the important differences between the sentences below. You have arrived late to work: a) would be used in a discussion in the office; b) would be used when you are out of the office; and c) is what the boss says to you the next day:

a)	zə kār ta na-'waxta rā-'orasedəm.	I came to work late.	زۀ کار ته ناوخته راورسېدم.
b)	zə kār ta leṭ war-'orasedəm.	I arrived late to work.	زۀ کار ته لېټ ورورسېدم.
c)	tə pa'run na-'waxta rā-'orasede.	You came late yesterday.	تۀ پرُون ناوخته راورسېدې.

Some more examples of verbs that add / o- / (و-) for the simple past

garze'dəl	ګرځېدل	to walk	čəle'dəl	چلېدل	to be in motion
ba'har tləl	بهر تلل	to go out	yeše'dəl	یشېدل	to boil itself
xa'təl	ختل	to climb	təxte'dəl	تښتېدل	to run away
ləge'dəl	لګېدل	to be fixed	sase'dəl	څڅېدل	to drip

Intransitive verbs that take an / o- / prefix in the past tense

tə də kor na rā-owate?	Did you get out of the house?	ته د کور نه راوتې؟
āw, zə də kor na rā-'owatəm ...	Yes, I got out, ...	آو، زۀ د کور نه راوتم،...
... 'lekın ha'ɣa rā-o-'nə-wato.	... but he did not get out.	... لېکن هغه راونۀ وتو.
ha'ɣa ɣar ta 'oxata?	Did she climb the hill?	هغه غر ته وخته؟
u'bə 'o-yešede?	Did the water boil?	اوبۀ وویشېدې؟
məǰ'rıma 'o-təxteda.	The criminal ran away. (*f.*)	مجرمه وتښتېده.

be'ṭək 'o-tsatsedə.	The guest room leaked.	بېټک وڅڅېدۀ.
ha'lək 'o-ɣorzedo.	The boy fell down.	هلک وغورځېدو.
ru'pəy nā'ləy ke 'o-ɣorzeda.	The rupee fell in the drain.	روپۍ نالۍ کښې وغورځېده.
bəs tsə waxt 'dəlta 'o-dredo?	When did the bus stop here?	بس څۀ وخت دلته ودرېدو؟
ləs 'mɪnṭa 'maxke 'o-dredo.	It stopped here ten minutes ago.	لس مينټه مخکښې ودرېدو.
stā 'wruṇa tso 'myašte 'maxke pa pexā'wər ke ose'dəl?	How many months ago did your brothers live in Peshawar?	ستا رونړه څو مياشتې مخکښې په پېښور کښې اوسېدل؟
dre 'myašte 'maxke 'halta ose'dəl.	They lived there three months ago.	درې مياشتې مخکښې هلته اوسېدل.

NOTE:

To make past sentences negative, add the negative marker *nə-* (نۀ -) between the / o- / (-و) and the verb. For example,

	/ o- / (-و)	nə- (نۀ -)	verb
ha'ɣa rā	o- -و	nə- نۀ -	wat وت

ha'ɣa rā-o-'nə-wat. He didn't come out. هغه را ونۀ وت.

This takes some practice, so have your helper make simple past sentences for you to make negative.

Irregular intransitive verbs

Some verbs do not follow the pattern of the verb 'to understand', nor do they take / o- / (-و) as a prefix. For example:

1. 'To go'

   The verb 'to go' occurs in two forms: *tləl* (تلل) and *'lāṛəl* (لاړل).

   'lāṛəl (لاړل) forms the past progressive tense, 'I went'. It is for events that just recently happened.

pa'run zə haspa'tāl ta 'lāṛəm.	Yesterday I went to hospital.	پرُون زۀ هسپتال ته لاړم.
pa'run zanā'na a'ṭək ta 'lāṛe.	Yesterday the ladies went to Attock.	پرُون زنانه اټک ته لاړې.
zə skul ta lā-'nə-ṛəm.	I did not go to the school.	زۀ سکُول ته لانۀ ړم.
'xəze ba'zār ta lā-'nə-ṛe.	The ladies did not go to the bazaar.	ښځې بازار ته لانۀ ړې.
bij'li 'lāṛa.	The electricity just left.	بجلی لاړه.

NOTE:
To make the verb negative, use the construction *lā-'nə-ṛel* (لا نۀ ړل) as in the example 'I did not go to school'.

2. 'To come'

The infinitive *rāt'ləl* (راتلل) becomes *'rā-ɣləl* (راغلل) in the simple past.

To say, "He came" an irregular ending is used: *rāɣey* (راغے).

Person	Singular			Plural		
1st	I came	rā-ɣləm	راغلم	we came	rā-ɣlu	راغلو
2nd	you came	rā-ɣle	راغلې	you came	rā-ɣləy	راغلئ
3rd m.	he came	rā-ɣey	راغے	they came	rā-ɣləl	راغلل
3rd f.	she came	rā-ɣla	راغله	they came	rā-ɣle	راغلې

ha'ɣə tsə waxt kor ta 'rā-ɣey āw tə tsə waxt 'rā-ɣle?	When did he come home and when did you come?	هغۀ څۀ وخت کور ته راغے او تۀ څۀ وخت راغلې؟
ha'ɣa kor ta ḍer nā-waxta 'rā-ɣey, xo zə wax'ti 'rā-ɣləm.	He came home very late, but I came early.	هغه کور ته ډېر ناوخته راغے، خو زۀ وختی راغلم.
tə rā-nə-ɣle.	You did not come.	تۀ رانۀ غلې.

The use of adjectives in the comparative degree

An adjective in the 'comparative degree' is used when comparing two things or persons. In English grammar this often done by adding / -er / or / -ier / to the adjective, as in the example, "Today's weather is warm-er than yesterday's."
Practice the sentences below to become familiar with the way comparisons are made in Pukhto.

kəm yo ki'tāb xə dey? 'haɣa ki'tāb āw kə dā ki'tāb?	Which book is good? That book or this book?	کُوم يو کتاب ښۀ دے؟ هغه کتاب او کۀ دا کتاب؟
'haɣa ki'tāb də de ki'tāb na xə dey.	That book is better than this one.	هغه کتاب د دې کتاب نه ښۀ دے.
dā ǰı'nəy də ha'ɣe na bad'ranga da.	This girl is uglier than that one.	دا جينۍ د هغې نه بدرنګه ده.

dā san'duq də ha'ɣe na drund dey.	This trunk is heavier than that one.	دا صندُوق د هغې نه درُوند دے.
'tāso sa'ra də de na ar'zān qa'ləm 'ništa?	Don't you have a cheaper pen than this?	تاسو سره د دې نه ارزان قلم نشته؟
na, də de na ar'zān qa'ləm 'ništa.	No, there is no cheaper pen than this.	نه، د دې نه ارزان قلم نشته.
nənə'ney mo'səm da parun na 'garəm dey.	Today's weather is warmer than yesterday's.	نننے موسم د پرُون نه گرم دے.
zə'mā pa xyāl fār'si də pəx'to na ā'sāna da.	I think Farsi is easier than Pukhto.	زما په خيال فارسى د پښتو نه آسانه ده.
tə də xpəl wror na 'məšar ye?	Are you older than your brother?	تهٔ د خپل ورور نه مشر يې؟
na, də ha'ɣə na 'kəšar yım.	No, I am younger than him.	نه، د هغهٔ نه کشر يم.

The use of adjectives in the superlative degree

An adjective in the 'superlative degree' is used when comparing three or more things or persons. In English grammar this often done by adding / -est / to the adjective, as in the example, "Of all of your children, which is the young-est?" Drill the sentences below and experiment with different adjectives to familiarise yourself with how the superlative degree is used in Pukhto.

də 'ṭolo-na xə me'wa 'kəma 'yəwa da?	Which is the best fruit of all?	د ټولو نه ښهٔ مېوه کُومه يوه ده؟
ma'ṇa pa 'ṭolo ke xə me'wa da.	The apple is the best fruit of all.	منړه په ټولو کښې ښهٔ مېوه ده.
stā mašu'māno ke də 'ṭolo na 'kəšar kəm yo dey?	Of all of your children which is the youngest?	ستا ماشُومانو کښې د ټولو نه کشر کُوم يو دے؟
stā 'mexo ke 'kəma 'yəwa də 'ṭolo na ḍer pəy ka'wi?	Of all of your buffaloes, which gives the most milk?	ستا مېښو کښې کُومه يوه د ټولو نه ډېر پئ کوى؟
'haɣa čər'gəy 'mexa də 'ṭolo na ḍer pəy ka'wi.	That one with a white forelock gives the most milk of all.	هغه چرګۍ مېښه د ټولو نه ډېر پئ کوى.

General comparisons

dā tsaˈpləy də de ˈbəle na baˈdəla da.	That sandal is different from the other.	دا څپلۍ د دې بلې نه بدله ده.
dā ǰāˈme pa mā bərāˈbəre di.	These clothes fit me.	دا جامې په ما برابرې دي.
ˈdwāṛa yo šey di.	Both of them are the same.	دواړه يو شے دي.
špəg ˈwāṛa yo bərāˈbər di.	All six of them are same.	شپږ واړه يو برابر دي.
ṭol ˈyo šey di.	They are all the same.	ټول يو شے دي.
ṭol yo ˈumra di.	They are all the same size.	ټول يو همره دي.
mā ta xo pa gul raˈsul āw ɪšˈfāq ke ˈhits farq ˈnə-xkāri.	To me there is no difference between Gul Rasoul and Ishfaq.	ما ته خو په ګُل رسول او اشفاق کښې هيڅ فرق نۀ ښکاري.

Memorising moment

mataˈluna

دَ سحر ورک چې ماښام کور ته راشي نو ورک نۀ دے.

də saˈhar wrək če māˈxām kor ta ˈrāši no wrək nə dey.

What is lost in the morning that shows up in the evening is not lost.

چې خُدائ يې نۀ کړي پير بابا به يې څۀ کړي.

če xoˈdey ye nə kṛi pir ˈbābā ba ye tsə kṛi.

If God doesn't do it, then what can Pir Baba do about it?

د پردي کلي په صبا څوک نۀ پوهېږي.

də praˈdi ˈkəli pa saˈbā tsok nə poˈhigi.

No one knows the dawn rituals of a foreign village.

اور له راغله د کور مېرمن شوه.

or la ˈrāɣla də kor merˈman šwa.

She came to get a burning coal and became mistress of the house.

څنګه حال دے؟

د دوؤ ښځو د خاوند نه مې ښۀ حال دے.

tsənga hāl dey?

də ˈdwəo ˈxəzo də xāˈwand na me xə hāl dey

How are you? I'm better off than a man with two wives.

Exercises for Lesson Nineteen

1. Change the following sentences into the simple past tense:

a. ˈxəza de ˈčerta zi? — ښځه دې چرته ځی؟

____

b. tə tsə ˈwaxt rāˈze? — تۀ څۀ وخت راځې؟

____

c. ˈluṇa ye nən ˈhalta raˈsigi? — لُونړه يې نن هلته رسيږی؟

____

d. duˈkān ta zəy? — دُوکان ته ځئ؟

____

e. haləˈkān tsə waxt skul ta nənˈuzi? — هلکان څۀ وخت سکُول ته ننوزی؟

____

f. zəˈmā pa xaˈbəro poheˈde? — زما په خبرو پوهيدې؟

____

2. Using the verbs listed earlier on in this Lesson (pages 272-277), have your helper call out a verb in the infinitive. You should then make positive and negative sentences in the simple past tense.

Vocabulary for Lesson Nineteen

an'dam / anda'muna	اندام / اندامُونه	*m.*	*n.*	limb, part of the body
isāre'dəl	ایساریدل [حصاریدل]		*v.i.*	to wait, to stay, to be(come) late
ba'dəla	بدله	*f.*		different
ba'dən	بدن	*m.*	*n.*	body
bərā'bər	برابر	*m.*	*adj.*	equal, even, on a par; fit, match
barbāde'dəl	بربادېدل		*v.i.*	to be destroyed, to be ruined
ba'har tləl	بهر تلل		*comp. v.i.*	to go out
pəṭe'dəl	پټېدل		*v.i.*	to become hidden, to be put away, to hide oneself
peǰan'dey ke'dəl	پېژندے کېدل		*comp. v.i.*	to be known
pexe'dəl	پېښېدل		*v.i.*	to happen, to occur, to take place, to meet
təxte'dəl	تښتېدل		*v.i.*	to run away, to flee, to escape
tere'dəl	تېرېدل		*v.i.*	to pass by, to overtake; to swallow
sa'bəta	ثابته		*adj.*	all, whole, complete
čər'gəy	چرګی	*f.*	*n.*	a white spot on the fore-head, a white forelock
hefā'zət	حفاظت	*m.*	*n.*	protection, safe
xarābe'dəl	خرابېدل		*v.i.*	to go bad, to be decayed, to be spoiled, to be ruined
'dwāṛa	دواړه	*f.*	*adj.*	both
zax'mi ke'dəl	زخمی کېدل		*comp. v.i.*	to be injured, to become hurt
zyāte'dəl	زیاتېدل		*v.i.*	to be increased
ǰo'bəl	ژوبل	*m.*	*adj.*	wounded, hurt, injured
sore'dəl	سورېدل		*v.i.*	to ride, to mount
šarike'dəl	شریکېدل		*v.i.*	to be shared, to be included
šmer	شمېر	*m.*	*n.*	count, number

san'duq	صندُوق	*m.*	*n.*	trunk, box
zaru'rət	ضرُورت	*m.*	*n.*	need, necessity
farq	فرق	*m.*	*n.*	difference, distinction
qā'sad	قاصد	*m.*	*n.*	*peon*, messenger
kəme'dəl	کمېدل		*v.i.*	to be decreased
gəḍwəḍ	ګډوډ	*m.*	*adj.*	mixed, intermingled, disordered
gəḍwəḍe'dəl	ګډوډ کېدل		*v.i.*	to be mixed
gar'dān	ګردان	*m.*	*n.*	repetition
'garəm	ګرم	*m.*	*adj.*	warm
'garma / 'garme	ګرمه / ګرمې	*f.*		
lax'tey	لختے	*m.*	*n.*	gutter, stream, drain
leṭ	لېټ	*m.*	*adj.*	late
'lekın	لېکن		*conj.*	but
məǰ'rım	مجرم	*m.*	*n.*	criminal
moxta'lıf	مُختلف	*m.*	*adj.*	different, various
na'sāpa	ناثاپه		*adv.*	suddenly
nā'la / nā'ləy	ناله / نالۍ	*f.*	*n.*	gutter, stream, drain
na-'waxta	ناوخته	*f.*	*adj.*	late
nənə'ney	ننني	*m.*	*adj.*	of the day, today's
hedā'yət	هدايت	*m.*	*n.*	guidance, direction, instruction, leading

šɪlˈəm saˈbəq شلم سبق

Lesson Twenty

Dialogue twenty: Make your own texts

☝ It is a huge step forward in your learning when you are able to speak on a short topic. Work with your helper to develop three topics about yourself. To do this explain to your helper how you would talk about yourself in three diferent tenses. Then have your helper prepare three short talks – as you might say them. Record each one; transcribe them; and then memorize them before going out to use them.

Present:

A text answering the common question, *tə ˈdəlta tsə key?* (تهٔ دلته څهٔ کې؟) "What do you do here?"

Future:

A text telling of your plans in the near future.

Past:

A text that tells of some interesting event you saw or something that happened to you a few days ago. Try to keep it in the simple past tense.

Pronunciation drill

Have fun with this tongue twister:

د ګنړو منړو په باغ کښې د رنړو اوبو په غاړه کنړه چنړ چنړه په کانړی اووله.

də gu'ṇo ma'ṇo pa bāɣ ke də ra'ṇo u'bo pa 'ɣāṛa ka'ṇa 'čaṇ 'čaṇa pa 'kāṇi u'wəla.

Transitive verbs in the simple past tense

The next two chapters deal with the simple past tense for transitive verbs. Unlike intransitive verbs, transitive verbs in the past tense agree with the object, not the subject of the sentence. It is this feature of Pukhto that makes it a challenging language to speak accurately in the past tense. Take your time as you study the next lessons.

Verbs taking / o- /

As with intransitive verbs, / o- / (-و) is added to the infinitive to form the simple past tense of a great many transitive verbs. *xo'ṛəl* (خوړل) 'to bite', 'to eat', 'to consume' is one example of a transitive verb:

Person	Singular			Plural		
1st	I ate an apple *(f.s.)*	mā ma'ṇa 'o-xoṛa ['o-xoṛəla]	ما منړه وخوړه [وخوړله]	We ate food *(f.)*	mung ro'ṭəy 'o-xoṛa ['o-xoṛəla]	مونږ روټۍ وخوړه [وخوړله]
2nd	You ate a banana *(f.s.)*	tā ke'la 'o-xoṛa ['o-xoṛəla]	تا کېله وخوړه [وخوړله]	You ate food *(f.)*	'tāso ḍo'ḍəy 'o-xoṛa ['o-xoṛəla]	تاسو ډوډۍ وخوړه [وخوړله]
3rd m.	He ate one potato *(m.s.)*	ha'ɣə yo ā'lu 'o-xoṛo	هغۀ يو آلُو وخوړو	They ate pears *(f.pl.)*	haɣ'wi našpā'təy 'o-xoṛəle	هغوی ناشپاتئ وخوړلې
3rd f.	She ate a mango *(m.s.)*	ha'ɣe yo ām 'o-xoṛo	هغې يو آم اوخوړو	They ate pears *(f.pl.)*	haɣ'wi našpā'təy 'o-xoṛəle	هغوی ناشپاتئ وخوړلې

NOTES:

1. If the verb *xo'ṛəl* (خوړل) is used in a sentence without an object the verb agrees with the implied object. In the examples below, *ro'ṭəy* (روټۍ) or *ḍo'ḍəy* (ډوډۍ), that is 'food' or 'a meal', is implied. The agreement in this case is feminine because the implied object is feminine.

tā 'oxoṛa?	Did you eat?	تا وخوړه؟
āw, mā 'oxoṛa.	Yes, I ate.	آو، ما وخوړه.

2. The masculine and feminine construction of the sentence refers to the <u>thing</u> eaten, not the gender of the one who ate.

Study these examples and then practice making lots of new sentences:

haɣe yo <u>ām</u> o-xoṛo.	She ate a mango. (*m.s.*)	هغې يو <u>آم</u> وخوړو.
haɣe ḍer <u>āmuna</u> o'xoṛəl?	Did she eat many mangoes? (*m.p.*)	هغې ډېر <u>آمونه</u> وخوړل؟
də 'yəwa <u>ma'na</u> o-xoṛa?	Did he eat an apple? (*f.s.*)	دۀ يوه <u>منړه</u> وخوړه؟
də 'ḍere <u>ma'ne</u> o-xoṛe.	He ate a lot of apples. (*f.p.*)	دۀ ډېرې <u>منړې</u> وخوړې.

NOTES:

1. In these sentences, fruit is the object (recipient of an action).
2. The verb form is based on the person, number and gender of the object.
3. The subject is inflected in the past tense in the following ways:

zə	→	mā	ما	←	زۀ
tə	→	tā	تا	←	تۀ
ha'ɣa	→	ha'ɣə (*m.*)	هغۀ	←	هغه
ha'ɣa	→	ha'ɣe (*f.*)	هغې	←	هغه
ha'ɣwi	→	ha'ɣwi (*pl.* – no change)	هغوی	←	هغوی

Practice the sentences below to become familiar with the way transitive verbs are used in the simple past tense.

mā 'doləs <u>ke'le</u> 'oxoṛe.	I ate twelve bananas. (*f.pl.*)	ما دولس <u>کېلې</u> وخوړې.
mā 'yəwa <u>ke'la</u> 'oxoṛa.	I ate a banana. (*f.s.*)	ما يوه <u>کېله</u> وخوړه.
hay'wi 'doləs <u>ke'le</u> 'oxoṛe.	They ate twelve bananas. (*f.pl.*)	هغوی دولس <u>کېلې</u> وخوړې.
hay'wi 'yəwa <u>ke'la</u> 'oxoṛa.	They ate a banana. (*f.s.*)	هغوی يوه <u>کېله</u> وخوړه.
ha'ɣə yo <u>ām'rud</u> 'oxoṛo.	He ate a guava. (*m.s.*)	هغۀ يو <u>امرُود</u> وخوړو.

mā ləg šat ˈoxoṛəl.	I ate some honey. *(m.pl.)*	ما لږ شات وخوړل.
mā ˈwriǰe ˈoxoṛe.	I ate rice. *(f.pl.)*	ما وريژې وخوړې.
haˈɣə yo teˈpər ˈoxoṛo.	He ate a turnip. *(m.s.)*	هغهٔ يو ټيپر وخوړو.
haˈɣe dwa pyāz ˈoxoṛəl.	She ate two onions. *(m.pl.)*	هغې دوه پياز وخوړل.
haˈɣe yo pyāx ˈoxoṛo.	She ate an onion. *(m.s.)*	هغې يو پياز وخوړو.
zə spi ˈoxoṛələm.	The dog bit me. *(s.)*	زهٔ سپي وخوړلم.
haˈɣa spi ˈoxoṛo.	The dog bit him. *(m.s.)*	هغه سپي وخوړو.
spi saˈṛi ˈoxoṛəl.	The dog bit the men. *(m.pl.)*	سپي سړي وخوړل.
spi ˈxəze ˈoxoṛe.	The dog bit the ladies. *(f.pl.)*	سپي ښځې وخوړې.
tə spi ˈoxoṛe?	Did the dog bite you? *(s.)*	تهٔ سپي وخوړې؟
ˈtāso spi ˈoxoṛəy?	Did the dog bite you? *(p.)*	تاسو سپي وخوړئ؟
mung ləg kəˈbāb ˈoxoṛəl.	We ate some kebabs. *(m.pl.)*	مونږ لږ کباب وخوړل.
haˈɣe yo ām o-nə-xoṛo.	She didn't eat a mango. *(m.s.)*	هغې يو آم ونهٔ خوړو.

NOTES:

1. The object is not inflected.
2. In the sentence, 'The dog bit me' the object is me, so the verb takes the first person singular ending / -əm / (م-).

Transitive verbs that take the / o- / (و-) prefix in the simple past tense

Infinitive			Masculine plural	
to forgive	baˈxəl	بخښل	ˈobaxəl	وبخښل
to know (recognise)	peǰanˈdəl	پېژندل	ˈopeǰanˈdəl	وپېژندل
to drink	skəl	څښل	ˈoskəl	وڅښل
to want	ɣoxˈtəl	غوښتل	ˈoɣoxtəḷ	وغوښتل
to sow	kaˈrəl	کرل	ˈokarəl	وکَرل
to look at	kaˈtəl	کتل	ˈokatəl	وکتل

Infinitive			**Masculine plural**	
to sew	gan'ḍəl	گنډل	'oganḍəl	وگنډل
to turn on	ləga'wəl	لگول	'oləgawəl	ولگول
to see	li'dəl	ليدل	'olidəl	وليدل
to send	le'gəl	ليږل	'olegəl	وليږل
to write	li'kəl	ليکل	'olikəl	وليکل
to catch	ni'wəl	نيول	'oniwəl	ونيول
to hit	wa'həl	وهل	'owahəl	ووهل
to extract	wis'təl	ويستل [وښکل]	'owis'təl	وويستل
to wash	win'zəl	وينځل	'owinzəl	ووينځل
to say	wa'yəl	وئيل	'owayəl	ووئيل

The use of the / o- / (-و) prefix in transitive verbs (simple past tense)

mā sa'ṛey 'obaxəlo.	I forgave the man. (*m.s.*)	ما سړے وبخښلو.
mā sa'ṛi 'obaxəl.	I forgave the men. (*m.pl.*)	ما سړی وبخښل.
mā 'xəza 'obaxəla.	I forgave the woman. (*f.s.*)	ما ښځه وبخښله.
mā 'xəze 'obaxəle.	I forgave the women. (*f.pl.*)	ما ښځې وبخښلې.
tā xat 'olikəlo?	Did you write the letter? (*m.s.*)	تا خط وليکلو؟
tā xa'tuna 'olikəl?	Did you write letters? (*m.pl.*)	تا خطُونه وليکل؟
tā qi'sa 'olikəla?	Did you write a story? (*f.s.*)	تا قيصه وليکله؟
tā qi'sa o-'nə-likəla?	Didn't you write a story?	تا قيصه ونهٔ ليکله؟
tā qi'se 'olikəle?	Did you write stories? (*f.pl.*)	تا قيصې وليکلې؟
də 'xpəla 'xəza 'owahəla.	He hit his wife. (*f.s.*)	دهٔ خپله ښځه ووهله.
gul ra'sul xpəle 'xəze 'owahəle.	Gul Rasoul hit his wives. (*f.pl.*)	گُل رسول خپلې ښځې ووهلې.
'tāso čay 'oskəle?	Did you drink tea? (*f.pl.*)	تاسو چائې وڅښلې؟
āw, mung čay 'oskəle.	Yes, we drank tea.	آو، مُونږ چائې وڅښلې.
tā 'haɣa ǰɪ'nəy 'olida?	Did you see that girl?	تا هغه جينۍ وليده؟

āw, o-me-li'da.	Yes, I saw her.	آو، ومې لیده.
tā ax'bār 'olosto?	Did you read the newspaper? (*m.s.*)	تا اخبار ولوستو؟
āw, 'o-me-los'to.	Yes, I read it.	آو، ومې لوستو.
mā xpəl zwe 'owahalo ['owahə].	I hit my son. (*m.s.*)	ما خپل زوئ ووهلو [ووهٔ].
tā xpəl mašu'mān 'owahəl?	Did you hit your children? (*m.pl.*)	تا خپل ماشُومان ووهل؟
mung 'xpəla lur 'owahəla.	We hit our daughter. (*f.s.*)	مُونږ خپله لُور ووهله.
xəze ye 'owahəle?	Did he hit (his) wives? (*f.pl.*)	ښځې یې ووهلې؟
mā ha'lək 'owahəlo.	I hit the boy. (*m.s.*)	ما هلک ووهلو.
tā zə'mā ka'mis 'oganḍəlo?	Did you sew my shirt? (*m.s.*)	تا زما قمیص وګنډلو؟
āw, o-me-gan'ḍəlo.	Yes, I sewed it.	آو، ومې ګنډلو.
la'ṛəm 'oči'čəle?	Did the scorpion sting you?	لړم وچیچلې؟
po'lis mung 'oniwəlu.	The police caught us.	پولیس مُونږ ونیولُو.
pa'run tā xpəl zwe du'kān ta 'olegəlo?	Did you send your son to the shop yesterday?	پرُون تا خپل زوئ دُوکان ته ولیږلو؟
tā zə pa'run 'olidələm?	Did you see me yesterday?	تا زهٔ پرُون ولیدلم؟
āw, mā tə pa'run 'olidəle.	Yes, I saw you yesterday.	آو، ما تهٔ پرُون ولیدلې.
āw, tə me pa'run 'olidəle.	Yes, I saw you yesterday.	آو، تهٔ مې پرُون ولیدلې.
tə me o-'nə-lidəle.	I didn't see you.	تهٔ مې ونهٔ لیدلې.

Transitive verbs when the object is 'you', 'us' or 'me'

Practice the following sentences, using substitution.

ha'ɣə zə 'owahələm.	He hit me.	هغهٔ زهٔ ووهلم.
mung mo'ṭər 'owahəlu.	A car hit us.	مُونږ موټر ووهلو.
mā tə 'owahəle.	I hit you.	ما تهٔ ووهلې.

lā'rəy 'tāso 'owahələy?	Did a truck hit you?	لارۍ تاسو ووهلئ؟
zə sa'ṛi 'olidələm.	A man saw me.	زهٔ سړي وليدم.
halə'kāno mung 'olidu?	Did the boys see us?	هلکانو مُونږ وليدو؟
'tāso hay'wi o-nə-lidəy?	Didn't they see you?	تاسو هغوی ونهٔ ليدئ؟
mung 'tāso o-nə-lidəy?	We didn't see you?	مُونږ تاسو ونهٔ ليدئ؟
tā zə 'opeǰandəm?	Did you know me?	تا زهٔ وپېژندم؟
tə me 'opeǰande.	I knew you.	تهٔ مې وپېژندې.
'tāso mung opeǰandu?	You knew us?	تاسو مُونږ وپېژندُو؟
mung 'tāso 'opeǰandəy.	We knew you.	مُونږ تاسو وپېژندئ.

NOTES:

1. Compare the present and past tense forms of the following sentences:

'ahmad pia'luy 'winzi.	Ahmad is washing the cups.	احمد پيالۍ وينځي.
'ahmad pia'luy 'owinzəle.	Ahmad washed the cups.	احمد پيالۍ ووينځلې.
tə mā 'wine.	You see me.	تهٔ ما وينې.
tā zə 'olidələm.	You saw me.	تا زهٔ وليدلم.

2. The subject in the past tense is always in the oblique case. For example, *'xəze* (ښځې) changes to *'xəzo* (ښځو). Note the following examples:

'xəze sa'ṛey 'olido.	The woman saw the man. *(m.s.)*	ښځې سړے وليدو.
'xəzo sa'ṛi 'olidəl.	The women saw the men. *(m.pl.)*	ښځو سړي وليدل.
sa'ṛi 'xəza 'olidəla.	The man saw the woman. *(f.s.)*	سړي ښځه وليدله.
sa'ṛo 'xəze 'olidəle.	The men saw the women. *(f.pl.)*	سړو ښځې وليدلې.

Transitive verbs that do not use the / o- / prefix in the simple past tense

Infinitive			**Masculine plural**	
to buy	āxɪs'təl	اخستل	'wāxistəl	واخستل
to wear	āɣos'təl	اغوستل	'wāɣostəl	واغوستل
to hear	āwre'dəl	اورېدل	'wawredəl	واورېدل
to take (animate)	bot'ləl	بوتلل	bot'ləl	بوتلل
to bring (inanimate)	rāw'ṛəl	راوړل	rāw'ṛəl	راوړل
to bring (animate)	rāwəs'təl	راوستل	rāwəs'təl	راوستل
to put	kexo'dəl	کېښودل	kexo'dəl	کېښودل
to take (inanimate)	o'ṛəl	وړل	'oṛəl	وړل

Some sentences

tā ma'ṇe čerta kexo'dəle?	Where did you put the apples? (*f.pl.*)	تا منړې چرته کېښودلې؟
mā pa mez 'bānde kexo'dəle.	I put them on the table.	ما په مېز باندې کېښودلې.
ha'ɣa mung xpəl kor ta 'botlu.	He took us to his own home.	هغه مُونږ خپل کور ته بوتلُو.

☝ Make more sentences with each of these verbs.

A note on the following comprehension drills

In this kind of drill your language helper gives a series of instructions on a topic, and demonstrates the activities. For example: "Put the onion on the board. Open the drawer, and take out the knife. Slice the onion." Mimic the actions a couple of times and then obey the instructions without your helper doing the actions. Then have him or her give the instructions at random. For some activities you can use real props and for others do it in mime.

You might find it helpful to record the drill on the first time through, and at a later time do the drill 'live'.

The following is the first of several comprehension drills using these instructions. Learn this one by mime.

Comprehension drill: Cooking

baˈzār ta lāṛ ša.	Go to the market.	بازار ته لاړ شه.
yo kiˈlo qiˈma ˈrāwṛa!	Bring one kilo of mince meat!	یو کیلو قیمه راؤړه!
warsara yo kiˈlo pyāz āw nim kiˈlo ṭamāˈṭər həm wāxla!	Also buy one kilo of onions and half a kilo of tomatoes!	ورسره یو کیلو پیاز او نیم کیلو ټماټر هم واخله!
byā pyāz ṭoˈṭe ṭoˈṭe ka!	Then chop the onions into pieces!	بیا پیاز ټوټې ټوټې که!
ṭamāˈṭər həm saˈfā ka.	Also clean the tomatoes.	ټماټر هم صفا که.
byā ˈɣwaxa, aˈgəy, pyāz āw ṭamāˈṭər warsara gəḍ ka.	Then mix the meat with an egg, onions and tomatoes.	بیا غوښه، اګۍ، پیاز او ټماټر ورسره ګډ که.
byā ye pa ɣwaˈṛo ke xə srə ka!	Then fry it well in oil!	بیا یې په غوړو کښې ښهٔ سرهٔ که!
byā ba ye mung ˈdoləs baǰe xoˈru.	Then we will eat it about twelve o'clock.	بیا به یې مُونږ دولس بجې خورُو.

Memorising moment

mataˈluna

دَ سحر په بانگ کښې مې نوے ټپه واورېده.

də saˈhar pa bāng ke me ˈneβey ṭapa ˈwāwreda.

I heard a new song in the morning call to prayer.

نمر په گوته نۀ پټيږي.

nwar pa ˈguta ˈnə-pəṭigi.

The sun cannot be hidden by a finger.

د دروغو مزل لنډ وی.

də darˈoɣo məˈzəl lənḍ wi.

The distance of untruth is short.

Rahman Baba

عقل څۀ کړې بخت ترې وغواړه رحمانه
عقلمند د بختورو غلامان وی.

ˈaqəl tsə kṛe bəxt tre ˈoɣwāṛa rahˈmāna

aqəlˈmənd də bəxtaˈwəro ɣlāˈmān wi.

What will you do with wisdom? Ask for luck Rahman.

The wise are slaves of the lucky.

Exercises for Lesson Twenty

1. Listen to your helper read the following story and see how much of it you understand. Work on it until you can tell it. Concentrate on the past tense verb endings.

يو ځل د تازهٔ ګُل درې زامن پټي ته لاړل. هلته يې د زيارت ګُل د زوئ سره خبرې ورانې شوې او دوئ يې بنهٔ ووهل. دوئ کور ته په ژړا راغلل او پلار ته يې ووئيل چې مُونږ د زيارت ګُل زوئ وُو هلُو. پلار يې حيران شو چې دا ولې او څنګه؟ هغوی ووئيل چې مُونږ بِلکل يواځې وُو.

2. Take one verb at a time from the lists of transitive verbs in the simple past tense included in this Lesson. Have your language helper supply masculine singular, feminine singular, masculine plural and feminine plural tenses, and also the subjects and objects that are normally used with each verb. Make sentences accordingly. Try not to use any English in these drills.

3. Make a recording putting the verb through its paces with the different subjects and objects, making sure that your helper stresses the endings. Say the sentence in English, then have the helper say the sentence in Pukhto. Progress down the verb charts in the Lesson (288-289, 292) one verb at a time.

Vocabulary for Lesson Twenty

po'lis	پولیس	*m.*	*n.*	police
ṭo'ṭe ka'wəl	ټوټې کول		*comp. v.t.*	to cut into pieces, to chop
či'čəl	چیچل		*v.t.*	to bite, to sting
ro'ṭəy	روټۍ	*f.s.*	*n.*	food, meal; bread
qi'ma	قیمه	*f.*	*n.*	mince meat, ground beef
gəḍa'wəl	ګډول		*v.t.*	to mix, to combine
lā'rəy	لارۍ	*f.*	*n.*	truck, lorry

yowiš'təm sa'bəq یوویشتم سبق

Lesson Twenty-One

Dialogue twenty-one: What happened yesterday?

L: pa'run tsə waxt rā'pasede? What time did you get up yesterday?	پرُون څۀ وخت راپاڅېدې؟
H: špəg 'baǰe Six o'clock.	شپږ بجې.
L: byā de tsə okṛəl? Then what did you do?	بیا دې څۀ وکړل؟
H: byā me pa brəš 'bānde ɣa'xuna sa'fā kṛəl. Then I brushed my teeth.	بیا مې په برش باندې غاښونه صفا کړل.
L: pa'run de 'čerta ḍo'ḍəy 'oxoṛəla? Where did you eat food yesterday?	پرُون دې چرته ډوډۍ وخوړله؟
H: pa kor ke me 'oxoṛəla. I ate at home.	په کور کښې مې وخوړله.
L: pa'run dəf'tər ta 'lāṛe? Did you go to the office yesterday?	پرُون دفتر ته لاړې؟
H: āw, tər yawe baǰe 'pore me kār oko. Yes, I worked until one o'clock yesterday.	آو، تر یوې بجې پورې مې کار وکړو.
L: mā'xām de tsə 'okṛəl? What did you do in the evening?	ماښام دې څۀ وکړل؟
H: mā'xām me sab'zi 'wāxista āw kor ta 'rāɣləm. In the evening I bought some vegetables and I came home.	ماښام مې سبزی واخسته او کور ته راغلم.
L: be'gā de xab'runa 'wāwredəl? Did you listen to the news last night?	بېگا دې خبرُونه واؤرېدل؟
H: na, wā-me-'nə-wredəl. No, I didn't listen to it.	نه، وامې نۀ ورېدل.
L: be'ga tsə waxt u'də šwe? What time did you go to sleep last night?	بېگا څۀ وخت اُودۀ شوې؟
H: 'yoləs baǰe. Eleven o'clock.	یوولس بجې.

NOTE:

Look carefully through the dialogue and identify which verbs are transitive and which are intransitive. See if the verb endings make sense to you.

Pronunciation practice

Focus on the / t / ت and / ṭ / ټ sounds in this tongue twister:

زما ټبر تبه په تبر ووهله!

zə'mā 'ṭabar 'təba pa 'tabar 'owahəla!

Compound transitive verbs in the simple past tense

Many compound verbs take a noun or adjective and add the past tense of the verb *ka'wəl* (کول) 'to be', becoming *kṛəl* (کړل).

The past verb endings are often shortened in normal conversation, but you will find that written text (for example, in books) retain the full verb ending.

Past verb endings of *kṛəl* کړل

	Shortened form		Full ending	
Masculine singular	ko	کو	kṛo	کړو
Feminine singular	ka	که	kṛa	کړه
Feminine plural	ke	کې	kṛe	کړې
Masculine plural	kṛəl	کړل	kṛəl	کړل

Noun-verb combinations with *kṛəl*

dəlta ye kār dar-sara okṛo?	Did he work here with you? (*m.s.*)	دلته يې کار درسره وکړو؟
na, kār ye rā-sa'ra o-'nə-kṛo.	No, he didn't work with me.	نه، کار يې راسره ونۀ کړو.
pa'roskāl de tsə kā'runa okṛəl?	What jobs did you do last year? (*m.pl.*)	پروسکال دې څۀ کارُونه وکړل؟
ḍer kā'runa me okṛəl.	I did many jobs.	ډېر کارُونه مې وکړل.
tā warsara ɪm'dād o-nə-kṛo?	Didn't you help them? (*m.s.*)	تا ورسره امداد ونۀ کړو؟
āw, ɪm'dād me warsara 'okṛo.	Yes, I helped them.	آو، امداد مې ورسره وکړو.

NOTE:

The masculine singular verb ending *okṛo* (وکړو) is commonly shortened to *oko* in ordinary speech.

Practice

You are probably getting the hang of transitive verbs by now.

☝ Try the verbs below to see if you have fluency. Ask your helper to supply words for you to make into sentences. Here is an example of how the drill might work.

H:	ha'ɣe / is'tri / ka'mis		هغې / اِستری / قمیص
L:	ha'ɣe ka'mis is'tri kṛo.	She ironed the shirt. *(m.s.)*	هغې قمیص اِستری کړو.
H:	kami'suna		قمیصُونه
L:	ha'ɣe kami'suna is'tri kṛəl.	She ironed the shirts. *(m.pl.)*	هغې قمیصُونه اِستری کړل.
H:	par'da		پرده
L:	ha'ɣe par'da is'tri kṛa.	She ironed the curtain. *(f.s.)*	هغې پرده اِستری کړه.
H:	par'de		پردې
L:	ha'ɣe par'de is'tri kṛe.	She ironed the curtains. *(f.pl.)*	هغې پردې اِستری کړې.

Questions and answers

Try to answer each of the following questions, first in the affirmative, then in the negative.

na'sime dā farš ǰā'ru kṛo?	Did Nasima sweep this floor? *(m.s.)*	نسیمې دا فرش جارُو کړو؟
ḍāk'ṭər halə'kān ček kṛəl?	Did the doctor examine the boys? *(m.pl.)*	ډاکټر هلکان چیک کړل؟
tā 'ɣwaxa pre kṛa?	Did you cut the meat? *(m.s.)*	تا غوښه پرې کړه؟
yo sa'ṛi 'dwəo 'xəzo sa'ra wā'də 'okṛo?	Did one man marry two wives? *(m.s.)*	یو سړی دوؤ ښځو سره وادهٔ وکړو؟

Other noun-verb combinations

'tāso ra'bāb xə 'owahəlo.	You played the *rabab* well. *(m.s.)*	تاسو رباب ښهٔ ووهلو.
ḍer ka'bān me 'oniwəl.	I caught a lot of fish. *(m.pl.)*	ډېر کبان مې ونیول.
lambo de 'wəle o-nə-wahəla?	Why didn't you swim? *(f.s.)*	لامبو دې ولې ونهٔ وهله؟
ha'yə be'gā maǰ'lıs okṛo?	Did he sing last night? *(m.s.)*	هغهٔ بېگا مجلس وکړو؟

'tāso nən 'mənḍe 'owahəle?	Did you run today? (*f.pl.*)	تاسو نن منډې ووهلې؟
na, 'mənḍe mo o-'nə-wahəle.	No, we didn't run.	نه، منډې مو ونۀ وهلې.
'tāso pa'run čə'kər 'owahəlo?	Did you take an outing yesterday?	تاسو پرُون چکر ووهلو؟
na, pa'run mo čə'kər o-nə-wahəlo.	No, we didn't take an outing yesterday.	نه، پرُون مو چکر ونۀ وهلو.

Adjective-verb combinations in the past tense

mis'tri stā 'gaḍey ṭik kṛo āw kə na?	Did the mechanic fix your car or not (*lit.* yes or no)? (*m.s.*)	مستری ستا ګاډے ټيک کړو او کۀ نه؟
na, ṭik ye 'nə-kṛo.	No, he did not fix it.	نه، ټيک يې نۀ کړو.
eh'mad ga'ni pre kṛəl?	Did Ahmad cut the sugar cane? (*m.pl.*)	احمد ګنی پرې کړل؟
āw, māt ye kṛəl.	Yes, he cut it.	آو، مات يې کړل.
xansā'ma 'ɣwaxa pa'xa kṛa?	Did the cook cook the meat? (*f.s.*)	خانسامه غوښه پخه کړه؟
na, pa'xa ye 'nə-kṛa.	No, he didn't cook it.	نه، پخه يې نۀ کړه.
paxwā'nəy tsa'pləy de za'ṛe kṛe?	Did you wear out your old sandals? (*f.pl.*)	پخوانۍ څپلۍ دې زړې کړې؟
āw, za'ṛe me kṛe.	Yes, I wore them out.	آو، زړې مې کړې.

pa'roskāl de me'we həm 'xartse kṛe?	Did you also sell fruit last year? (*f.pl.*)	پروسکال دې مېوې هم خرڅې کړې؟
āw, me'we me həm 'xartse kṛe.	Yes, I also sold fruit.	آو، مېوې مې هم خرڅې کړې.
ha'ɣe də ɣar'me ḍo'ḍəy də'pāra tsə ta'yār kṛəl?	What did she prepare for lunch? (*m.pl.*)	هغې د غرمې ډوډۍ د پاره څهٔ تيار کړل؟
'wriǰe āw qorma ye ta'yāra kṛa.	She prepared rice and a meat sauce. (*f.s.*)	وريژې او قورمه يې تياره کړه.

NOTES:

1. The last sentence has several potential objects for the verb to agree with. Usually the verb agrees with the last object named (in this case *qorma* قورمه). However, some speakers will group all the objects together to make the verb plural, in which case *ta'yār kṛəl* تيار کړل will be used.
2. *qorma* (قورمه) is a meat sauce prepared with chickpeas (*ča'ṇa* چڼه) and either served with rice or eaten with *ro'ṭəy* (روټۍ).

Some irregular transitive verbs

Some verbs have no object, and are always used in the masculine plural form. This makes them the easiest past tense transitive verbs to use!

mā ḍer 'oxandəl.	I laughed a lot.	ما ډېر وخاندل.
sa'ṛo rā-'pore 'oxandəl.	The men laughed at me.	سړو راپورې وخاندل.
de 'xəze 'wəle 'oǰaṛəl?	Why did this woman cry?	دې ښځې ولې وژړل؟
haɣ'wi be'gā 'oǰaṛəl.	They cried last night.	هغوی بېگا وژړل.
spo 'ṭola špa 'oɣapəl.	The dogs barked all night.	سپو ټوله شپه وغپل.
mašu'māno pa 'ɣoli ke 'odangəl.	The children jumped in the courtyard.	ماشُومانو په غولی کښې ودنگل.
mung pa pārk ke 'ozangəl.	We swung in the park.	مُونږ په پارک کښې وزنگل.
mā pa sind ke 'olāmbəl.	I bathed in the river.	ما په سيند کښې ولامبل.

NOTE:

In Pukhto laughing is done at someone, and is considered transitive.

Phrases that express time

bəl kāl ba baˈhar zəm.	Next year I am going abroad.	بل کال به بهر ځم.
pa rātˈlunki kāl ke ba baˈhar zəm.	In the coming year I am going abroad.	په راتلُونکی کال کښې به بهر ځم.
pa rātˈlunki ˈmyāšt ba moˈsəm ˈgaram ši.	In the coming month the weather will become warm.	په راتلُونکی میاشت کښې به موسم ګرم شی.
də ˈos na ˈpas ba ˈdā kār ˈdā šān key.	From now on, do this work like this.	د اوس نه پس به دا کار دا شان کے.
pa rātˈlunki ˈwrəzo ke stā də liˈdo koˈšiš kaˈwəm.	In the coming days I will try to see you.	په راتلُونکی ورځو کښې ستا د لیدو کوشش کوم.
pa āynˈda ke ba səxt koˈšiš kaˈwəm.	I will try harder in the future.	په آئینده کښې به سخت کوشش کوم.
pa de ˈwrəzo ke ḍer ˈxalak waˈǰəley kigi.	Many people are being killed these days.	په دې ورځو کښې ډېر خلق وژلے کیږی.
nən saˈbā zə ḍer masˈruf yım.	I am very busy these days.	نن صبا زۀ ډېر مصرُوف یم.
pa de špo āw ˈwrəzo ke moˈsəm ḍer ˈyəx dey.	These days and nights the weather is very cold.	په دې شپو او ورځو کښې موسم ډېر یخ دے.
pa de waxt ke zə ḍer ˈstəṛey yım.	At this time I am very tired.	په دې وخت کښې زۀ ډېر ستړے یم.

Common responses to questions

dā kār de ˈwəle ˈokṛo?	Why did you do that?	دا کار دې ولې وکړو؟
ˈzəka če zə ḍer ɣaˈrib yım.	Because I am very poor.	ځکه چې زۀ ډېر غریب یم.
ˈhalta ˈwəle ze?	Why are you going there?	هلته ولې ځې؟
ˈzəka če zəˈmā plār ˈdəlta nəˈrāˈzi.	Because my father is not coming here.	ځکه چې زما پلار دلته نۀ راځی.

ˈdəlta ˈwəle ˈrāɣle?	Why did you come here?	دلته ولې راغلې؟
zə stā dəˈpāra ˈrāɣləm.	I came for you.	زۀ ستا د پاره راغلم.
haˈɣa de ˈwəle wā-nə-ɣəsto?	Why didn't you buy it?	هغه دې ولې وانۀ غستو؟
ḍer grān wo, pa de ˈwəǰa me wā-nə-ɣəsto.	It was very expensive, so for this reason I didn't buy it.	ډېر ګران وو، په دې وجه مې وانۀ غستو.
tə ıslāmāˈbad ta ˈwəle lāˈnə-ṛe?	Why didn't you go to Islamabad?	تۀ اسلام آباد ته ولې لانۀ ړې؟
ˈzəka če mā saˈra peˈse nə we.	Because I didn't have money.	ځکه چې ما سره پېسې نۀ وې.
paˈrun de kār ˈwəle o-nə-kṛo?	Why didn't you work yesterday?	پرُون دې کار ولې ونۀ کړو؟
ˈzəka če zə nāˈǰoṛa wəm.	Because I was sick.	ځکه چې زۀ ناجوړه وم.
ˈwəle warsara xaˈbare nə-kawe?	Why are you not speaking with them?	ولې ورسره خبرې نۀ کوې؟
ˈzəka če war-na ˈxəfa yım.	Because I am upset with them.	ځکه چې ورنه خفه یم.
haˈɣa ˈwəle rā-nə-ɣlo?	Why didn't he come?	هغه ولې رانۀ غلو؟
ˈzəke če uzˈgār nə-wo.	Because he was not free.	ځکه چې وزګار نۀ وو.

Comprehension drill: Housework

ǰāˈru ˈwāxla āw ˈbāwarči xāˈna ǰāˈru ka!	Take the broom and sweep the kitchen!	جارُو واخله او باورچی خانه جارُو که!
dastarˈxān āw ˈluxi owinza!	Wash the table cloth and the dishes!	دسترخوان او لوښی ووینځه!
byā beˈṭək ta lāṛ ša, meˈzuna āw kurˈsəy saˈfā ka.	Then go to the guest room and clean the table and chairs.	بیا بېټک ته لاړ شه، مېزونه او کُرسئ صفا که.
farš ǰāˈru ka, byā ye ˈowinza!	Sweep the floor, then wash it!	فرش جارُو که، بیا یې ووینځه!
də beˈṭək qāˈlin baˈhar ˈosanḍa!	Beat the *betuk* rug outside!	د بېټک قالین بهر وسنډه!

byā ye wa'pas 'rāwṛa āw we ɣwaṛa'wa!	Then bring it back and spread it out!	بيا يې واپس راؤړه او وې غوړه وه!
po'ṛəy həm ǰā'ru ka āw xa'zəla ye pa ṭo'krəy ke 'wāčawa.	Sweep the stairs and put the rubbish in the dustbin.	پوړۍ هم جارُو که او خزله يې په ټوکرۍ کښې واچوه.
byā 'rāša āw zān ta čay 'ǰoṛa ka!	Then come and make yourself some tea!	بيا راشه او ځان ته چائې جوړه کړه!

Memorising moment

mata'luna

نۀ په مينه مړېدل شته نۀ په مال

نۀ په عُمر څوک مړيږي نۀ په سوال.

nə pa 'mina maṛe'dəl šta, nə pa māl

nə pa 'umar tsok maṛ'igi, nə pa swāl.

There is no satisfaction in love, nor by things,

Not by age are people filled, nor by begging.

دَ باران نه تښتيدم دَ ناوے لاندې مې شپه شوه.

də bā'rān na təxte'dəm də 'nāwey 'lande me špa šwa.

I got out of the rain but ended up spending the night under a drain-pipe.

ṭa'pa

په دُنيا مۀ نازيږئ خلقه!

د شاه جهان بادشاه نه پاتې شول تختُونه.

pa dun'yā mə-nāzegəy 'xalka!

də šā ǰe'hān bād'šā na 'pāte šwəl tax'tuna.

Don't love the world, Oh people!

King Shah Jehan has left the throne.

Exercises for Lesson Twenty-One

1. Translate the following sentences into Pukhto:

   a. The dog barked all night.

   b. Why did you laugh at me?

   c. The children swung in the park.

   d. She cried last night.

2. Change the following into the simple past tense.

   a. hayˈwi pa ˈkəli ke ǰang kaˈwi. — هغوی په کلی کښې جنګ کوی.

   b. ˈwəle haˈɣa kɪṛˈkəy bandaˈwi? — ولې هغه کړکئ بندوی؟

   c. saˈkāl haˈɣa wāˈdə kaˈwi. — سخکال هغه وادۀ کوی.

   d. ˈɣwaxa pre kaˈwi. — غوښه پرې کوی.

   e. tarˈkāṇ zəˈmā mez tsə waxt ǰoṛaˈwi? — ترکاڼ زما مېز څۀ وخت جوړوی؟

   f. tə də ɣarˈme ḍoˈḍəy dəˈpāra tsə paxaˈwe? — تۀ د غرمې ډوډۍ د پاره څۀ پخوې؟

   g. haˈɣa ḍere xe sanˈdəre ˈwayi. — هغه ډېرې ښې سندرې وائی.

h. noˈkər parˈde isˈtri kaˈwi. نوکر پردې اِستري کوي.

---

i. zəˈmā niˈkə nən maˈyānˈnisi. زما نيکهٔ نن مهيان نيسي.

---

j. ˈtāso raˈbāb xə waˈhəy. تاسو رباب ښهٔ وهئ.

Vocabulary for Lesson Twenty-One

āyn'da	آئينده	*m., f.*	*n.*	coming, future
brəš	برش	*m.s.*	*n.*	brush
ba'har	بهر		*adv., prep.*	out, outside, abroad
pārk	پارک	*m.*	*n.*	park
par'da / par'de	پرده / پردې	*f.*	*n.*	curtain, screen, drape
pre ka'wəl	پرې کول		*comp. v.t.*	to cut
po'ṛəy	پوړۍ	*f.*	*n.*	stairs
ṭo'krəy	ټوکرۍ	*f.*	*n.*	basket, bin, dustbin
ǰā'ru	جارُو	*m.*	*n.*	broom
ǰang ka'wəl	جنګ کول		*v.t.*	to fight
čə'kər	چکر	*m.*	*n.*	stroll, walk, trip, outing
ček ka'wəl	چېک کول		*comp. v.t.*	to check, to examine
xān'dəl	خاندل		*v.t.*	to laugh
xa'zəla	خزله		*n.*	rubbish, litter, trash
dān'gəl	دانګل		*v.t.*	to jump, to run
dastar'xān	دسترخوان	*m.*	*n.*	tablecloth
rāt'lunkey	راتلُونکے	*m.*	*n., adj.*	coming, future, forth-coming, 'next'
zān'gəl	زانګل		*v.t.*	to swing
za'ṛe ka'wəl [zəṛa'wəl]	زړې کول [زړول]		*v.t.*	to wear out, to make old
ǰa'ṛəl	ژړل		*v.t.*	to cry, to weep
san'ḍəl	سنډل		*v.t.*	to dust, to beat
ɣax / ɣa'xuna	غاښ / غاښونه	*m.*	*n.*	tooth / teeth
ɣa'pəl	غپل		*v.t.*	to bark, to yelp
ɣa'rib / ɣa'rib, ɣari'bān, ɣari'bānān	غريب / غريب، غريبان، غريبانان	*m.*	*n., adj.*	poor
ɣa'riba / ɣa'ribe	غريبه / غريبې	*f.*	*adj.*	

ˈɣoley	غولے	*m.*	*n.*	courtyard
qāˈlin	قالین	*m.*	*n.*	rug, carpet
kab / kaˈbān	کب / کبان	*m.*	*n.*	fish
gaˈni	گنی	*m.pl.*	*n.*	sugar cane
lamˈbəl	لامبل		*v.i.*	to bathe, to shower
masˈruf	مصرُوف	*m.*	*adj.*	busy, engaged, occupied
masˈrufa / masˈrufe	مصروفه / مصرُوفې	*f.*		
ˈwəǰa	وجه	*f.*	*n.*	reason, cause
waˈǰəl	وژل		*v.t.*	to kill, to slaughter, to murder

dwa-išˈtəm saˈbəq دوه ويشتم سبق

Lesson Twenty-Two

Dialogue twenty-two: Friendship

L: nən zə də dostāˈne motaˈlıq xaˈbare ızˈda kəm. Today I am learning to talk about friendship.	نن زۀ د دوستانې مُتعلق خبرې زده کوم.
H: ˈḍera xə xaˈbara da. That's very good news.	ډېره ښۀ خبره ده.
L: stā dosˈtān tsok di? Who are your friends?	ستا دوستان څوک دي؟
H: zəˈmā dosˈtān zəˈmā həmˈzoli di. My friends are my peers.	زما دوستان زما همزولي دي.
L: stā dosˈtān ˈtsumra xə di? How good are your friends?	ستا دوستان څومره ښۀ دي؟
H: zəˈmā xo ḍer xə dosˈtān di. My friends are very good.	زما خو ډېر ښۀ دوستان دي.
L: də dostāˈne mətˈləb tsə dey? What is the meaning of friendship?	د دوستانې مطلب څۀ دے؟
H: yo bəl saˈra xoˈlus, waˈfā āw xeˈgəṛa da. Devotion to one another, faithfulness and help.	يو بل سره خلُوص، وفا او ښېګړه ده.
L: də dostāˈne tsə uˈsul di? What are the principles of friendship?	د دوستانې څۀ اصُول دي؟
H: če də dost də ıhsāˈsāto xyāl sāˈti. To care for a friend's feelings.	چې د دوست د احساساتو خيال ساتي.
L: kə stā dost stā na ˈxəfa ši, tə ba tsə key? If your friend is angry with you, what will you do?	کۀ ستا دوست ستا نه خفه شي تۀ به څۀ کړې؟
H: zə ba ye raˈzā kaˈwəm. I would reconcile with him (*lit.* 'reconcile him').	زۀ به يې رضا کوم.

Rhythm and stress

☝ Mimic your helper reading this poem until you sound similar. Pukhto is a musical language with a strong emphasis on rhyme and rhythm. Try to get a feel of these new patterns.

ˈbata (بطحه) 'duck'

زۀ کۀ جوړه شوې په کاغذ باندې غلطه يم
بيا هم په مېښوکه پيژندے شم چې زۀ بطحه يم
غوا ړم شپه او ورځ دې په اوبو کښې لامبوزنه وے
ښکار مې د چينجو کولے دا شانې تورزنه وے
سيند وی کۀ تالاب وی کۀ وله وی زۀ وردانګمه
ښۀ تېزه هوا کښې د اوبو په چپو زانګمه.
ډېر ځلې سيلاب د اوبو راشی ما په مخه کړی
د خپلو پښو په زور مې قِسمت بيا د چا په برخه کړی
زۀ طوفان نوح کښې بې خطرې ورګډيدے شمه
بل سيلاب کۀ راشی زۀ ترې کله تښتيدے شمه
څوک هم د موجونو د څپيړو تاب راوړے نۀ شی
زۀ يم چې په دې کښې څوک زمانه برے اوړے نۀ شی
شکل په صُورت باندې زۀ ډېره مزېداره يم
دا راکښې غضب دے چې زۀ ډېره وزن داره يم

NOTE:
There are strong regional differences in the way in which *ˈbata* (بطحه) 'duck' is spelt. These include بته and بطخه.

'was doing': The past progressive tense

The past progressive tense is formed from the past endings added to the infinitive.

Study these examples:

	Infinitive		Past progressive	
I was going.	rāt'ləl	راتلل	zə rāt'ləm.	زۀ راتلم.
He was dying.	məṛ ke'dəl	مړ کېدل	ha'ɣa məṛ ke'do.	هغه مړ کېدو.
They were sleeping.	u'də ke'dəl	اُودۀ کېدل	haɣ'wi u'də ke'dəl.	هغوی اُودۀ کېدل.
Were you walking?	garze'dəl	ګرځېدل	'tāso garze'dəy?	تاسو ګرځېدئ؟
She was sleeping.	u'da ke'dəl	اُودۀ کېدل	ha'ɣa u'da ke'da.	هغه اُودۀ کېده.

NOTE:

The / -əl / (ل-) ending (*m.pl.*) is often dropped in everyday speech.

Intransitive verbs in the past progressive

zmung lur də xob-na pāseda 'kəla če or 'olegedo. — Our daughter was waking up when the fire started. — زمونږ لُور د خوب نه پاڅېده کله چې اور ولګېدو.

zə'mā 'xəza uda ke'da 'kəla če ṭele'fun rāɣey. — My wife was going to sleep when the telephone rang. — زما ښځه اُودۀ کېده کله چې ټیلیفون راغے.

ha'ɣə məṛ ke'do 'kəla če ḍāk'ṭər rāɣey. — He was dying when the doctor came. — هغۀ مړ کېدو کله چې ډاکټر راغے.

bā'rān šo'ro ke'do 'kəla če dəf'tər ta 'orasedəm. — It was starting to rain when I reached the office. — باران شروع کېدو کله چې دفتر ته ورسېدم.

pa'run zə'mā xpe xuge'de. — Yesterday my feet were hurting. (*f.pl.*) — پرُون زما خپې خوږېدې.

zə 'hara wrəz bi'māregəm. — I am getting sick every day. — زۀ هره ورځ بیمارېږم.

NOTE:

Using the sentences below as practice, contrast the simple past tense with the past progressive:

'haɣa sa'ṛey məṛ šo. — That man died. — هغه سړے مړ شو.

'haɣa sa'ṛey məṛ ke'do. — That man was dying. — هغه سړے مړ کېدو.

mašu'mān u'də šwəl?	Did the children go to sleep?	ماشُومان اُودهٔ شول؟
mašu'mān u'də ke'dəl?	Were the children going to sleep?	ماشُومان اُودهٔ کېدل؟

Passives

ke'dəl (کېدل) acts as a passive form in the past progressive:

stā mo'ṭər də xa'li pa wrəz səmedə [səmedo].	Your car was being repaired on Saturday.	ستا موټر د خالی په ورځ سمېدهٔ [سمېدو].
pa'run zə'mā kam'ra rang keda.	Yesterday my room was being painted.	پرُون زما کمره رنګ کېږده.
ḍo'ḍəy paxe'de 'kəla če ṭa'ləy 'owahəley šwa.	The food was being cooked when the doorbell rang.	ډوډۍ پخېدې کله چې ټلۍ ووهلے شوه.

More intransitive past progressive verbs

tā sa'ra tsok tlo?	Who was going with you?	تا سره څوک تلو؟
šā'hıd mā sa'ra tlo.	Shahid was going with me.	شاهد ما سره تلو.
'tāso 'kəla garze'dəy?	When were you walking?	تاسو کله ګرځېدئ؟
zə sa'har ā'tə baǰe garze'dəm.	I was walking at eight o'clock in the morning.	زهٔ سحر اتهٔ بجې ګرځېدم.
tə 'čerta tle?	Where were you going?	تهٔ چرته تلې؟
zə ba'zār ta tləm.	I was going to the market.	زهٔ بازار ته تلم.
ha'ɣa də dəf'tər na rāt'la?	Was she coming from the office?	هغه د دفتر نه راتله؟
na, ha'ɣa də ba'zār na rāt'la.	No, she was coming from the market.	نه، هغه د بازار نه راتله.
tsə waxt če 'xəze də ho'ṭəl na rāwa'təle, no tsə čəl 'ošo?	When the ladies were coming out of the hotel, what happened?	څهٔ وخت چې ښځې د هوټل نه راوتلې، نو څهٔ چل وشو؟
tsə waxt če haɣ'wi 'rāwate no 'wawra ware'dəl šo'ro šo.	When they were coming out it started to snow.	څهٔ وخت چې هغوی راوتې نو واؤره ورېدل شروع شو.
zə nən sa'har pa sāy'kəl skul ta rāt'ləm, 'kəla če ...	This morning I was going to school by cycle, when ...	زهٔ نن سحر په سائیکل سکُول ته راتلم کله چې ...

tsə waxt če ha'ɣa də ās na ɣorze'do no tā 'olido?	When he was falling from the horse did you see him?	څهٔ وخت چې هغه د اس نه غورزېدو نو تا وليدو؟
āw, mā 'olido.	Yes, I saw him.	آو، ما وليدو.
'kəla če zə pa pexā'wər ke ose'dəm, tā zə peǰan'dəm?	When I was living in Peshawar did you know me?	کله چې زهٔ په پېښور کښې اوسېدم، تا زهٔ پېژندم؟
āw, mā tə peǰan'de.	Yes, I knew (*lit.* 'was knowing') you.	آو، ما تهٔ پېژندې.
če zə 'rāɣləm no tə prot we?	When I was coming were you lying down?	چې زهٔ راغلم نو تهٔ پروت وې؟
na, zə də xob na 'pasedəm.	No, I was waking up from sleep.	نه، زهٔ د خوب نه پاڅېدم.

'was coming': *rāt'ləl* in the past progressive tense راتلل

Person	Singular			Plural		
1st	rāt'ləm	راتلم	I was coming	rāt'lu	راتلو	we were coming
2nd	rāt'le	راتلې	you were coming	rāt'ləy	راتلئ	you were coming
3rd m.	rāt'lo	راتلو	he was coming	rāt'ləl	راتلل	they were coming
3rd f.	rāt'la	راتله	she was coming	rāt'le	راتلې	they were coming

NOTE:
tləl (تلل) follows the same pattern at *rāt'ləl* (راتلل), but in the second masculine singular it is *tlo* (تلو).

Transitive verbs in the past progressive

As in the simple past, transitive verbs agree with the object, but if / o- / (-و) was used in the simple past tense it is not used in the past progressive. For example:

'tāso tsə kawəl?	What things were you doing? (*m.pl.*)	تاسو څهٔ کول؟

A great many sentences have past progressive followed by simple past:

'kəla če ha'ɣə zə'mā pə'ṭey re'bəlo mā pa ṭopak 'owišto.	When he was reaping my field I shot him with the gun.	کله چې هغهٔ زما پټے رېبلو ما په ټوپک وويشتو.

mā mo'ṭər čəla'wə 'kəla če zə ye 'owahələm.	I was driving the car when he hit me.	ما موټر چلاوهٔ کله چې زهٔ يې ووهلم.
mā pa ǰu'māt ke munz ka'wəlo 'kəla če ɣəl zə'mā tsa'pləy 'pəṭe kṛe.	I was praying in the mosque when a thief stole my sandals.	ما په جُماعت کښې مُونځ کولو کله چې غل زما څپلۍ پټې کړې.

Finish the story

☝ Have your teacher say these sentences then use them to start a story in the simple past in any way you like.

'kəla če mā xpe win'zəle ...	While I was washing my feet ...	کله چې ما خپې وينځلې ...
'kəla če mā ka'pṛe ɣwaṛa'wəle ...	While I was spreading out the clothes ...	کله چې ما کپړې غوړولې ...
'kəla če ha'ɣe čay 'skəle ...	While she was drinking tea ...	کله چې هغې چائې څښلې ...

What were you doing when?

It is a useful skill to get people to talk and expand on what they are saying as they tell a story. A good question can trigger a whole conversation. Try some of these phrases when your friends are relating a past event:

'tāso tsə ka'wəl?	What were you doing?	تاسو څهٔ کول؟
ha'ɣa 'kəla zax'mi šo?	When was he wounded?	هغه کله زخمی شو؟
ha'ɣa tsə waxt xa'bər kṛey šwa?	When did she become informed?	هغه څهٔ وخت خبر کړے شوه؟
xpo la de tsə čəl 'ošo?	What happened to your feet?	خپو له دې څهٔ چل وشو؟
tā re'ḍyo āwre'do?	Were you listening to the radio?	تا ريډيو اورېدو؟
tā be'gā sa'bəq we?	Were you studying last night?	تا بېګا سبق وې؟
tā pa'run lam'bo wa'həla?	Were you swimming yesterday?	تا پرُون لامبو وهله؟
tā də špe 'čəɣe wa'həle?	Were you screaming in the night?	تا د شپې چغې وهلې؟

☝ Now get your helper to ask you questions about what you did yesterday.

Compound verbs in the past progressive

stā xor tsə ka'wəl?	What was your sister doing?	ستا خور څهٔ کول؟
zə'mā xor ḍo'ḍəy paxa'wəla.	My sister was baking bread. (*f.s.*)	زما خور ډوډۍ پخوله.

haˈɣa saˈṛo tsə rang kaˈwəl?	What were those men dyeing?	هغه سړو څۀ رنګ کول؟
haɣˈwi zəˈmā ǰāˈme rang kaˈwəle.	They were dyeing my clothes. (*f.pl.*)	هغوی زما جامې رنګ کولې.
ˈhaɣa saˈṛi tā ta kənˈzəl ˈwəle kaˈwəl?	Why was that man cursing you?	هغه سړی تا ته کنځل ولې کول؟
ˈzəka če mā də haˈgə xra naˈgā kəṛe wa.	Because I was holding his donkey.	ځکه چې ما د هغۀ خره ناګا کړې وه.
če zə ˈrāɣləm no tə uˈdə we?	When I came were you sleeping?	چې زۀ راغلم نو تۀ اُودۀ وې؟
tsə čəl ˈošo če tā kiˈtāb we?	What happened as you were reading the book?	څۀ چل وشو چې تا کتاب وې؟
ˈkəla če mā kiˈtāb we, no wror me rāˈɣey.	As I was studying, my brother came.	کله چې ما کتاب وې نو ورور مې راغے.
tsə waxt če me kabuˈḍi kaˈwəla no xpa me mā ta šwa.	When I was playing Kubudi then my leg [*lit.* foot] broke.	څۀ وخت چې مې کبډی کوله نو خپه مې ما ته شوه.
tsə waxt če ɣəl ɣlā kaˈwəla, tsokiˈdār ˈčerta wo?	When the thief was robbing, where was the watchman?	څۀ وخت چې غل غلا کوله څوکیدار چرته وو؟
haˈɣə pa baˈzār ke xwaˈrāk kaˈwu.	He was in the market eating food.	هغۀ په بازار کښې خوراک کوو.
tā də de na ˈmaxke pəxˈto waˈyəla?	Were you speaking in Pukhto before this?	تا د دې نه مخکښې پښتو وئیله؟
na, mung pəxˈto nə waˈyəla.	No, we were not speaking Pukhto.	نه، مُونږ پښتو نۀ وئیله.

Contrasting simple and progressive past tenses

mā pa dəfˈtər ke kār oko.	I worked in the office.	ما په دفتر کښې کار وکړو.
mā pa dəfˈtər ke kār kaˈwəlo.	I was working in an office.	ما په دفتر کښې کار کولو.
mašuˈmāno ˈyəwa ˈloba ˈokṛa.	The children played a game.	ماشُومانو یوه لوبه وکړه.
mašuˈmāno ˈyəwa ˈloba kaˈwəla.	The children were playing a game.	ماشُومانو یوه لوبه کوله.

tā pa pəx'to ke xa'bare 'okṛe?	Did you speak in Pukhto?	تا په پښتو کښې خبرې وکړې؟
tā pa pəx'to ke xa'bare ka'wəle?	Were you speaking in Pukhto?	تا په پښتو کښې خبرې کولې؟

NOTE:

The / o- / (و-) is dropped for the past progressive.

When the verb *ka'wəl* (کول) is used in compound verbs in the past progressive tense the initial / k- / (ک-) is dropped in some cases.

mā yo mez ǰoṛ kṛo.	I built a desk. (*m.s.*)	ما يو ميز جوړ کړو.
mā yo mez ǰoṛa'wəlo.	I was building a desk.	ما يو ميز جوړولو.
'tāso lar'gi ṭo'ṭe kṛəl?	Did you chop the wood? (*m.pl.*)	تاسو لرګی ټوټې کړل؟
'tāso lar'gi ṭo'ṭe ka'wəl?	Were you chopping the wood?	تاسو لرګی ټوټې کول؟
ha'ɣe kam'ra sa'fā kṛa.	She cleaned the room. (*f.s.*)	هغې کمره صفا کړه.
ha'ɣe kam'ra sa'fā ka'wəla.	She was cleaning the room.	هغې کمره صفا کوله.
ha'ɣə kıṛ'kəy 'bānde kṛe.	He closed the windows. (*f.pl.*)	هغۀ کړکۍ بندې کړې.
ha'ɣə kıṛ'kəy banda'wəle.	He was closing the windows.	هغۀ کړکۍ بندولې.

How to practice this tense?

Memorise a story of something dramatic that happened to you and tell it to your friends.

Tell it to your helper, and ask him or her to tell it back to you in the two past tenses we have met so far. Practice these versions with your helper – paying particular attention to the verb endings.

Prepositions showing location

1. *məxā'məx* 'facing', 'opposite' مخامخ

zə'mā kor haspa'tāl ta məxā'məx dey.	My house is opposite the hospital.	زما کور هسپتال ته مخامخ دے.
sıne'mā də benk ku'se ta məxā'məx da.	The cinema is opposite to the street of the bank.	سنيما د بينک کوڅې ته مخامخ ده.

2. *pa xwā ke* 'next to', 'beside' — په خوا کښې

zə də or pa xwā ke ˈkenəm ˈzəka če yəxˈni me ˈkigi.	I am sitting beside the fire because I am getting cold.	زۀ د اور په خوا کښې کښېنم ځکه چې يخنى مې کېږى.
də pasˈporṭ dəfˈtər də afˈɣān hoˈṭəl pa xwā ke dey.	The Passport Office is beside the Afghan restaurant.	د پاسپورټ دفتر د افغان هوټل په خوا کښې دے.

NOTE:
Confusingly, the English loan word hoˈṭəl (هوټل) is mainly used in Pukhto to mean a place to eat, rather than to sleep and is equivalent to 'restaurant'.

3. *ˈməxe ta* and *maxke* 'in front of' — مخې ته، مخکښې

mā paˈrun haˈɣa də sabˈzəy də duˈkān maxke ˈolido.	Yesterday I saw him in front of the grocery store.	ما پرُون هغه د سبزئ د دُوکان مخکښې وليدو.
zmung də kor ˈməxe ta yo waˈṛukey xwaṛ dey.	In front of our house there is a small stream.	زمُونږ د کور مخې ته يو وړُوکے خوړ دے.

4. *ˈšāta* 'behind', 'at the back of', 'in back of' — شاته

də ǰamˈrud saˈṛək zmung də kor ˈšāta terigi.	Jamrud road passes behind our house.	د جمرود سړک زمُونږ د کور شاته تېرېږى.
nən haˈɣa zəˈmā ˈšāta nāst wo.	Today he was sitting behind me.	نن هغه زما شاته ناست وو.

5. *ǰoxt* 'right next to', 'alongside' — جوښت

zəˈmā kor də bɪˈlor kor saˈra ǰoxt dey.	My house is next to Bilour's house.	زما کور د بلور کور سره جوښت دے.
pa munz ke dumra ǰoxt oˈdregəy če uˈge yo bəl saˈra ˈləgi.	In prayer stand so close that your shoulders touch.	په مُونځ کښې دومره جوښت اودرېږئ چې اوږې يو بل سره لږى.

6. *pe, pre* 'on' — پې، پرې

xpa pe ˈmə-ɪgda, ˈzəka če guˈnā da.	Don't put your foot on it, as that's a sin.	خپه پې مۀ ږده، ځکه چه ګُناه ده.

ha'ɣa pa kor ke nāst wo āw čət pe ra prewato.	He was sitting in the house and the roof fell on him.	هغه په کور کښې ناست وو او چت پې را پرېوتو.

Comprehension drill: Laundry

'spine āw rang'dāre kap'ṛe byele kəy!	Separate the white and coloured clothes!	سپینې او رنګدارې کپړې بېلې کئ!
'spine kap'ṛe pa 'garmo u'bo ke āw rang'dāre pa 'yəxo u'bo ke 'wāčawa.	Put the white clothes in hot and the coloured in cold water.	سپینې کپړې په ګرمو اوبو کښې او رنګدارې په یخو اوبو کښې واچوه.
xo dā na'rəy kap'ṛe pa lā'suno 'owinzəy.	But wash these thin clothes by hand.	خو دا نرۍ کپړې په لاسونو ووینځئ.
byā ye pa tār 'oɣwaṛawəy.	Later spread them on the line.	بیا یې په تار وغوړوئ.
če 'uče ši, byā ye rā'ɣonḍe kṛəy āw is'tri ye kṛəy!	When they become dry, collect them and iron them!	چې وچې شي، بیا یې راغونډې کړئ او اِستري یې کړئ!

☝ Add at least five more commands that you have to use often.

Memorising moment

mata'luna

چې یارانه په شلتالو شوه نو ما نه پاتې ده.

če yār'āna pa šəlta'lo šwa no mā na 'pāte da.

If friendship is for a peach then I can't live with it.

دوست له دومره قوت مه ورکوه چې برابري درسره وکړي.

dost la 'dumra qu'wət mə war'kawa če bərābə'ri dar-sa'ra o'kṛi.

Don't give that much power to a friend that they can become equal to you.

هر چا سره پنج، خو یار اشنا سره نهٔ پنج.

har ča sa'ra panǰ, xo yār āš'nā sa'ra nə panǰ.[22]

Compete with everyone but not with friends and companions.

دَ کم عقل دوست نه هوښیار دُشمن ښهٔ وی.

də kəm 'aqəl dost na ux'yār duš'man xə wi.

The wise enemy is better than a stupid friend.

هندُو د یار د پاره غته غوښه خوړلې ده.

hın'du də yār də'pāra, 'ɣaṭa 'ɣwaxa xo'ṛəle da.

For a friend a Hindu has eaten beef.

Exercises for Lesson Twenty-Two

1. Use the prepositions: *məxā'məx* (مخامخ) 'facing', 'opposite'; *'maxke* (مخکښې) 'in front'; *pa xwā ke* (په خوا کښې) 'beside'; and *'šāta* (شاته) 'behind' in the following sentences.

   a. xpəl sāy'kəl zə'mā də kor _______________ ta mə-pregda!

   خپل سائیکل زما د کور _______________ ته مهٔ پرېږده!

   b. 'yəwa xkwəle ǰı'nəy zə'mā _______________ 'nāsta da.

   یوه ښکُلې جینۍ زما _______________ ناسته ده.

   c. də ha'ɣa du'kān zə'mā də kor _______________ prot dey.

   د هغه دُوکان زما د کور _______________ پروت دے.

   d. zmung də kor _______________ yo wa'ṛukey 'laxtey dey.

   زمُونږ د کور _______________ یو وړُوکے لختے دے.

[22] panǰ (پنج) means 'five', but here it is being used idiomatically to mean 'claws' (pan'ǰa پنجه). To give 'five' means to come against someone competitively.

2. Say the following sentences in the past progressive tense, and then finish the story.
   a. As he was lying on the ground ...
   b. As they approached the mountain pass ...
   c. One day Ariq was hunting ...
   d. One day he was ploughing his field ...
   e. He was going to the village barber for a hair cut ...
   f. As she was returning to her village ...
   g. One day he was sitting under a shady tree ...

3. In the following sentences change the simple past tense verbs to the progressive past.

a.	mal'gəre de 'tāso ta tsə dar-kṛəl?	ملګرې دې تاسو ته څهٔ درکړل؟
b.	mā ha'ɣə ta yo xat 'olego.	ما هغهٔ ته يو خط ولېږو.
c.	mor me rāta xwanda'nāka ḍo'ḍəy pa'xa kṛa.	مور مې راته خوندناکه ډوډۍ پخه کړه.
d.	plār me war sa'ra həm lāṛo.	پلار مې ورسره هم لاړو.
e.	wror me pa bāɣ ke kār 'okṛo āw ḍer 'stəṛey šo.	ورور مې په باغ کښې کار وکړو او ډېر ستړے شو.
f.	mā ki'tāb xlās kṛo 'kəla če tə rāɣle.	ما کتاب خلاص کړو کله چې تهٔ راغلې.
g.	stā qi'sa me 'wawreda āw ḍera me 'xwaxa šwa.	ستا قيصه مې واؤريده او ډېره مې خوښه شوه.

h.	mašu'māno də bāɣ na ma'ṇe 'pəṭe kṛe.	ماشُومانو د باغ نه منړې پټې کړې.
i.	mā də ta kən'zəl okṛə xo zə'mā xa'bara ye wā-'nə-wreda.	ما دۀ ته کنځل اوکړۀ خو زما خبره يې وانۀ وريده.
j.	səxt bā'rān 'ošo āw 'ṭole me'we xa'rābe šwe.	سخت باران وشو او ټولې مېوې خرابې شوې.
k.	ḍer 'xəfa šəm če tā mā sa'ra ḍo'ḍəy o-'nə-xoṛa.	ډېر خفه شوم چې تا ما سره ډوډۍ ونۀ خوړه.
l.	mā xpəl zwi ta ma'ṇa 'war-kṛa.	ما خپل زوئ ته منړه ورکړه.

Vocabulary for Lesson Twenty-Two

ıhsā'sāt	احساسات	*m.pl.*	*n.*	feelings, emotions
u'sul	اصُول	*m.pl.*	*n.*	principles, methods, rules
u'ga / u'ge	اوږه / اوږې	*f.*	*n.*	shoulder
byela'wəl	بېلول		*v.t.*	to separate, to disunite, to disconnect
benk	بېنک	*m.*	*n.*	bank
pas'porṭ	پاسپورټ	*m.*	*n*	passport
pəṭa'wəl	پټول		*v.t.*	to hide, to cover, to conceal, to put away; to steal
pə'ṭey	پټے	*m.*	*n.*	field, farmland
pre	پرې		*prep.*	on
pa xwā ke	په خوا کښې		*prep.*	next to, beside
pe	پې		*prep*	on
tār	تار	*m.s.*	*n.*	rope; shalwar cord
ṭa'ləy	ټلۍ	*f.*	*n.*	doorbell
ṭo'pak	ټوپک	*m.*	*n.*	gun, rifle
ǰoxt	جوښت		*prep.*	right next to, alongside
čəl	چل	*m.*	*n.*	manner, method, event, trick, occurrence
xa'bər	خبر	*m.*	*n.*	news, information
xo'lus	خلوص	*m.*	*n.*	devotion, sincerity
xwaṛ	خوړ	*m.*	*n.*	gully, stream
dostā'ne	دوستانې	*f. pl.*	*n.*	friendship
rāwa'təl	راوتل		*v.i.*	to come out, to exit, to leave
ra'zā ka'wəl	رضا کول		*comp. v.t.*	to reconcile
rang'dāre	رنګدارې		*adj.*	coloured

ranga'wəl [rang ka'wəl]	رنګول [رنګ کول]		*v.t.*	to colour, to paint, to dye, to polish
range'dəl	رنګېدل		*v.i.*	to be dyed, to be coloured, to be painted
re'bəl	رېبل		*v.t.*	to reap, to harvest
zax'mi	زخمی	*m., f.*	*adj.*	wounded, injured
səme'dəl	سمېدل		*v.i*	to be repaired, to become straight, to right
'šāta	شاته		*prep.*	behind, at the back of, in back of
xe'gəṛa	ښېګړه	*f.*	*n.*	favour, kindness, help
qɪs'mət	قِسمت	*m.*	*n*	fate, luck
ɣonḍa'wəl	غونډول		*v.t.*	to gather, to collect
kabu'ḍi ka'wəl	کبډی کول		*comp. v.t.*	to play Kubudi
kən'zəl ka'wəl	کنځل کول		*comp. v.t.*	to curse
mota'lɪq	مُتعلق	*m.*	*adj.*	belonging, pertaining, depending
məxā'məx	مخامخ	*m.*	*adj.*	opposite, facing
'məxe ta	مخې ته		*prep.*	in front of
mət'ləb	مطلب	*m.*	*n.*	meaning, purpose, aim, object
na'gā ka'wəl	ناګا کول		*v.t.*	to hold an animal that strays into someone's crops
'wawra ware'dəl	واوره ورېدل		*v.t.*	to snow
wa'fā	وفا	*f.*	*n.*	fidelity, loyalty, faithfulness
wiš'təl	ویشتل		*v.t.*	to shoot, to hurl, to throw

dər-wišˈtəm saˈbəq درویشتم سبق

Lesson Twenty-Three

Dialogue twenty-three: Ladies' home-life

L: stā ǰwənd ˈtsənga terˈigi? How is your life going?	ستا ژوند څنګه تېرېږي؟
H: də ālˈlā ˈfəzəl dey. By God's grace.	د الله فضل دے.
L: wāˈdə de pa ˈxpəla ˈxwaxa ˈkəṛey dey? Was your wedding of your own choosing?	وادۀ دې په خپله خوښه کړے دے؟
H: na, da mor plār pa xwaxa me kəˈṛey dey. No, I have gone with my parents' choice.	نه، د مور پلار په خوښه مې کړے دے.
L: xāˈwənd dar-sara xə dey? Is your husband good to you?	خاوند درسره ښۀ دے؟
H: na, ḍer trix dey. No, he is very harsh.	نه، ډېر تریخ دے.
L: ˈwəle, ṭaˈkəy de tsə? Why, does he hit you?	ولې ټکې دې څۀ؟
H: na, ṭaˈkəy me nə, xo har waxt ˈɣosa ˈkigi. No, he doesn't hit me, but he is always angry.	نه، ټکې مې نۀ خو هر وخت غُصه کېږي.
L: haˈɣa ˈwəle ˈdase kaˈwi? Why is he like that? (*Lit.* 'Why does he do that?')	هغه ولې داسې کوي؟
H: haˈɣa har waxt ˈɣwāṛi če zə də sād xyāl ˈosatəm. He always wants me to take care of Saad.	هغه هر وخت غواړي چې زۀ د سعد خیال وساتم.
L: xo tə ba tsə oke, də kor kārˈuna həm ḍer wi. But what can you do, there is also a lot of housework.	خو تۀ به څۀ وکې، د کور کارُونه هم ډېر وي.

Men's dialogue: Enmity

L: zə nən dā ɪzˈda kaˈwəm, če dušmaˈni ˈtsənga pedaˈkigi. Today I am learning how feuds start.	زۀ نن دا زده کوم چې دُشمنی څنګه پیدا کېږي.
H: dušmaˈni yā pa ˈxəzo, yā pa ˈzməko, yā pa doˈlət, āw yā pa ɣlā pedaˈkigi. Feuds start over women, land, money or theft.	دُشمنی یا په ښځو یا په زمکو یا په دولت او یا په غلا پیدا کېږي.

L:	bad'la āxɪs'təl xə kār dey? Is taking revenge a good thing?	بدله اخستل ښۀ کار دے؟
H:	āw, pa tsə ha'lāto ke xə kār dey. Yes, in some situations it's good.	آو، په څۀ حالاتو کښې ښۀ کار دے.
L:	kə tsok 'qatal kṛey ši, no ā'wal tsok də ha'ɣə ba'dəl 'axli? If someone is killed, then who is the first one to take revenge?	کۀ څوک قتل کړے شي، نو اول څوک د هغۀ بدل اخلي؟
H:	'wruṇa āw zā'mən ye ba'dal 'axli. Brothers and sons take revenge.	وروُنړه او زامن يې بدل اخلي.
L:	če dušma'ni 'yəwa pe'ra šo'ro ši, no byā 'tsənga xatme'dey ši? Once a feud starts, then how can it be stopped?	چې دُشمنې يوه پېره شروع شي، نو بيا څنګه ختمېدے شي؟
H:	haɣ'wi la ba swa'ra āw yā pe'se warka'wi. They will give *swara* or money to them.	هغوی له به سوره او يا پېسې ورکوي.
L:	mā ta də dušma'ni 'yəwa qi'sa 'oka. Tell me a story about a feud.	ما ته د دُشمنۍ يوه قيصه وکه.

NOTE:
swa'ra (سوره) is the tradition in some villages in which a girl of marriageable age is given to the aggrieved party in the hope that her marriage to the enemy will end the enmity.

Pronunciation drill

Practice these tongue twisters:

wa'li, də waley wa'le 'wale 'oli?	ولی د ولے ولې ولې ولی؟
tayāra pa tyārə ke tayāra šwa.	طياره په تيارۀ کښې تياره شوه.

'used to': The habitual past

The habitual past is formed by adding *ba* (به) in the same way as the future tense. The difference is that the / o- / (و-) prefix is dropped in verbs that would normally take it, and past endings are added to the infinitive. As with other past verbs, the verb endings agree with the object for transitive verbs and with the subject for intransitive verbs.

Intransitive verbs in the habitual past

bəs ba 'dəlta odre'do?	Did the bus used to stop here?	بس به دلته ودرېدو؟

āw, pa'roskāl ba 'dəlta odre'do.	Yes, last year it used to stop here.	آو، پروسکال به دلته ودرېدو.
'tāso ba pa pexā'wər ke ose'dəy?	Did you used to live in Peshawar?	تاسو به په پېښور کښې اوسېدئ؟
āw, mung ba 'halta ose'du.	Yes, we used to live there.	آو، مُونږ به هلته اوسېدُو.
ha'ɣa ba tsə waxt kār ta rāt'lo?	When did he used to come to work?	هغه به څۀ وخت کار ته راتلو؟
ha'ɣa ba wax'ti kār ta rāt'lo.	He used to come to work early.	هغه به وختی کار ته راتلو.
tə ba hame'ša 'čerta tle?	Where did you always used to go?	تۀ به همیشه چرته تلې؟
zə ba bāɣ ta tləm.	I used to go to the park.	زۀ به باغ ته تلم.

NOTE:
The third sentence makes a very good one for substitution drills.

'used to become': *ba ke'dəl* — به کېدل

ḍo'dəy ba tsə waxt paxe'da?	When did the bread used to be cooked?	ډوډۍ به څۀ وخت پخېده؟
špəg baǰe ba paxe'da.	It used to be cooked at six o'clock.	شپږ بجې به پخېده.
tə ba tsə waxt 'wəgey kede?	When did you used to become hungry?	تۀ به څۀ وخت اوږے کېدې؟
zə ba mā'xām 'wəgey ke'dəm.	I used to become hungry in the evening.	زۀ به ماښام اوږے کېدم.
barā'nuna ba 'kəla šo'ro ke'dəl?	When did it used to start raining? (*m.pl.*)	بارانونه به کله شروع کېدل؟
pa paša'kāl ke ba šo'ro ke'dəl.	It used to rain in Pashakal.	په پشکال کښې به شروع کېدل.
ka'pṛe ba 'kəla win'zəley ke'de?	When did your clothes used to be washed?	کپړې به کله وينځلے کېدې؟
hara haf'ta ba win'zəley ke'de.	They used to be washed every Saturday.	هره هفته به وينځلے کېدې.
xpa ba de xuge'da?	Did your foot used to hurt?	خپه به دې خوږېده؟
āw, xuge'da ba, xo os ṭik da.	Yes, it used to hurt, but now it is fine.	آو، خوږېده به، خو اوس ټیک ده.

NOTES:

1. Reminder: getting agreement with the object is the key to using *ba ke'dəl* (به کېدل).
2. *paša'kāl* (پشکال) is the hot and humid time prior to the monsoon. Explore this and other traditional Pukhtun names for the months.

Transitive verbs in the habitual past

tā ba ka'pṛe gan'ḍəle?	Did you used to sew clothes? (*f.pl.*)	تا به کپړې گنډلې؟
āw, mā ba gan'ḍəle.	Yes, I used to sew them.	آو، ما به گنډلې.
ha'ɣə ba 'čerta ḍo'ḍəy xo'ṛa?	Where did he used to eat food? (*f.s.*)	هغهٔ به چرته ډوډۍ خوړه؟
ha'ɣə ba hara wrəz 'dəlta xo'ṛa.	He used to eat here every day.	هغهٔ به هره ورځ دلته خوړه.
tā ba hara špa ša'rāb skəl?	Did you used to drink alcohol every night? (*m.pl.*)	تا به هره شپه شراب څښل؟
āw, mā ba skəl xo os me 'prexodəl.	Yes, I used to drink it, but now I've stopped it.	آو، ما به څښل خو اوس مې پرېښودل.
tā ba rozā'na ax'bār we?	Did you used to read the newspaper every day?	تا به روزانه اخبار وې؟
āw, mā ba we.	Yes, I used to read it.	آو، ما به وې.
ha'ɣə ba tə wa'həle?	Did he used to beat you?	هغهٔ به تهٔ وهلې؟
āw, zə ba ye rozā'na wa'hələm.	Yes, he used to beat me every day.	آو، زهٔ به يې روزانه وهلم.

Compound transitive verbs

tā ba pa 'qatar ke kār ka'wəlo?	Did you used to work in Qatar?	تا به په قطر کښې کار کولو؟
āw, 'halta ba me kār ka'wəlo.	Yes, I used to work there.	آو، هلته به مې کار کولو.
tā ba də haɣ'wi ma'dəd ka'wəlo?	Did you used to help them?	تا به د هغوی مدد کولو؟
na, mā ba 'hits-kəla də haɣ'wi ma'dəd 'nə-kawəlo.	No, I never used to help them.	نه، ما به هېڅ کله د هغوی مدد نهٔ کولو.
tā ba 'mexe sa'təle?	Did you used to keep buffaloes?	تا به مېښې ساتلې؟
ha'ɣe ba mā sa'ra xa'bare ka'wəle.	She used to talk with me.	هغې به ما سره خبرې کولې.

ter kāl ba me də dwi saˈra ˈḍere ˈṭoqe kaˈwəle.	I used to joke with them a lot last year.	تېر کال به مې د دوئ سره ډېرې ټوقې کولې.
če tə zwān we tā ba ˈgāḍi səmaˈwəl?	When you were young did you used to fix cars?	چې تهٔ ځوان وې تا به ګاډی سمول؟
āw, səmaˈwəl ba me.	Yes, I used to fix them.	آو، سمول به مې.
stā noˈkər ba peˈse pəṭaˈwəle?	Did your servant used to steal money?	ستا نوکر به پېسې پټولې؟
na, haˈɣa də hameˈša na imanˈdār wo.	No, he was always honest.	نه، هغه د همېشه نه ایماندار وو.
haˈɣe ba hameˈša ˈdumra xə xwaˈrāk taˈyārawəlo?	Did she always used to prepare so much good food?	هغې به همېشه دومره ښهٔ خوراک تیارولو؟
pa garˈməy ke ba de tsə waxt xpəl duˈkān kolāˈwəlo āw bandaˈwəlo?	In the summer when did you used to open and close your shop?	په ګرمۍ کښې به دې څهٔ وخت خپل دُوکان کولاولو او بندولو؟
mā ba saˈhar špəg baǰe kolāˈwəlo āw də špe ləs baǰe ba me bandaˈwəlo.	I used to open it at six in the morning and close it at ten at night.	ما به سحر شپږ بجې کولاولو او د شپې لس بجې به مې بندولو.
dāˈdā me, xoˈdey de ˈobaxi, haˈɣə ba we ...	My dad, may God forgive him, used to say ...	دادا مې، خُدائ دې وبخښی، هغهٔ به وې ...
xeza me, de xoˈdey ˈobaxi, haˈɣa ba we ...	My wife, may God forgive her, used to say ...	ښځه مې، دې خُدائ وبخښی، هغه به وې ...

NOTE:

The past continuous tense is often used in story telling. Practice it as much as you can in telling short stories.

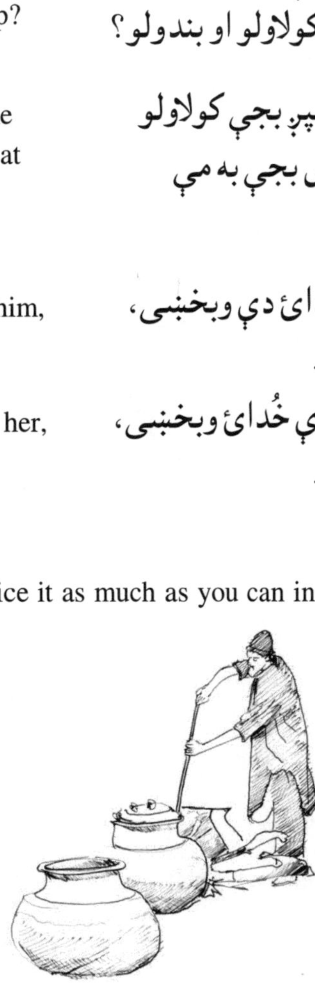

Useful time words

baˈsir təl ˈḍere peˈse gaˈṭi.	Basir always earns a lot of money.	بصیر تل ډېرې پیسې ګټي.
tə ˈwəle təl haˈɣə saˈra ǰang kaˈwe?	Why are you always fighting with him?	تهٔ ولې تل هغهٔ سره جنګ کوې؟
mung ba ṭol ˈumar ˈpore haˈɣa yādaˈwu.	We will be thinking of him our whole lives.	مُونږ به ټول عُمر پورې هغه یادوُو.
gulāˈləy hameˈša xoˈšāla wi.	Gulalay is always happy.	ګُلالۍ همیشه خوشحاله وي.
mung akˈsər saˈbəq ˈwayu.	We usually study.	مُونږ اکثر سبق وایُو.
zə haˈɣa har zəl ˈwinəm.	I see him every time.	زهٔ هغه هر ځل وینم.
haɣˈwi xār ta ḍer nə-zi.	They don't go to the city very often.	هغوی ښار ته ډېر نهٔ ځي.
ˈkəla ˈkəla penṭ-šərṭ ˈāɣondəm.	I sometimes wear western clothes.	کله کله پېنټ شرټ اغوندم.
dā ˈkəla na ˈkəla ˈmāla rāˈzi.	She sometimes comes to see me.	دا کله نا کله ما له راځي.
haɣˈwi ḍer kəm pa kor ke wi.	They are seldom at home.	هغوی ډېر کم په کور کښې وي.
ḍer kəm haˈɣa ˈdəlta ˈwinəm.	I seldom see him here.	ډېر کم هغه دلته وینم.
tə ˈhıčere zəˈmā kor ta ˈnə-rāze!	You never come to my house!	ته هېچرې زما کور ته نه راځې!
zə ˈhits-kəla də špe kār ˈnə-kawəm.	I never work at night.	زهٔ هېڅ کله د شپې کار نهٔ کوم.

Seasons

spring	سپرلے	sparˈley	بهار	baˈhār
summer	اوړے	ˈoṛey		
autumn	منے	ˈməney		
winter	ژمے	ˈǰımey		

pa sparˈli ke moˈsəm ˈtsənga wi?	How is the weather in the spring?	په سپرلی کښې موسم څنګه وي؟
bərāˈbər wi.	It is moderate.	برابر وي.
pa ˈǰımi ke ˈwāwra waˈrigi?	Does it snow in winter?	په ژمی کښې واوره وریږي؟
na, nə waˈrigi.	No, it doesn't snow.	نه، نهٔ وریږي.

Comprehension drill: Pictures

☝ Collect some photographs of a wide range of local life, or cut out pictures from newspapers and magazines. You can also use the illustrations in *Picture It in Dari and Pashto.* Choose a photo or picture and talk about it in the following way:

1. Have your helper name the objects. For example,

dā ˈwəna da. dā saˈṛey dey.	This is a tree. This is a man.	دا ونه ده. دا سړے دے.

2. The helper points to the objects and you name them.

ˈwəna ˈčerta da? saˈṛey ˈčerta dey?	Where is the tree? Where is the man?	ونه چرته ده؟ سړے چرته دے؟

3. Use the picture to show simple relationships between objects.

da ˈwəne ˈlānde raˈwān saˈṛi ta išaˈra ˈoka.	Point to the man walking under the tree.	د ونې لاندې روان سړی ته اشاره وکه.

4. Make up a story about the picture in different tenses.

When conversation drags in the *hujra* or guest room, it is helpful to have a small booklet of pictures with you. It turns any helpful person into a language teacher. It will also keep the conversation focused on a topic with which you are familiar.

Memorising moment

mataˈluna

وروری خوری به کوُو خو حساب کتاب تر مینځه.

ˈwrori xoˈri ba kaˈwu xo hiˈsāb kiˈtāb tər ˈmenza.

We will be like brothers and sisters but will keep accounts between us.

دا گز او دا میدان.

dā gaz āw dā meˈdān.

This the yardstick and this the open ground.

پښتُون سل کاله پس بدل واغستو او وې وئيل چې زر مې واغستو.

pəx'tun sıl 'kāla pas ba'dəl 'wāɣəsto āw we wa'yəl če zər me 'wāɣəsto.

A Pukhtun took revenge after a hundred years and said, "I took it quickly."

په زور کلی نۀ کېږی.

pa zor 'kəli 'nə kigi.

Community is not created by force.

ښځې له يا کور دے يا ګور دے.

'xəze la yā kor dey yā gor dey.

For the woman either the house or the grave.

Exercises for Lesson Twenty-Three

1. This week record a short story about a feud, or some other event. Write out what your friend has told you using phonetics or script. Pay special attention to the verb endings. The following phrase may help you get started:

   mā ta də dušma'ni 'yəwa qi'sa 'oka! Tell me a story about a feud! ما ته د دُشمنئ يوه قيصه وکه!

   Now look for chances to retell the story.

2. Tell a short story that starts like this:
   a. There used to be a rich man ...
   b. He used to graze his sheep on a nearby mountain ...
   c. He used to eat a lot ...
   d. She used to be very poor ...
   e. We used to sell vegetables ...
   f. She used to attack the villagers ...

Vocabulary for Lesson Twenty-Three

iman'dār	ايماندار	*m.*	*adj.*	honest, faithful
iman'dāra / iman'dare	ايمانداره / ايمانداري	*f.*		
bad'la āxɪs'təl	بدله اخستل		*comp. v.t.*	to take revenge
bərā'bər	برابر	*m.*	*adj.*	equal, even, on a par; fit, match
ba'hār	بهار	*m.*	*n*	spring (season)
trix / trā'xə	تريخ / تراخهٔ	*m.*	*adj.*	bitter
tra'xa / tra'xe	ترخه / ترخي	*f.*		
təl	تل		*adv.*	always
ṭa'kəy	ټکی	*f.*	*n.*	strike, hit
'ṭoqe ka'wəl	ټوقي کول		*comp. v.t.*	to joke, to jest
prexo'dəl	پرېښودل		*v.i.*	to quit, to stop (doing something), to leave, to let go, to forsake
paša'kāl	پشکال	*m.*	*n.*	hot humid weather prior to the monsoon
pe'ra	پېره	*f.*	*n.*	one time period, one turn
penṭ-šərṭ	پېنټ شرټ	*m.*	*n.*	western style trousers (pants) and shirt
hā'lat	حالت	*m.*	*n.*	state, condition
xwaxa'wəl	خوښول		*v.t.*	to like, to choose
dušma'ni	دُشمني		*n.*	feud, enmity
do'lət	دولت	*m.*	*n.*	riches, wealth
ḍer kəm	ډېر کم		*adv.*	seldom, hardly ever
'zməka	زمکه	*f.*	*n.*	land
'ǰɪmey	ژمے	*m.*	*n.*	winter
ǰwənd	ژوند	*m.*	*n.*	life
səma'wəl	سمول		*v.t*	to fix, to correct, to mend, to straighten, to adjust

swaˈra	سوره	*f.*	*n.*	forced marriage to end a feud
šaˈrāb	شراب	*m.pl.*	*n.*	alcoholic drink
tayāra	طیاره	*f.*	*n.*	plane, aeroplane [airplane]
ˈumar	عُمر	*m.*	*n.*	life; age
ˈqatal kaˈwəl	قتل کول		*comp. v.t.*	to kill, to murder
ˈkəla ˈkəla	کله کله		*adv.*	sometimes, now and again
ˈməney	منے	*m.*	*n.*	autumn, fall

tsalerišˈtəm saˈbəq ځليرېشتم سبق

Lesson Twenty-Four

Dialogue twenty-four: Sickness

H: zə naˈǰoṛa yım, zəˈmā zoˈkām dey, ˈtəba me həm da, āw sər me həm xoˈgigi. I'm sick, I have a cold, I also have a fever and my head hurts.	زهٔ ناجوړه يم، زما زُکام دے، تبه مې هم ده، او سر مې هم خوږېږي.
L: ḍākˈṭər la lāṛ ša! Go to the doctor!	ډاکټر له لاړ شه!
H: na, dəwaˈi xoˈṛəm. No, I'm taking medicine.	نه، دوائ خورم.
L: də zoˈkām saˈra tsə parˈhez kaˈwəl paˈkār di? What restrictions are needed for a cold?	د زُکام سره څهٔ پرهېز کول پکار دي؟
H: də ɣwaˈṛo, də ˈyəxo āw trāˈwo siˈzuno na ba zān sāˈte. You should keep away from oil, 'cold' and sour things.	د غوړو، د يخو او تراوو څيزُونو نه به ځان ساتې.
L: tə hameˈša naˈǰoṛa kege? Are you always getting sick?	تهٔ هميشه ناجوړه کېږې؟
H: na, ˈkəla na ˈkəla. No, now and then.	نه، کله نا کله.
L: pa tā ˈbānde ˈčere tsə draˈna bimaˈri ˈtera šɪβe da? Have you ever had any serious disease?	په تا باندې چرې څهٔ درنه بيمارى تېره شوې ده؟
H: āw, yo zəl me meāˈdi ˈtəba tera kəṛe da. Yes, one time I have had typhoid.	آو، يو ځل مې ميعادى تبه تېره کړې ده.
L: tə zān də bimaˈro na ˈtsənga bəč key? How can you keep yourself from sickness?	تهٔ ځان د بيمارو نه څنګه بچ کے؟

NOTE:

☝ Explore the concept of 'hot' and 'cold' foods with your friends.

Pronunciation drill

زما د دوست مور په يو موړ کښې مړه شوه.

zəˈmā də dost mor pa yo moṛ ke mṛa šwa.

'to have done': The present perfect tense

The present perfect tense is formed from the past participle and the appropriate present tense endings. The past participle consists of the infinitive form of the verb plus one of three masculine or feminine suffixes: / -ey / (ـے -), / -i / (ـی-) or / -e / (ـې-). The / o- / (و-) prefix is not used. See the example 'to have arrived' below.

The present perfect tense is one of the most commonly used past tenses. It indicates that the result of an action continues to be in some way important to the present situation.

The present perfect of the verb *rasc'dəley* – 'to have arrived' رسېدلے

past participle infinitive	+	 endings	+	present tense endings				
رسېدل rase'dəl	+	ـې / ـی / ـے ey / i / e	+	یم yım		=	رسېدلے یم rase'dəley yım	I have arrived, etc

NOTES:

1. The three suffixes are declined according to the gender and number of the subject.
2. The verb *rase'dəley* (رسېدلے) is an example of how most regular intransitive verbs are inflected in the present perfect tense.

Person	Singular			Plural		
1st m.	rase'dəley yım	I have arrived	رسېدلے یم	rase'dəli yu	we have arrived	رسېدلی یُو
1st f.	rase'dəle yım	I have arrived	رسېدلې یم	rase'dəle yu	we have arrived	رسېدلې یُو
2nd m.	rase'dəley ye	you have arrived	رسېدلے يې	rase'dəli yəy	you have arrived	رسېدلی یئ
2nd f.	rase'dəle ye	you have arrived	رسېدلې يې	rase'dəle yəy	you have arrived	رسېدلې یئ
3rd m.	rase'dəley dey	he has arrived	رسېدلے دے	rase'dəli di	they have arrived	رسېدلی دی
3rd f.	rase'dəle da	she has arrived	رسېدلې ده	rase'dəle di	they have arrived	رسېدلې دی

Intransitive verbs in the present perfect

nən 'čerta garze'dəley ye?	Where have you walked today? (*m.*)	نن چرته ګرځېدلے يې؟
zə 'ṭola wrəz pa xār ke garze'dəley yım.	I have walked all day in the city.	زۀ ټوله ورځ په ښار کښې ګرځېدلے یم.

ha'ɣa 'kəli ta rase'dəle da?	Has she reached the village?	هغه کلي ته رسېدلې ده؟
na, tər 'osa nə-da rase'dəle.	No, she hasn't reached it yet.	نه، تر اوسه نۀ ده رسېدلې.
tə 'maxke ko'hāṭ ta 'təley ye?	Have you gone to Kohat before? (*m.*)	تۀ مخکښې کوهاټ ته تلے يې؟
āw, 'təley yım.	Yes, I have gone.	آو، تلے يم.
hami'da čā sa'ra rā'ɣəle da?	Who has Hamida come with?	حميده چا سره راغلې ده؟
ha'ɣa xor sa'ra rā'ɣəle da.	She has come with her sister.	هغه خور سره راغلې ده.
ba'šir də po'lis na təxte'dəley dey?	Has Bashir run away from the police?	بشير د پوليس نه تښتېدلے دے؟
āw, təxte'dəley dey.	Yes, he has run away.	آو، تښتېدلے دے.
tə 'čerta də mərg na yere'dəley ye?	Have you ever been afraid of death? (*m.*)	تۀ چرته د مرګ نه يرېدلے يې؟
āw, 'kəla na 'kəla 'flāying koč ke yere'dəley yım.	Yes, sometimes I have been afraid in a 'flying coach.'	آو، کله نا کله فلائينګ کوچ کښې يرېدلے يم.

Negatives in the present perfect tense:

Short answers that are negative often involve splitting up the verb.

☝ Have your helper read the question and answer him in the negative.

'maxke 'kəla pa swāt ke ose'dəley ye?	Have you ever lived in Swat before?	مخکښې کله په سوات کښې اوسېدلے يې؟
na, 'halta nə-yu ose'dəli.	No, we have not lived there.	نه، هلته نۀ يُو اوسېدلی.
bəs tər 'osa 'dəlta odre'dəḷey dey?	Has the bus stopped here yet?	بس تر اوسه دلته ودرېدلے دے؟
na, tər 'osa 'pore nə-dey odre'dəley.	No, it has not stopped here yet.	نه، تر اوسه پورې نۀ دے ودرېدلے.

Practice:

Now take the list of intransitive verbs from earlier chapters (for example, the twelve intransitive verbs in Lesson Twelve) and make sentences from them. Pay special attention to the three endings that go onto the infinitive. Try the negative forms too. Try to use as many verbs as you can and speak as fast as you can!

Compound intransitive verbs in the present perfect

ˈstəṛey ˈšɪβey – 'to have become tired' ستړے شوے

Person	Masculine		Feminine	
1st s.	ˈstəṛey ˈšɪβey yɪm	ستړے شوے یم	ˈstəṛe ˈšɪβe yɪm	ستړې شوې یم
1st pl.	ˈstəṛi ˈšɪβi yu	ستړی شوی یُو	ˈstəṛe ˈšɪβe yu	ستړې شوې یُو
2nd s.	ˈstəṛey ˈšɪβey ye	ستړے شوے یې	ˈstəṛe ˈšɪβe ye	ستړې شوې یې
2nd pl.	ˈstəṛi ˈšɪβi yəy	ستړی شوی یئ	ˈstəṛe ˈšɪβe yəy	ستړې شوې یئ
3rd s.	ˈstəṛey ˈšɪβey dey	ستړے شوے دے	ˈstəṛe ˈšɪβe da	ستړې شوې ده
3rd pl.	ˈstəṛi ˈšɪβi di	ستړی شوی دی	ˈstəṛe ˈšɪβe di	ستړې شوې دی

Example sentences using compound intransitive verbs in the present perfect tense:

haˈɣa uˈdə ˈšɪβey dey?	Has he gone to sleep?	هغه اُودۀ شوے دے؟
na, haˈɣa nə-dey uˈdə ˈšɪβey.	No, he has not gone to sleep.	نه، هغه نۀ دے اُودۀ شوے.
marˈyam tər ˈosa wāˈdə ˈšɪβe nə-da?	Hasn't Miriam become married yet?	مریم تر اوسه وادۀ شوې نۀ ده؟
na, nə-da ˈwādə ˈšɪβe.	No, she hasn't become married.	نه، نۀ ده وادۀ شوې.
də ˈdə ˈxəza həm mṛa ˈšɪβe da?	Has his wife also died?	د دۀ ښځه هم مړه شوې ده؟
na, nə-da mṛa ˈšɪβe.	No, she hasn't died.	نه، نۀ ده مړه شوې.
gulaˈləy xug ˈšɪβe da?	Has Gulalay been hurt?	ګُلالۍ خوږ شوې ده؟
stā ˈwruṇa xpəl plār saˈra raˈzā ˈšɪβi di?	Have your brothers become reconciled with their father?	ستا رونړه خپل پلار سره رضا شوی دی؟
na, nə-di raˈzā ˈšɪβi.	No, they haven't become reconciled.	نه، نۀ دی رضا شوی.

mašu'mān wix 'šɪβi di?	Have the children woken up?	ماشُومان ويښ شوی دی؟
na, nə-di wix 'šɪβi.	No, they haven't woken up.	نه، نهٔ دی ويښ شوی.
no'kəra də 'maxke na 'stəṛe 'šɪβe da?	Has the servant become tired already?	نوکره د مخکښې نه ستړې شوې ده؟

Passive sentences in the present perfect

Passive sentences are similar to transitive verbs in the way that the verb agrees with the object.

klās 'xatəm 'šɪβey dey.	The lesson has become finished. (*m.s.*)	کلاس ختم شوے دے.
ka'pṛe me za'ṛe 'šɪβe di.	My clothes have become old. (*f.pl.*)	کپړې مې زړې شوې دی.
lur me xə 'šɪβe da.	My daughter has become well. (*f.s.*)	لُور مې ښهٔ شوې ده.
'wrije pa'xe 'šɪβi di?	Has the rice become cooked? (*f.pl.*)	وريژې پخې شوی دی؟
stā kār 'xatəm 'šɪβey dey?	Has your work been completed? (*m.s.*)	ستا کار ختم شوے دے؟
na, nə-dey 'xatəm 'šɪβey.	No, it hasn't been completed.	نه، نهٔ دے ختم شوے.
jā'me win'zəley 'šɪβe di?	Have the clothes been washed?	جامې وينځلے شوې دی؟
na, tər'osa 'pore nə-di win'zəley 'šɪβe.	No, they haven't been washed yet.	نه،تر اوسه پورې نهٔ دی وينځلے شوې.
jɪ'nəy zax'mi 'šɪβe da.	The girl has been hurt.	جينۍ زخمی شوې ده.
tə či'čəley 'šɪβey ye?	Have you been stung? (*m.*)	تهٔ چيچلے شوے يې؟
na, nə-yɪm či'čəley 'šɪβey.	No, I haven't been stung. (*m.*)	نه، نهٔ يم چيچلے شوے.

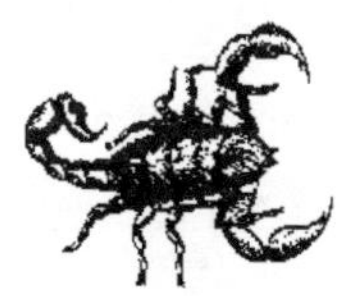

Transitive verbs in the present perfect

Like all transitive verbs in the past tense, agreement must be shown between the object and the verb. Both the past participle and the present endings are inflected.

mā ki'tāb a'xɪstey dey.	I have bought a book. (*m.s.*)	ما کتاب اخستے دے.
mā kita'buna a'xɪsti di.	I have bought books. (*m.pl.*)	ما کتابونه اخستی دی.

mā kā'pi a'xıste da.	I have bought a notebook. (*f.s.*)	ما کاپی اخستې ده.
mā kā'pyāne a'xıste di.	I have bought notebooks. (*f.pl.*)	ما کاپیانې اخستې دی.
tā dey mwaf 'kəṛey dey?	Have you forgiven him?	تا دے معاف کړے دے؟
tā hay'wi mwaf kəṛi di?	Have you forgiven them? (*m.pl.*)	تا هغوی معاف کړی دی؟
tā ha'ya mwaf kəṛe da?	Have you forgiven her? (*f.s.*)	تا هغه معاف کړې ده؟
tā hay'wi mwaf kəṛi di?	Have you forgiven them? (*f.pl.*)	تا هغوی معاف کړی دی؟
ha'ye xat wa'yəley dey.	She has read the letter. (*m.s.*)	هغې خط وئیلے دے.
ha'ye xa'tuna wa'yəli di.	She has read the letters. (*m.pl.*)	هغې خطُونه وئیلی دی.
ha'yə qi'sa wa'yəle da.	He has read the story. (*f.s.*)	هغۀ قیصه وئیلې ده.
ha'yə qi'se wa'yəli di.	He has read the stories. (*f.pl.*)	هغۀ قیصې وئیلی دی.
mung spey nə-dey wiš'təley.	We haven't hit the dog. (*m.s.*)	مُونږ سپے نۀ دے ویشتلے.
mā spi nə-di wiš'təli.	I haven't hit the dogs. (*m.pl.*)	ما سپی نۀ دی ویشتلی.
ha'yə ǰı'nəy nə-da wa'həle.	He hasn't hit the girl. (*f.s.*)	هغۀ جینۍ نۀ ده وهلې.
ha'yə ǰına'kəy nə-di wa'həle.	He hasn't hit the girls. (*f.pl.*)	هغۀ جینکۍ نۀ دی وهلې.
tā zə li'dəle yım.	You have seen me. (*m.s.*)	تا زۀ لیدلې یم.
tā mung li'dəli yu.	You have seen us. (*m.pl.*)	تا مُونږ لیدلی یو.
mā tə li'dəley ye.	I have seen you. (*f.s.*)	ما تۀ لیدلے یې.
mā 'tāso li'dəli yəy.	I have seen you. (*f.pl.*)	ما تاسو لیدلی یئ.
stā 'guta 'wrəka 'šıβe da?	Has your ring become lost? (*f.s.*)	ستا گوته ورکه شوې ده؟
tā 'guta 'monte da?	Have you found the ring? (*f.s.*)	تا گوته موندې ده؟
tsə de li'kəli di?	What have you written? (*m.s.*)	څۀ دې لیکلی دی.
yo maz'mun me də sṭuḍan'ṭāno də'pāra li'kəley dey.	I have written one article for the students. (*m.s.*)	یو مضمُون مې د سټوډنټانو د پاره لیکلے دے.
hay'wi ḍo'ḍəy xo'ṛəle da?	Have they eaten the food? (*f.s.*)	هغوی ډوډۍ خوړلې ده؟
āw, hay'wi xo'ṛəle da.	Yes, they have eaten it.	آو، هغوی خوړلې ده.

tā ha'ɣa 'maxke zān sa'ra pexā'wər ta bo'təle da?	Have you taken her with you to Peshawar before? (*f.s.*)	تا هغه مخکښې ځان سره پېښور ته بوتلې ده؟
na, ha'ɣa me zān sa'ra nə-da bo'təle.	No, I haven't taken her with me.	نه، هغه مې ځان سره نهٔ ده بوتلې.
'tāso os os 'xpəla mal'gəre li'dəle da?	Have you seen your friend recently? (*f.s.*)	تاسو اوس اوس خپله ملګرې ليدلې ده؟
na, mā nə-da li'dəle.	No, I haven't seen her.	نه، ما نهٔ ده ليدلې.
tā mo'ṭər rāwəs'tey dey?	Have you brought the car? (*m.s.*)	تا موټر راوستے دے؟
āw, mā rāwəs'tey dey.	Yes, I have brought it.	آو، ما راوستے دے.
ha'ɣə kaɣa'zuna rā'wəṛi di?	Has he brought the papers? (*m.pl.*)	هغهٔ کاغذونه راوړی دی؟
na, nə-ye di rā'wəṛi.	No, he hasn't brought them.	نه، نهٔ يې دی راوړی.
ǰe'hāz 'maxke na 'təley dey?	Has the plane left already? (*m.s.*)	جهاز مخکښې نه تلے دے؟
āw, nən də 'maxke na 'təley dey.	Yes, it has already gone today.	آو، نن د مخکښې نه تلے دے.
tā xab'runa āwre'dəli di?	Have you listened to the news? (*m.pl.*)	تا خبرُونه اورېدلی دی؟
āw, mā də rus xab'runa āwre'dəli di.	Yes, I have listened to the Russian news.	آو، ما د رُوس خبرُونه اورېدلی دی.
mā nən ḍer xān'dəli di.	I have laughed a lot today. (*m.pl.*)	ما نن ډېر خاندلی دی.
tā ǰa'ṛəli di?	Have you been crying?	تا ژړلی دی؟
tā zə 'wəle 'oṭaka'wələm?	Why have you hit me?	تا زهٔ ولې وټکولم؟

Compound transitive verbs in the present perfect

The verb *ka'wəl* (کول) 'to do' has a past participle verb stem *kəṛ-* (-کړ), as in the following examples:

ha'ɣə 'dəlta ḍer kār 'kəṛey dey.	He has done a lot of work here. (*m.s.*)	هغهٔ دلته ډېر کار کړے دے.
tā zə'mā də'pāra yo'so ka'runa kəṛi di.	You have done a few jobs for me. (*m.pl.*)	تا زما د پاره يوڅو کارُونه کړی دی.

mā ˈmaxke də hayˈwi maˈdəd nə-dey ˈkəṛey.	I haven't given them help before. (*m.s.*)	ما مخکښې د هغوی مدد نهٔ دے کړے.
haˈɣə zəˈmā ḍer maˈdəd ˈkəṛey dey.	He has given me a lot of help. (*m.s.*)	هغهٔ زما ډېر مدد کړے دے.
tarˈkāṇ mā dəˈpāra yo mez ǰoṛ ˈkəṛey dey.	The carpenter has made a table for me. (*m.s.*)	ترکاڼ ما د پاره يو مېز جوړ کړے دے.
tā zəˈmā ˈgāḍey tər ˈosa ˈpore nə-dey səm ˈkəṛey?	Haven't you fixed my car yet? (*m.s.*)	تا زما ګاډے تر اوسه پورې نهٔ دے سم کړے؟
haˈɣə kıṛˈkəy ˈsəma ˈkəṛe da?	Has he repaired the window? (*f.s.*)	هغهٔ کړکۍ سمه کړې ده؟
hayˈwi ˈḍere xe kurˈsəy ˈǰoṛe ˈkəṛi di.	They have made very good chairs. (*f.pl.*)	هغوی ډېرې ښې کُرسۍ جوړې کړی دی.
mā nən yo kaˈbāb pox ˈkəṛey dey.	I cooked a kabab today. (*m.s.*)	ما نن يو کباب پوخ کړے دے.
tā ˈɣwaxa paˈxa ˈkəṛe da?	Have you cooked the meat? (*f.s.*)	تا غوښه پخه کړې ده؟
haˈye ˈḍere xaˈrābe ˈwriǰe paˈxe kəṛi di.	She has cooked very bad rice. (*f.pl.*)	هغې ډېرې خرابې وريژې پخې کړی دی.

Answering questions in the present perfect

When you are asked a question make a habit of answering in the same tense. Listen carefully to the question, the speaker will have solved any difficulties of agreement for you. Use that knowledge to answer flawlessly.

☝ Answer the following questions postively and negatively, staying in the same tense. Use this pattern:

Question:	haˈɣə xpəl qaˈləm her ˈkəṛey dey?	هغهٔ خپل قلم هېر کړے دے؟ Has he forgotten his pen?
Positive reply:	āw, her ˈkəṛey ye dey.	آو، هېر کړے يې دے. Yes, he has forgotten it.
Negative reply:	na, haˈɣa nə-dey her ˈkəṛey.	نه، هغهٔ نهٔ دے هېر کړے. No, he hasn't forgotten it.

stā xpəl sarˈwi yād ˈšɪβi di?

ستا خپل څاروی یاد شوی دی؟

Have you remembered your livestock? (*m.pl.*)

Positive: ______________________

Negative: ______________________

tā xpəl kiˈtāb wrək ˈkəṛey dey?

تا خپل کتاب ورک کړے دے؟

Have you lost your book? (*m.s.*)

Positive: ______________________

Negative: ______________________

tā hayˈwi saˈra xaˈbare kəṛi di?

تا هغوی سره خبرې کړی دی؟

Have you spoken with them? (*f.pl.*)

Positive: ______________________

Negative: ______________________

tā bijˈli ləgaˈwəle da?

تا بجلی لګولې ده؟

Have you turned on the electricity? (*f.s.*)

Positive: ______________________

Negative: ______________________

tə zmung də ˈnewi sɪkreˈṭri saˈra meˈlaw šɪβey ye?

تهٔ زمونږ د نوی سکرټری سره مِلاو شوے يې؟

Have you met our new secretary? (*m.s.*)

Positive: ______________________

Negative: ______________________

tā tsə fesaˈla ˈkəṛe da?

تا څهٔ فيصله کړې ده؟

What decision have you made? (*f.s.*)

Positive: ______________________

Negative: ______________________

tā nən ra'bāb 'wəle nə dey wa'həley? — تا نن رباب ولې نۀ دے وهلے؟

Why haven't you played *rabab* today? (*m.s.*)

Positive: ______________________________

Negative: ______________________________

Self: *pa 'xpəl* — په خپل

mašu'mān pa 'xpəla ba'zār ta tley ši?	Can the children go to the bazaar by themselves?	ماشُومان په خپله بازار ته تلے شی؟
āw, tley ši 'zəka če zwa'nān di.	Yes, they can go by themselves, they are teenagers.	آو، تلے شی ځکه چې ځوانان دی.
tə pa 'xpəla čərg paxa'wəley še?	Can you cook chicken by yourself?	تۀ په خپله چرګ پخولې شې؟
āw, zə pa 'xpəla čərg paxa'wəley šəm.	Yes, I can cook it by myself.	آو، زۀ په خپله چرګ پخولے شم.
tə ba hay'wi sa'ra xa'bare kawe?	Will you speak with them?	تۀ به هغوی سره خبرې کوې؟
zə ba pa 'xpəla də hay'wi sa'ra xa'bare kawəm.	I will speak with them myself.	زۀ به په خپله د هغوی سره خبرې کوم.
ṭol pa 'xpəla mə-xora!	Don't eat it all yourself!	ټول په خپله مۀ خوره!
ga'ṛəy pa 'xpəla mā ta šwa.	The clock broke by itself.	ګړی په خپله ما ته شوه.
tə ɣari'bāno ta pe'se pa 'xpəla warka'we?	Do you give money to the poor yourself?	تۀ غریبانو ته پیسې په خپله ورکوې؟
āw, zə pa 'xpəla pe'se warka'wəm.	Yes, I give them money myself.	آو، زۀ په خپله پیسې ورکوم.
zə pa 'xpəla xa'bare ka'wəm.	I'll talk myself.	زۀ په خپله خبرې کوم.

Using *xpəl* and *pa 'xpəl* in the same sentence — خپل، په خپل

ha'ɣə xpəla kam'ra pa 'xpəla sa'fā kṛa?	Did he clean his own room by himself?	هغهٔ خپله کمره په خپله صفا کړه؟
na, də ha'ɣə mor sa'fā kṛa.	No, his mother cleaned it.	نه، د هغهٔ مور صفا کړه.
xpəl kār pa 'xpəla nə'še ka'wəley?	Can't you do your own work by yourself?	خپل کار په خپله نهٔ شې کولے؟
āw, zə xpəl kār pa 'xpəla ka'wəley šəm.	Yes, I can do my own work by myself.	آو، زهٔ خپل کار په خپله کولے شم.

Medical talk

Questions:

tsə tək'lif dey?	What is the problem?	څهٔ تکلیف دے؟
tə ṭu'xege?	Are you coughing?	تهٔ ټوخیږې؟
'tāso 'ulṭəy ka'wəy?	Are you vomiting?	تاسو اُلټۍ کوئ؟
čin'ǰi šta?	Do you have worms?	چینجی شته؟
mɪt'yāze 'swazi?	Is your urine burning?	متیازې سوزی؟
ɣwəg bā'igi?	Is the ear draining?	غوږ بهیږی؟
pa 'xeṭa mā'šum šta?	Are you pregnant?	په خېټه ماشُوم شته؟
stā 'xeṭa xa'rāba da, das'tuna šta?	Is your stomach upset, do you have diarrhoea?	ستا خېټه خرابه ده، دستُونه شته؟

Answers:

'spine gu'ləy mā xo'ṛəli di, xo xə 'šɪβey nə-yɪm.	I took some white tablets, but I have not got better.	سپینې ګولۍ ما خوړلی دی، خو ښهٔ شوې نهٔ یم.
dre, tsa'lor 'wrəzo-na zə na'ǰoṛa yɪm.	I've been ill for three or four days.	درې څلور ورځو نه زهٔ ناجوړه یم.
ḍo'ḍəy me zṛə ta 'nə kigi.	I don't feel like eating food.	ډوډۍ مې زړهٔ ته نهٔ کیږی.

Memorising moment

Parts of the body

Use the drawings to drill the names of these parts of the body:

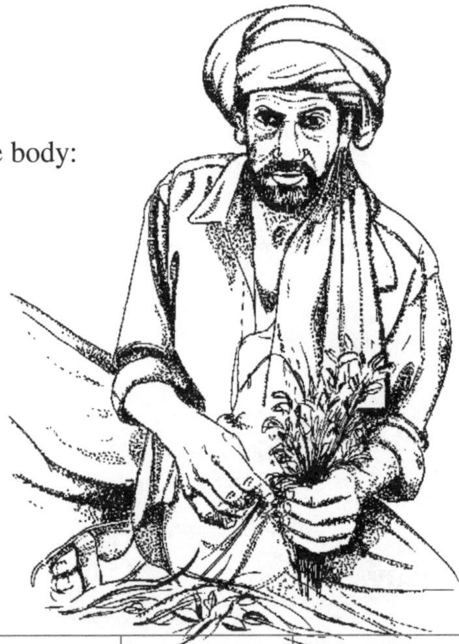

u'ga	اوږه	shoulder
ta'ley	تلے	palm
tsan'gəl	څنګل	elbow
xpa	خپه	foot
'xeṭa	خېټه	stomach
zan'gun	زنګون	knee
sər	سر	head
si'na	سينه	chest
šā	شا	upper back
'guta	ګوته	finger
gi'ṭəy	ګيټئ	ankle
lās	لاس	hand
'leča	لېچه	arm

'məṭa	مټه	upper arm
maṛ'wand	مړُوند	wrist
mlā	ملا	back
me'da	مېده	stomach
na'rəy mlā	نرئى ملا	lower back
nuk	نُوک	fingernail

Face

'wruza	ورُوځه	eyebrow
'ɣwəg	غوږ	ear
'ǰıba	ژبه	tongue
'zına	زنه	chin
səṭ	څټ	back of neck
wex'tə	وېښتهٔ	hair
'poza	پوزهٔ	nose
'šunḍe	شُونډې	lips
ɣā'xuna	غاښُونه	teeth

ma'rəy	مرى	throat (inside)
'ɣāṛa	غاړه	throat (outside, front of neck)

mataˈluna

چې بل ته کُوهے کنی، هغه پخپله پکښې پرېوزی.

če bəl ta kuˈey kəni, haˈɣa paxˈpəla paˈke preˈuzi.

The one who digs a well for another, will himself fall in it.

دَ خپلو نه پردی ښهٔ وی. دَ پردو نه اپریدی ښهٔ وی.

də xpəlo na praˈdi xə wi. də praˈdo na āpridi xə wi.

Outsiders are better than relatives, and Afridis are better than outsiders.

دَ تورے پرهر به روغ شی خو دَ ژبے پرهر نهٔ روغیږی.

də ˈturey parhar ba roɣ ši xo də ˈǰɪbey parhar nə roˈɣigi.

The wound of the sword can be healed, but the tongue's wound won't be healed.

چې مرګ وینی، تبې ته رضا شی.

če mərg ˈwini, ˈtəbe ta raˈzā ši

If he sees death, he will be satisfied with a fever.

Exercises for Lesson Twenty-Four

1. Substitution drill:

   Have your helper point to various parts of the body, and substitute the names into the sentence below:

   sər me xuˈgigi. — My head hurts. — سر مې خوږیږی.

   Then have your helper make up similar drills.

2. Answer the following questions giving both positive and negative short answers.

   ˈtāso čeȓta āfɣānɪˈstān ta ˈtəli yəy? — تاسو چرته افغانستان ته تلی یئ؟

wā'də de 'kəṛey dey?

وادهٔ دې کړے دے؟

nən mo kəm maz'mun wa'yəley dey?

نن مو کُوم مضمُون وئيلے دے؟

'tāso nən xpəle korwa'lā sa'ra pa pārk ke garze'dəli yəy?

تاسو نن خپلې کور والا سره په پارک کښې گرځېدلی يئ؟

tā tər 'osa 'pore xpəl mal'gərey lidəley nə-dey?

تا تر اوسه پورې خپل ملگرے ليدلے نهٔ دے؟

☝ Have your helper make up lots more.

Vocabulary for Lesson Twenty-Four

ul'ṭəy ka'wəl	اُلټې کول		comp.v.t.	to vomit
bā'edəl	بهېدل		v.i.	to flow, to run
par'hez ka'wəl	پرهېز کول		comp.v.t.	to avoid, to abstain, to diet
pa 'xpəl	په خپل		pro.	-self, -selves; automatic
'təba	تبه	f.s.	n.	fever
triw / trā'wə	تریو / تراوۀ	m.	adj.	sour
tra'wa / tra'we	تروه / تروې	f.		
təxte'dəl	تښتېدل		v.i.	to run away, to flee, to escape
ta'ley	تلے	m.	n.	palm
ṭuxe'dəl	ټوخېدل		v.i.	to cough
ǰe'hāz	جهاز	m.	n.	aeroplane [airplane]
čin'ǰi	چینجی	f.	n.	worm
səṭ	څټ	m.	n.	back of neck
tsan'gəl	څنګل	m.	n.	elbow
xoge'dəl	خوږېدل		v.i.	to hurt
das'tuna	دستُونه	f.	n.	diarrhoea
ra'zā ke'dəl	رضا کېدل		comp.v.i.	to become reconciled
rus	رُوس	m.	n.	Russia
zo'kām	زُکام	m.	n.	cold
zan'gun	زنګُون	m.	n.	knee
zına / zıne	زنه / زنې	f.	n.	chin
sıkre'ṭri	سکرټری		n.	secretary
šā	شا	f.	n.	upper back
'šunḍe	شُونډې	f.pl.	n.	lips
'ɣāṛa	غاړه	f.	n.	neck, throat; collar
'flāying koč	فلائینګ کوچ		n.	'flying coach', minivan

fesa'la	فېصله	*f.*	*n.*	decision
'guta / 'gute	ګوته / ګوتې	*f.*	*n.*	finger; toe; ring
gi'ṭəy	ګيټۍ	*f.*	*n.*	ankle
'leča	لېچه	*f.*	*n.*	arm, wrist
mıt'yāze [mi'čāze]	متيازې [ميچازې]	*f.pl.*	*n.*	urine
'maṭa	مټه	*f.*	*n.*	upper arm
ma'rəy	مرۍ	*f.*	*n.*	throat
mwaf ka'wəl	معاف کول		*comp.v.t.*	to forgive
mlā	ملا	*f.*	*n.*	lower back
mon'dəl, māluma'wəl	مُوندل، معلُومول		*v.t.*	to find out, to know, to understand, to look for, to discover, to acquire, to get
me'da	مېده	*f.*	*n.*	stomach
meā'di 'təba	ميعادي تبه	*f.*	*n.*	typhoid
na'rəy mlā	نرئۍ ملا	*f.*	*n.*	lower back
nuk / nu'kuna	نُوک / نُوکنو	*m.*	*n.*	fingernail
wrəke'dəl	ورکېدل		*v.i.*	to become lost
wixe'dəl	ويښېدل		*v.i.*	to awaken, to wake up
hera'wəl	هېرول		*v.t.*	to forget
yere'dəl	يرېدل		*v.i.*	to be afraid, to be frightened, to fear

pinzə-wiš'təm sa'bəq پینځۀ ویشتم سبق

Lesson Twenty-Five

Dialogue twenty-five: Pukhto

L:	də pəx'tun 'ṭıki mət'ləb tsə dey? What is the meaning of the word Pukhtun?	د پښتُون ټکی مطلب څۀ دے؟
H:	pe də pət də'pāra, xin də xe'gəre də'pāra, te də torzan'tob də'pāra, wow də wa'fā də'pāra āw nun də nangyā'li də'pāra. p is for dignity, x for help, t for bravery, w for faithful and n for self-sacrifice.	پ د پت د پاره، ښ د ښیگړې د پاره، ت د تورزنتوب د پاره، و د وفا د پاره او ن د ننگیالی د پاره.
L:	xa, no pa sa'hi pəx'tun ke ba dā si'fət wi. Ah, so a good Pukhtun will have these characteristics.	ښه، نو په صحیح پښتُون کښې به دا صِفت وی.
H:	pa'kār dey če ye pa'ke. It is necessary that they have them.	پکار دے چې یې په کښې.
L:	də pəx'tun pa nə'zər ke ɣe'rat tsə dey? What do Pukhtuns understand by 'ghairat'?	د پښتُون په نظر کښې غیرت څۀ دے؟
H:	də pəx'tun pa nə'zər ke, ɣe'rət də har yo najā'eza kār na moxalı'fət dey. From the Pukhtun's point of view, 'ghairat' is opposed to everything that is unfair.	د پښتُون په نظر کښې، غیرت د هر یو ناجائزه کار نه مُخالفت دے.
L:	najā'ez kār tsə ta wayi? What is the meaning of unfair things?	ناجائزه کار څۀ ته وائی؟
H:	najā'ez har 'haɣa kār-ta wa'yəley ši, kəm če də māša're āw də ma'zəb də u'sulo na xı'lāf wi. Unfair things are everything which opposes the rulers of society and religion.	ناجائزه هر هغه کار ته وئیلے شی کُوم چې د معاشرې او د مذهب د اصولو نه خِلاف وی.

Life story

L:	tə zə'mā 'ḍera xə mal'gəre ye. You are a very good friend of mine.	ته زما ډېره ښۀ ملگرې یې.

L: zə nən ˈɣwāṛəm če stā də zındaˈgəy qiˈsā ˈwāwrəm āw dā ba zəˈmā pa pəxˈto ke maˈdəd oki. dā ˈsıraf zəˈmā də āwreˈdo dəˈpāra da. Today I want to hear the story of your life and this will help my Pukhto. It is just for my listening.	زۀ نن غواړم چې ستا د زندګۍ قيصه واؤرم او دا به زما په پښتو کښې مدد وکی. دا صرف زما د اورېدو د پاره ده.
H: ṭik da. OK, fine.	ټيک ده.
L: zə ba swāˈluna kaˈwəm āw ˈtāso ba ǰawāˈbuna rākaˈwəy. I will ask questions and you will give the answers.	زۀ به سوالُونه کوم او تاسو به جوابُونه راکوئ.

Some questions

L: stā pa ǰwənd ke āwalaˈne wāqiˈa tsə da? What is the first event you remember in your life?	ستا په ژوند کښې اولنې واقعه څۀ ده؟
haˈɣa waxt tə də tso ˈkālo we? How old were you then?	هغه وخت تۀ د څو کالُو وې؟
stā pa waṛukˈwāli ke tsə xošāˈləy we? What happiness did you have in childhood?	ستا په وړوکوالی کښې څۀ خوشحالئ وې؟
tā ta pa waṛukˈwāli ke tsə təkˈlif wo? What trouble did you have as a child?	تا ته په وړوکوالی کښې څۀ تکليف وو؟
tā ˈkəla wāˈdə ˈokṛo? When did you get married?	تا کله وادۀ وکړو؟
stā də wāˈdə na pas žwənd ˈtsənga dey? What is life after your marriage like?	ستا د وادۀ نه پس ژوند څنګه دے؟

L: tā ta os tsə muškɪ'lāt šta? Do you have any difficulties now?	تا ته اوس څۀ مُشکلات شته؟
stā də mustaq'bɪl də'pāra tsə xwāhe'šāt di? What are your future wishes?	ستا د مُستقبل د پاره څۀ خواهشات دی؟

Pronunciation drill

Practice this tongue twister:

چې د تورو وريځو نه واؤره وربده نو ورور مې ورو ورو د ورنداري خواله وراغے.

če də 'toro wa'rezo na 'wawra ware'da no 'wror me wro wro də wran'dāre xwā la 'waraɣey.

When it was snowing from the black clouds then my brother slowly went to my sister-in-law's.

'had done': The past perfect tense

Pukhto, like many Indo-European languages, has a past perfect tense, which is used to show which of two past events happened first. For example, "she had arrived when ...". The tense is formed by adding past endings to a past participle.

Intransitive verbs in the past perfect

rase'dəl رسېدل (to arrive) is a good example of how most regular intransitive verbs are conjugated in the past perfect:

Person	Singular		Plural	
1st m.	rase'dəley wəm I had arrived	رسېدلے وم	rase'dəli wu we had arrived	رسېدلی وُو
1st f.	rase'dəle wəm I had arrived	رسېدلې وم	rase'dəli wu we had arrived	رسېدلی وُو
2nd m.	rase'dəley we you had arrived	رسېدلے وې	rase'dəli wəy you had arrived	رسېدلی وئ
2nd f.	rase'dəle we you had arrived	رسېدلې وې	rase'dəle wəy you had arrived	رسېدلې وئ
3rd m.	rase'dəley wo he had arrived	رسېدلے وو	rase'dəli wu they had arrived	رسېدلی وُو
3rd f.	rase'dəle wa she had arrived	رسېدلې وه	rase'dəle we they had arrived	رسېدلې وې

Example sentences using intransitive verbs in the past perfect tense:

pa'run tə čerta 'təley we?	Where had you gone yesterday? (*m.*)	پرُون تهٔ چرته تلے وې؟
zə xār ta 'təley wəm.	I had gone to the city.	زهٔ ښار ته تلے وم.
ha'ɣa də špe na 'maxke xār ta rase'dəle wa?	Had she reached the city before night?	هغه د شپې نه مخکښې ښار ته رسېدلې وه؟
na, ha'ɣa nə-wa rase'dəle.	No, she had not arrived.	نه، هغه نهٔ وه رسېدلې.
yo tso 'wrəze 'maxke 'tāso 'halta 'təli wəy?	Had you gone there a few days ago?	يوڅو ورځې مخکښې تاسو هلته تلی وئ؟
āw, mung 'təli wu.	Yes, we had gone.	آو، مُونږ تلی وُو.
dāud čā sa'ra rāɣəley wo?	Who had David come with?	داؤد چا سره راغلے وو؟
ha'ɣa də 'xpəle xor sa'ra rāɣəley wo.	He had come with his sister.	هغه د خپلې خور سره راغلے وو.
'maxke tə də foǰ na təxte'dəley we?	Had you run away from the army before?	مخکښې ته د فوج نه تښتېدلے وې؟
āw, ter kāl həm.	Yes, last year also.	آو، تېر کال هم.
hay'wi tā sa'ra xa'bare 'kəṛe we?	Had they talked with you?	هغوی تا سره خبرې کړې وې؟
na, hay'wi mā sa'ra nə-we 'kəṛe.	No, they hadn't talked with me.	نه، هغوی ما سره نهٔ وې کړې.
če tə swāt ta 'təley we, tā 'halta 'tsumra waxt ter 'kəṛey wo?	When you (*m.*) had gone to Swat, how long did you stay there?	چې تهٔ سوات ته تلے وې تا هلته څومره وخت تېر کړے وو؟
mā 'halta yo kāl ter 'kəṛey wo.	I stayed there for one year.	ما هلته يو کال تېر کړے وو.
ɣəl zmung kor ta rā'ɣəley wo.	The thief had come to our house.	غل زمُونږ کور ته راغلے وو.
'tāso pa'xwā pa mingo'ra ke ose'dəli wəy?	Had you lived in Mingora long ago?	تاسو پخوا په مينگوره کښې اوسېدلی وئ؟
na, mung 'halta nə-wu ose'dəli.	No, we had not lived there.	نه، مُونږ هلته نهٔ وُو اوسېدلی.

Compound intransitive verbs in the past perfect

In the past perfect the past participle of the verb agrees with the number and gender of the subject:

Person	Masculine		Feminine	
1st s.	ˈstəṛey ˈšɪβey wəm	سترېےشوے وم	ˈstəṛe ˈšɪβe wəm	سترې شوې وم
1st pl.	ˈstəṛi ˈšɪβi wu	سترى شوى وُو	ˈstəṛe ˈšɪβe wu	سترې شوې وُو
2nd s.	ˈstəṛey ˈšɪβey we	سترېےشوے وې	ˈstəṛe ˈšɪβe we	سترې شوې وې
2nd pl.	ˈstəṛi ˈšɪβi wəy	سترى شوى وئ	ˈstəṛe ˈšɪβe wəy	سترې شوې وئ
3rd s.	ˈstəṛey ˈšɪβey wo	سترېےشوے وو	ˈstəṛe ˈšɪβe wa	سترې شوې وه
3rd pl.	ˈstəṛi ˈšɪβi wu	سترى شوى وُو	ˈstəṛe ˈšɪβe we	سترې شوې وې

moˈṭər paˈxwā xaˈrāb ˈšɪβey wo?	Had the car gone bad before? (*m.s.*)	موټر پخوا خراب شوے وو؟
āw, haˈɣa ter kāl həm xaˈrāb ˈšɪβey wo.	Yes, it had also gone bad last year.	آو، هغه تېر کال هم خراب شوے وو.
tə hayˈwi ta pa ˈqəhar ˈšɪβey we?	Had you become angry with them?	ته هغوى ته په قهر شوے وې؟
na, mung hayˈwi ta nə-wu pa ˈqəhar ˈšɪβi.	No, we had not been angry with them.	نه، مُونږ هغوى ته نۀ وُو په قهر شوى.
ˈtāso ˈmaxke ˈwādə ˈšɪβe wəy?	Had you been married before?	تاسو مخکښې وادۀ شوې وئ؟
āw, zə ˈwādə ˈšɪβe wəm xo xāˈwənd me məṛ šo.	Yes, I had been married but my husband died.	آو، زۀ وادۀ شوې وم خو خاوند مې مړ شو.

Passive sentences in the past perfect

As in the present perfect, the passive construction has verb agreement with the object.

ˈhaɣa waxt kār ˈxatəm ˈšɪβey wo?	Had the job been completed at that time? (*m.s.*)	هغه وخت کار ختم شوے وو؟
āw, ˈxatəm ˈšɪβey wo.	Yes, it had been completed.	آو، ختم شوے وو.
ˈstāso parˈde šleˈdəle we?	Had your curtains become torn? (*f.pl.*)	ستاسو پردې شلېدلې وې؟
stā zwe ˈkəla naˈǰoṛa ˈšɪβey wo?	When had your son become sick? (*m.s.*)	ستا زوئ کله ناجوړه شوے وو؟

ha'ɣa ter kāl na'ǰoṛa 'šɪβey wo.	He had become sick last year.	هغه تېر کال ناجوړه شوے وو.
kā'pi 'ḍera 'maxke 'wrəka 'šɪβe wa?	Had the notebook been lost long before? (*f.s.*)	کاپی ډېره مخکښې ورکه شوې وه؟
zi'ā wiš'təley 'šɪβey wo?	Had Zia been shot? (*m.s.*)	ضیاء ویشتلے شوے وو؟
āw, wiš'təley 'šɪβey wo, xo qā'tɪl pa 'haɣa sāt 'bānde oni'wəley šo.	Yes, he had been shot, but the assassin was caught at the same time. (*m.s.*)	آو، ویشتلے شوے وو، خو قاتِل په هغه سات باندې ونیولے شو.
ṭol lar'gi māt 'šɪβi wu.	All the wood had been cut. (*m.pl.*)	ټول لرګی مات شوی وُو.
tə pa'xwā ni'wəley 'šɪβey we?	Had you been caught before? (*m.s.*)	تهٔ پخوا نیولے شوے وې؟
na, zə nə-wəm ni'wəley 'šɪβey.	No, I hadn't been caught.	نه، زهٔ نهٔ وم نیولے شوے.

Transitive verbs in the past perfect

As with other past tenses, agreement is with the object:

ki'tāb me li'kəley wo.	I had written a book. (*m.s.*)	کتاب مې لیکلے وو.
kita'buna me li'kəli wu.	I had written books. (*m.pl.*)	کتابونه مې لیکلی وُو.
'yəwa 'late'fā me li'kəle wa.	I had written a joke. (*f.s.*)	یوه لطیفه مې لیکلې وه.
late'fe me li'kəle we.	I had written jokes. (*f.pl.*)	لطیفې مې لیکلې وې.
xor'wā ye 'skəle nə-wa.	He hadn't drunk the soup. (*f.s.*)	ښوروا یې څښلې نهٔ وه.
pəy me 'skəli nə-wu.	I hadn't drunk the milk. (*f.pl.*)	پئ مې څښلی نهٔ وُو.

Substitution drill

Have your helper call out the names of different objects and subjects for you to substitute in the sentence below. You can use *Picture It in Dari or Pashto* or a magazine to help you.

ha'ɣə ḍo'ḍəy xo'ṛəle wa.	He had eaten food.	هغهٔ ډوډۍ خوړلې وه.

Questions and answers in the past perfect

haɣ'wi 'wəle tər'osa 'pore kor nə wo a'xɪstey?	Why hadn't they bought a home until now?	هغوی ولې تر اوسه پورې کور نهٔ وو اخستے؟

hayˈwi saˈra peˈse nə we.	They had no money.	هغوی سره پېسې نه وې.
ˈtāso xpəle ǰāˈme ˈpāke winˈzəle we?	Had you washed your own clothes?	تاسو خپلې جامې پاکې وينځلې وې؟
na, doˈbi winˈzəle we.	No, the washerman had washed them.	نه، دوبی وينځلې وې.
tā ˈmaxke kaˈǰure xoˈṛəle we?	Had you eaten dates before?	تا مخکښې کجُورې خوړلې وې؟
tā zān saˈra kaˈǰure rāwˈṛəle we?	Had you brought dates with you?	تا ځان سره کجُورې راوړلې وې؟
na, mā saˈra zay nə wo.	No, I didn't have room.	نه، ما سره ځای نه وو.
hayˈwi zān saˈra ḍer saˈmān rāˈwəṛey wo?	Had they brought a lot of luggage with them?	هغوی ځان سره ډېر سامان راوړے وو؟
na, har yo saˈra dwa beˈguna wu.	No, they had only brought two bags each.	نه، هريو سره دوه بيګُونه وُو.
ˈtāso xpəḷ malˈgərey pa axıraˈnəy peˈra ˈkəla liˈdəley wo?	When is the last time you had seen your friend? (*m.s.*)	تاسو خپل ملګرے په آخرنۍ پېره کله ليدلے وو؟
haˈɣa mā dre ˈkāla ˈmaxke liˈdəley wo.	I had seen him three years ago.	هغه ما درې کاله مخکښې ليدلے وو.
xpəl baˈnen de pa ˈxpəla ǰoṛ ˈkəṛey wo?	Had you knitted your own sweater?	خپل بنين دې په خپله جوړ کړے وو؟
āw, ǰoṛ ˈkəṛey me wo.	Yes, I had.	آو، جوړ کړے مې وو.
haˈɣe zəˈmā baks xə taˈṛəley wo?	Had she wrapped my box well? (*m.s.*)	هغې زما بکس ښۀ تړلے وو؟
na, haˈɣe səm nə wo taˈṛəley.	No, she hadn't wrapped it well.	نه، هغې سم نۀ وو تړلے.
ˈtāso ˈmaxke də haˈɣe pa baˈra ke tsə āwreˈdəli wu?	What had you heard about her before?	تاسو مخکښې د هغې په باره کښې څۀ اورېدلی وُو ؟
āw, āwreˈdəli me wu, xo bāˈwər me pe nə rātˈlo.	Yes, I had heard about it, but I didn't believe it was true.	آو، اورېدلی مې وُو خو باور مې پې نۀ راتلو.

hayˈwi paˈxwā tə peǰanˈdəley we?	Had they known you before? (*m.s.*)	هغوی پخوا تهٔ پېژندلے وې؟
na, hayˈwi zə nə wəm peǰanˈdəley.	No, they had not known me.	نه، هغوی زهٔ نهٔ وم پېژندلے.
ḍer waxt kigi če ˈdāse me nə wu xānˈdəli!	It has been a long time since I had laughed like this!	ډېر وخت کېږی چې داسې مې نهٔ وُو خاندلی!
ḍer mahˈyān de niˈwəli wu?	Had you caught many fish?	ډېر مهیان دې نیولی وُو؟
tā ter kāl raˈbāb waˈhəley wo?	Had you played *rabab* last year?	تا تېر کال رباب وهلے وو؟
na, mā saˈra waxt nə wo.	No, I didn't have time.	نه، ما سره وخت نهٔ وو.

NOTE:

Colloquial expressions like, *bāˈwər me pe nə rātˈlo* (باور مې پې نهٔ راتلو) should be practiced with your helper in different sentences. However, you will only get to really remember this expression if you then use it in real settings.

Compound transitive verbs in the past perfect

stā niˈkə də mərg na ˈmaxke kəm axıraˈne kār ˈkəṛey wo?	What was the last thing your grandfather had done before he died?	ستا نیکهٔ د مرګ نه مخکښې کُوم آخېرنے کار کړے وو؟
zəˈmā niˈkə xpəḷ ṭoˈpak saˈfā ˈkəṛey wo.	My grandfather had cleaned his gun.	زما نیکهٔ خپل ټوپک صفا کړے وو.
ˈtāso pa pexāˈwər ke tso ˈkāla ter kəṛi wu?	How many years had you spent in Peshawar?	تاسو په پېښور کښې څو کاله تېر کړی وُو ؟
mung yo kāl ˈhalta ter ˈkəṛey wo.	We had spent a year there.	مُونږ یو کال هلته تېر کړے وو.
haˈyə kıṛˈkəy ˈǰoṛa kəṛe wa?	Had he made the window? (*f.s.*)	هغهٔ کړکۍ جوړه کړې وه؟
na, haˈyə nə wa ˈǰoṛa kəṛe.	No, he had not made it.	نه، هغهٔ نهٔ وه جوړه کړې.
haˈyə tsə ˈqisəm kurˈsəy stā dəˈpāra ˈǰoṛe kəṛe we?	What type of chairs had he made for you? (*f.pl.*)	هغهٔ څهٔ قسم کُرسۍ ستا د پاره جوړې کړې وې؟

haˈɣə də larˈgi kurˈsəy ˈǰoṛe kəṛe we.	He had made wooden chairs.	هغهٔ د لرګی کُرسۍ جوړې کړې وې.
xpəl moˈṭər de paṛačiˈnār ke xars ˈkəṛey wo?	Had you sold your car in Parachinar?	خپل موټر دې پاړه چنار کښې خرڅ کړے وو؟
āw, mā xarts ˈkəṛey wo.	Yes, I had sold it.	آو، ما خرڅ کړے وو.
tā byā dā her ˈkəṛey wo?	Had you forgotten it again?	تا بیا دا هېر کړے وو؟
na, mā nə wo her ˈkəṛey.	No, I hadn't forgotten it.	نه، ما نهٔ وو هېر کړے.
haˈɣə dā yād ˈkəṛey wo?	Had he remembered it?	هغهٔ دا یاد کړے وو؟
āw, haˈɣə yād ˈkəṛey wo.	Yes, he had remembered.	آو، هغهٔ یاد کړے وو.
tā də haˈɣe maˈdəd ˈkəṛey wo?	Had you given her help? (*m.s.*)	تا د هغې مدد کړے وو؟
na, mā də haˈɣe maˈdəd nə wo ˈkəṛey.	No, I hadn't given her help.	نه، ما د هغې مدد نهٔ وو کړے.

Are you busy? *masˈruf, axˈta* and *ləgˈyā* مصرُوف، اخته، لګیا

stā xāˈwənd sāˈbəta špa pa tsə masˈruf wo?	What was your husband busy doing all night long?	ستا خاوند ثابته شپه په څهٔ مصرُوف وو؟
haˈɣa ˈṭola špa pa ǰawāˈrəy ˈbānde masˈruf wo.	He was busy gambling all night long.	هغه ټوله شپه په جوارئ باندې مصرُوف وو.
tə špa, wrəz pa čay ˈskəlo axˈta ye!	You are busy drinking tea night and day!	تهٔ شپه ورځ په چائې څښلو اخته یې!
zə pa xpəl ˈnewey kār ke masˈruf ˈšɪβey yɪm.	I have become busy with my new job.	زهٔ په خپل نوے کار کښې مصرُوف شوے یم.
də ɣarˈme na pa kiˈtāb waˈyəlo ləgˈyā ˈšɪβey ye!	You have been busy reading the book since noon!	د غرمې نه په کتاب وئیلو لګیا شوے یې!
ˈhaɣa ˈxəze pa tsə kār ke masˈrufe di?	What have those women been busy with?	هغه ښځې په څهٔ کار کښې مصرُوفې دی؟

haɣ'wi pa gul'kārəy də sa'har na ləg'yā di.	They have been busy embroidering since morning.	هغوی په ګُلکارئ د سحر نه لګیا دی.

NOTES:

1. All three adjectives are interchangeable in most contexts.
2. Although *ax'ta* (اخته) and *ləg'yā* (لګیا) are adjectives, they do not change according to gender.
3. In addition to meaning 'busy', 'engaged' and 'occupied', the words *ax'ta* (اخته) and *ləg'yā* (لګیا) can also refer to someone who has a bad habit, or is suffering from a disease. In that context they carry a negative meaning.

yār'ān de pa na'šo tamā'šo ləg'yā di.	Your friends are involved in bad things.	یاران دې په نشو تماشو لګیا دی.
ha'ɣa də 'ḍere mu'de na pa ranz ax'ta dey.	He has been sick for a long time.	هغه د ډېرې مودې نه په رنځ اخته دے.

4. *ax'ta* (اخته) is often used with a negative meaning in Pukhto idioms. The idiom below is used by an offended person about the one who offended them. It can be used by anyone, but it is most commonly said by women:

də zṛə pa ranz ax'ta še!	May you stay sad for ever! (*Lit.* May you suffer the sickness of the heart!)	د زړهٔ په رنځ اخته شې!

Memorising moment

Rahman Baba

ژوندے ځان په زمکه ښخ کړه لکه تخم
کهٔ لوئی غواړې د خاورو په مقام شه.

ǰwən'dey zān pa 'zməka xəx-kṛa 'ləka 'toxəm
kə luy 'ɣwāṛe, də 'xāwro pa ma'qām ša.

Plant yourself alive, like a seed in the ground
If you desire greatness, be in the place of dust.

mata'luna

اتفاق کښې برکت وی.

ɪtɪ'fāq ke bara'kət wi.

There is blessing in unity.

چرته ډب وی هلته ادب وی.

'čerta ḍəb wi 'halta a'dəb wi.

Where there is beating there is obedience.

د اُوښ په شا سپو وخوړم.

də ux pa šā, spo 'oxoṛəm.

I was bitten by dogs while sitting on the back of a camel.

Comprehension drill: Tense production

In this drill you will talk about an activity in different tenses.

☝ Your helper will give you an instruction and then you will say what you are about to do (future), what you are doing (present), what you did (simple past) and then add the other past tenses.

For example your helper might say:

qa'ləm pa ba'kəs ke 'keda!	Put the pen in the box!	قلم په بکس کښې کېده!

You respond with a series of sentences:

zə ba qa'ləm pa 'bakəs ke 'kedəm.	I will put the pen in the box.	زۀ به قلم په بکس کښې کېدم.
zə qa'ləm pa 'bakəs ke kedəm.	I am putting the pen in the box.	زۀ قلم په بکس کښې کېدم.
mā qa'ləm pa 'bakəs ke 'kexodo.	I put the pen in the box.	ما قلم په بکس کښې کېښودو.
mā qa'ləm pa 'bakəs ke kexo'dəley dey.	I have put the pen in the box.	ما قلم په بکس کښې کېښودلے دے.
mā qa'ləm pa ba'kəs ke kexo'dəley wo.	I had put the pen in the box.	ما قلم په بکس کښې کېښودلے وو.
də sa'bəq na pas mā xpəl qa'ləm pa ba'kəs ke kexo'do.	After class I used to put the pen in the box.	د سبق نه پس ما خپل قلم په بکس کښې کېښودو.

Try the same drill by talking about someone else doing the same thing: he is, she is, they (*m./f.*) are, etc. Then try the same process using different verbs. For example,

take out	rā'ob āša	راؤباسه
give	war-ka	ورکه
go	za	ځه
come	'rāša	راشه
stand up	o'driga	ودرېږه
sit down	'kena	کښېنه

Look at the lists of verbs from past chapters and drill these for a few days. Remember to keep the object the same and keep the sentence very simple. You are trying to learn verbs not new vocabulary.

Exercises for Lesson Twenty-Five

1. In the following sentences change the following present perfect verbs to their past perfect verb forms. For example:

   mā tər'osa 'pore 'kābəl nə dey li'dəley. — ما تر اوسه پورې کابل نۀ دے لیدلے.

   becomes:

   mā tər'osa 'pore 'kābəl nə wo li'dəley. — ما تر اوسه پورې کابل نۀ وو لیدلے.

   a. kəm waxt de li'dəley wu? — کُوم وخت دې لیدلے وُو؟

   ____

   b. dwa 'wrəze kigi če rā'ɣəli yu. — دوه ورځې کېږی چې راغلی یُو.

   ____

   c. də pa 'xpəla ǰā'me win'zəle di. — دۀ په خپله جامې وینځلې دی.

   ____

   d. ze'bā tso baǰe 'təle da? — زیبا څو بجې تلې ده؟

   ____

   e. tā ǰa'ṛəli di? — تا ژړلی دی؟

   ____

   f. tā pa'run zə lidəley yım? — تا پرُون زۀ لیدلے یم؟

   ____

2. Give both negative and affirmative short answers to the following questions. For example:

zān sa'ra de bo'təle wa? — ځان سره دې بوتلې وه؟

becomes:

āw, bo'təle me wa. — آو، بوتلې مې وه.

na, nə-me wa-bo'təle. — نه، نه مې وه بوتلې.

a. ki'tāb de lāybre'rəy ta raw'ṛəley wo? — کتاب دې لائبريرئ ته راوړلے وو؟

....

....

b. tā war sa'ra kār 'kəṛey wo? — تا ورسره کار کړے وو؟

....

....

c. pa'run de 'lāmbo wa'həle wa? — پرُون دې لامبو وهلې وه؟

....

....

d. ha'ɣwi alu'gān spin kəṛi wu? — هغوی آلوګان سپين کړی وُو؟

....

....

3. Complete the following questions with the past perfect forms of the verbs given in the right-hand column and then answer them. For example:

ha'ɣa tsə waxt ________________? هغه څۀ وخت ______________؟	tləl تلل

becomes

ha'ɣa tsə waxt 'təley wo? — هغه څۀ وخت تلے وو؟

ha'ɣa sa'har wax'ti 'təley wo. — هغه سحر وختی تلے وو.

a. ki'tāb de tso kāla 'maxke ________________? کتاب دې څو کاله مخکښې ______________؟	li'kəl ليکل

b.	ˈtāso war saˈra həm ________________? ؟________________ تاسو ورسره هم	maˈdəd kaˈwəl مدد کول
c.	haˈɣə pa ˈxpəla zəˈmā koˈṭa ________________? ؟________________ هغهٔ په خپله زما کوټه	saˈfā kaˈwəl صفا کول
d.	tərˈosa de xaˈbər nə ________________? ؟________________ تر اوسه دې خبر نهٔ	āwreˈdəl اورېدل
e.	pa klās de ḍer xə noˈṭuna ________________? ؟________________ په کلاس دې ډېر ښهٔ نوټونه	niˈwəl نيول
f.	tā paˈxwā həm zə ________________? ؟________________ تا پخوا هم زهٔ	liˈdəl ليدل
g.	pa tsə ši ləgˈyā we ˈkəla če ________________? ؟________________ په څهٔ شی لګيا وې کله چې	liˈdəl ليدل
h.	ˈwəle de ˈhaɣa haˈlək ________________? ؟________________ ولې دې هغه هلک	waˈhəl وهل
i.	ˈtāso ḍer ˈmaxke ˈdəlta ________________? ؟________________ تاسو ډېر مخکښې دلته	rasedəl رسېدل
j.	tā tso kiˈlo maˈṇe ________________? ؟________________ تا څو کيلو مڼې	āxɪsˈtəl اخستل

Vocabulary for Lesson Twenty-Five

axıraˈnəy	آخرنۍ	*f.*	*adj.*	the last
axˈta	اخته	*m., f.*	*adj.*	engaged, busy, occupied, involved
bāˈwər	باور	*m.*	*n.*	trust, assurance
baˈnen	بنین	*m.*	*n.*	sweater
pət	پت	*m.*	*n.*	respect, dignity, honour
taˈṛəl	تړل		*v.t.*	to bind, to wrap, to close, to tie
torzanˈtob	تورزنتوب	*m.*	*n.*	bravery, courage, fearlessness
ǰaˈwāb / ǰawāˈbuna	جواب / جوابُونه	*m.*	*n.*	answer, reply
ǰawāˈri	جواری	*f.*	*n.*	gambling
doˈbi	دوبی	*m.*	*n.*	washerman, launderer
ranz	رنځ	*m.*	*n.*	sickness
ǰwənd	ژوند	*f.*	*n.*	life
sāˈmān	سامان	*m.*	*n.*	luggage, equipment, furniture, tools
swāl / swālˈuna	سوال / سوالونه	*m.*	*n.*	request, question, query; begging
šarˈbət	شربت	*m.*	*n.*	sweet drink, juice, syrup
šleˈdəl	شلیدل		*v.i.*	to be torn, to be ripped
xorˈwā	ښوروا	*f.*	*n.*	soup, broth
siˈfət	صِفت	*m.*	*n.*	character, quality
foǰ	فوج		*n.*	army
qāˈtıl	قاتِل	*m.*	*n.*	murderer, killer, assassin
ˈqisəm	قسم	*m.*	*n.*	kind, sort, variety, type
ˈqəhər	قهر	*m.*	*n., adj.*	anger, rage, fury
kaˈǰure	کجُورې	*f.pl.*	*n.*	dates
gulˈkāri	گُلکاری	*f.*	*n.*	embroidery

ləgˈyā	لګيا	*m., f.*	*adj.*	busy, engaged
moxalıˈfət	مُخالفت	*m.*	*n.*	opposition, contradiction, antagonism
maˈzəb	مذهب	*m.*	*n.*	religion, faith
mustaqˈbıl	مُستقبل	*m.*	*n.*	future
muškıˈlāt	مُشکلات	*m.pl.*	*n.*	difficulties, problems
masˈruf	مصرُوف	*m.*	*adj.*	busy, engaged, occupied
masˈrufa / masˈrufe	مصرُوفه / مصرُوفې	*f.*		
muašeˈra	معاشره	*f.*	*n.*	society
muˈde / muˈde-na	مودې / مودې نه	*f.pl.*	*n.*	a period of time
naǰāˈez	ناجائز	*m.*	*adj.*	unjust, unfair
naˈši tamāˈši	نشی تماشی		*ph.*	rhyming idiomatic expression meaning 'bad things'
nəˈzər	نظر	*m.*	*n.*	opinion, viewpoint; view, sight, look
nangyāˈli	ننګیالی	*m.*	*adj.*	honourable, reputable
wāqiˈa	واقعه	*f.s.*	*n.*	happening, event, accident, incident
waṛukˈwāley	وړُوکوالے	*m.*	*n.*	childhood

špəgiš'təm sa'bəq شپږ ویشتم سبق

Lesson Twenty-Six

Dialogue twenty-six: Questions, questions, questions

With your helper prepare full answers to these common questions. You should memorise your answers. Make them longer as your fluency increases.

tə də kəm zay ye? Where are you from?	تهٔ د کُوم ځایٔ یې؟
tə də kəm məlk na rā'ɣəley ye? What country have you come from?	تهٔ د کُوم ملک نه راغلے یې؟
Answer:	
tə 'dəlta tsə key? What do you do here?	تهٔ دلته څهٔ کې؟
Answer:	
stā pa pakı'stān ke 'tsona 'kāla 'kigi? How many years have you been in Pakistan?	ستا په پاکِستان کښې څونه کاله کیږی؟
Answer:	
stā tan'xā 'tsumra da? What is your pay?	ستا تنخا څومره ده؟
Answer:	
tə mā xpəl məlk ta bot'ley še? Can you take me to your country?	تهٔ ما خپل ملک ته بوتلے شې؟
Answer:	
tə musal'mān 'šıβey ye? Have you become a Muslim?	تهٔ مُسلمان شوے یې؟

Answer:	
tə ˈwəle musalˈmān nə-ǰoˈṛege? Why don't you become a Muslim?	تهٔ ولې مُسلمان نهٔ جوړېږې؟
Answer:	
tə ˈdəlta ˈwəle ˈrāɣəley ye? Why did you come here?	تهٔ دلته ولې راغلے يې؟
Answer:	
tə ba tər ˈkəla ˈpore ˈdəlta ye? How long will you stay here?	تهٔ به تر کله پورې دلته يې؟
Answer:	
stā dā zay xwax dey? Do you like this place?	ستا دا ځائ خوښ دے؟
Answer:	
zmung pa məlk ke stā tsə xwax šo? What did you like in our country?	زمونږ په ملک کښې ستا څهٔ خوښ شو؟
Answer:	
stā pa məlk ke, həm ˈdāse garˈmi šta? Is it as hot as this in your country?	ستا په ملک کښې هم داسې ګرمی شته؟
Answer:	

This week listen very carefully to any other questions you are asked. Write them down or record them and transcribe them here. Learn to answer them too.

'should have': The subjunctive mood in the past tense

There are several ways to indicate 'should' or 'ought'.

1. Using a past participle and the past tense auxiliary form of the 'be' verb form *we* (وي) to communicate the idea of necessity, possibility and responsibility.

zaru'ri nə wa če pe'se ye war-ta le'gəle we.	It wasn't necessary to have sent them money.	ضرُوری نۀ وه چې پیسې یې ورته لیږلې وې.
pa'kār di če haɣ'wi os 'dəlta rā-rase'dəley wey.	They should have arrived here by now.	پکار دی چې هغوی اوس دلته را رسېدلے وے.
pa'kār di če tə ye 'wištey we, xo we-nə-wište.	They should have shot you, but they didn't shoot you.	پکار دی چې تۀ یې ویشتے وې، خو وې نۀ ویشتې.
ha'ɣə gox'təl če 'dəlta 'pāte 'šɪβey wey xo maǰ'bur wo, no lāṛo.	He wanted to stay here, but was compelled, so he went.	هغۀ غوښتل چه دلته پاتې شوے وے خو مجبُور وو، نو لاړو.
kə tə 'təley we, no zə ba həm 'təley wəm.	If you had gone, I would have gone too.	کۀ تۀ تلے وې، نو زۀ به هم تلے وم.
kə pa'run mo'səm xə wey, no zə ba xpəl kor ta rā'ɣəley wəm.	If the weather had been good yesterday, I would have come to my house.	کۀ پرُون موسم ښۀ وے، نو زۀ به خپل کور ته راغلے وم.
kə xo'dey ha'ɣə ta šɪ'fā war-'kəṛey wey, no ha'ɣa ba os ǰwən'dey wey.	If God had healed him, he would have been alive now.	کۀ خُدائ هغۀ ته شفا ورکړے وے، نو هغه به اوس ژوندے وے.
kə tā mā ta wa'yəle wey če tə 'təgey ye, no mā ba tā la u'bə dar-kəṛe we.	If you had told me you were thirsty, I would have given you some water. (*m.*)	کۀ تا ما ته وئیلې وے چې تۀ تږے یې، نو ما به تاله اوبۀ درکړې وې.

kə mā ha'ɣa wa'həley wey, no ha'ɣa ba xug 'šɪβey wo.	If I would have hit him, he would have been hurt. (*m.*)	کۀ ما هغه وهلے وے، نو هغه به خوږ شوے وو.
kə dā kā'sa mā ta 'šɪβe wey, no zə'mā mor ba 'xəfa 'šɪβe wa.	If this bowl had been broken my mother would have been upset.	کۀ دا کاسه ما ته شوے وے، نو زما مور به خفه شوې وه.
kə tə nə-wey rā'ɣəley, no mā ba tā ta nə-wu wa'yəli.	If you had not come, I wouldn't have told you. (*m.*)	کۀ تۀ نۀ وے راغلے، نو ما به تا ته نۀ وُو وئیلی.
pa'kār wu če pe'se ye tre a'xɪstey wey āw war-ta ye war-'kəṛey wey.	He should have taken the money and given it to him.	پکار وُو چې پېسې يې ترې اخستے وے او ورته يې ورکړے وے.

2. Using the participle *ba* (به) to indicate blame, regret or failure.

tə ba rā'ɣəley we!	You should have come!	تۀ به راغلے وې!
mung ba ha'ɣa li'dəle wa.	We should have seen her.	مُونږ به هغه لیدلې وه.
mung ba haɣ'wi li'dəli wu.	We might have seen them.	مُونږ به هغوی لیدلی وُو.
zə ba 'halta 'təley wəm, xo tley nə-šwəm.	I might have gone there, but I couldn't go.	زۀ به هلته تلے وم، خو تلے نۀ شوم.

3. Using *pa'kār dey* (پکار دے) 'need', *šā'ɪd če* (شاید چې) 'maybe', *mom'kɪn* (ممکن) 'possible', *xyāl* (خیال) 'thought' and *ke'dey ši če* (کېدے شی چې) 'possible' to indicate a past possibility. That is, something that might have happened in the past.

zə'mā pa xyāl ha'ɣa 'təley wo.	I think he may have gone.	زما په خیال هغه تلے وو.
šā'ɪd če haɣ'wi zə li'dəley wəm.	Perhaps they might have seen me.	شاید چې هغوی زۀ لیدلے وم.
mom'kɪna wa če ha'ɣe kār šo'ro 'kəṛey wey kə ha'ɣa 'dəlta wey.	She might have started work by now if she had been here.	ممکنه وه چې هغې کار شروع کړے وے کۀ هغه دلته وے.
ke'dey ši če xpəl ki'tāb ye her 'kəṛey wo.	It is possible that he had forgotten his book.	کېدے شی چې خپل کتاب يې هېر کړے وو.
zə'mā xyāl wo če ha'ɣa ba 'təley wi.	I thought he would have been gone.	زما خیال وو چې هغه به تلے وی.

mung la ha'ɣa waxt də haɣ'wi ma'dəd ka'wəl pa'kār wo.	We should have assisted them at that time.	مُونږ له هغه وخت د هغوی مدد کول پکار وو.
ha'ɣə la ko'šiš ka'wəl pa'kār wu, xo ha'ɣa fel šo.	He should have tried, but he failed.	هغۀ له کوشش کول پکار وُو خو هغه فیل شو.
'māla pa'kār wu če xpəl pəx'to sa'bəq ke me meh'nət 'kəṛey wey.	I should have been more diligent in my Pukhto studies.	ماله پکار وُو چې خپل پښتو سبق کښې مې مِحنت کړے وے.
ke'dey ši zə 'halta 'maxke 'təley wəm.	I might have gone there earlier.	کېدے شی زۀ هلته مخکښې تلے وم.
mung la ha'ɣa li'dəl pa'kār wu.	We should have seen them.	مُونږ له هغه لیدل پکار وُو.

Expressing an unfulfilled desire

zə'mā pa angre'zəy ız'da ka'wəlo ke dılčas'pi da, xo zə'mā sa'ra waxt 'ništa.	I have an interest to learn English, but I don't have the time.	زما په انګرېزۍ زده کولو کښې دلچسپی ده، خو زما سره وخت نشته.
pa'kār dey če nən yo xə xa'bər rā'ɣəley wey!	I wish some good news would have come today!	پکار دے چې نن یو ښۀ خبر راغلے وے!
zə'mā dā u'mıd wo če ha'lək ba 'oši, xo ǰınəy 'ošwa.	I had hoped a boy would have been born, but it was a girl.	زما دا اُمید وو چې هلک به وشی، خو جینۍ وشوه.
pa'run mā lām'bəl gox'təl.	I wanted to bathe yesterday.	پرُون ما لامبل غوښتل.
mā gox'təl če zə 'kəli ta lāṛ šəm, xo zə'mā af'sər mā ta də ču'ṭəy eǰā'zət rā-nə-kṛo.	I wanted to go to the village, but my boss wouldn't give me permission for leave.	ما غوښتل چې زۀ کلی ته لاړ شم، خو زما افسر ما ته د چُھټۍ اِجازت رانۀ کړو.

Expressing something that is doubtful or contrary to fact

The following phrases provide useful ways in which to communicate expressions of 'if only' or 'would have':

1. Intransitive

kə mā ta 'pata wey ...	If I had known ...	کۀ ما ته پته وے ...
kə tā ta 'pata wey ...	If you had known ...	کۀ تا ته پته وے ...

zə ba ˈtəley wəm.	I would have gone.	زۀ به تلے وم.
mung ba ˈtəli wu.	We would have gone.	مُونږ به تلی وُو.
baˈsir ba ˈtəley wo.	Basir would have gone.	بصير به تلے وو.
zahıˈda ba ˈtəle wa.	Zahida would have gone.	زاهده به تلې وه.

2. Transitive

kə mā tā ta waˈyəle we …	If I had told you ...	کۀ ما تا ته وئيلې وے ...
kə tā mā ta waˈyəle we …	If you had told me ...	کۀ تا ما ته وئيلې وے ...
mā ba haˈɣa waˈhəley wo.	I would have hit him.	ما به هغه وهلے وو.
mung ba haˈɣa waˈhəley wo.	We would have hit him.	مُونږ به هغه وهلے وو.
haˈɣə ba zə waˈhəley wəm.	He would have hit me.	هغۀ به زۀ وهلے وم.
haˈɣa ba waˈhəley ˈšıβey wo.	He would have been hit.	هغه به وهلے شوے وو.
kə ahˈmad ye waˈhəley wo ...	If Ahmad had been hit by him ...	کۀ احمد يې وهلے وو ...
kə ḍoˈḍəy paˈxa ˈšıβe wa ...	If the bread had been cooked ...	کۀ ډوډۍ پخه شوې وه ...

The all purpose *če* 'who', 'whom', 'that' and 'which' چې

tsok če ḍer kār kaˈwi ḍera ḍoˈḍəy xoˈri.	The one who works a lot eats a lot of food.	څوک چې ډېر کار کوی ډېره ډوډۍ خوری.
tsok če ˈdəlta oˈsigi, də haˈɣə xə ǰwənd wi.	He who lives here has a good life.	څوک چې دلته اوسېږی، د هغۀ ښۀ ژوند وی.
tsok če xə udə ˈkigi haˈɣa xə kār həm kaˈwəley ši.	The person who sleeps well is also able to work well.	څوک چې ښۀ اُودۀ کېږی هغه ښۀ کارهم کولے شی.
ˈhaɣa saˈṛey če čā saˈra peˈse ˈzyāte we, os pirˈpāi ke dey.	The person who had a lot of money is now in Pirpai.	هغه سړے چې چا سره پېسې زياتې وې اوس پيرپائی کښې دے.
čā če haˈɣə saˈra xaˈbare kəṛi di, haˈɣa xə ˈpeǰani.	Anyone who has talked with him knows him well.	چاچې هغۀ سره خبرې کړی دی، هغه ښۀ پېژنی.
ˈhaɣa haˈlək ta āˈwāz ka čā če spin koṭ ačaˈwəley dey.	Call the boy who has put on the white coat.	هغه هلک ته آواز که چاچې سپين کوټ اچولے دے.

ˈhaɣa kaˈsān čāta če də kor zaruˈrət dey, tā ta kamˈra ke nāst di.	Those people who are in need of a house are waiting for you in the room.	هغه کسان چاته چې د کور ضرورت دے، تا ته کمره کښې ناست دی.
ˈhaɣa ˈxəza če tā paˈrun liˈdəle wa, haˈɣa ṛanˈda wa.	The woman whom you had seen yesterday was blind.	هغه ښځه چې تا پرون ليدلې وه، هغه ړنده وه.
zə ˈhaɣa ḍākˈṭər la zəm če ḍera xə dəwaˈi war-kaˈwi.	I am going to that doctor who gives very good medicine.	زهٔ هغه ډاکټر له ځم چې ډېره ښهٔ دوائي ورکوی.
ˈhaɣa šey če tā aˈxɪstey wo, zə ba ye həm ˈaxləm.	That thing which you have bought, I will also buy.	هغه شے چې تا اخستے وو، زهٔ به يې هم اخلم.
če stā tsə šey paˈkār dey, haˈɣa ˈdəlta ˈništa.	That thing which you want isn't here.	چې ستا څهٔ شے پکار دے، هغه دلته نشته.
ˈhaɣa kār če tā ˈkəṛey dey, ḍer zaruˈri dey.	The work which you have done is very important.	هغه کار چې تا کړے دے، ډېر ضروری دے.
če ˈkuma ṭoˈṭa tā aˈxɪste da, haˈɣa ḍera ˈgrāna da.	The piece of cloth which you have bought is very expensive.	چې کومه ټوټه تا اخستې ده، هغه ډېره ګرانه ده.
haˈɣa pen če stā xwax dey, haˈga mā saˈra os ˈništa.	The pen which you like, I don't have now.	هغه پن چې ستا خوښ دے، هغه ما سره اوس نشته.
kəm zay ta če haˈɣa ˈtəle da, zə (*m.*) war-ta nə-yɪm ˈtəley.	The place to which she has gone, I haven't gone to. (*m. speaker*)	کوم ځائ ته چې هغه تلې ده، زهٔ ورته نهٔ يم تلے.
kəm zay ke če haˈɣa ˈosi, ˈhalta moˈsəm ḍer ˈyəx wi.	The place where she lives has very cold weather.	کوم ځای کښې چې هغه اوسی، هلته موسم ډېر يخ وی.
čerta če zə ˈosəm, haˈɣa zay də xār na ˈləre dey.	The place where I live is a long way from the city.	چرته چې زهٔ اوسم، هغه ځائ د ښار نه لرې دے.

NOTES:

1. The word *če* (چې) can be used by itself or in combination with other words, such as *tsok* (څوک) 'who', *čā* (چا) 'whom', *ˈčerta* (چرته) 'where', etc.
2. *če* (چې) often links two clauses in a sentence. For example,

če zə ˈdarāɣləm, tā tsə kaˈwəl?	When I came to you, what were you doing?	چې زهٔ دراغلم، تا څهٔ کول؟

če tə rā'ɣle, mā ro'ṭəy xo'ṛəla.	When you arrived, I was eating food.	چې تهٔ راغلې ما روټۍ خوړله.

3. The same kind of linking may also be done by *xo* (خو), *no* (نو) *byā* (بیا) and *āw* (او):

ha'ɣa 'rāɣey āw u'da šo.	He came and went to sleep.	هغه راغے او اُودهٔ شو.
ha'ɣa 'rāɣey, xo u'da nə šo.	He came, but didn't go to sleep.	هغه راغے، خو اُودهٔ نهٔ شو.
kə ha'ɣa rā'ɣəley wey, no byā ba u'da 'šɪβey wo.	If he had come, then he would have gone to sleep.	کهٔ هغه راغلے وے، نو بیا به اُودهٔ شوے وو.
yā xo rā'ɣəley dey, āw yā 'uda 'šɪβey dey.	Either he has come, or he has gone to sleep.	یا خو راغلے دے، او یا اُودهٔ شوے دے.
rāt'lo na pas, ha'ɣa u'da šo.	After coming, he went to sleep.	راتلو نه پس، هغه اُودهٔ شو.
če ha'ɣa 'kəla 'rāɣey, no u'da šo.	When he came he went to sleep.	چې هغه کله راغے، نو اُودهٔ شو.

The conjunction *če*

če (چې) is an all purpose conjunction used to mark the transition between ideas in Pukhto. It is used in two main ways.

1. *če* (چې) as a simple conjunction.

By itself *če* (چې) means 'that', 'when', 'if', and 'in order that', and is used to introduce a dependent clause.

če laila rā'zi no mung ba he'rān šu.	We will be surprised <u>if</u> Laila comes.	چې لیلی راځی نو مُونږ به حیران شُو.

NOTE:

You will note that the dependent clause *če laila rā'zi* (راځی لیلی چې) comes before the main clause. This is a common occurrence in Pukhto.

če (چې) is also used to introduce reported speech, commands or questions. For example,

umār ghani way če laila ba xāma'xā rā'zi.	Umar Ghani says <u>that</u> Laila will definitely come.	عمرغنی وائی چې لیلی به خامخا راځی.

2. *če* in combination with other words.

če (چې) is used in combination with other words, particularly adverbs. Here are a few of the more common uses:

har ˈkəla če	whenever	هر کله چې
ˈkəma (wrəz) če	whatever (day), whichever (day)	کُومه (ورځ) چې
tar so ˈpore če	as long as, until	تر څو پورې چې
ˈləka če	as if, like	لکه چې
bey də de na če	unless	بې د دې نه چې
ˈtsumra če	however much	څومره چې
ˈwəle če	because	ولې چې
ˈzəka če	since, because	ځکه چې

☝ Make sentences using *če* (چې) in these ways and practice using them with your helper.

The prefix *har* 'ever-' and 'any-' هر-

har tsok če ˈdəlta rāˈzi, kiˈtāb ˈaxli.	Everybody who comes here buys a book.	هر څوک چې دلته راځی، کتاب اخلی.
har tsə če stā paˈkār di, ˈdəlta šta.	Everything that you need is present.	هر څهٔ چې ستا پکار دی، دلته شته.
če tə har čerta tləl ˈɣwāṛe, ˈhalta lāṛ ša.	Wherever you want to go, go there.	چې تهٔ هر چرته تلل غواړې هلته لاړ شه.
har čerta mə-za!/ har xwā mə za!	Don't go everywhere!	هر چرته مهٔ ځه!/ هر خواه مهٔ ځه!
de ke har tsə če tə āxɪsˈtəl ɣwāṛe wāxla.	Take anything in it which you want to buy.	دې کښې هر څهٔ چې تهٔ اخستل غواړې واخله.
har šey mə-xora!	Don't eat everything!	هر شے مهٔ خوره!
har yo kum če stā xwax wi, zān saˈra raˈwāla!	Bring with you everything you like!	هر يو کُوم چې ستا خوښ وی ځان سره راوله!
har šey kum če de ke nə dey xə, xarts ye ka!	Everything in it which is not good, sell it!	هر شے کُوم چې دې کښې نهٔ دے ښهٔ، خرڅ يې که!
har ˈkəla če rātˈley še, ˈrāša!	Whenever you can come, come!	هر کله چې راتلے شې، راشه!

Improving fluency in the tenses

☝ You've probably realized by now that the fluent use of verbs in the past tense is one of the biggest challenges in learning Pukhto. The following five pages have lists of commonly used verbs, the basic tenses, and various pictures of people and objects. Each page can be used as a drill that involves pointing at pictures to make sentences in different tenses. This has the advantage of moving straight into Pukhto and not using translation from English to Pukhto. You may need to show your helper how to do this kind of drill.

The people grouped on each page can be used to represent first, second, and third persons, singular and plural, masculine and feminine.

Drills:

1. Sentences with confusing word order. Get your helper to make sentences using one verb, working through it tense by tense. Point to the combination of people and tense that you want to use to make a sentence.

For example, using the verb *pohe'dəl* (پوهېدل) 'to understand':
Point to a picture representing *zə* (زۀ) [yourself] and then to one of the illustrations that represent the masculine singular tense, and lastly to the verb, 'to understand'. The sentence you would say in the present tense (in Pukhto) would be 'I understand him'. You can then work through the same process, still in the same tense with masculine plural, feminine singular and feminine plural. You can then reverse the whole thing – for example, 'He understands me' – and methodically go through all the possibilities in the same tense: That is, 'You understand him', 'She understands them', etc.

When you think you grasp the use of a verb in one tense, get your helper to point to people and other verb tense combinations for you to try to produce sentences. With each verb progress down the tenses; have your helper say the sentences each time before you produce them.

2. Using animals (in feminine singular, and plural and masculine singular and plural) as objects of sentences, and people as the subjects. For example, 'He milked a buffalo'. However, some sentences only make sense if people are the objects. For example, 'The donkey bit the ladies', etc.

3. Objects of different gender, for example, 'She bought two pots'. You can complicate it further by pointing back to a person, and saying, 'He bought a candle for her', etc.

4. Intransitive verbs. Your helper can add any other words or phrases. Do not try and learn any new vocabulary here, but concentrate on the verbs and their uses.

5. Transitive verbs. Again supply words that fit each sentence.

Drill one

Tenses

- Present
- Imperative
- Future
- Past
- Past progressive
- Habitual past
- Present perfect
- Past perfect
- Subjunctive

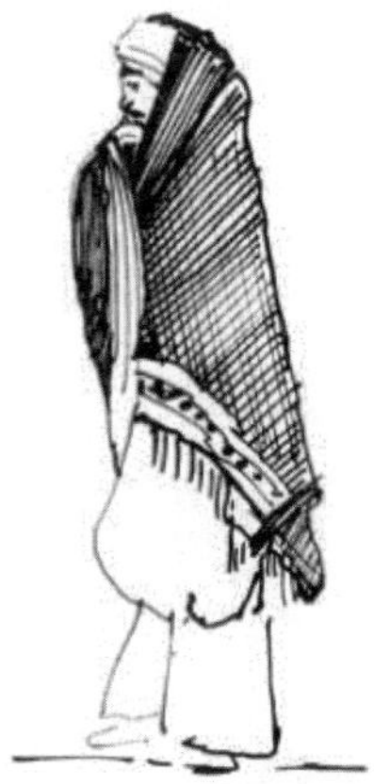

Verbs

poheˈdəl	to know (understand)	پوهېدل	waˈyəl	to say	وئیل
peǰanˈdəl	to know (recognise)	پېژندل	xaˈbare kaˈwəl	to talk	خبرې کول
warkaˈwəl	to give	ورکول	rātˈləl	to come	راتلل
āxɪsˈtəl	to buy, to get, to take	اخستل	tləl	to go	تلل
taˈpos kaˈwəl	to ask	تپوس کول			

Drill two

Tenses

- Present
- Imperative
- Future
- Past
- Past progressive
- Habitual past
- Present perfect
- Past perfect
- Subjunctive

Verbs

wiš'təl	to shoot	ويشتل	ose'dəl	to live, to stay	اوسېدل
məṛ ka'wəl	to kill	مړ کول	xura'wəl	to feed	خورول
ka'təl	to look at	کتل	ni'wəl	to hold	نيول
či'čəl	to bite (sting)	چيچل	di'ka warka'wəl	to push	ديکه ورکول
wa'həl	to hit	وهل			

Drill three

Tenses

- Present
- Imperative
- Future
- Past
- Past progressive
- Habitual past
- Present perfect
- Past perfect
- Subjunctive

Verbs

qarz warkaˈwəl	to lend	قرض ورکول	xarsaˈwəl	to sell	خرڅول
mātaˈwəl	to break	ماتول	winˈzəl	to wash	وینځل
rākaˈwəl	to give me	راکول	səmaˈwəl	to mend	سمول
monˈdəl	to find out	مُوندل	ǰoṛaˈwəl	to make	جوړول
āxɪsˈtəl	to buy	اخستل			

Drill four

Tenses

- Present
- Imperative
- Future
- Past
- Past progressive
- Habitual past
- Present perfect
- Past perfect
- Subjunctive

Verbs

wāˈdə keˈdəl	to become married	وادهٔ کېدل	tləl	to go	تلل
ˈɣosa keˈdəl	to become angry	غُصه کېدل	məṛ keˈdəl	to die	مړ کېدل
yereˈdəl	to fear	يرېدل	ˈpāte keˈdəl	to stay	پاتې کېدل
rāwaˈtəl	to come out	راوتل	taβeˈdəl	to turn	تاوېدل
kenasˈtəl	to sit	کښېناستل	ˈstəṛe keˈdəl	to become tired	ستړى کېدل

Drill five

☝ Use the same tenses as before; the verbs are on the following page.

Verbs

šıla'wəl	to tear (rip)	شلول
le'gəl	to send	لیږل
pāk-a'wəl	to clean	پاکول
'ləre ka'wəl	to extract	لرې کول
mon'dəl, māluma'wəl	to find out	مُوندل، معلُومول
xo'ṛəl	to eat	خوړل
lām'bəl	to bathe	لامبل
o'rəl	to carry, to take	وړل
āxıs'təl	to take	اخستل
šor ka'wəl	to make noise	شور کول
rāw'ṛəl	to bring	راوړل
tawa'wəl	to spin	تاؤول
paxa'wəl	to cook	پخول
pəta'wəl	to hide	پټول
ıstemāla'wəl	to use	اِستعمالول
wā'də ka'wəl	to marry	وَادهٔ کول
banda'wəl	to close	بندول
ga'ṭəl	to gain	ګټل
hasıla'wəl	to obtain	حاصلول
taqsima'wəl	to divide	تقسیمول
'ǰama ka'wəl	to collect	جمع کول
o'ṛə ka'wəl	to powder	وړهٔ کول
ni'wəl, ni'səl	to catch	نیول، نیسل
sambāla'wəl	to dress	سمبالول
kexo'dəl	to put	کېښودل
awre'dəl	to hear	اورېدل
skəl	to drink	څښل
li'kəl	to write	لیکل
bot'ləl	to take	بوتلل
prexo'dəl	to quit	پرېښودل
šarika'wəl	to share	شریکول
re'bəl	to reap	رېبل
ǰang ka'wəl	to fight	جنګ کول
wa'həl, ṭaka'wəl	to beat	وهل، ټکول
sa'ṭəl	to lick	څټل
šma'rəl	to count	شمارل
ča'kər wa'həl	to take a trip	چکر وهل
ka'wəl	to do	کول
təxta'wəl	to kidnap	تښتول
bəč ka'wəl	to save (rescue)	بچ کول

Comprehension drill: Speed counting

Ask and answer quick questions using mental arithmetic. For example:

dwa ˈǰama dre ˈǰama tsaˈlor tso šwe?	دوه جمعه درې جمعه څلور څو شوې؟
dre ˈzəla špəg ˈtsumra wi?	درې ځله شپږ څومره وی؟
če ˈdoləs pa dreo kaˈsāno taqˈsim ke, ˈtsumra yo kas ta ˈrasi?	چې دولس په درېو کسانو تقسیم کړې، څومره یو کس ته رسی؟
če də špəgo-na dre ˈləre kṛe, no tso ˈpāte šo?	چې د شپږو نه درې لرې کړې، نو څو پاتې شو؟

Memorising moment

mataˈluna

دَ املوکو په تول کښې راغلے دے.

də āmˈluko pa tol ke raˈɣəley dey.

It came in the weighing of persimmons.

پیشو خلق په اوله شپه وژنی.

pišo ˈxalak pa āˈwala špa wəǰni.

People kill a cat on the first night.

څۀ مو رانۀ کړل خو ما هم درته ټول مُونځونه بې اودسه کړی دی.

tsə mo rā-nə kṛəl xo mā həm ˈdarta ṭol munzˈuna be āwˈdasa kəˈṛi di.

You didn't give me a thing, but I also have done all the prayers without ablution.

Exercises for Lesson Twenty-Six

Complete the following sentences in the past tense in the subjunctive mood.

a. kə ______________ mula'qāt ba me war-sa'ra kəṛe ______________.

کهٔ ______________ ملاقات به مې ورسره کړې ______________.

b. ke'de ši če li'dəle me ______________.

کېدے شي چې ليدلې مې ______________.

c. kə roɣ ______________ ke'dey ši če 'dəlta rāɣəley ______________.

کهٔ روغ ______________ کېدے شي چې دلته راغلے ______________.

d. zaru'ri da če zə war-sa'ra xa'bare ______________.

ضرُوری ده چې زهٔ ورسره خبرې ______________.

e. lā'zɪm wu če ma'dəd me war-sa'ra ______________.

لازم وُو چې مدد مې ورسره ______________.

f. 'uče ro'ṭəy me la mal'gəro sa'ra xwa'ṛəley ______________.

وچې روټۍ مې له ملګرو سره خوړلے ______________.

g. zə bā'ɪd la də sa'ra haspa'tāl ta 'təley ______________.

زهٔ بايد له دهٔ سره هسپتال ته تلے ______________.

h. ke'dey ši če nas'rin 'roɣa nə ______________.

کېدے شي چې نسرين روغه نهٔ ______________.

i. kə tə rāɣəley ______________ zə ba 'halta ______________.

کهٔ تهٔ راغلے ______________ زهٔ به هلته ______________.

j. kə tā xan'dəḷey nə ______________, no zə ba nə ______________.

کهٔ تا خاندلے نهٔ ______________ نو زهٔ به نهٔ ______________.

Vocabulary for Lesson Twenty-Six

āˈrām kaˈwəl	آرام کول		*comp. v.t.*	to rest
afˈsər	افسر	*m.s.*	*n.*	officer, boss
bəč kaˈwəl	بچ کول		*comp. v.t.*	to save, to rescue
bey də de na če	بې د دې نه چې		*conj.*	unless
prexoˈdəl	پرېښودل		*v.i.*	to leave, to abandon, to quit, to forsake, to let go
tawaˈwəl	تاؤول		*v.t.*	to spin
tar so ˈpore če	تر څو پورې چې		*conj.*	as long as, until
tre, tre-na	ترې، ترې نه		*pro.*	from someone or something
taqsimaˈwəl	تقسيمول		*v.t.*	to divide, to distribute, to share
tanˈxā	تنخا	*f.s.*	*n.*	salary, wage, pay
ṭoˈṭa	ټوټه	*f.s.*	*n.*	piece, segment, part
ˈǰama kaˈwəl	جمع کول		*comp. v.t.*	to collect, to gather, to deposit
ˈzəka če	ځکه چې		*conj.*	since, because
čaˈkər waˈhəl	چکر وهل		*comp. v.t.*	to take a trip, to take a walk, to stroll, to go on an outing
če	چې		*conj.*	that, who, whom, which, in order that, when, if
saˈṭəl	څټل		*v.t.*	to lick
ˈtsumra če	څومره چې		*conj.*	however much
ˈtsona	څونه		*q., adj.*	how many, how much
hasılaˈwəl	حاصلول		*v.t.*	to get, to acquire, to obtain
xuraˈwəl	خورول		*v.t.*	to feed, to cause to eat
xyāl	خيال	*m.*	*n.*	thought, idea, notion
dılčasˈpi	دلچسپی	*f.s.*	*n.*	interest, enthusiasm
diˈka warkaˈwəl	دیکه ورکول		*comp. v.t.*	to push
zyāt	زيات	*m.*	*adv.*	much, more, many, most, excess

sambāla'wəl	سمبالول		*v.t.*	to organise, to make orderly, to store; to dress, to attire
šarika'wəl	شریکول		*v.t.*	to make a partner, to share, to join in
šma'rəl	شمارل		*v.t.*	to count, to calculate
šor ka'wəl	شور کول		*comp. v.t.*	to make noise
zaru'ri	ضرُوری	*f.*	*adj.*	necessary, essential, urgent, indispensable
fel kedəl	فیل کېدل		*comp. v.i.*	to fail
qarz warka'wəl	قرض ورکول		*comp. v.t.*	to give a loan, to lend
kā'sa	کاسه	*f.s.*	*n.*	bowl
'kəma (wrəz) če	کُومه (ورځ) چې		*conj.*	whatever (day), whichever (day)
ga'ṭəl	گټل		*v.t.*	to gain, to win, to earn, to profit
'ləre ka'wəl	لرې کول		*comp. v.t.*	to throw away, to remove, to extract
'ləka če	لکه چې		*conj.*	as if, like
meh'nət	محنت	*m.*	*n.*	toil, struggle
meh'nət ka'wəl	محنت کول		*comp. v.t.*	to toil, to work hard
məṛ ka'wəl	مړ کول		*comp. v.t.*	to kill; to turn off, to extinguish
mom'kın	ممکن	*m.*	*adj.*	possible
'mənḍa wa'həl	منډه وهل		*comp. v.t.*	to run
mon'dəl	مُوندل		*v.t.*	to find out, to know, to understand, to look for, to discover, to acquire, to get
o'ṛə ka'wəl	وړه کول		*comp. v.t.*	to grind to a powder
'wəle če	ولې چې		*conj.*	because
har tsok če	هر څوک چې		*pro.*	everybody
har 'kəla če	هر کله چې		*conj.*	whenever

uwiš'təm sa'bəq اووۀ ويشتم سبق
Lesson Twenty-Seven

Dialogue twenty-seven: Expressing sympathy

L: baši'ra yāra, nən 'wəle xə'fa xə'fa ya'wāze nāst ye? Dear Bashira, why are you sitting alone, so sad today?	بشيره ياره، نن ولې خفه خفه يواځې ناست يې؟
H: trə me məṛ 'šɪβey dey. My uncle has died.	ترۀ مې مړ شوے دے.
L: de sa'ra zə ḍer xə'fa šwəm, dā tsə waxt? This makes me very sad, when was it?	دې سره زۀ ډېر خفه شوم، دا څۀ وخت؟
H: nən sa'har rāta xa'bər me'lāw šo. The news came to me this morning.	نن سحر راته خبر مِلاؤ شو.
L: zama ḍer afsos dey. ǰanā'za ba 'kəla wi? I am very sorry. When will the funeral be?	زما ډېر افسوس دے. جنازه به کله وی؟
H: ǰanā'za ba tsa'lor baǰe wi. The funeral will be at four o'clock.	جنازه به څلور بجې وی.
L: zə tā sa'ra ǰenā'ze ta tləl 'ɣwāṛəm. I want to go with you to the ceremony.	زۀ تا سره جنازې ته تلل غواړم.
H: zə xo 'halta os ra'wān yɪm, tə os mā sa'ra 'halta ze? I am going there now, will you come with me?	زۀ خو هلته اوس روان يم، تۀ اوس ما سره هلته ځې؟
L: zə ḍer xə'fa yɪm, če də 'de dun'yā na yo xə sa'ṛey 'lāṛo. I am very sad, that a good man has left the world.	زۀ ډېر خفه يم، چې د دې دُنيا نه يو ښۀ سړے لاړو.
H: xo xo'dey ta ba dā man'zura wa. har yo sa'ṛey če de dun'yā ta rā'ɣəley dey, wā'pas ba zi. But that was God's will. Every man who has come into the world will return.	خو خُدائ ته به دا منظوره وه. هر يو سړے چې دې دُنيا ته راغلے دے، واپس به ځی.
L: xo'dey de 'obaxi. May God forgive him.	خُدائ دې وبخښی.
L: xo'dey de 'tāso la 'səbər 'dar kṛi. May God give you patience.	خُدائ دې تاسو له صبر درکړی.

The past potential

tā war sara ma'dəd ka'wəley šo?	Could you have helped them?	تا ورسره مدد کولے شو؟
āw, mā də hayˈwi ma'dəd ka'wəley šo, xo o-me-nə-ko.	Yes, I could have helped them, but I didn't.	آو، ما د هغوی مدد کولے شو، خو ومې نۀ کو.
ha'ɣe pa 'xpəla paxa'wəley šwa?	Could she have cooked it herself?	هغې په خپله پخولے شوه؟
zə pa'run 'stāso 'kara nə-šwəm rāt'ley.	I couldn't come to your house yesterday.	زۀ پرُون تاسو کره نۀ شوم راتلے.
mung xpəl kār xlāsa'wəley šo, xo zmung ḍer melmā'nə wu.	We could have finished the work, but we had lots of guests.	مُونږ خپل کار خلاصولے شو، خو زمُونږ ډېر مېلمانۀ وُو.
ha'ɣe dwa 'wrəze 'maxke xpəl kār nə-šo xlāsa'wəley.	She couldn't have finished her work two days ago.	هغې دوه ورځې مخکښې خپل کار نۀ شو خلاصولے.
ha'ɣə zə bot'ley nə-šwəm.	He couldn't take me.	هغۀ زۀ بوتلے نۀ شوم.
hayˈwi me nən nə-šu li'dey.	I couldn't see them today.	هغوی مې نن نۀ شُو لیدے.
fātı'ma ax'bār nə-ši wa'yəley.	Fatima couldn't read the paper.	فاطمه اخبار نۀ شی وئیلے.
'wəle tā lar'gi nə-šu māta'wəley?	Why couldn't you have broken the wood?	ولې تا لرګی نۀ شُو ماتولے؟
mung pa'law nə-šu xo'ṛey, zəka če 'wrije xa'rābe we!	We couldn't eat the pulao, because the rice was bad!	مُونږ پولاؤ نۀ شُو خوړے، ځکه چې وریژې خرابې وې!
'tāso ara'bi həm wa'yəley šwa?	Could you speak Arabic too?	تاسو عربی هم وئیلے شوه؟
tā xpəl af'sər sa'ra xa'bare ka'wəley šwe, xo tā o'nə-ke.	You could have talked to your boss, but you didn't.	تا خپل افسر سره خبرې کولے شوې، خو تا ونۀ کې.
zə də ziā'rət pa wrəz tley šwəm.	I could have gone on Thursday.	زۀ د زیارت په ورځ تلے شوم.
tə pa'run 'wəle nə-šwe rāt'ley?	Why couldn't you have come yesterday?	تۀ پرُون ولې نۀ شوې راتلے؟
kə zə 'halta tley šwey, zə ba 'halta ke wəm.	If I could have gone there I would have been there.	کۀ زۀ هلته تلے شوے، زۀ به هلته کښې وم.

NOTES

1. The past potential (could, could not) is expressed by the past participle of the verb *ka'wəl* (کول) or applicable verb, plus the simple past tense forms of the verb *šwəl* (شول).

2. All the past tense forms of the verb *šwəl* (شول) are used in the intransitive and transitive forms. However, in the intransitive form they are conjugated for number and gender based on the subject.

3. Conditional sentences can also occur with the past potential. In such sentences, the auxiliary verb *'šwe* (شوي) 'could have' is used with the past participle of a given verb. Note the examples below:

kə zə rāt'ley 'šwey, no tā tə ba me wa'yəle wu.	If I could have come, I would have told you.	کۀ زۀ راتلے شوے، نو تا ته به مې وئيلې وُو.
kə me ka'wəley 'šwey, mrəsta ba me dar-sa'ra kəṛe wa.	If I could have done it, I would have helped you.	کۀ مې کولے شوے، مرسته به مې درسره کړې وه.

Emphatic and exclamatory

'tsumra zər zər lw'ege!	How quickly you are growing!	څومره زر زر لوئيږې!
'ogora! 'tsumra wro wro ha'ɣa ra'wāna da!	Look! How slowly she is moving!	وګوره! څومره ورو ورو هغه روانه ده!
ha'ɣa 'tsumra ḍo'ḍəy xo'ri!	How much food he eats!	هغه څومره ډوډۍ خوري!
ah! ha'ɣa 'tsona 'xkwəle da!	Oh! How beautiful she is!	آه! هغه څونه ښکُلې ده!
'dumra luy kor!	Such a big house!	دومره لوئ کور!
'tsumra zər rā-'o-rasede!	How quickly you arrived!	څومره زر راورسيدې!
zə 'dumra 'stəṛey 'šıβey yım če wa'yəley nə-šəm!	I'm so tired I can't say!	زۀ دومره ستړے شوے يم چې وئيلے نۀ شم!
ha'ɣa 'dumra na'rāsta dey, če ta'pos ye mə-kawa!	He's so lazy, don't even ask him!	هغه دومره ناراسته دے، چې تپوس يې مۀ کوه!
ha'ɣa 'dumra sa'bəq 'wayi, če wa'yəley nə-šəm!	He studies so much, that I can't say!	هغه دومره سبق وائی، چې وئيلے نۀ شم!
tsə aǰi'ba sa'ṛey dey!	What a strange man!	څۀ عجيبه سړے دے!

NOTE:

In the first two sentences the adverbs *zər zər* (زر زر) and *wro wro* (ورو ورو) are repeated for emphasis. You will often hear this type of emphasis in spoken Pukhto.

Rhyming words

You have probably heard words that are combined with a second one in a delightful rhyming couplet. Often the second word starts with an / m- / (م-) although this has no meaning. For example:

ḍo'ḍəy mo'ḍəy ta'yāra da? Is the food-mood ready? ډوډۍ موډۍ تیاره ده؟

Make sentences with the following words that are commonly combined in this way.

چائې	čay [če]	tea
پېنټ	penṭ	trousers
لامبل	lām'bəl	bathe
خوږ	xog	sweet
پکے	pa'key	fan
هلک	ha'lək	boy
جرابې	ǰərā'be	socks
سترګې	'stərge	eyes
بلب	'bələf	light bulb
جامې	ǰā'me	clothes
کتابونه	kitā'buna	books
سړے	sa'ṛey	man

Some useful idioms

The normal sequence of learning is first the pronunciation, then the grammar, and finally the vocabulary is mastered. Idioms are an important part of this process. Like proverbs, the use of an idiom at the right time and place in a conversation will always be appreciated by your friends. Here are a few to get you started:

1. Equating people with animals:

nən zə də ha'ɣa zanā'warāno nu'muna ɪz'da kəm če 'xalak ɪnsa'nāno ta 'wayi.	Today I'm learning names of animals that people use to call others by.	نن زۀ د هغه ځناورانو نُومُونه زده کوم چې خلق انسانانو ته وائی.
ha'ɣa də azma'ri pa'šān bahā'dər dey.	He is as brave as a lion.	هغه د زمری په شان بهادر دے.
dumra 'ɣaṭa da 'ləka 'mexa.	She is as fat as a buffalo.	دومره غټه ده لکه مېښه.
'stərge ye də o'səy pa'šān 'xkwəle di.	Her eyes are as beautiful as a deer's.	سترګې يې د اوسۍ په شان ښکُلې دی.
'dāse 'garzi 'ləka 'zərka.	She walks like a partridge.	داسې ګرځی لکه زرکه.
'dāse haṇ'ke če 'ləka spey.	She makes a noise like a dog [eating].	داسې هنړکې چې لکه سپے.
də spi pa'šān ɣa'pigi.	He barks like a dog.	د سپی په شان غپيږی.
os tə mā ta nor 'dāse nu'muna 'owaya.	Now tell me some more names like this.	اوس ته ما ته نور داسې نُومُونه ووايه.

2. Equating parts of the body with special meaning:

pa pəx'to ke 'xalak 'wayi če ...	In Pukhto people say that ...	په پښتو کښې خلق وائی چې ...
ha'ɣa də sər na tər xpo 'pore də gu'nā na ḍək dey.	He is full of sin from head to foot.	هغه د سر نه تر پښو پورې د ګُناه نه ډک دے.
ḍer nura'ni max la'ri.	He has a very shining (holy) face.	ډېر نورانی مخ لری.
ɣwə'guna me ni'wəli di če byā ba 'dāse nə kom.	I pulled my ears (in repentance), so that I will not do it again.	غوږُونه مې نيولی دی چې بيا به داسې نۀ کوم.
ha'ɣə zə'mā ɣwə'guna 'oxoṛəl.	He ate my ears off (with talk).	هغۀ زما غوږُونه وخوړل.

zə ye tər ˈpoze ˈrāwastəm.	I've had it with him up to my nose.	زۀ يې تر پوزې راوستم.
dā zəˈmā də zṛə ṭoˈṭa da!	She is a piece of my heart!	دا زما د زړۀ ټوټه ده!
də zṛə pa ˈɣwəgo ye ˈwāwra!	Listen with your heart's ear!	د زړۀ په غوږو يې واؤره!
ɣwəˈguna ye ˈrāta paˈxə ka.	He cooked my ears off.	غوږُونه يې راته پاښۀ که.
tə os mā ta ˈdāse nor mısaˈluna ˈowaya če də baˈdən də andāˈmuno saˈra ˈləgi.	Now give me some more examples related to parts of the body.	ته اوس ما ته داسې نور مِثالُونه ووايه چې د بدن د اندامونو سره لږي.

Comprehension drill: Body language

☝ Much communication is without words. Below is a list of some common body language. Have your helper read the command, and show the unspoken way to 'say' the same. Then you show the right sign at the given command. Finally you give the meaning of signs that your helper gives.

ˈdəlta ˈrāša!	دلته راشه!	pa ˈguta ye šmār ka!	په ګوته يې شمار که!
pe'sc mə rāobasa!	پېسې مۀ راوباسه!	peˈse šmār ka!	پېسې شمار که!
heˈran šo!	حېران شو!	pāˈgəl dey!	پاګل دے!
za!	ځه!	dəˈnəna rāzəy!	دننه راځئ!
tsə key!	څۀ کړے!	ˈguru ba!	ګورُو به!
xəˈfa!	خفه!	xə kār dey ˈkəṛey wo!	ښۀ کار دے کړے وو!
xoˈšāla!	خوشحاله!	ˈxəze!	ښځې!
čəp ša!	چپ شه!	haˈɣə ta ˈmə-waya!	هغۀ ته مۀ وايه!
ˈodrega!	ودرېږه!	šarˈmege!	شرمېږې!
kena!	کښېنه!	za če zu!	ځه چې ځُو!
ḍer xə!	ډېر ښۀ!	mwāf ka!	معاف که!
zə tabıˈdār yım!	زۀ تابعدار يم!	ˈmə-kawa!	مۀ کوه!

Memorising moment

Rahman Baba

زمونږ دومره قِسمت چرته دے؟

zmung ˈdumra qɪsˈmət ˈčerta dey?

Where would be so much luck for us?

چې اختر تېر شی نکریزے په دېوال اوتپه.

če āxˈtar ter ši naˈkrizey pa diˈwāl utapa.

When the festivities have ended, henna is pasted on the wall.

هر زِنده چې د مُرده په قبر ورشی،

دومره بس دے نصیحت په دې دُنیا.

har zɪnˈda če də mərˈda pa ˈqəbər warši,

ˈdumra bas dey nəsiˈhət pa de dunˈyā.

Any living person who sees a grave,

For him this advice is enough.

کۀ هزار هزار پشتۍ ورله څوک ورکړی

بې بُنیاده دے بُنیاد ددې دُنیا.

kə haˈzār, haˈzār pašˈtəy warla tsok ˈwarkṛi

be bunˈyāda dey bunˈyād də de dunˈyā.

Even if someone gives thousands and thousands of supports,

The foundation of this world is baseless.

Exercises for Lesson Twenty-Seven

Complete the following sentences in the past potential.

a. zə ˈtera špa ˈtləley ________________.

زۀ تېره شپه تللے ________________.

b. ḍer ˈobaxa, dar-ˈtləley nə ________________.

ډېر وبخښه، درتللے نۀ ________________.

c. ḍer grān wo axəsˈtəley me nə ________________.

ډېر ګران وو اخستلے مې نۀ ________________.

d. ḍer bāˈrān wareˈdo, tə me liˈdəley nə ________________.

ډېر باران ورېدو، تۀ مې ليدلے نۀ ________________.

e. haˈwā ˈḍera ˈyaxa wa, uˈbə me ˈskəley nə ________________.

هوا ډېره يخه وه، اوبۀ مې څکلے نۀ ________________.

f. mā ˈhaɣa moˈṭər čalaˈwəley ________________.

ما هغه موټر چلولے ________________.

g. zāˈhid xə raˈbāb waˈhəley ________________.

زاهد ښۀ رباب وهلے ________________.

h. haɣˈwi ˈḍere xe qiˈse liˈkəley ________________.

هغوی ډېرې ښې قيصې ليکلې ________________.

Vocabulary for Lesson Twenty-Seven

āf'sos	افسوس	*m.*	*n.*	regret, sigh, sorrow
ɪn'sān / ɪnsa'nān	انسان / انسانان	*m.*	*n.*	man, mankind, a human, person, people
o'səy	اوسی	*f.s.*	*n.*	deer, gazelle
bahā'dər	بهادر	*m.*	*adj.*	brave
pā'gəl	پاگل	*m.*	*adj.*	crazy, mad, insane; foolish, stupid
pa'law	پولاو		*n.*	pulao [pilau, pilaf] (an Afghan-style rice dish)
tabɪ'dār	تابعدار	*m.*	*adj.*	at your service
ǰərā'be	جرابي	*pl.*	*n.*	socks
ǰanā'za	جنازه	*f.s.*	*n.*	funeral
'zərka	زرکه	*f.s.*	*n.*	partridge
aǰi'ba	عجيبه	*f.*	*adj.*	interesting, surprising, strange
ara'bi	عربی		*n.*	Arabic
ɣa'pəl	غپل		*v.t.*	to bark, to yelp
man'zur	منظور	*m.*	*adj., n.*	aim, object, intention, hope; approved, accepted
na'rāsta	ناراسته	*m., f.*	*adj.*	lazy
nura'ni	نورانی	*f.*	*adj.*	shining
haṇ'ke	هنړکي		*n.*	chomp, noise of dog eating

Users' Index

Index: English - Pukhto

Index: Pukhto phonetics - English

Index: Pukhto script - English

Book List

Bartlotti, Leonard and Khattak, Raj Wali Shah (editors). *Rohi Mataluna: Pashto Proverbs.* Revised and Expanded Edition of the original work by Tair, Mohammad Nawaz and Edwards, T. C.. Peshawar: InterLit Foundation and Pashto Academy, Peshawar University. 2007, reprinted 2008, 2011.

Enevoldsen, Jens. *Sound the bells, O moon, arise and shine! A collection of Pashto proverbs and tappas*. Peshawar: InterLit Foundation. 2000

Enevoldsen, Jens. *The Nightingale of Peshawar: Selections from Rahman Baba.* Peshawar: InterLit Foundation. 1993

InterLit Foundation. *Pashto Phrasebook: A Guide for Newcomers.* Peshawar: InterLit Foundation. 2004, reprinted 2010.

Language and Orientation Programme, International Assistance Mission. *Picture It in Dari and Pashto*. Peshawar: InterLit Foundation. 2004, reprinted 2011.

Sampson, Robert. *A Dictionary of Spoken Pukhto.* Peshawar: InterLit Foundation. 2004, reprinted 2010.

Sampson, Robert and Khan, Momin. *Sow Flowers, Selections from Rahman Baba, The Poet of the Afghans*. Peshawar: InterLit Foundation. 2003, reprinted 2004, 2008.

Sampson, Robert and Khan, Momin. *The Poetry of Rahman Baba: Poet of the Pukhtuns.* Peshawar: University Book Agency. 2005, reprinted 2010

For other books by the InterLit Foundation see www.interlitfoundation.org